Wellsprings of Knowledge

Wellsprings of Knowledge

Building and Sustaining the Sources of Innovation

DOROTHY LEONARD

Harvard Business School Press
Boston, Massachusetts

Published by the Harvard Business School Press in hardcover, 1995;
in paperback, 1998
Copyright 1995 President and Fellows of Harvard College
All rights reserved
Printed in the United States of America
02 01 00 99   5 4 3   (pbk)

Library of Congress Cataloging-in-Publication Data

Leonard-Barton, Dorothy.
  Wellsprings of knowledge : building and sustaining the sources of innovation /
  Dorothy Leonard-Barton.
     p.   cm.
  Includes bibliographical references and index.
  ISBN 0-87584-612-2
  1. Information technology—Management.   2. Information resources
management.   3. Management information systems.   I. Title.
HD30.2.L46   1995
658.4'038—dc20   95-14582
                                                                        CIP

ISBN 0-87584-859-1 (pbk)

The paper used in this publication meets the requirements of the American
National Standard for Permanence of Paper for Printed Library Materials
Z39.49–1984.

To Ron, my best critic and personal wellspring,
and to my unfailing supporters, Gavin and Michelle.

C O N T E N T S

PREFACE

My former professor and longtime friend Everett Rogers, whose prodigious output of books and articles always awed me, once surprised me with the comment that he never knew enough material to write a book when he *started* it. I had naively assumed that his remarkable syntheses and insights were mostly, if not wholly, formed when he first set fingers to keyboard. As is common with the wisdom of teachers, the remark took on more significance when I experienced it in my own life. In one sense, this book is a compilation of observations accumulated over several decades. Threading through this volume are traces of long-ago Peace Corps experiences with the development of technological capabilities in Thailand and later memories of steelmaking equipment rusting in the sands of an Indonesian beach, mutely denying the effectiveness of a Russian technology-transfer program. My preoccupation throughout this book with *behavioral* interaction with technology, as opposed to attitude or opinion, has roots in research on the diffusion of innovations conducted at Stanford and, later, at MIT. I can also trace my interest in the role of technology users in its development to that earlier work. However, the book most directly derives from research done over the past decade at Harvard Business School, where I have learned to focus on key managerial actions and their link to competitiveness. I draw heavily herein on teaching cases I have written and research I have published in journals while at Harvard. At the same time, Everett's comment applies to me as well in that the process of writing has occasioned much discovery and learning. I have continually revised this manuscript to take advantage of new insights gained from my immersion in industry and academia; incorporating the new material has added greatly to the pleasure of writing.

As will become obvious to the reader, I am tremendously indebted to managers in dozens of companies, who generously allowed me to blend their ideas with mine (and despite best efforts, no doubt sometimes to distort those ideas). Many of these managers are named; some preferred anonymity. Less obvious perhaps is the debt I owe to a number of research associates over the years who lent me their intellectual muscles, researching and coauthoring almost all of the teaching cases and helping on a few of the published articles: Paul Barese, Cynthia Costello, Brian DeLacey, Isabel Deschamps, Marianne Hedin, Fred Johnson, Brook Larmer, Mark Leiter, Joshua Macht, Marilyn Matis, Linda Moffat, Gil Preuss, Paul Sagawa, Deepak Sinha, Sarah Tabler, George Thill, Robert Valletta, Alistair Williamson, and Allegra Young. All of their work, and mine since coming to Harvard, has been generously supported by the Harvard Business School Division of Research.

Over the years, I have greatly profited from the support of Dean McArthur and my colleagues in the Technology and Operations Management area. A few of my colleagues here at Harvard and elsewhere stole time from far more personally important activities to read this entire manuscript in draft and comment in detail: Kim Clark, Margaret Graham, and Gary Lilien as well as two anonymous reviewers. Readers will unknowingly benefit from their excellent suggestions and suffer from my incomplete ability to respond. I am also personally most grateful to the midwife of innumerable Harvard Business School publications, Barbara Feinberg. Her unfailing enthusiasm for this book buoyed me up, and her calm reason, based on decades of experience, steered me away from excesses of various kinds.

Despite all this aid, everyone knows that helping authors is like training cats; in the end, we pursue our goals with a certain degree of feline independence and incomprehension. We must therefore accept final responsibility for the flaws that remain in our work. I trust that feedback from readers of this book will improve my next one.

INTRODUCTION

This book is about a process that sounds abstract and yet is concrete, practical, and profoundly important—managing a firm's knowledge assets. Companies, like individuals, compete on the basis of their ability to create and utilize knowledge; therefore, managing knowledge is as important as managing the finances. In other words, firms are knowledge, as well as financial, institutions. They are repositories and wellsprings of knowledge. Expertise collects in employees' heads and is embodied in machines, software, and routine organizational processes. Some of this knowledge and know-how is essential simply to survive or to achieve parity with the competition. However, it is *core* or *strategic* capabilities that distinguish a firm competitively. Management of these strategic knowledge assets determines the company's ability to survive, to adapt, to compete. Drawing on managers' experiences—both successes and failures—from a number of firms in various manufacturing industries, I have tried to show how through systematic decision making and actions, both routine and strategic, core technological capabilities can be built and changed.

The focus herein is on companies whose core capabilities are technology-based—i.e., on organizations that compete on the basis of technological advantage (rather than, say, personal services, access to natural resources, artistic talent, or distribution rights). These strategic technological capabilities are organic systems of interdependent dimensions that are created over time and can be sustained over time. They are not easily imitated, transferred, or redirected on short notice. And as bodies of knowledge, core capabilities cannot be managed in the same way as are the tangible assets of the firm.

Managing knowledge is not a simple task, and despite our national proclivity for sound bites, this is not a quick-read book. Nor is it a "how-to" book, with recipes for instant success (although there are many implications for managerial action). In order to manage knowledge assets, we need not merely to identify them but to *understand* them—in depth—in all their complexity: where they exist, how they grow or atrophy, how managers' actions affect their viability. We also need to understand the manager's role in designing an organization for learning, for continual renewal.

Companies survive on their ability to adapt when necessary, and it is increasingly necessary for them to do so. Successful adaptation is not, however, a chameleonlike response to the most immediate stimuli—a quick switch to a new enterprise or an impulse acquisition. Rather, successful adaptation seems to involve the thoughtful, incremental redirection of skills and knowledge bases so that today's expertise is reshaped into tomorrow's capabilities. Of course, companies do sometimes require a dramatic shift in priorities and/or leadership; progress need not be plodding. The point is that successful adaptation builds thoughtfully from where we are. Because we cannot foresee the future, we can prepare for it only by planning for continuous rejuvenation of a firm's strategically important knowledge assets—its core capabilities.

Within our individual life spans, we may observe the waxing and waning of corporate competitive advantage. We can remember when IBM was considered the safest, if not the only, source for computers and when photocopying was "Xeroxing"—period. When the fortunes of such technology-based giants are on the downswing, critics abound and managers sometimes despair. In the 1980s, AT&T and Xerox were popular targets for cynicism. In the early 1990s, it was fashionable to decry IBM's management and to pontificate on the failures of Kodak. Unquestionably, the traditional competitive bases of these companies have been somewhat undermined, but experience suggests it may be too early to count them out, for they have vast reservoirs of deep knowledge on which to draw. It remains to be seen whether their managers can continuously transform the technology into commercializable products, but we may be witnessing a temporary (albeit sizable) dip in fortunes rather than a one-way plunge to obscurity.

Many companies display amazing resilience, enduring through generations, albeit often in altered forms. Motorola, producer of semiconductor chips as well as cellular phones, started out making automobile radios and walkie-talkies. Sharp Corporation, maker of the world's most advanced liquid crystal displays, was a mechanical-pencil shop at its birth. Harris Corporation, a contender in the new multimedia industry, was founded to produce printing presses. Today, 3M is as well known for its tapes and Post-it Notes as for its origins in abrasives and minerals. Such companies exploited traditional capabilities even as they grew entirely new ones.

The primary engine for the creation and growth of technological capabilities is the development of new products and processes, and it is within this development context that we shall explore managing knowledge. However, this context is extremely extensive; it encompasses every function from research to service, including marketing as well as engineering, and design as well as manufacturing. Indeed, this book has grown from a desire to understand what difference it makes to managers involved in *any* aspect of product or process development to view every day's activities from the perspective of knowledge management and growth. Products are physical manifestations of knowledge, and their worth largely, if not entirely, depends on the value of the knowledge they embody. The management of knowledge, therefore, is a skill, like financial acumen, and managers who understand and develop it will dominate competitively.

The word *wellsprings* appears in the title of this book because a wellspring, the source of a stream, sustains life within and beyond the riverbanks or, by becoming dammed up or polluted, denies its existence. The most useful wellsprings are constant, reliable, and their waters pure. As flows of water from such wellsprings feed the biological systems around them, so in the same way, flows of appropriate knowledge into and within companies enable them to develop competitively advantageous capabilities. However, without sources of renewal, wellsprings can run dry; moreover, the channels feeding out of them require tending, clearing, adapting. Within corporations, managers *at all levels* of the organization are the keepers of the wellsprings of knowledge. To them falls the responsibility for selecting the correct knowledge sources, for understanding how knowledge is accessed and channeled, and for redirecting flows or fighting contamination.

Although *Wellsprings of Knowledge* has its intellectual roots in research conducted over the past decade, its most immediate stimulus was a second-year MBA course taught at Harvard Business School on the topic of managing strategic technological capabilities. From my research in industry and the cases I wrote, my students and I discovered that managers in many companies were convinced they needed to identify strategically vital capabilities. What puzzled them was what to do once they had made that identification. The link between strategic technological capabilities and daily routines was unclear. That is, once a company knew how to position itself relative to the competition, how should managers build the capability to support that position? What should they be doing differently if they wanted to create, nurture, enhance, or adapt core technological capabilities? I therefore wrote this book in the hopes that it may stimulate—and help—managers *to think constantly about the potential knowledge-building import of every single technology-related decision they make.* Those decisions must originate in an understanding of the long-term, systemic, and people-based nature of technological advantage.

My secondary purpose is to provide academics with material that can be used in training managers in this kind of thinking. Therefore, the book contains extensive (albeit not comprehensive) references to the works of my fellow researchers.

In every chapter, I rely heavily upon illustrations of both successful and failed attempts to manage knowledge. Some examples are mentioned in passing; others are described at some length. Most are drawn from field research, much of it personally conducted. The recitation of failures is an important element in the overall theme of the book because managers' candid reflections on what they have learned from missteps are often more revealing than postproject rationalizations about successes.

Wellsprings of Knowledge is organized in three parts. In Part I, I lay out the conceptual frameworks that will shape the rest of the discussion and also present a dilemma central to the entire process of managing knowledge—that core capabilities, in all the dimensions described, are simultaneously core rigidities. Strategic technological capabilities have a dark side. The very system that conveys competitive advantage can also disadvantage the company, either when it is carried to an extreme or when the competitive environment changes. Managers must be highly sensitive to the signals that indicate when a core capability is strangling growth and adaptation—i.e., is functioning as a core rigidity.

Since core capabilities (and rigidities) are interlocked *systems* of knowledge bases and flows, they are not easily described in the abstract. Therefore, much of the first two chapters is devoted to grounding subsequent discussion very concretely in the real-life situation of particular companies and to detailed exploration of the nature of capabilities. This first part of the book also briefly introduces four key activities that create flows of knowledge and direct them into the core capabilities.

Part II, is the heart of the book, drawing upon extensive field studies to describe and illustrate those four key *activities.* Well managed, these activities enable companies to tap the wellsprings consistently and continuously. Thus, this second segment of the book directs attention to some very specific managerial behaviors that build—or undermine—capabilities. Time-constrained readers and those with a bent toward immediate action may wish to focus relatively more attention on these chapters. Knowledge wellsprings are tapped and renewed through such new-product and new-process development-related activities as: (1) integrated problem solving across different cognitive and functional barriers (Chapter 3), (2) implementation of new methodologies and process tools (Chapter 4), (3) experimentation (Chapter 5), and (4) importing know-how from outside technological and market sources (Chapters 6 and 7). These four activities are not the sole province of research departments, as most R&D managers would be the first to admit. As a Bell Laboratories researcher has noted, "[I]nnovation . . . is a connected process in which many and sufficient creative acts, from research through service, couple together in an integrated way for a common goal. . . ."[1] Managers at all company levels and in all functions are gatekeepers for the flow of information and knowledge. Because life is simplified by the *closing* of gates, a manager's first impulse may be to do just that—to close off new ideas or to direct them into well-worn channels where they will be gradually eroded into recognizable, comfortable shapes. Yet to grow, organizations, like individuals, require the stimulus of challenge and innovation. Therefore, managing knowledge requires designing an environment that encourages *creative* enactments of these four activities. That is, the management of these activities distinguishes organizations that learn from those that do not.

In Part III, I return to a more holistic perspective on core technological capabilities, first by devoting a chapter to their development in global companies. Then the book concludes with a brief summary of some general characteristics of organizations and managers who engender, nurture, discipline, and encourage technological knowledge—who do a good job of creating core technological capabilities. The key to managing wellsprings of knowledge is to emphasize the constant rebirth of expertise. That rebirth, in turn, is determined by the attitude managers and organizations foster toward learning. Thus, this final chapter attempts to capture the components of the managerial mind-set that keep the knowledge wellsprings open and flowing.

P A R T   O N E

THE NATURE OF CORE CAPABILITIES AND RIGIDITIES

C H A P T E R   O N E

Core Capabilities

Product development and product-based competition is often only the last 100 yards of a marathon.
—Gary Hamel
 Visiting Professor, London Business School[1]

To stand still is to fall behind.
—Gordon Forward
 CEO, Chaparral Steel

Despite the Greek myth about goddess of wisdom Athena, who burst full-grown from Zeus's forehead, knowledge does not appear all at once. Rather, knowledge accumulates slowly, over time, shaped and channeled into certain directions through the nudging of hundreds of daily managerial decisions. Nor does knowledge occur only one time; it is constantly aborning. As suggested in the introduction to this book, knowledge reservoirs in organizations are not static pools but wellsprings, constantly replenished with streams of new ideas and constituting an ever-flowing source of corporate renewal. Therefore, the development of core capabilities is inextricably linked to learning; knowledge is both raw material and finished goods in today's corporations.

Core Capabilities: Definitions

The starting point for managing knowledge in an organization is an understanding of core capabilities and, for technology-based companies, core *technological* capabilities. Thus, at the outset, we need to define these terms carefully in preparation for a detailed look at them later in Part I.

"Core" capabilities constitute a competitive advantage for a firm; they have been built up over time and cannot be easily imitated.[2] They are distinct from both supplemental and enabling capabilities, neither of which is sufficiently superior to those of competitors to offer a sustainable advantage. (See Figure 1-1.) *Supplemental* capabilities are those that add value to core capabilities but that could be imitated—for example, particular distribution channels or strong but not unique packaging design skills. *Enabling* capabilities are necessary but not sufficient in themselves to competitively distinguish a company. World-class quality in manufacturing, for instance, is increasingly the price for entering the game rather than the certain road to superiority. Technology-based companies cannot compete without manufacturing capabilities at least on a par with those of their competitors. However, such capabilities are core only if they embody proprietary knowledge (unavailable from public sources) and are superior to those of competitors.[3] Thus, even excellent assembly operations are unlikely to constitute a core technological capability because the knowledge content (including automated equipment) required to bring such operations to peak quality performance is available to all competitors.

To create and maintain core technological capabilities, managers need at least two abilities: they must (1) know how to manage the *activities* that create knowledge and (2) possess an understanding of exactly what constitutes a core capability—what are its *dimensions.* There is a continuous interaction between the activities that managers encourage and the core capabilities of the firm. That is, core capabilities are created through knowledge-creating activities, but those activities are also dependent on, and enabled by, core

Figure 1-1 Strategic Importance of Technological Capabilities

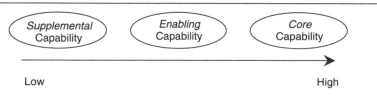

Strategic Importance of Technological Capabilities to the Firm

capabilities. *This book zeros in on managing the interaction between activities pursued in the course of developing new products and processes, and the organization's core technological capabilities.*

We begin our exploration of both the systems that constitute core capabilities and four of the most critical knowledge-building activities interacting with those capabilities by way of a tour through a company obsessed with learning—Chaparral Steel. Chaparral managers think seriously about the potential knowledge-building import of these four activities and, in fact, of every technology-related decision they make. We shall first learn how Chaparral employees (1) draw upon cross-functional expertise to solve operating problems, (2) integrate new tools and methodologies, (3) experiment, and (4) import knowledge from outside the company. We shall then scrutinize the core capability that interacts with these knowledge-creating activities. Chaparral management defines its core capability as *the ability to transform technology rapidly into new product and process.* We examine the four dimensions of that capability—physical systems, skills, managerial systems, and values. Following this tour through Chaparral, which illustrates both knowledge-creating activities and the resultant core capability, we return to look in depth at the four dimensions of a core capability as a generic system framework that applies to *any* company.

The four *activities* introduced in this chapter and the four interactive *dimensions of core capabilities* provide the conceptual armature on which the body of the book is built.

Chaparral Steel: A Knowledge-Based Organization

What does an organization managed by and for the growth of knowledge look like? How do managers think and behave in a learning organization? What activities create the knowledge assets? There are probably no perfect exemplars. In fact, many institutions have knowledge management and learning capabilities.[4] However, to penetrate the mist of vagueness that enshrouds the term *knowledge management,* let us place a real organization under the microscope. Chaparral Steel,[5] a minimill that is the tenth largest U.S. steel producer, offers an interesting example of a company focused on knowledge management. As a basis for a generic discussion of knowledge assets—i.e., competencies and capabilities—we can look at the workplace *activities* that characterize Chaparral's operations and see this unusual culture in action. As management scholars have pointed out, "espoused theory" tells us little about real behavior; we need to study "theory in practice"—i.e., view the actions that reflect managerial attitudes and values.[6]

Chaparral CEO Gordon Forward claims that "[O]ne of our core competencies is the rapid realization of new technology into [steel] products. We are a learning organization." The claim is not baseless. Although no one company is a paragon, Chaparral's policies are highly consistent with prescriptions of organizational learning theorists.[7] More important, Chaparral's high quality standards have been rewarded by the market, and company productivity compares favorably to both U.S. and Asian competitors. In its almost two-decade-long history, Chaparral has set world records for productivity a number of times; in 1990, its 1.5 person-hours per rolled ton of steel compared to a U.S. average of 5.3, a Japanese average of 5.6, and a German average of 5.7. Chaparral was the first American steel company (and only the second company outside of Japan at the time) to be awarded the right to use the Japanese Industrial Standard certification on its general structural steel products. Individual managers as well as the company as a whole have won numerous awards.

The company has not sought rapid growth and geographic expansion (as have some of its primary competitors), in large part due to a deep concern for retaining the culture that has yielded the rapid development capability. Chaparral is compact, and its size (fewer than a thousand employees) renders it accessible to analysis; the observer can see how the system works in some detail. Placing a real organization under such an intense microscope runs some risks. Not only is no company totally invariant in performance, but the modest size that enables close scrutiny of Chaparral invites readers in large organizations to dismiss the example as atypical. Yet the fact that everyone can know almost everyone else in the company does not explain Chaparral's extraordinary environment, since few small organizations look like this one. Moreover, throughout the rest of the book, we will see illustrations from very different settings of the strategy, the activities, the principles, the managerial practices that characterize Chaparral at its best.

Making Steel

Visualize a steel mill: the mammoth hollowed-out foundry building is as big as an airplane hanger. The air is so heavy with the stench of hot steel you can taste iron and carbon on your tongue. Indoor lightning flashes as electrodes liquefy old car bodies into a 3,000-degree-Fahrenheit bath. Burly workers look puny and hellishly vulnerable beside a two-story-high pot of molten metal so hot that a splash would explode if it hit the floor. You are struck by the awesome fury of barely contained churning liquid as it is poured through a constraining, forming mold. Even a small protrusion on the mold's precisely smooth side or an oxygen bubble can rend the fragile skin formed around the steel, releasing uncontrolled torrents of white-hot, liquid metal onto machinery below in a fearsome "breakout." The operator controlling the pour from a pulpit high above the floor cannot relax vigilance for a second. Emerging from the mold, the steel threads through the mill in long, glowing strips. A succession of rollers knead the metal, pliant only as long as it is red-hot, into square, rectangular, then increasingly flat shapes. The steel passes through the various apertures, and rollers are skillfully designed to create the desired crystalline structure in reinforcement bars or beams used in the construction of buildings and motor homes.

The steel production process is a weird combination of impressive brute physical force and highly skilled finesse. How can one apply a fragile, academic-sounding term like *learning organization* to a production facility where raw physical power so predominates and where productivity is such a major concern that every second counts? Do these people really think about "knowledge management"? They do, from the CEO down to the line operator who is standing, stopwatch in palm, persistently trying to better the speed of the rolling mills—just because he thinks it is possible.

An Organic Learning System

A close look at Chaparral reveals an organic learning system so tightly coupled that CEO Forward says he can tour competitors through the plant, show them almost "everything and we will be giving away nothing because they can't take it home with them." His confidence derives from the fact that the knowledge management organization is comprehensible only as an organic whole.[8] Moreover, it is in continuous flux, constantly self-regenerating. Even if a competitor identifies important elements of the system, emulation will require time. By then, Chaparral managers trust they will have moved on to the next innovation. This system has evolved in response to a turbulent competitive environment.[9] Forward observes: "We have to go like hell all the time. If the price of what we sell goes up too high . . . all of a sudden lots of folks will be jumping in. And they can get into business in 18 months or so. . . . We constantly chip away the ground we stand on. We have to keep out front all the time. . . ."[10]

Keeping out in front for Chaparral means leading the world in the low-cost, safe production of high-quality steel. The test of such an explicitly stated strategic vision is the extent to which it permeates the whole organization, guiding every micro- and macrodecision. Unless it can be directly translated into operational principles—that is, into guidelines for running the factory lines—it may have little effect on actual shop floor behavior. The goal of leading the world requires innovating beyond the current cutting edge of production techniques. Maintaining a cost advantage requires constant improvements in productivity. The vision dictates that those improvements cannot come at the expense of quality or employee safety. Therefore, the goal for every hour, the criterion for every person's activity, is crystal clear: make ever more steel—increasingly better than anyone else.[11]

Knowledge-Building Activities

The clarity of the goal enables managers and operators alike to concentrate their attention on those activities that add obvious value. *Activities*—not goals or financial rewards or even skills (until they are activated)—create a firm's capabilities. A firm like Chaparral nurtures and creates knowledge through certain characteristic activities. These activities do not constitute a sterile checklist of "to-dos." Nor do the activities have any meaning separate from the people who conduct them since those individuals bring to the activities a set of idiosyncratic abilities, histories, personalities. Each person or team conducts the activity in a distinct manner. Thus, knowledge building for an organization occurs by combining people's distinct individualities with a particular set of activities. It is this combination that enables innovation, and it is this combination that managers manage. For as we shall see, managing the activities as a sterile process, without consideration for the innovation potential the actors bring to it, is dangerous.

At Chaparral, four primary learning activities create and control the knowledge necessary for its current and future operations. Three of these activities are internally focused: (1) shared, creative problem solving (to produce current products); (2) implementing and integrating new methodologies and tools (to enhance internal operations); and (3) formal and informal experimentation (to build capabilities for the future). The final activity is externally focused: (4) pulling in expertise from outside.[12] (See Figure 1-2.) Throughout the book, we will examine the activities that create, channel, and control knowledge, and we will draw on many examples besides Chaparral. However, by looking even superficially at a particular set of such activities in a real factory, we start with our feet on the managerial ground.

Shared Problem Solving. In a learning environment, progress must be everyone's business—not just the province of a few specialists.[13] As a foreman explains, "We are all out here to make it run. Probably 90 percent of the problems never even make it to the morning meetings [held among everyone on the shift to discuss problems]. They are fixed in the field."

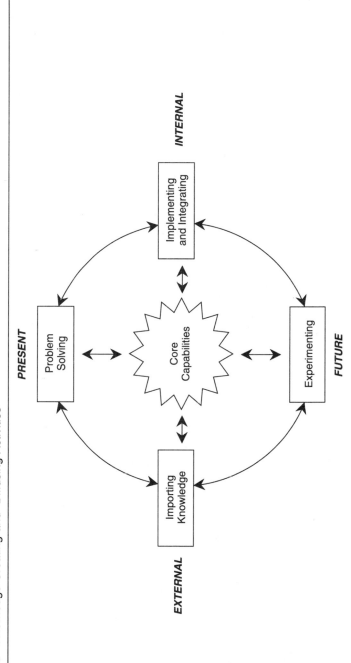

Figure 1-2 Knowledge-Creating and -Diffusing Activities

One of the greatest advantages of this attitude, as a Chaparral maintenance foreman points out, is that "[i]deas come from just about everybody. The operators working on the equipment have a lot of input because they see the exact problems when they happen. . . ." For instance, when cooling hoses burst during the first few weeks of starting up the new near-net-shape[14] project, a group of operators, a welder, foremen, and a buyer spontaneously gathered to discuss the problem, then scattered to seek solutions. "When something like that comes up, and there seems no immediate solution," explained a senior operator, "you go see what the problem is. You don't say, 'That's not my area,' or 'I don't know that much about it.' You just show up." In this case, "everyone telephoned some person they thought might know how to fix the problem—vendors, experts—and within three to four hours, we were getting calls back. Servicepeople were showing up, and we worked the problem out. If it had been just one guy, probably a foreman, and everyone walked out . . . it would have taken him ten times longer to find a solution."

This kind of shared problem solving sounds chaotic, and it undoubtedly is at times. Yet the interesting assumptions are that any employee will willingly apply his or her intelligence to the problem until it is solved—and that, in the absence of evidence to the contrary, five or six heads are better than one. However, as noted below, when the problems to be solved require invention or innovation, as distinct from merely locating expertise, the activity is quite different.

Knowledge management demands the ability to move knowledge in all directions—up, down, across. At Chaparral, knowledge flows readily not only because of the company's size but because considerable effort has been made to minimize both vertical and horizontal barriers. A scant two levels separate the CEO from operators in the rolling mill, and employees have little hesitation in approaching anyone. A millwright notes: "If you have tact, you can tell anybody from Mr. Forward on down exactly what is on your mind. There is no problem in expressing your opinion here." Visitors to the factory will see evidence of this free information flow—for example, an operator stopping Gordon Forward on a walk through the plant to discuss problems with a new product. Similarly, a group of workers gathered by the clothes lockers strategically located near a vice president's office get an immediate response to questions as the VP walks by.

Horizontal boundaries are similarly minimal. "At Chaparral," a maintenance foreman notes, "we get involved with the whole process. We are not just tied to one area." Operators—not separate inspectors—identify quality problems on the line and report them to the quality control department. Production workers do 40 percent of the maintenance tasks. Though there is a marketing department, everyone in the firm is considered a salesperson. Every employee from CEO to receptionist has a business card to use with customers. Security guards enter data while on night duty—and are trained paramedics as well.

Integrating New Technologies and Methodologies. Chaparral competes through constantly improving production processes. Managers assume that the performance of any purchased equipment can be improved; innovation accompanies implementation of new tools. Some improvements are novel enough to be patented. The rolling mill equipment its vendor believed limited to 8-inch slabs is turning out 14-inch slabs, and the vendor has tried to buy back the redesign. The two electric arc furnaces, designed originally to melt annual rates of 250,000 and 500,000 tons of scrap metal, now produce over 600,000 and 1 million tons, respectively. The physical processes following the molding step are also knowledge-intensive. When Chaparral set up "hot-link" rolling, whereby hot cast steel is sent directly into the rolling mills, only one other steel mill in the world had that capability.

This is a do-it-yourself company, with no acknowledged staff positions and only a few positions that seem stafflike (e.g., personnel). Although there are fifty graduate engineers and technicians, all have line duties, tied directly to steel production. Decisions about production methodologies are pushed down to the lowest possible supervisory level, "where the knowledge is." Process improvements are immediately enacted, with no wait for management approval or standardization of "best practices." If it works, it is the de facto standard. If it improves performance, everyone will imitate it. "Whoever can come up with an idea on how to fix it, from the millwrights or myself right on up to the top . . . does it right then," explains a foreman. Lead operators are selected for their knowledge-transmitting as well as knowledge-creating skills, for much process knowledge flows horizontally among peers. Work is structured with the objective of disseminating knowledge. For instance, in "commissioning" (ramping up to problem-free production) the new mill that receives the near-net-shape product, only two teams of operators are being trained. Each team works a twelve-hour shift (with paid overtime). After the initial eight weeks of this grueling schedule, these operators will be dispersed among the rest of the crews, to diffuse the knowledge they have created and assimilated about the idiosyncrasies of this new process.

Constant Formal and Informal Experimenting. No separate R&D facility exists at Chaparral.[15] Production Manager Paul Wilson takes a stance unusual for someone in charge of getting product out the door: "In other companies, the word is, Don't rock the boat. Here we rock the hell out of the boat. We don't know the factory's limits. We want it to change, to evolve."

Chaparral employees are often unable to identify the source of production innovation. Wilson explains, "It is hard to say who fathers an idea. It doesn't make any difference. Everyone shares in the pride of doing, and if the experiment fails, everyone shares in the failure. In other places, a few people do a lot of innovating. Here a lot of people do little bits that add up." At Chaparral, there is no formal requirement (as at some Japanese companies) for a certain number of suggestions for improvement. Vice President of Operations Dave Fournie says of Chaparral, "You don't have to have credit for particular ideas to be thought good at your job. Lots of innovations take more than one good idea. They go through a gestation period, and lots of people figure out how to make sense of it. The point is to focus on the good of the whole. That's why we don't have suggestion boxes, where you hide ideas so someone else won't steal them."

Creating knowledge requires constant pushing beyond the familiar, and Chaparral employees are skilled experimenters. The nature of the experimentation, however, is shaped by both the skills of the actors and the risk of the endeavor. A visitor was surprised to find extensive overhead slides prepared for the board of directors elaborating formal Taguchi experimental designs guiding the development of the horizontal caster, a high-risk project. This extremely technical presentation was to help directors understand the methodical knowledge-creation process, enable them to identify critical decision points, and thereby better equip them to evaluate the risk.

Yet at the same time, much ad hoc, inexpensive, and unscientific experimentation goes on. Chaparral employees are experts at cut-and-try. In one project, a prototype of metal splashboards was first constructed out of plywood. By continuously soaking the wood in water, the crews were able to keep it from being consumed by molten steel just long enough to prove the concept. "We were the local hardware store's favorite plywood customers for a while," one employee recalled. In another experiment, employees welded together copper prototypes of a new steel mold. The pure copper, which was less expensive than sturdier alloys, held together just long enough for observation and learning.

Pulling in Expertise from Outside. An important source of knowledge is found in other organizations. Chaparral employees constantly benchmark and scan the world for technical expertise.[16] Managers never hesitate to invent when necessary, but only after assuring themselves through extensive searches that no available system will suit their needs. The company works with the best suppliers it can identify in the world—and then pushes those suppliers to innovate, often far beyond current designs and products. Possibly because of CEO Forward's early career experience as a research metallurgist, the company is very aggressive in pursuing the latest industry knowledge. Chaparral sought its much-coveted steel certification from the Japanese not because management ever expected to sell much steel in Japan but because it was convinced that the Japanese would go through the company's process carefully—and Chaparral would learn from the exercise.

Chaparral personnel also very actively scan external sources of expertise through more than the usual publication channels. Forward applies the perspective of a researcher to environmental scanning for his factory: "By the time you hear about a technology in a paper at a conference, it is too late." This philosophy explains why Chaparral invests in unorthodox knowledge-gathering mechanisms—for instance, cosponsoring a research conference with the Colorado School of Mining about a new alloy under investigation, in order to garner the latest knowledge.

These four sets of characteristic activities at Chaparral both feed into and derive from the company's core capabilities—its knowledge assets. What, then, are those knowledge assets? We turn next to a close look at the dimensions of Chaparral's core capabilities, starting with the reservoir of knowledge housed in (1) the skills and (2) the physical systems that distinguish this minimill. Then we look at (3) the management systems and (4) the norms, or values, that support the growth of knowledge.

Skills and Physical Technical Systems at Chaparral

Chaparral's expertise is embodied in the energy and skills of every person, from its industry-acknowledged expert on mold making or Gordon Forward, with his formidable qualifications as an MIT-educated metallurgist, to the foreman who has accumulated experience since he started on the very first line eighteeen years ago. Although much of the knowledge is tacit, in people's heads, it is also embedded in superior physical equipment and systems. Chaparral boasts such cutting-edge equipment as an automobile shredder it believes to be the fastest and most efficient in the world, an unusual horizontal (instead of vertical) caster, and some of the most advanced digital furnace controls anywhere.

Managerial Systems at Chaparral

The accumulation of knowledge in the physical systems and in people's heads is encouraged by managerial systems that have evolved to enable and reward learning.[17] Since they must be innovators, constantly challenging the status quo, employees are carefully selected as much for their potential, their attitude toward learning, and their enthusiasm as they are for a specific background. And their future colleagues on the line make hiring decisions.

The compensation structure embodies respect for the contribution of each individual to the whole enterprise. There are no time clocks at Chaparral. CEO Forward explains, "When I am ill, I get a day off. Why shouldn't everyone else?" He is fond of saying that the management system was designed for the 97 percent of employees who are "conscientious people who want to put in a full day's work." The 3 percent who abused the system when the company switched to salaries from hourly paychecks were let go. Bonus schemes are linked to company profits—for everyone (including janitors and secretaries). An operator comments, "The more money the company makes, the more money I make. The profit-sharing system creates built-in pride." Further, 93 percent of the employees are stockholders and, together, own 3 percent of the stock. Employee shareholding started in 1988, when each worker received one share for every year worked at the company; 62 percent buy additional shares every month through payroll deductions. Although the monetary implications are small, this policy is consistent with the rest of the rewards structure, and some employees find it symbolically important. A furnace controls operator comments: "I feel like this company partly belongs to me. Owning part of the company makes you care. I take better care not to waste anything, because I feel like I am paying for it."[18]

There are formal and informal educational programs, too. Although Chaparral management has sent some employees back to school to obtain advanced degrees, it also invests heavily in an unusual formal apprenticeship program for everyone in the plant, developed with the Bureau of Apprenticeship and Training in the U.S. Department of Labor. (Most apprenticeships are run by unions.) As Forward notes, "Expertise must be in the hands of the people that make the product."

The roughly 3.5-year-long program allows apprentices to progress to the level of senior operator/craftsman by successfully completing 7,280 hours of on-the-job training and designated formal schooling. The foremen of individual crews schedule the on-the-job training and evaluate the candidates' systematic progression through various tasks in the factory—e.g., 2,200 hours in steel-pouring operations is one qualification in ladle metallurgy apprenticeship.

Chaparral also invests in people through informal practices such as "vicing." At other companies, when a foreman is absent, the foreman from a prior shift is often required to stay on in that role. At Chaparral, the foreman is asked to work the extra hours at the usual pay rate but in a subordinate position. The most senior operator is temporarily promoted to "vice-foreman" to cover the supervisory position. This practice benefits the company in that the prior shift foreman's experience is still available, while the senior operator is being trained for a future role as foreman.

Underlying Values at Chaparral

Such incentive and educational systems are supported by a strong set of very clear and consistent values. Values critical to creating a learning environment are: respect for the individual, tolerance of failure, and openness to ideas from outside. Assuming that all employees have potential to contribute (if they are willing to learn), Forward has said, "We figured that if we could tap the egos of everyone in the company, we could move mountains."[19] Chaparral has many of the outward symbols of egalitarianism characteristic of other minimills: no assigned parking places, no different-colored hard hats or uniforms reflecting title or position—and the local diner is a company dining room.

One of the most unusual values for a highly competitive operation under pressure to get product out the door is the tolerance for risk taking and failure. In fact, Chaparral managers avoid riskless projects because a "sure thing" holds no promise of competitive advantage—no opportunity to out-learn competitors. Says Forward, "We look at risk differently from other people. We always ask what is the risk of doing *nothing*. We don't bet the company, but if we're not taking some calculated risks, if we stop growing, we may die." This positive attitude toward risk permeates the company. "Everybody makes mistakes," a Chaparral foreman remarks. "You don't have to cover up a mistake here. You just fix it and keep on going."

Ample evidence indicates this attitude permeates actions, not just words. As further discussed in Chapter 5, in 1986, Dave Fournie (Medium Section Mill superintendent at the time) championed the ultimately disastrous installation of a $1.5 million arc saw for cutting finished beams. He was not penalized—but promoted. This propensity to reward risk taking, however, does not equate to a myopic obsession with invention as the only path to creating value. "Not *reinvented* here" is the operative slogan. There is no value in recreating something—only in building on the best existing knowledge. Therefore, openness to external ideas is another critical value.

Chaparral's Interdependent System

Chaparral's skills, physical systems, learning activities, values, and managerial philosophies and practices are obviously highly interdependent. Competitively advantageous equipment can be designed and constantly improved *only* if the workforce is highly skilled. Continuous education is attractive *only* if employees are carefully selected for their willingness to learn. Sending workers throughout the world to garner ideas is cost-effective *only* if they are empowered to apply what they learned to production problems. Hence, continuous learning and knowledge accumulation depend on the sense of ownership derived from the incentive systems, on the pride of accomplishment gained from special educational systems, on values embedded in policies and managerial practices, as well as on specific technical skills.

When Gordon Forward claims rapid product development as a core competency, then, he is referring to the entire dynamic system of knowledge-generation and knowledge-channeling activities, interacting with the knowledge already captured in employee skills and in physical equipment, reinforced by carefully crafted rewards and incentives. This *system* gives Chaparral its distinctive advantage over other steel producers, including almost all other minimills.

Now that we have toured Chaparral, we can generalize from our observations in this particular company to discuss the nature of core technological capabilities in any organization. In the remainder of the chapter, we consider the essence of core capabilities: What is the history of the concept? Where in the corporation are capabilities located? What comprises each of the four dimensions making up a core technological capability, and what does each look like as part of a core capability in companies other than Chaparral?

The Essence of Core Capabilities

The idea that certain core capabilities bestow a competitive advantage on a company is not new. Various authors have called them distinctive, firm-specific, or organizational competencies; resource deployments; or invisible assets.[20] Researchers for several decades have noted that a strategy of building on such distinctive capabilities appears to lead to superior performance. For instance, Rumelt[21] discovered that of nine diversification strategies identified, the two that built on an existing skill or resource base in the firm were associated with the highest overall corporate performance. Recent research has supported that finding by showing that industry-specific capabilities increased the likelihood that a firm could exploit a new technology within that industry.

Such work has led management researchers to advise managers to "build capabilities and then encourage the development of plans for exploiting them."[22] This advice is often accompanied by the observation that effective competition is usually based less on dramatic, strategic leaps than on steady, more incremental innovation.[23] However, the proponents of this view (sometimes called the "learning school" of strategy)[24] do not suggest a static view of competence. Rather, they recognize that although organizations, like the people who populate them, have invested in knowledge building over the years and have developed particular skills, they still must continue to build and change those skills in response to changing environments. In fact, as Gary Hamel has pointed out, a "core" competence or capability (terms he considers interchangeable) "provides a gateway to new opportunities."[25] Continuous innovation is an act of "creative destruction."[26] Even "seemingly minor" innovations that alter the architecture of a product can undermine the usefulness of deeply embedded knowledge.[27] Of course, radical changes in the environment can necessitate an organization's totally remaking itself. However, most organizations face a somewhat less dramatic and (ironically) almost *more* challenging situation: they must continually enhance their capabilities, absent an obvious life-or-death crisis to motivate change.

The Locus of Core Capabilities

There is much debate over whether core capabilities should be defined at the corporate level only[28] or whether a core capability can be located in a division or function within the organization. If a core capability is one that provides competitive advantage, it would seem logical that it might reside at any line-of-business level. Some quite successful corporations are composed of divisions that have little technical synergy. Johnson & Johnson's Ethicon Division, producing instruments for endoscopic surgery, has relatively little technological knowledge in common with J&J's Consumer Division, which produces baby shampoo, among other things. Hewlett-Packard's Medical Instruments Division is dissimilar in technological knowledge from the Mass Storage Products Division. This is not to say that such divisions cannot combine technological capabilities at a market or product level to produce something that neither could have delivered alone. Managers at HP, for example, have announced that they wish to take advantage of their competencies in measurement, communications, and computation (MC^2) to create synergistic products. When HP won a $63 million contract from Ford to create a diagnostic system that monitors engine performance, reports the data back to a central computer, and analyzes the data, it had an advantage over IBM, which could deliver the computation and communications—but had no competence in measurement, in the sensors and monitoring equipment needed.[29]

Moreover, even corporations serving quite different markets can reduce their technological diversity to some common component. At 3M, the company's business is "disposable chemicals," a term that covers everything from coatings to the transparencies used in its overhead projectors. Xerox is the "document" company. However, such reductions to the lowest common denominator are useful only if they serve to guide the identification, nurturing, and exploitation of knowledge bases—i.e., if they help managers design and control daily activities. The test of a useful description of a core capability is the extent to which it can be meaningfully operationalized. That is why this book emphasizes the design of *activities* that create and channel knowledge rather than the process of agreeing upon a phrase or statement that captures a company's technological identity.

Before examining the process of developing, nurturing, and enhancing internal capabilities in depth, we need to establish a framework and vocabulary for discussion. Today, many companies are struggling to define their capabilities. It is obviously inadequate to note merely that such capabilities are "unique" or "superior to the competition" or even to describe them as "resource deployment." We need some way of discussing such capabilities quite specifically. Only then can we decide whether we have initiated the *right* knowledge-creation activities. The next section revisits the four dimensions of a core capability first seen at Chaparral and discusses each more fully.

The Nature of Core *Technological Capabilities*

In this book, the term *technological capability* is used to encompass the *system* of activities, physical systems, skills and knowledge bases, managerial systems of education and reward, and values that create a special advantage for a company or line of business.[30] As noted earlier, such systems may be considered *supplemental, enabling,* or *core.* Supplemental capabilities, as the name implies, are nice to have—but unessential. Enabling technological capabilities are those that are important to a company as a minimum basis for competition in the industry but that, by themselves, convey no particular competitive advantage.[31] Core technological capabilities, by contrast, are those that set the company apart from the rest of the pack and at least potentially provide a competitive edge.

Labeling certain capabilities "technological" risks implying that such competitive advantages consist solely of technical knowledge. However, even those capabilities with a strong technical component are multidimensional *systems* only one of whose dimensions is wholly or principally technical in nature.[32] As the description of Chaparral Steel suggests, core, or strategic, capabilities comprise at least four interdependent dimensions, two of which may be thought of as dynamic knowledge reservoirs, or competencies, and two of which are knowledge-control or -channeling mechanisms. (See Figure 1-3).

1. *Employee knowledge and skill:* This dimension is the most obvious one.

2. *Physical technical systems.* But technological competence accumulates not only in the heads of people; it also accumulates in the physical systems that they build over time—databases, machinery, and software programs.

3. *Managerial systems:* The accumulation of employee knowledge is guided and monitored by the company's systems of education, rewards, and incentives. These managerial systems—particularly incentive structures—create the channels through which knowledge is accessed and flows; they also set up barriers to undesired knowledge-creation activities.

4. *Values and norms:* These determine what kinds of knowledge are sought and nurtured, what kinds of knowledge-building activities are tolerated and encouraged. There are systems of caste and status, rituals of behavior, and passionate beliefs associated with various kinds of technological knowledge that are as rigid and complex as those associated with religion. Therefore, values serve as knowledge-screening and -control mechanisms.

Figure 1-3 Dimensions of a Core Capability

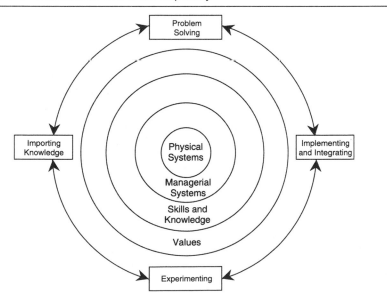

Although, at least potentially, aspects of these four dimensions may be readily absorbed by outsiders, it is those portions of the system, and especially the synergy from unique combinations of them, that are neither readily transferred nor imitated. These provide the company strategic advantage.

Skills and Knowledge Base

The skills and knowledge embodied in employees is the dimension most often associated with core capabilities.[33] This skills/knowledge dimension encompasses both techniques specific to the firm and scientific understanding.[34] For instance, at Chaparral, one engineer is a recognized industry expert on the design of molds—the shaping aperture through which molten steel is poured on its way to the rolling mills. Residing at Hewlett-Packard is one of a handful of people anywhere who have contributed to setting atomic time standards. The fruits of his scientific leadership are available to the world. However, he also helped design a set of measurement instruments including a clock accurate to one second in two million years. Millipore Corporation's recently divested Waters Division produces high-pressure liquid chromatography systems. An important component is the pump that stimulates the flow of the chemical compound to be analyzed through the separation process. Designing such pumps requires knowledge about the physics of fluids and application of these principles to separating fluids according to molecular size. The scientific principles are public knowledge, available to anyone. However, Waters employs one of the foremost experts in the world on the application of those principles to pumping fluids under pressure.

Such skills have been called T-shaped,[35] meaning that they are both very deep (the stem of the *T*) yet broad enough (the cross of the *T*) to enable their possessors to explore the interfaces between their particular knowledge domain and various applications of that knowledge in particular products. It is the understanding of those interfaces that makes the skills especially critical to the organization's core capabilities. I will discuss their cultivation in Chapter 3.

Although the deep skill may be rare, it is probably not exclusive to a particular organization and may be accessed through consultants or by hiring in an expert. For instance, Chaparral Steel metallurgists frequently augment their knowledge through consultation with experts from their president's alma mater, the Massachusetts Institute of Technology. At the same time, the unique advantage that Chaparral's in-house molds expert provides is his understanding of how the geometry and metal composition of a particular mold interact with the evolving crystalline structure of the steel to create particular shapes. That knowledge is unobtainable in the laboratory or from textbooks: it has been created through on-line experimentation. Moreover, he knows the idiosyncrasies of Chaparral equipment and the skills of other employees.

Such knowledge became critical when, in 1991, Chaparral management decided to launch into a market usually avoided by minimills—namely, large structural beams for construction. In order to stay true to its strategic intent of remaining the low-cost producer, Chaparral had to come up with a highly innovative design. The challenge was to cast, right out of the mold, a strip of molten steel that so closely approximated the final desired shape ("near net-shape") that the need for subsequent highly energy intensive and expensive rolling was greatly reduced. The company achieved its purpose by purchasing some expertise from outside specialists (mold suppliers), but the extremely unusual mold rendering the project feasible was *designed* in-house by its own specialist. Why design in-house? "To keep the knowledge here," a mill manager explains.

As these examples suggest, there are at least three kinds of skills and knowledge constituting this dimension of a core capability: (1) scientific (public), (2) industry-specific, and (3) firm-specific. Moving from 1 to 3, these types of skills and knowledge are increasingly less codified and transferable.[36] (See Figure 1-4.) In the Chaparral example, the science of metallurgy is public (although, of course, the written, codified communication of this science in professional journals and textbooks lags behind the continual

Figure 1-4 Three Types of Skills and Knowledge

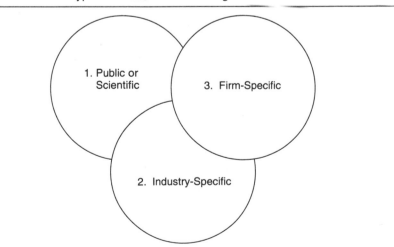

discovery process). Industry-specific knowledge about the manufacture of steel is diffused among many experts, including suppliers and consultants available to all comers.

In-house (firm-specific) knowledge, however, is not so easily duplicated. Although a Chaparral competitor can access the scientific knowledge of metallurgy, can hire the same MIT consultants, and can work with the same European suppliers, this competitor would also have to hire the in-house mold expert to begin to approximate Chaparral's near-net-shape process. Even then, the competitor would need the complementary skills of Chaparral operators, such as the man who spent time working with the German firm that actually constructed the innovative mold. Suppose the competitor hired *all* these individuals. It might then be able to imitate this one near-net-shape casting process. But that competitor would still not have duplicated what Chaparral considers its core capability—the ability to transfer technology rapidly into viable products. To understand why, we need to explore the other three dimensions of a core capability.

Physical Technical Systems

One reason that a competitor could imitate, but not duplicate, Chaparral's near-net-shape casting process is that both mold and process are patented. Thus, a portion of knowledge and skills integrated from public, industry-specific, and firm-specific know-how has been embedded in proprietary and protected form. However, patents are not the only (or necessarily the best) way to protect firm-specific knowledge. The tacit knowledge of various experts that accumulates in firms, structured and codified over time, becomes embedded in software, hardware, and accepted procedures. Because such compilations of knowledge derive from multiple individual sources, the whole technical system can be greater than the sum of its parts. The skills and knowledge of multiple experts (who need not have communicated with each other) are combined. Moreover, like a coral bed in the ocean, physical systems *preserve* the knowledge of individuals who have moved on to other functions, other jobs, other organizations.

The nature of the physical systems constituting part of a core capability depends on the bases of competition in the industry. Such systems can consist of software as well as hardware and equipment, and may confer temporary or long-lived advantage. For instance, in the airline industry, American Airline's computerized reservation system represented a competitive advantage until other major airlines constructed their own. American's system was proprietary and was not immediately imitated, but the information contained in it was not proprietary. Eventually, competitors developed comparable systems. As one of the primary architects of American Airline's capability in information systems noted in 1990, "In this new era, information technology will be at once more pervasive and less potent—table stakes for competition, but no trump card for competitive success."[37] What had once been a core capability was downgraded to an enabling capability.

When the knowledge embedded in databases is proprietary, software programs can constitute a longer-lived dimension of a core capability. Ford Motor Company has accumulated years of test data, including that on the crashing of cars. These data feed into computerized simulations that allow rapid concepts testing; an entrant into the automobile industry would certainly find it difficult to imitate such simulations. Even some current competitors have less readily accessible and usable data. Consequently, Ford considers its simulations a significant contributor to its core capability of total vehicle design.[38] Using these simulations, Ford engineers found, for instance, that a noise apparently originating in the floorboards could be traced instead to the acoustical interaction of sound waves reverberating between roof and floor. Since elimination of noise is a critical success factor in the industry, such discoveries are highly significant.

Managerial Systems

Managerial systems—the organized routines guiding resource accumulation and deployment—are a less obvious dimension of core capabilities. Yet incentive and educational programs or promotional practices can induce beneficial behaviors particular to a firm. One reason why Chaparral operators are technically proficient enough to contribute to the construction of a patented mold is the corporation's unique apprenticeship program for the entire production staff, involving both classroom education and on-the-job training. The program is unusual in at least two respects: first (unlike those sponsored by trade unions), it is a general rather than trade-specific apprenticeship; second, the classes are taught on a rotating basis by mill foremen. The combination of mill-specific information and general education (including such unusual offerings as enhancing interpersonal communication skills) would be difficult to imitate, if only because of the diverse abilities required of instructors. The foremen know what to teach, having experienced problems on the factory floor; they then have the no doubt sobering opportunity to judge the success of their teaching by working with their students on the factory floor.

Critically important managerial systems can be much less formal—yet still contribute to distinctive capabilities. For instance, in some consulting firms or universities, entering personnel are informally apprenticed to experienced consultants or professors and learn particular styles of behavior and delivering services. At Harvard Business School, the teaching groups delivering the required first-year curriculum serve as important socialization mechanisms. New professors learn the school's very highly interactive case teaching methods through observation, formal and informal feedback, and daily group discussions about pedagogy. Newcomers to the teaching faculty are always surprised at the amount of time devoted to helping new faculty gain the discussion-facilitating and Socratic-questioning skills, which are perceived to distinguish the school's pedagogy from that of other schools that employ cases in their classrooms less intensively.

Values and Norms

Skills and knowledge, both embodied in people and embedded in physical systems as well as managerial systems all exhibit a particular character depending on what is valued in the company. In most companies, the basic assumptions about human nature and the personal values of the founders led to the growth of a set of corporate values. Researchers studying organizations over time have noted that many retain the character, or company "personality,"[39] from their earliest days.

Some corporate values are generic: they apply to human interactions within the corporation in general or to a general outlook on life. Strongly held basic values fit what Ed Schein termed a "cultural paradigm": they are "a set of interrelated assumptions that form a coherent pattern."[40] Employees of Hitachi like to quote their founder, who said, "Though we cannot live 100 years, we should be concerned about 1,000 years hence." The Johnson & Johnson "Credo," which guides many daily decisions in that organization, dates to the days of Robert Wood Johnson, the son of the company founder. Chairman of J&J from 1938 to 1963, he held very strong convictions about the ability of sensible people to work together and the public and social responsibilities of any business firm. Traditionally, the Credo has been prominently displayed in every manager's office.

J&J top management credited the values expressed in this Credo for the company's superb, public-spirited, and principled handling of the 1982 Tylenol crisis, in which seven people died after ingesting cyanide-laced Tylenol capsules. Prominent in the Credo is the following statement: "We believe our first responsibility is to the doctors, nurses and patients, to mothers and all others who use our products and services." This guiding value underlay the speedy but financially costly decision to pull all Tylenol capsules off the shelves across the United States. The J&J Credo also covers values governing relations among employees and with the community at large: "Everyone must be considered as an individual. We must respect their dignity and recognize their merit. . . . Employees must feel free to make suggestions and complaints. . . . We must be good citizens. . . . We must experiment with new ideas. . . ."[41] When Chairman and CEO James Burke feared that the Credo was becoming mere formula, he and J&J President David Clare traveled to all 150 J&J companies to "challenge" the Credo. The resulting discussions with employees led to a recommitment to company values.

Hewlett-Packard has a similar set of values embodied in the "HP Way," which founder Bill Hewlett says comes down to "respecting the integrity of the individual." The official HP Way lists trust and respect for individuals, uncompromising integrity, and teamwork among the corporate values.[42] Such generic values are what I consider "big *V*s"; they define how employees are expected to act toward each other and toward customers. Big *V*s contribute mightily to corporate culture, and some authors have argued that such strong cultures in and of themselves can be competitive advantages.[43]

At the same time, values can be more limited in scope. Rather than addressing human nature or human relationships, these "little *v*s" are concerned with the choice of technology, the value placed on *types of knowledge*, or *the way in which generic values are* operationalized. In essence, little *v*s are norms of behavior. Values placed on certain kinds of technical knowledge contribute to the strategically significant *technological* capabilities that distinguish one company from another.

For instance, at Kodak, the chemical-engineering knowledge associated with film design was highly valued for many years—certainly more than the mechanical engineering associated with equipment design. The reason was obvious: Kodak's superior ability to suspend silver halide particles in a smoothly spread emulsion of gelatin was a capability perceived to depend more directly on chemistry than on mechanics. The pinnacle of engineering success was traditionally represented by the 5 percent of engineers who could claim the title of film designers. For years at Kodak, as at other large companies whose capabilities predated the invasion of software into controls, software-engineering skills were not as highly regarded. Consequently, although Kodak could attract the very best chemical-engineering graduates—who were assured of good facilities, challenging assignments, and top-notch colleagues in their field—the company was not likely to be the first choice for top mechanical and software engineers. The managerial systems of hiring and rewarding engineers had

Figure 1-5 Positive Reinforcing Cycle

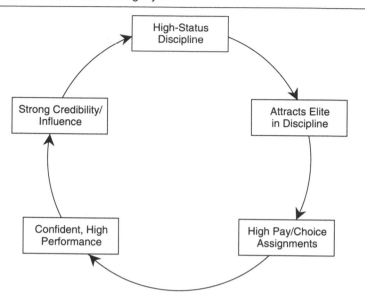

to be consonant with the values placing film designers above equipment designers in order to protect Kodak's preeminence in film making. These values, and the aligned selection criteria and incentive systems, ensured that the right skills were acquired and the right knowledge bases accumulated.

Thus, these little *vs* interact with the other dimensions of a core technological capability in a self-reinforcing "virtuous cycle,"[44] as suggested in Figure 1-5. All organizations have such sets of values that determine the kinds of skilled people who are attracted to the company and rewarded by choice assignments and/or higher pay than their colleagues. These individuals, drawn from the top ranks of their discipline, generally are confident and perform well, thereby reinforcing the credibility and influence invested in that skill base by the company culture. The kind of knowledge possessed by such individuals (be it engineering, marketing, finance, or other valued knowledge) is considered legitimate evidence to back up new-product development decisions; moreover, this expertise often paves the road to the top.

Deep Roots into the Past

Because values have a profound effect on the buildup of capabilities, to perhaps a surprising degree, many companies that appear to have evolved over time still have deep roots in their technological origins. To be sure, Motorola is better known today for cellular telephones and microprocessor chips than for home radios (where it started) or car radios (which gave the company its name). Yet Motorola still produces car radios. Moreover, its mobile wireless communications business began back in 1934–1935, when the company designed one of the first two-way radio communications systems in the world for the Chicago Police Department.[45] One of its strongest businesses during World War II was mobile communications—walkie-talkies and radios. Similarly, Raychem started business in 1957 in heat-shrunk polymers and today is still known for highly sophisticated heat-shrunk coatings. Genrad began life in 1915, as General Radio (*radio* then being a general term, comparable to today's *electronics*), to produce instruments to measure currents, voltage, and resistance at the high frequencies used in radio transmission.[46] Measurement instrumentation for electronic equipment is still a major business today. And Pall Corporation traces its beginnings to a steel screen that David Pall created to separate two types of uranium when he worked on the (atomic bomb) Manhattan Project as a recent Ph.D. in 1941.[47] Pall Corporation currently makes filters so fine they can trap bacteria and impurities over .04 micron in diameter, or about one four-thousandth the diameter of a human hair.

Such deep roots convey advantage to the capabilities that have evolved over time—but they also make them difficult to change. In the next chapter, we will examine the flip side of core capabilities—core rigidities. In subsequent chapters, we turn to the internally and externally focused activities that challenge core rigidities and ultimately explore differing strategies and bases for core capabilities.

Summary

This chapter has examined the nature of core technological capabilities, beginning with the example of Chaparral Steel, which claims as a core capability its ability to transform technology rapidly into product. We then saw that a core technological capability is a *system* partly comprising technical competencies in the form of: (1) people's *skills* and (2) the knowledge embedded in *physical systems*. In addition to these important knowledge repositories, capabilities have two other highly interdependent dimensions that channel and control knowledge: (3) *managerial systems* that support and reinforce the growth of knowledge through carefully designed education and incentives and (4) *values* that serve to screen and encourage or discourage the accumulation of different kinds of knowledge.

A central question is, *How* do these capabilities grow over time? The remainder of this book is devoted to addressing that question. We can readily see the accretion of physical systems—rolling mills in Chaparral, computers housing software programs in airline offices, or engineering simulation and design systems in electronics firms. Much less visible are the skills embedded in employees' heads and hands, the managerial systems that encourage some behaviors and discourage others, the values that permeate the organization but may be unspoken or even unrecognized. How do these invisible assets of the firm come into being? Although values may be idiosyncratic to founders, employees over time reinforce or erode them. The managerial systems evolve as managers discover unexpected and anticipated responses to incentives and rewards among employees. The skills accumulate according to the attitudes and behaviors that are encouraged.

In short, capabilities grow through the actions of the members of the firm—through the behaviors of employees at all organizational levels. The critical task for managers is to identify, implant, nurture, and enhance those activities that create the knowledge to be absorbed and retained by the organization and its employees. At Chaparral Steel, important activities included shared problem solving, integrating new methodologies and process tools, constant formal and informal experimentation, and pulling in expertise from outside. Although these activities characterize Chaparral Steel, they are also generic externally focused and internally focused activities that build core capabilities at any manufacturing company. In Part II (Chapters 3–7), we explore these activities in depth.

However, before doing so, we need to examine a prior question: why focus on managing these particular activities rather than any number of other important ones? The rationale for their selection is: these are the activities that, if managed intelligently, provide the best hope for successfully addressing the central paradox of a core capability—namely, that *every core capability is also inherently a core rigidity.* The next chapter answers the question, What constitutes a core rigidity?

CHAPTER TWO

Core Rigidities

While it is difficult to change a company that is struggling, it is next to impossible to change a company that is showing all the outward signs of success. Without the spur of a crisis or a period of great stress, most organizations—like most people—are incapable of changing the habits and attitudes of a lifetime.

—John F. McDonnell
   McDonnell Douglas Corporation[1]

How would you like to move from a house after 112 years? . . . We've got 112 years of closets and attics in this company. We want to flush them out, to start with a brand new house with empty closets, to begin the whole game again.

—Jack Welch
   Chairman and CEO, General Electric[2]

We have to be willing to cannibalize what we're doing today in order to ensure our leadership in the future. It's counter to human nature but you have to kill your business while it is still working.

—Lewis Platt
   Chairman and CEO, Hewlett-Packard[3]

"Torawarenai sunao-na kokoro," which means "Mind that does not stick."

—Favorite phrase of Konosuke Matsushita
   Founder, Matsushita Electric Industrial[4]

The perplexing paradox involved in managing core capabilities is that they are core rigidities.[5] That is, a firm's strengths are also—*simultaneously*—its weaknesses. The dimensions that distinguish a company competitively have grown up over time as an accumulation of activities and decisions that focus on one kind of knowledge at the expense of others. Companies, like people, cannot be skillful at everything. Therefore, core capabilities both advantage and disadvantage a company.

Since core rigidities are but the flip side of core capabilities, the same conceptual models examined in Chapter 1 apply here. The four dimensions mirror those associated with the company's core capabilities. So long as conditions remain constant, managers experience the advantages of that interdependent system. In the face of a changing business environment, or when the system itself matures into mindless routine, managers find themselves fighting the very underpinnings of the firm's success. One or more of the dimensions are pathological, are clogging up the flow of knowledge.

The Pathology of Core Rigidities

Core rigidities are built through the same activities that create core capabilities, albeit in mutated form. The activities themselves—problem solving, implementation of new processes, experimentation, and importing knowledge from outside—are essentially neutral and inescapable in new-product development. *The management of those activities determines whether they foster or inhibit the unimpeded flow of critical knowledge.* The rest of the book is dedicated to demonstrating how innovative managers have successfully focused those activities on feeding the wellsprings of knowledge. This chapter seeks to establish the importance of those creative approaches by defining the nature of core rigidities and illustrating their growth. Since the activities can be managed for either benefit or dysfunction, it is well to be aware of their dual potential. Constant vigilance over core capabilities and the activities that create them may obviate the necessity for "managing change" in revolutionary form.

In the following subsections, we first look at why core rigidities matter. Then we turn to an examination of why core capabilities transform so readily into rigidities and how the activities that create knowledge for core capabilities can inhibit knowledge flows. Finally, we take a close look at the four interwoven dimensions of a core rigidity.

Insularity

Often the flip side, the dark side, of core capabilities is revealed due to external events—when new competitors figure out a better way to serve the firm's customers, when new technologies emerge, or when political or social events shift the ground underneath. However, as we shall see, many pressures conspire to keep managers internally focused and comfortable with the status quo long after disquieting signs should have made them edgy. The scent of a conflagration miles away can be dismissed as the harmless emissions of a neighbor's woodstove—even if the fiery inferno is advancing rapidly in our direction. These days it may seem impossible that any managers could be so inwardly focused as to believe that their company is insulated from change or that the skills and markets relevant to today's success will be identically relevant tomorrow. Yet the front pages of the popular press are full of accounts of former flagship companies now apparently struggling to stay afloat—Digital Equipment Corporation, Wang Corporation, and Sears, among others.

Of course, multiple events—including some beyond the control of these companies—conspired to threaten them. However, a contributing factor seems to have been activities that flowed in well-worn and successful paths— unchallenged. Sears counted on its excellent store sites, its decades of dominance in retail, its mighty purchasing power to maintain its position in the market. Some critics aver that Sears managers disdained to notice Wal-Mart's incursion into their merchandising territory: well into the 1980s, Sears' position papers did not even *list* that company among competitors to be watched. Sam Walton, Wal-Mart's founder, claimed in his autobiography, "One reason Sears fell so far off the pace is that they wouldn't admit for the longest time that Wal-Mart and Kmart were their real competition. They ignored both of us, and we both blew right by them."[6] A former senior executive at Sears recalled that inattention to outside events was compounded by the existence of a whole library of "bulletins" dictating responses to problems. "God forbid there should be a problem that comes up for which there isn't a bulletin," he observed. "That means the problem's *new!*"[7]

Managers in some of the companies currently undergoing massive change—such as IBM, AT&T, and Kodak—are on record as believing that their companies should have heeded warning signs more quickly. Like cattle in a snowstorm, managers turned their heads inward and ignored the winds of change. "We had fallen in love with ourselves," a former IBMer admits.[8] One of the reasons that top management in large, successful companies can ignore a breaking storm is that no one seems ready to challenge those who led the company to preeminence. When, in 1991, Digital Equipment's nosedive as a result of the swing in the industry toward smaller, faster machines seemed to steepen, former Digital executive Gordon Bell observed that Ken Olsen, Digital's founder and leader since 1957, had "been essentially talking to himself for a decade."[9]

Overshooting the Target

One of the most common, but least recognized, causes of core capabilities' functioning as rigidities is overshooting the target—that is, succumbing to the simplistic notion that more of a good thing is always better. Formerly beneficial activities are carried so far that they hamper rather than help. This attitude is by no means confined to multinationals based in the United States. Former McKinsey principal Kenichi Ohmae describes the destructive effects of thinking that competitive strategy means doing what you've always done, but doing it better or simply working harder:

> Japanese managers are victims of their own success and of the habits that success creates. . . . Rowing harder does not help if the boat is headed in the wrong direction. . . . It is human nature to resist change, to stick with what you've got, to do more better of what you know how to do well but that only makes it more important for managers consciously to refuse to take their business systems or their definitions of customer value as givens.[10]

In the 1980s, the world automobile industry focused attention on the superior practices of the Japanese. An exhaustive study of automobile manufacturers in Japan, Europe, and the United States found that Japanese firms on average designed and developed products a year faster than, and with almost twice the development productivity (measured in engineering hours) of, the average American or European firm. Japanese carmakers producing high-volume models introduced many more new products with shorter model lives and expanded their product lines more rapidly than Western competitors. This performance advantage was "based on fundamental capabilities that firms applied throughout the 1980s and these capabilities make a difference in competition."[11] Toyota, in particular, became a role model in manufacturing. Its just-in-time inventory delivery, multitask work assignments for employees, total quality control system, small-lot production—all were recognized as providing a competitive advantage in international competition. Such activities in Japanese car companies did not spring from a coherent strategy but "were often adopted unintentionally as the firms were forced to respond to certain historical imperatives, or at least without knowing the potential competitive benefits. Solutions often existed prior to the competitive problems."[12] Nevertheless, this essentially experimental process "eventually created a rational system in terms of competitive advantages."[13]

Some of the most admired features, and those identified in research as conveying a competitive advantage, were: (1) overlapping problem solving among the engineering and manufacturing functions, leading to shorter model change cycles; (2) small teams with broad task assignments, leading to high development productivity and shorter lead times; and (3) using a "heavyweight" product manager—a competent individual with extensive project influence (not just coordinating and administrative duties) who led a cohesive team with autonomy over product design decisions.[14] By the early 1990s, many of these features had been emulated or even improved upon by U.S. automobile manufacturers, and the gap between the U.S. and Japanese companies in development lead time and productivity had virtually disappeared.[15]

However, according to industry experts, there was another reason for the loss of the Japanese competitive edge—"fat product designs." The "fat" referred to was an excess in product variety, speed of model change, and unnecessary options. This did not mean that the Japanese automakers had built the wrong set of capabilities. Rather, " 'overuse' of the same capability that created competitive advantages in the 1980s has been the source of the new problem in the 1990s."[16] The formerly "lean" Japanese producers such as Toyota had overshot their targets of customer satisfaction and overspecified their products, catering to a "long laundry list" of features and carrying their quest for quality to an extreme that could not be cost-justified when the yen appreciated in 1993. "[E]ngineers in leading Japanese firms emphasized customer satisfaction and product integrity in their designs (a good thing) to the point of making cost a secondary consideration in design (a real problem today)."[17] Moreover, the practice of using heavyweight managers to guide important projects led to excessive complexity of parts because these powerful individuals disliked sharing common parts with other car models.

As one industry specialist noted, "[T]he US firms once became competitive through a mass production system of specialization, but subsequently they suffered from 'over-specialization.' The Japanese once enjoyed competitive advantages in product variety, but now they may be suffering from over-variety."[18] Within the Japanese auto industry, exceptions to the trend toward "fat products"—such as the Mazda Miata and the Toyota Lexus LS 400—led industry experts to observe that competition is not so much between countries (Japan versus the United States) as between companies, based on the ability to hit the market target—without overshooting it.[19]

The tendency to "overshoot" with core capabilities until they function as core rigidities has affected many firms. Danny Miller has characterized initially successful companies in terms of four types and described the downward trajectories experienced by those whose "victories and . . . strengths . . . seduce them into the excesses that cause their downfall. Success leads to specialization and exaggeration, to confidence and complacency, to dogma and ritual."[20] Formerly strong "craftsmen" companies turn into mere "tinkerers," he argues, when employees become obsessed with technical details and forget about satisfying customers. "Builder" companies develop into "imperialists" when they evolve from strategies of aggressive growth into irresponsible expansion and mergers. "Pioneers" become "escapists" when their focus on inventiveness becomes a futile pursuit of technology for its own sake. "Salesmen" companies are transformed over time into "drifters" when marketing absorbs their energies to the exclusion of good design and manufacturing.

Why It Is So Easy for Core Capabilities to Become Core Rigidities: Alternative Explanations

As Miller's analysis suggests, once a system is set up to deliver a certain capability, that system acquires a momentum of its own and becomes difficult to dismantle—even if it is now outmoded or has become so excessive as to be a caricature of its original self. In a culture that prizes innovation, as the United States does, why is it that our institutions seem so impervious to the most vigorous assaults from outside and from within?

Multiple (and interacting) explanations exist for this seemingly self-defeating behavior.[21] One of these is economics. Attacking core rigidities often means undermining the current economic foundations of the firm—cannibalizing current product lines, making obsolete current knowledge bases and skills, lessening the value of current assets.[22] IBM ignored the promise of the RISC architecture that originated in its own laboratories. Why? This simplified, faster computing technology was particularly well suited to the minicomputers coming on the scene in the mid-1970s, which threatened to steal customers from IBM's existing mainframe business.

The politics of power offer another reason. Altering current capabilities may dislodge organizational royalty from their thrones atop functional, market-based, or other fiefdoms.[23] Such revolutions can reach clear to the top of the organizational ladder, and managers are understandably reluctant to give up political power. After continuous-aim firing at sea was invented and proved superior to current practice in a number of British and American ships, with performance carefully documented and reports submitted to Washington to urge its adoption, the innovation still met with indifference, then argument, then hostility. The redoubtable champion, a mere lieutenant in the U.S. Navy, had to appeal directly to President Theodore Roosevelt to be heard. Superior officers in the Navy opposed the innovation because they rightly foresaw a disruptive reorganization of their military society based on this innovation. Among other changes, the lowly position of gunnery officer gained power and became a route to the top ranks.[24]

A third explanation for the difficulty in overcoming rigidities is behavioral: organizational routines are ingrained, and various forms of habit govern.[25] In fact, all three of these reasons interact to create a complex system that is difficult to dismantle. A threat to the economics of current business is also a threat to the political coalitions that support retaining individuals' skills and traditional organizational routines.

Since institutionalized activities are at the heart of core rigidities, the emphasis here is on this last explanation—the behavioral aspects of a core rigidity. Thus, we now explore how activities designed to support core capabilities also build core rigidities.

Knowledge-Inhibiting Activities

A firm's habitual activities concentrate on augmenting current knowledge. (See Figure 2-1.) That is, the problems on which people focus are the ones most relevant to current markets and current operations. The functional and disciplinary groups responsible for creating and integrating knowledge are specialized to deliver benefits within the current system, and their influence on product development derives from their historical importance in that development process. The future is implicitly assumed to look much like the present, so that experimentation addresses doing what we do now, better—not differently. Information from outside passes through screens designed to reject knowledge that is irrelevant to current core capabilities. These activities build strengths and define weaknesses. The following subsections explore the activities featured in Figure 2-1, starting at the top and moving clockwise.

Limited Problem Solving: The Power of the Past

Decisions and events from the past intrude on the present and shape the future. Economists have dubbed this connection "path dependency" because the footsteps of the past cannot be undone; the actions of the present are influenced by the paths followed to get here. Conditions at the time of the company's founding, including its initial strategy, create an internal consensus about the way things should be done to succeed; over the years, organizational routines solidify.[26]

Figure 2-1 Knowledge-Inhibiting Activities

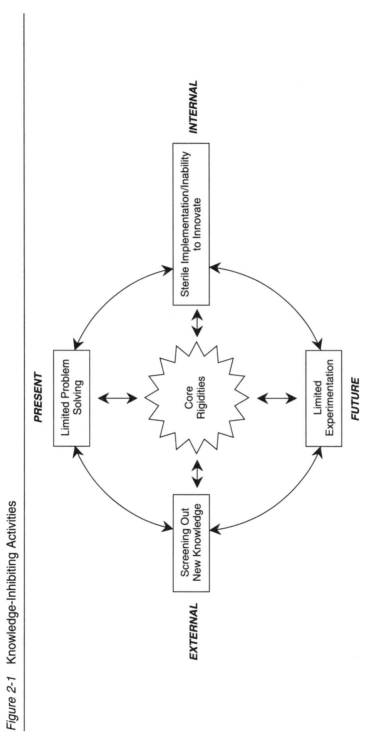

The disciplinary and functional specialties that grow up to create and control the knowledge critical to an organization's products and services inevitably experience difficulty integrating their different knowledge bases. An inability to involve relevant constituencies leads to suboptimal decisions. One reason RCA lost its leadership in the videocassette recorder market to the Japanese can be traced to technological choices RCA's central laboratories made in the 1960s and 1970s. Researchers there, charged with developing videoplayers for the burgeoning consumer electronics market, decided to emphasize a lower-cost capacitance approach over higher-performance videoplayer alternatives. RCA's own Consumer Electronics Division disagreed with the choice, wanting to emphasize performance, but the historic isolation of the central laboratories from the business division and the discord between the two precluded cooperation. The Consumer Electronics Division eventually marketed a Japanese-produced videocassette recorder in direct competition with the internally developed videodisc.[27]

One of the simplest explanations for a rigid adherence to prior approaches for solving development problems is that alternatives don't occur to employees. People have a natural selection bias toward the familiar in designing new products.[28] When Dow Jones & Company, publisher of the *Wall Street Journal,* and Knight-Ridder, owner of newspapers such as the *Philadelphia Inquirer,* decided to launch computerized services to business, both corporations seemed to be building on strong capabilities. They had both been delivering information to people for years. The design problem was apparently simple: provide that information electronically. However, their computerized systems had one critical and competitively disadvantageous characteristic: they were designed as if their users were, like newspaper readers, passive recipients of data. Computer users wanted different functionality—primarily, the ability to manipulate, chart, and analyze the data they received electronically. Consequently, Dow Jones & Company's Telerate system supplying government bond prices has been overrun by competing services that provide more interactivity.[29]

To overcome such outmoded ways of identifying and solving problems, managers must actively encourage people to break from the past. Instead, as discussed in more detail in Chapter 5, the tendency is to discourage innovation and train people as fleas used to be for a circus. Enclosed in a glass tube, the fleas slammed into the invisible force above them every time they hopped. Thus trained, they "learned" to crawl, so that they could be docilely harnessed to tiny wagons and encouraged to crawl across minuscule tightropes. Employees can likewise be trained to adhere to the past, mindlessly. Thus trained, they may continue routines long since outdated.[30]

The story of the British artillery team using an old gun during the waning days of the Second World War illustrates the point. Old as they were, the guns were useful as mobile units hitched to trucks and moved about in the defense of the English coast. A time-and-motion expert was asked to simplify and speed up the firing procedures drilled into the team of soldiers over the years. From studying slow-motion pictures he took of the procedures, the expert was puzzled: just before the firing,

> two members of the gun crew ceased all activity and came to attention for a three-second interval extending throughout the discharge of the gun. He summoned an old colonel of artillery, showed him the pictures, and pointed out this strange behavior. What, he asked the colonel, did it mean? The colonel too, was puzzled. He asked to see the pictures again. "Ah," he said when the performance was over, "I have it. They are holding the horses."[31]

Inability to Innovate with New Tools and Methods

Internal hardening of organizational arteries can cause paralysis even if people within a company recognize the need for process innovation and strive mightily to bring it about. Consider the situation of USX (originally United States Steel).[32] The company had a history of investing in state-of-the-art steelmaking processes, including, in the late 1950s, the continuous-casting technology that allowed molten steel to be cast directly into shapes approximating the end product, instead of ingots. In 1990, the company faced the choice between investing in a continuous caster and concomitant modernization of its hot-rolling mill at Mon Valley or launching a new thin-slab casting technology, "compact strip production" (CSP). The CSP process was being aggressively pursued by an important competitor, the minimill company Nucor Steel. Nucor claimed the new process would lower the costs of sheet and strip steel by 10 percent to 15 percent of gross margin, giving it a significant competitive edge over the large integrated steel producers.

USX had been an early investor in developing the CSP technology, and some managers believed thin-slab casting was critical for the company's future. However, these champions were tied by hundreds of rules, constraints, and existing conditions that rendered them as immobile as Jonathan Swift's Gulliver, held down with thousands of threads by Lilliputians. USX management chose the more conservative investment in upgrading for a number of reasons. First, USX's current process methodologies had significant near-term financial advantages. Projected operating costs for CSP at Mon Valley were much higher than those Nucor anticipated, probably because Nucor used electric furnaces and its nonunion workers accepted flexible work rules.

Tied to the Mon Valley site by an agreement with its labor unions, USX had to work within the constraints of that existing facility—both physical and human resource. Although the CSP process would actually entail less capital cost per ton, the immediate cash flow would be greater for the innovation. Moreover, the new CSP process could not produce the quality of surface finish demanded by USX's traditional customers—at least initially. As a senior USX executive observed, "Mon Valley sells surface, not bulk."

For all these reasons, USX very rationally rejected thin-slab casting. The paralyzing inability to innovate in the face of a desire to do so may not hurt in the short term, as the old technology continues to perform well. USX's Mon Valley mill was competitive and profitable in 1993. However, Nucor meantime doubled its capacity and went on to build more CSP mills, which outperform traditional steel mills over three-to-one in labor content. More important, CSP continues to improve in surface finish, as new technologies typically do. (See the discussion of technological S curves in Chapter 6.) The very real threat exists, therefore, that innovative minimills will overtake old integrated mills in finished steel as they have in structural steel.

Time will tell whether USX's decision was a "competency trap," which "can occur when favorable performance with an inferior procedure leads an organization to accumulate more experience with it, thus keeping experience with a superior procedure inadequate to make it rewarding to use."[33] If CSP follows the usual pattern of improved performance parameters in technological innovations, USX will have locked itself into an investment that precludes developing core capabilities in the new technology.[34] If USX should decide to switch to the new technology, Nucor still has an experience advantage. "When we went into structure beams six years ago," Nucor CEO Ken Iverson said in 1992, "imports had 35% of the market. Now they have 8% of the market. We took their share, and companies like Inland and U.S. Steel [USX] got out. Thin-slab casting will do the same thing to weaker operations in the flat-rolled market." Asked about the possibility of U.S. Steel's adopting the CSP technology, Iverson was unconcerned: "It will take two years to build a plant and another year to get it running properly. We've got at least 3½ to four years on them."[35]

Limited Experimentation

The third activity, experimentation, is limited when knowledge extension flows along well-worn paths rather than creating new options for the corporation. The interests and abilities of technical staff often constrain the bounds of innovation. In the 1960s, when Du Pont wished to reduce dependency on textile fibers, management launched some sixty new ventures. However, to the disappointment of top management, of the ten most costly ventures, six were still in textile fibers. Since each department made the decision independently, the limited pattern of experimentation was visible only at the top of the corporation.[36] This concentration of ventures around familiar technologies and markets was not surprising, however: the technologists could readily conceive of experiments within their realm of expertise but could not imagine those based on totally different technical knowledge.

Screening Out External Knowledge

The fourth activity featured in this book is importing knowledge from outside. As Chapters 6 and 7 discuss in detail, knowledge critical to new-product development originates from outside sources of technology and from the market. At the same time, the screen through which such external knowledge must travel, and the channels by which it must flow, may be heavily biased toward the types of knowledge already known to feed core capabilities. Indeed, these capabilities have been nurtured so as to support business success. Unchecked and unexamined, however, predilections toward existing core capabilities can choke off enriching knowledge from unexpected sources.

Biased Evaluations of New Technology. Decisions about investments in new technologies often pit the new against the old in a skewed struggle. One reason for this, of course, is the new's being disadvantaged in its infancy. People traveling on horseback at the end of the nineteenth century, galloping past broken-down automobiles, used to yell "Get a horse" as they left the newfangled mode of transportation literally in the dust. Earlier, sailing ships were faster (in a wind) than steamships years after that mode of transportation had arrived. Although these are obvious examples, there are less obvious biases built into the evaluation of new technologies; for example, considering a new technology a straightforward substitute for the old, and using time-honored criteria for evaluation, can mislead. When jet airplanes were first introduced in the 1950s, airplane manufacturers such as Curtiss-Wright hesitated to adopt the new technology because the operating cost per seat-mile was higher. However, because jets could fly faster, they could fly far more seat-miles per day; therefore, the capital cost of seat-miles was actually lower. By the time Curtiss-Wright realized how profitable jet aircraft could be, Boeing and Lockheed were far ahead.[37]

Listening to Customers—Too Hard. Given the ubiquitous examples of misunderstanding user needs, one would think it impossible to listen too hard to customers. However, the problem of "overshooting" often arises precisely because the corporation is bombarded by demands from current customers. As we shall see in more detail in Chapter 7, customers tend to demand better versions of what they have, and the importunate voices of today's market drown out fainter signals from future potential users. Indeed, for both IBM and USX, booming customer demand was an important contributor to their core rigidities. On the other hand, consumers are also very rationally concerned about the costs of switching to new versions of, or substitutes for, current products—especially when the products are embedded in a system.[38] Consumer reluctance to invest in new learning on a frequent basis is another pressure that focuses corporate attention on the needs of current customers—and away from those of potential new customer sets.

Variation in Resistance to Change: The Four Dimensions of Core Rigidities

Core rigidities are most dangerous when a company is poised on the brink of a technological discontinuity—when the technology on which it is based is shifting massively to an entirely new paradigm. Such discontinuities can enhance or destroy existing competencies within an entire industry.[39] Of the twenty largest companies worldwide (by stock market valuation) in 1972, only three (Exxon, AT&T, and General Electric) remained on the list twenty years later. Giants in 1972—including IBM, Eastman Kodak, General Motors, and Sears, Roebuck—had slipped out of the top ranking; in fact, in 1992, IBM was twenty-sixth and GM fortieth. Sears was down to eighty-first![40]

Intel's chairman, Andrew Grove, believes that there is "at least one point in the history of any company when you have to change dramatically to rise to the next performance level. Miss the moment, and you start to decline."[41] National Cash Register faced such a moment in 1972. Its transition into the computer age appeared threatened by rigidities—born both of internal excesses and of immobility in the face of changes in the external world—that had to be overcome before the company could build on its emerging capabilities. Each of the dimensions of this company's core capabilities that had led to success now contributed to core rigidities.

Addressing Core Rigidities

NCR's difficulties exemplify one type of situation in which core rigidities have to be addressed: the organization has fully ossified, and most of its

THE NCR STORY

NCR, which, in 1916, sold 95 percent of the cash registers in the United States,[42] shipped its first computer (the 304) in 1959. However, its early foray into this business bogged down severely, and by the end of the 1960s, the company was in serious trouble.[43] Worldwide employment stood at 102,000 in 1969. Revenues for 1971 were flat; earnings per share fell from $1.37 in the prior year to $.04. The quarterly dividend was reduced for the first time since the Great Depression forty years earlier. NCR's ratio of sales per employee was $16,000 compared to Burroughs' $23,000 and IBM's $31,000. The board of directors reacted by bringing in a new president, William Anderson, previously vice president, Far Eastern operations.

Anderson inherited a company full of core rigidities; its management had underestimated the leap required to move from cash registers and adding machines to computer systems. Perhaps surprisingly, the largest barriers to change lay not so much in technical skills and knowledge, although these were problematic, as in the other three dimensions of the company's core capabilities in producing mechanical and electromechanical accounting equipment.

Values

A history of experience with cash registers led the company to value small, stand-alone machines over large systems that could handle accounting. The chairman of the corporation preferred "to sell a million Chevrolets than 100,000 Cadillacs."[44] "Uneasy" with larger computer systems, managers were reluctant to provide options for upgrading to bigger systems as their requirements grew.

Moreover, antagonism toward competing technologies and a strong preference for NCR-sanctioned technologies sometimes dictated counterproductive decisions. For instance, when Computer Research Corporation was acquired, the acquisition was forced to change both its more efficient internal control systems and its popular product design to avoid the punched-card technology associated with archrival IBM.[45] Loyalty to traditional designs died hard at NCR. Product developers stubbornly resisted designing a ten-key adding machine, arguing that the full-keyboard models the company had always produced were "superior." Eventually, market pressures forced the more efficient operating design—but even then, the new NCR cash registers were offered in both ten-key and full-keyboard models. The full keyboards were discontinued when they failed to sell.[46]

Physical Systems

The physical plant and operating procedures in 1972 still reflected the philosophy on which the company was founded in 1884—fully integrated manufacture. For instance, when the executive offices were refurbished, the walnut paneling came from wood dried in NCR kilns and cut and shaped in the NCR woodworking department. The thirty-building Dayton plant made everything from screws to plastic key tips. There were over 8,000 pieces of production machinery and 390,000 different tools. An inventory in 1969 showed that 30,000 different parts were in stock, including 2,700 types of springs and 9,500 different types and sizes of washers.[47] When a vice president of rival Burroughs Corporation visited the Dayton complex in the 1960s, he reported back to his chairman, "You can stop worrying about NCR. They're making more and more commitments to mechanical technology. They're getting into deep trouble and they don't even know it."[48]

Managerial Systems

The incentive systems in both marketing and manufacturing that had worked very well for NCR when it produced cash registers were tremendous barriers to change. The computer business was regarded as a diversion from the much more profitable traditional markets; most marketing branch managers had grown up selling cash registers and accounting machines.

"A number of managers said openly, 'I have only a few years left. If I convert our best accounting machine salesmen into computer salesmen it could be two or three years before they begin producing. However, if I keep them selling accounting machines they'll continue to produce for as long as I'm here and I'll share in the profits.' "[49]

Afraid that pushing computers too hard might cause the collapse of the traditional business, NCR introduced no incentives to promote computer sales. In fact, sales commissions on computers were initially discouragingly small. When the NCR 315 computer came out, for instance, sales personnel were offered .006 percent—a potential commission of $1,200 on a $200,000 machine. They could make more than that selling a single accounting machine.[50]

Manufacturing incentive systems similarly hobbled progress. NCR hung on to payment for piecework long after other U.S.-based businesses had concluded that the practice was dysfunctional. Contracts negotiated with unions in the late 1930s tied NCR pay scales to those of General Motors—with disastrous results for this very different business. Manufacturing supervisors' reward systems led them to build up huge inventories of parts—often obsolete.

Skills and Knowledge

NCR was aggressive in entering the world of electronics but had little experience. Therefore, it encountered severe difficulties with its Century Series, which was launched with numerous technical innovations—plated-wire main memory (rather than the emerging industry standard of magnetic core), nickel-cobalt-plated disk memory, and a very sophisticated read-write head for the disk unit that could scan twelve disk tracks simultaneously. NCR management ran into two primary difficulties. First, it failed to foresee a sharp drop in the cost of traditional magnetic-core memories as other producers gained experience and fine-tuned the technology, with the result that the plated-wire memory lost its initial cost advantage;[51] second, the company was unable to manufacture the innovative units. Disk heads "crashed" repeatedly, damaging the fragile aluminum disks and thus destroying data; short-rod memories couldn't be manufactured reliably. The company finally had to buy traditional magnetic cores and reengineer the disk heads to use ceramic materials. Besides these problems with hardware, the company had difficulty building software skills. Anderson with Truax recall that "most NCR people were afraid to be involved with computers."[52]

Source: This description of NCR draws heavily from William Anderson with Charles Truax, *Corporate Crisis: NCR and the Computer Revolution* (Dayton, Ohio: Landfall Press, 1991).

former capabilities are outdated. Managers must completely rebuild and renew the organization. This is a turnaround situation, a call for creative destruction of the old core capabilities in order to build new ones.[53]

In 1992 and 1993, top executives in some of the largest U.S. corporations were cleaning out their desk drawers and heading for unexpected retirement at an unprecedented rate. General Motors' Robert Stempel, Digital Equipment Corporation's Kenneth Olsen, IBM Chief Executive John Akers, Westinghouse Electric Corporation's Paul Lego, American Express's James Robinson, Apple's John Sculley—all resigned or were forced out. The cause of their demise was the perception that the corporation needed drastic change and that these leaders were too tied to the past to effect such a switch. Louis Gerstner reported that the IBM board of directors that hired him to replace Akers told him "they didn't need a technocrat. They needed a manager—a change agent."[54]

New top executives recognized they would have to address rigidities lying at the heart of the companies they took over. George Fisher, who moved from Motorola to Kodak, commented: "Rather than simply take an ax to budgets and manpower, we are trying to change, in significant ways, how this company operates."[55] Robert Palmer, who replaced Ken Olsen, said of Digital Equipment Corporation, the company "is going to change. It will take time but we are going to begin today. Digital will undergo a transformation."[56] Louis Gerstner emphasized that the alterations at IBM could not be superficial: "No more endless meetings about the need to change and then going back to business as usual."[57]

Such changes are so challenging because, like core capabilities, core rigidities comprise a *system*. Although we must keep in mind that the four dimensions of a core rigidity are interlocking and interacting, it is useful to consider each separately, as we did for core capabilities in Chapter 1. The four dimensions differ in the ease with which they may be changed and therefore in the amount of managerial attention required. (See Figure 2-2.)

Physical Systems: Tools and Methodologies

The easiest dimension to alter is the physical system. New equipment or new software programs can be purchased off the shelf. The more the innovation is fully embodied in the equipment and requires little user training, the more easily it is accepted.[58] This is not to say that implementing new technical systems is simple, as the following tale of woe from an aluminum smelter illustrates. The change was apparently very minor—switching from a clumsy manual way of stirring aluminum ingots down into a molten bath to an elegant electromechanical pump. What could be so difficult about that? A lot. The jumping ring circulator served as a honey pot for an extraordinarily large and vicious swarm of unfortunate decisions, design features, and luck. Almost anything that could go wrong with the new equipment did.

The JRC pump was apparently a small innovation, affecting just a single process in a long production chain and requiring no massive skills shift. It

Figure 2-2 Susceptibility of Core Rigidity Dimensions to Change

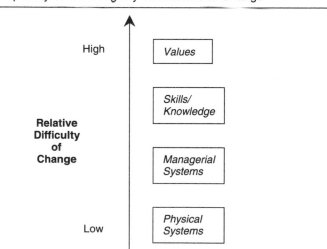

THE JUMPING RING CIRCULATOR AT WORLD ALUMINUM

In 1984, "WORAL" corporation experimented with an electromagnetic pump that "jumped" up and down in a furnace to circulate molten aluminum. The inventor of the jumping ring circulator (JRC), Charles Vendikicharian, proved the feasibility of his invention in the laboratory, and WORAL licensed the technology to an outside vendor that developed the pump and sold it mostly in the steel industry.

Despite Vendikicharian's involvement and a successful pilot project using water to model the effects of the pump, the project became a nightmare. The material in the nose cone that had survived the lower temperatures in steel furnaces cracked in aluminum baths. The operators who tended the furnaces were accustomed to loading them with large chunks of metal and leaving them unattended while the furnace digested; the JRC required constant feeding because it was designed to stir in very much lighter batches of aluminum scrap (recycled cans). By occupying space in the furnace, the pump reduced its capacity, and yet the production quota of 4,000 pounds per furnace per day was unchanged. Impatient with the constant attention demanded by the new process, the operators overloaded the furnace and then augmented the action of the JRC by reverting to their prior method of "truck stirring." Truck stirring involved attaching a metal rake to a fork truck and running the truck back and forth to manually agitate the molten bath. The waves caused by this agitation, in turn, lifted the JRC out of the bath, exposing it to greater swings in temperature and burning out the motor of the automatic hoist that sought to maintain a consistent depth in the metal bath.

Meanwhile, the vendor company suffered a change in leadership and in the turmoil was very unresponsive to requests for replacement parts and help on the initial installment. Furthermore, the experiments set up to test the JRC were wildly uncontrolled. Not only were the experiments interrupted by the frequent breakdowns of the JRC, but the engineers were also very uncertain about the best positioning of the pump in the furnace and consequently repositioned it a number of times, each time rendering the measurements not comparable to the outcomes of prior trials. The pump suffered a number of unexplained "accidents" while it sat outside the furnace during the night shifts. A final series of blows killed the project. First, the recycling supervisor found that his colleagues in downstream operations regarded recycled metal as a contaminant and were not eager to receive the output of the furnace. Second, if the JRC worked as desired, the output would be greater than the capacity of the trucks in the next manufacturing step. Finally, demand for aluminum had fallen recently. Unsurprisingly, the project was canceled.

Source: Based on Dorothy Leonard-Barton, "New Technology at World Aluminum Corporation: The Jumping Ring Circulator," case 687-050, Harvard Business School, Boston, 1987.

was an unexciting, routine change of equipment—hardly cutting-edge stuff. Yet consider what massive changes in the aluminum production process would have been necessary to make it succeed. Setting aside the fact that it was never really given a true trial because of inept experimentation, the JRC failed because its installation implied a host of other alterations—some of them diving into the heart of WORAL capabilities. The first change would be in operator incentives. The operators were rewarded for pushing as much metal through as possible; they therefore loaded the furnace incorrectly—and then exacerbated the situation by manually stirring the molten bath so that the JRC was subjected to extremes of physical pressure and temperature that it was not designed to withstand. Second, the next step in the aluminum production process did not have the capacity to accommodate higher furnace output, so installing the JRC implied capital investments. Third, increasing production output turned out to be an unimportant issue to the company in the face of falling demand. Finally, downstream receivers in the aluminum smelter disliked the "contaminated" aluminum produced by recycling cans.

Yet as the trend to recycle aluminum gained momentum in the 1980s, WORAL would in fact be required to receive and process cans. Therefore, although the JRC was apparently a simple, insignificant switch in technical systems, *it was potentially key to a change in core capabilities.* If this particular technical system turned out to be inadequate (a fact to be established through better experimentation), some other method would have to be devised to accommodate scrap aluminum—and whatever system was adopted, it would threaten the same core rigidities.

Alterations in technical systems are some of the most visible and most easily understood changes managers can make. Yet as further discussed in Chapters 4 and 5, their implementation rarely goes as planned. Temporary reductions in productivity are inevitable, and the most assiduous planning often results in merely a waste of paper and time.[59] Moreover, as the JRC story illustrates, the largest problem is that this dimension of a capability is almost never independent of the other three dimensions—and they are decidedly *more* difficult to alter.

Managerial Systems

Because managerial systems grow up in a company to encourage and reward the accretion of particular kinds of knowledge and to bestow status on certain functions, disciplines, and roles, other skills and knowledge are shortchanged by those same systems. Some such systems are overt and embedded in physical hardware or software systems. Hitachi's accounting system "remembers" losses product-by-product, whereas Toshiba's accounts start afresh every year. This difference probably plays a role in Toshiba's record as a market leader and Hitachi's as a follower—almost never first to market.[60]

The role of managerial systems in supporting core rigidities, however, is often less overt; it is more subtle, harder to pin down. Consider the flip side of the virtuous cycle reinforcing the status of engineering design at Kodak described in Chapter 1. Because the film design knowledge was highly valued, everything was geared toward hiring, rewarding, and celebrating engineering design people in that organization. In many first-rate manufacturing companies, such a cycle can be viewed from the perspective of another function—say, marketing or manufacturing—as a *negative* cycle. (See Figure 2-3.) In an engineering-dominated company, for instance, the marketing function has traditionally played a minor role in new-product design, which is more focused on outgoing communication than on collecting information from the marketplace. Because marketing's role is regarded as less relevant to the product development process, the company does not spend the kind of effort on recruiting and rewarding top marketing people that it does on engineers. Since the function is relatively less well paid, managers seek people with less experience. These people, knowing they are paid less and considered less vital to the process (and in fact, often having too little experience), perform hesitantly and deferentially in product development meetings. They sit in

Figure 2-3 Negative Reinforcing Cycle

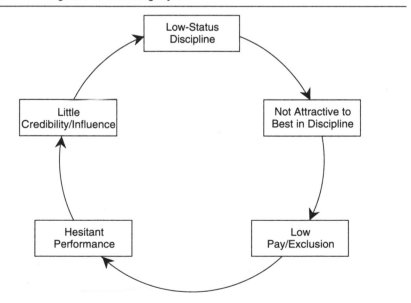

the chairs against the wall rather than at the table. They consequently *do* in fact have less influence on the product design process and are not personally associated with either failure or success. This lack of association, in turn, reinforces the low status of the function.

Of course, the obverse could be true in a marketing-dominated organization—say, a consumer product company—where perhaps engineering occupies the low position on the totem pole. The point is, in every organization that has developed a strong technology-based capability, the very system that attracts, nurtures, and reinforces the status of one function, discipline, or type of knowledge tends to downgrade others.

Software applications engineers felt like second-class citizens for years in hardware and operating systems companies such as Digital Equipment, IBM, or Xerox. Customer service representatives still have trouble being heard in many companies. Motorola is unusual in bestowing surprising visibility and influence on industrial designers; in many companies, IDs feel they are ignored, even when they know they have important information. (Yet even at Motorola, these designers naturally have more clout on teams developing consumer products such as cellular phones than on those developing industrial products such as semiconductors.)

Such differentials in status, rooted in the heart of a company's core capabilities, become dysfunctional when low-status roles or functions have information that is systematically ignored in new-product development—to the detriment of the project. Informal management systems grow into implicit routines that systematically support status differentials and subtly undermine the credibility of some disciplines. As noted above, a primary result is the inability of companies to integrate knowledge across specialties.

A team of academics and practitioners studying new-product development in five companies reported that the inequality in status of manufacturing relative to design engineers showed up in numerous apparently minor ways.[61] Representatives from manufacturing engineering on the new-product development team always traveled to the design engineers' site. The design engineers almost never went to the factory where the product was to be produced. This custom was sanctioned by tradition and by the recognition that, in the product development process, design preceded manufacturing sequentially. At the same time, the custom reinforced the perception that design engineers had the more highly valued knowledge base and that manufacturing's influence was at least secondary, if not nonexistent. The one-way travel also confirmed the role of manufacturing as a passive service organization, with little value to add to the design process. Consequently, products reaching the manufacturing floor experienced unanticipated problems in production.

Yet in these companies, managers were striving to augment the influence of manufacturing on design, knowing that earlier input from manufacturing would increase their speed to market. Their efforts were undermined by their own failure to recognize the subtle influence that accepted behaviors had on the perceptions and attitudes they were trying to change. Routine is amazingly resilient.

One should not conclude from these examples that marketing always possesses more insight than engineering. We will see cases of the opposite in Chapter 7. Rather, the point is that corporate history tends to confer greater credibility on the dominant function—whatever the function—and voices from lower-status functions are ignored. The inability of lower-status functions to influence product design becomes a problem only if their members have important information, of course. However, as has become increasingly obvious in recent years, failure to listen to a variety of different perspectives during product design often leads to rework, redesign, and fire fighting.

Skills and Knowledge

Altering the skills and knowledge base of a core capability is as simple and as devastatingly difficult as hiring new people. Much depends on which of the three types of knowledge mentioned in Chapter 1 is required—public, industry-specific, or firm-specific. Knowledgeable employees possessing public knowledge can be hired out of formal educational programs. Industry specialists can be lured from competitors. Indeed, raids on competitors' top technological "gurus" make the newspapers because of the potential competitive advantage transferred to the hiring company. When David Cutler left Digital Equipment Corporation for Microsoft Corporation because his "Prism" project on the RISC Alpha chip was canceled, his move was seen as a coup for Microsoft. Gordon Bell, one of the chief architects of DEC's VAX machines on which much of the company's early success was founded, and himself a legendary computer "guru," characterized Cutler as "one of the best system designers in the world."[62] Digital's loss was a definite gain for Microsoft: Gates put Cutler in charge of the critical project to create Windows NT.[63] A couple of years later another of the Digital Alpha chip designers, Richard Witek, left the company for Apple Computer.[64]

Such movement within the computer industry is not only well documented but expected and regarded as beneficial to the growth of the industry. The tacit and explicit knowledge disseminated through such informal networks as a restaurant in Silicon Valley famous as a watering hole for engineers is part of the attraction of the area for businesses.[65] The cross-hiring that occurs has at least two, opposing effects. On the one hand, movement of people tends to homogenize the knowledge pool and encourage the emergence of de facto technical standards within a given geographic area. (At one time, two versions of the software language LISP flourished—one on the East Coast and one on the West.) On the other hand, an influx of new people challenges established ways of doing things and thereby provides a guard against rigidity. Industry-specific knowledge is also diffused through "informal trading" by engineers. In a study of eleven U.S. steel minimills, von Hippel found that at all but one (and that one was selected precisely because behavior there differed), personnel reported "routinely trading proprietary process know-how, sometimes with direct competitors."[66] The managers interviewed emphasized that this knowledge flow had to be reciprocal: the knowledge was traded, not given away. Nevertheless, this kind of knowledge swap, at least within the industry, tends to make industry-specific knowledge more readily obtained than firm-specific skills.

In sum, firm-specific knowledge cannot be hired; it must grow up over time. Proprietary knowledge—especially that not captured in explicit form but still residing in people's heads—is clearly part of a core capability. It is also often the hardest to dislodge when it becomes a core rigidity. As extensively discussed in Chapter 3, skills frequently become closely entwined with people's identity, so that the imperative to switch skill bases is experienced as an attack on their very being. Moreover, attacks on outdated skills often seem almost immoral to longtime employees because knowledge bases are tied up with norms of behavior and implicit value systems. And values, as discussed below, are by far the most difficult dimension to alter.

Values

As explained in Chapter 1, there are really two kinds of values—generic (or big *V*) and knowledge-base-specific (or little *v*). The first are associated with attitudes and beliefs about relations with other people, including customers; the latter, "little" values, are tied to prizing particular ways of carrying out activities, with specific disciplinary approaches or with certain ways of operating.

Even if they departed the world generations ago, company founders and early leaders continue to influence the organization profoundly. Values, in particular, bear their "imprint."[67] As we saw in Chapter 1, the values of Robert Wood Johnson, son of the founder, and chairman of Johnson &

Johnson from 1938 to 1963, are enshrined in the company's "Credo," which was formalized in the 1940s and is displayed on corporate factory and office walls throughout the world today. Similarly, the "HP Way" set of corporate values has its roots in the birth of the company, when Hewlett and Packard stood in a garage in 1939 and flipped a coin to see whose name would go first in the company logo.

One of the difficulties of changing corporate norms and routines is that employees confuse the two different levels of values and are uncertain as to whether they are being asked to alter the big *V* or whether the change involves only the way in which existing values are being *operationalized.* That is, are basic values regarding the mission of the company being altered—or only the way that the activities in support of that mission are being carried out? At Cross Corporation, the maker of fine writing instruments, quality has long been a big *V*—synonymous with the company name. In the 1940s, Ellery Boss gave his factory floor operators the unprecedented right to personally reject any pen that was visually flawed, even if the imperfection was tiny and did not affect performance at all. Visitors touring the factory were shown with pride the bins of rejected products that had in some very minor way failed to meet the stringent quality requirements of the people who produced them. Over the years, as ever more sophisticated equipment allowed the identification of even more microscopic flaws, the workers pursued their obsession with perfection with unwavering dedication. However, in the early 1990s, Cross managers recognized the need to define quality through the eyes of the users rather than the producers, and their research into consumers' first interactions with the products produced some surprises. Consumers did not visually inspect the pen as they took it out of the box. Rather, they hefted it, felt the surface, and then checked its function. They were not concerned about minute variations in surface color or finish.

In response to this realization, company managers set about reeducating their employees. Quality, they explained, was in the eye of the customer—and had to be defined in those terms. Employees were initially alarmed, fearing that quality was being sacrificed: their long-held ways of operationalizing quality were being revised, and they were asked to consider mechanical function as more critical than appearance. Some protested vehemently, feeling that the very essence of the company was being challenged. Only if the Cross name remained synonymous with quality would they be comfortable with the change; they had to feel that quality itself was not being challenged or sacrificed. In fact, the company was changing the little *v*—the way that quality was defined and operationalized. The two *is* had to be separated in the minds of the employees in order to change behavior.

Management went to great lengths to help employees understand the reason for reformulating the activity of quality assurance. A selection of employees joined managers in observing, from behind one-way windows in an adjoining room, focus groups of individuals who had purchased a writing instrument priced at ten dollars or more within the last few months. The group members were asked first to examine a large assortment of writing instruments (not just Cross products) and comment on what they liked and disliked. Then they sorted the instruments into three piles, according to the degree to which the products (1) were flawless, (2) met high quality standards, or (3) did not meet such standards. Finally, focus group members were asked to explain *why* they made those judgments.

Cross employees were able to see for themselves that the members of the focus groups assessed instruments by determining how the pens felt in the hand, how well the propel/repel action to extend/retract the writing nib worked, and how smoothly they wrote. A condensed videotape of the research was then shown to all the employees, who subsequently met in small groups with their first-line supervisors to discuss what they had seen. Finally, management instituted new processes to reinforce the new ways of assessing product quality.[68] The big *V* of quality was preserved; it was *enacted* differently.

As the above examples of capability dimensions suggest, it is usually impossible to alter one dimension of a rigidity without also confronting the necessity of changing another dimension. It is possible to introduce change in relatively small steps, but the definition of "small" depends on the perspective. After all, Cross managers initially thought they were introducing a relatively minor process change (and so did the managers at WORAL). As we will see throughout the book, each individual employee has a lens through which he or she views the world, and the perceived size of the change depends on the focal range of that lens.

When the core capabilities have almost *all* become core rigidities, as in the case of NCR, the managerial options are fairly clear, if both drastic and extremely painful. As Anderson found at NCR, the managers were, of course, quick to believe (and insist) that the rigidities resided in departments other than their own. Actually, as Anderson understood, the rigidities were pervasive throughout the organization because they were born of the company's long-standing core capabilities. Consider all the changes—in all four dimensions—that Anderson needed to make to move NCR into the computer age.

THE TURNAROUND AT NCR

It is not surprising, given the problems that he inherited, that Anderson believed "success tends to spoil both companies and their managers."[69] After assuming NCR's presidency in 1972, Anderson immediately began dismantling many of the old systems and challenging the old values. He brought to the task strong personal beliefs in frugality and discipline. Adopting a strategy of NCR's becoming a full-fledged computer systems company, he discontinued mechanical products and focused the company on some key markets. Businesses that were profitable but not related to computer systems were divested, and others were acquired to fill out product lines. NCR developed a full line of data terminals and a broader range of computer "engines."

The old norm of manufacturing principally in Dayton was altered in favor of sourcing according to cost and of very decentralized manufacturing. Managerial systems were completely overhauled in manufacturing and marketing. Plants became cost centers; marketing was reorganized from a product-line focus to an industry/market responsibility. The ratio of salary to commission for the salesforce was increased. A new value was placed on moving managers around in the company—among divisions, functions, and countries—to break down the barriers that had caused some of the rigidity. New technical systems were adopted, including computerized control systems in manufacturing, order processing, product costing, and financial reporting. New products were designed in modules, to facilitate the delivery of complex systems.

Between 1975 and 1979, NCR revenues grew from $2 billion to $3 billion. Net income in that time period more than tripled (from $72 million to $235 million). Return on shareholder equity grew from 6.7 percent to 16.9 percent. In 1982, NCR's revenues reached $3.5 billion, and by the time Anderson retired in 1983, *Forbes* magazine reported:

> NCR . . . is far better poised for the future than many erstwhile stars of California's Silicon Valley or Boston's Route 128. [CEO Charles] Exley and retiring Chairman William Anderson have shaken the 99-year-old company to its roots. As a result, in the last 18 months the company has introduced products at an unprecedented pace, many aimed at completely new markets. Even with the major development costs, profits held up well during the recession. This year record earnings should approach $300 million, a 20% increase.[70]

In 1990, AT&T, in need of a partner for its computer business, approached NCR for a merger. NCR fought the deal for ten months, but in September 1991, the two companies merged. AT&T exchanged $7.4 billion of its stock for all of NCR's shares outstanding. The companies' combined revenues of $43.6 billion made it the eighth-largest company in the *Fortune* 500, and the merger was pronounced "successful beyond my wildest expectations" by then NCR president Gilbert Williamson in 1992.[71]

The process of change, however, is never finished. In a 1993 address at Harvard Business School, Jerre L. Stead, chairman and CEO of NCR (now a wholly owned subsidiary of AT&T), focused on his continuing need to change the organization. He favors three rules for policies: if rules don't support the company's core values, eliminate them; if rules don't elicit trust, eliminate them; if rules don't help in doing the job, eliminate them.[72]

Summary

The major point of this chapter has been that the flip side of a core capability, coexisting with it, is a core rigidity. Fully as complex a system as the capability, a core rigidity is comprised of the same four dimensions: physical systems, skills and knowledge, managerial systems, and values—both "big *Vs*" and "little *vs*." A critical managerial task is being aware of the flip side of capabilities as we grow and nurture the knowledge that will propel our institutions into success. Core rigidities are activated when companies fall prey to insularity or overshoot an optimal level of best practices. There are many explanations for these self-defeating tendencies; herein we have focused on the dysfunctional behaviors of managers in fostering them. As Peter Drucker often points out, every failure is a failure of management. Many companies discover core rigidities only when they have become so obvious that customers desert and the company's market value plummets. Then the board or shareholders or some extraordinarily courageous leader takes out a large hammer and bludgeons the organization into realizing that change, in one or more dimensions, truly is necessary.

We would all like to avoid the hammer. As Kenichi Ohmae notes, it is managers' "high responsibility to rethink . . . business systems on a regular basis, to take them apart in their minds, to go through a disciplined mental process of decomposing them and then restructuring them from scratch, from a zero-based foundation."[73] It is encouraging to recall that a number of large companies have very successfully segued from old core capabilities to new ones, overcoming rigidities along the way. As we saw, NCR did manage the transition from electromechanical to computer equipment. Harris Corporation, founded as a printing press company, is moving into multimedia. General Electric innovated in CT and MRI technologies.[74] We will see more examples throughout the book and will return to this theme in Chapter 9. Core rigidities can be avoided and new core capabilities encouraged to emerge.

In the remainder of this book, we consider the key activities that nurture new capabilities and hence open the organization to change. New-product development projects, new production processes, experimentation of all kinds, new avenues into knowledge from outside technology sources and market intelligence, new geographic sites—all challenge static thinking. These activities protect the firm against core rigidities, constantly clearing the channels so that the wellsprings of knowledge can flow freely.

The next chapter addresses the first of the four featured activities, exploring how managers can create intellectual variety within their organizations and yet integrate the disparate types of knowledge. To address operational issues in new-product development creatively, we must understand the psychological and organizational bases for different approaches to problem solving and build a repertoire of managerial responses.

PART TWO

KEY INNOVATION ACTIVITIES

CHAPTER THREE

Shared Problem Solving

[C]reative synthesis [is] the sudden interlocking of two previously unrelated skills, or matrices of thought.

—Arthur Koestler
  The Act of Creation[1]

Multiple disciplines in the same studio, fighting over radio stations and modes of dress and work hours and what's perceived as work . . . , all of that I saw as a rich and yeasty opportunity for a kind of abrasion that I wanted to turn into light rather than heat.

—Gerald Hirshberg
  Vice President, Nissan Design International[2]

As suggested in the last chapter's discussion of organizational rigidities, corporations foster certain skills, values, and knowledge bases at the expense of others. By virtue of being excellent in one knowledge domain, an organization is relatively unreceptive to ideas from others. This tendency to pay attention to and collect certain kinds of knowledge at the expense of others is echoed at all levels of the company—by individuals, by project teams, and by functions. These islands of knowledge (and the "political" fiefdoms that grow up around and support them) are potent barriers to the shared problem-solving activities featured in this chapter. (See Figure 3-1.)

Figure 3-1 Capability-Creating Activities: Shared Problem Solving

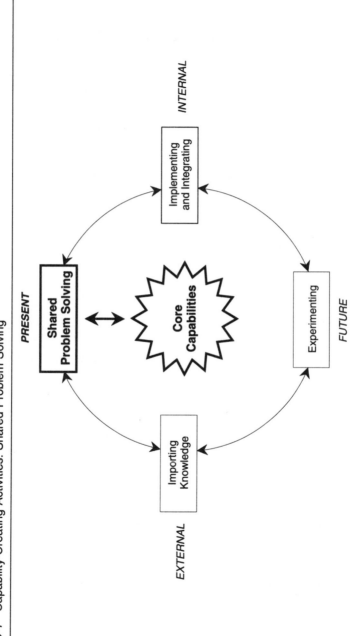

Increasingly, the complexity of the problems, the proliferation of formally educated specialties, and the pace of globalization require that the problem-solving activities involved in new-product development be shared across disciplinary, cognitive, geographic, and cultural boundaries. This chapter examines three sources of individual differences in problem solving—specialization, preferred cognitive style, and preferences in tools and methodologies. These three sources of intellectual diversity can promote divisiveness and often constitute formidable barriers to the shared problem solving so critical to new-product development. However, the same three also provide enormous opportunities for creativity. In the following pages, we will first discuss briefly how such intellectual differences shape problem-solving approaches; then we consider why and how some innovative managers and organizations have deliberately fostered such knowledge heterogeneity in their organizations. Finally, we look at various managerial levers available to transform the energy generated by such diversity into positive output or, as Hirshberg puts it, "light rather than heat."

The Trap of Mind-Set

In problem solving, search patterns of even the most intelligent people can be bound by prior experience and successes.[3] In fact, people fall into habits of thought precluding innovative problem solving with amazing ease and speed—even for the most minor of tasks. In experiments conducted a generation ago, researchers discovered what they dubbed "functional fixedness"—i.e., the tendency for people to be quite fixed in their perception of how objects could be used once that use was suggested. For example, two groups of people were given identical supplies (a stack of papers, a stapler, and a paper clip) and a simple task—to fasten the papers to each other and to the wall. The experimental group's papers were fastened together with the clip, whereas the control group received its clip in an envelope. This seemingly small difference created a mind-set among members of the experimental group: they were significantly slower to think of unbending the paper clip into a wire hook to fasten the papers to the wall.[4] A number of researchers replicated this experiment in various ways, demonstrating that even slight prior experience with an object negatively affected people's ability to think creatively about its use.[5] As one pair of early researchers concluded, "[F]unctional fixedness . . . interferes with problem solving."[6]

The phenomenon underlying the development of such mind-sets as functional fixedness seems to be the brain's natural tendency to store, process, and retrieve information in related blocks. Without some way of bundling information for parsimonious handling, we could not manage its continual flow from the environment. These blocks constitute mental models, or schema, against which we calibrate information and that we use to solve problems.[7] Mind-sets, therefore, are highly useful in routine activities. In fact, if the technique toward which prior experience biases us provides the best solution to a particular problem, applying that solution is both efficient and effective.[8] In an organization, when such techniques are reinforced over time by success, the patterns of thought fall into well-worn grooves[9] and become part of a business capability. The problem is that, as we have already seen, the limited range of problem-solving responses developed can become dysfunctional and contribute to core rigidities.[10]

Signature Skills

Limitations on problem-solving responses in an organization start with the individual. People become highly skilled in applying certain solutions to problems; moreover, people can become emotionally attached to their mind-sets, or problem-solving biases. In this case, they grow what I term *signature skills.*

A signature skill is an ability by which a person prefers to identify himself or herself professionally. *Signature* evokes the idiosyncratic nature of the skill—a personally defining characteristic, as much a part of someone's identity as the way the individual signs his or her name. Signature skills may be acquired through schooling or by experience, but they are ones to which we bond our professional identity because we have *chosen* to do so. (In addition, we may possess nonsignature skills—also acquired through education or of necessity—but we do not feel as invested in these.) Further, I would argue, the extent to which a new procedure, technology, or capability is "deskilling" depends on whether such an innovation makes a signature skill obsolete.[11] Therefore, a change in problem-solving solutions and technology in an organization may be welcomed by one person in a given job category yet resisted by another in that same position, depending on whether or not the supplanted skill was signature.[12]

A signature skill is an outgrowth, an interactive expression, of three interdependent preferences—preferred type of task, preferred cognitive approach to problems (sometimes considered cognitive style), and preferred technology for performing the task. (See Figure 3-2.) In our technically advanced society, specialists are rewarded for pursuing their signature skills in depth—at least

Figure 3-2 Composition of Signature Skills

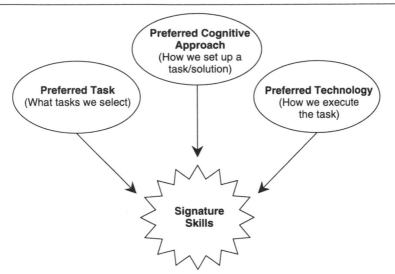

until and unless those skills are rendered obsolete. In consequence, our organizations have created and encouraged enclaves of specialized skills emotionally tied to people's egos and identities.[13] A task critical to organizational well-being and the integration of knowledge bases is managing across and among these enclaves of talent and signature skills.

Creative Abrasion

The first step in this management task is to recognize the potential inherent in a portfolio of often conflicting signature skills. Some managers of innovative organizations select people *because* their ideas, biases, personalities, values, and skills conflict—not in spite of their differences. Why? Because an effective guard against people's considering only a few problem-solving alternatives or, worse, framing problems so that they can be solved only with familiar solutions is to involve a variety of people, with their diverse signature skills, in the task. As different ideas rub against each other, sparks fly. However, in a well-managed process, the sparks are creative, not personal.

Gerald Hirshberg, director of Nissan Design International, coined the phrase *creative abrasion* to emphasize that energy generated by the conflict can be channeled into creating rather than destroying, into synthesis rather than fragmentation. Such managers build an atmosphere that encourages people to respect each other's viewpoint without always agreeing with it. In these environments, individuals are able to accept cognitive diversity without enthroning divisiveness. Obviously, nothing productive can come of the conflict without compromise and integration—but the innovation occurs at the boundaries between mind-sets, not within the provincial territory of one knowledge and skill base.

This concept of creative abrasion differs radically from several more familiar sources of friction. First, creative abrasion is *not* equivalent to a celebration of diversity on the basis of gender, sexual preference, or ethnic background. Although diversity on these bases surely introduces different perspectives and problem-framing approaches, managing creative abrasion requires both more and less than structuring an organization to attract and hold a group of people with mixed backgrounds. It requires *more* because merely introducing diversity in this general sense does not ensure that different kinds of creative problem solving occur. Assembling a group of people with different back-grounds and perspectives often generates some degree of abrasion but does not in and of itself ensure that the conflict will be creative. And creative abrasion requires *less* because people of similar ethnic backgrounds or of the same gender can draw upon extremely different sources and types of creativity. In short, "diversity," as popularly conceived, is not essential to the presence of creative abrasion between contrasting cognitive styles. Creative abrasion involves much more specific attention to people's *cognitive* approaches to problem solving and innovation.

Nor is creative abrasion identical to the "constructive confrontation" en-couraged at Intel and other fast-paced companies where, as Jelinek and Schoonhoven observed, corporate culture encourages employees to confront problems very openly and aggressively and not to allow politeness to mask important differences of opinion and lapses in needed action.[14] Such confron-tation does not necessarily arise from different perspectives on the world, and the norm applies to all interpersonal behavior. Thus, although creative abrasion is one form of constructive confrontation, its purpose is specifically to support innovation and encourage the integration of different problem-framing and problem-solving approaches—to create something that no single perspective could have.

Creative abrasion is also unlike personal confrontation and abuse. The controversial former head of Simon & Schuster, Richard Snyder, explained his management philosophy as follows: "Business is conflict. That's the creative process. You don't get excellence by saying yes. You get love, but you don't get excellence. Simon & Schuster is a company that raised the hurdles on excellence every bloody day."[15] Superficially, this could resemble the philosophy of Gordon Forward, CEO of Chaparral Steel. Yet, as Charles Hayward, who left his presidency of Simon & Schuster's consumer division to run Time Warner's Little, Brown & Company, recalls, Snyder's "remarks in meetings were either vulgar or he attacked personal style or a person's business style. . . . [He] would rarely get through a single meeting without going after someone."[16] Personally demeaning someone is antithetical to creative abrasion; managers expecting the abrasion thus engendered to result in creativity risk misdirecting much energy into nonproductive paths.

Before considering how to manage abrasion for its creative potential, let us consider each of the three elements of a signature skill and look at a few company situations in which managers deliberately set up conditions to encourage the diversity of specialization, cognitive style, and methodologies that leads to the abrasion.

Specialization

Preferences for certain types of tasks determine the kinds of work toward which we gravitate. Most people in the world are given little choice, of course, but those who end up in management generally began life with enough education, health, and opportunity to have made some choices along the way. These are rooted in our preference for careers offering various rewards—from autonomy to service to security[17]—and within those careers, for specific work that we enjoy. So, for instance, when a group of sales representatives at Digital Equipment Corporation was offered a software program automating the initial configuration of the complex computer systems they sold, the reps reacted differently, depending on whether or not they enjoyed manual configuration. Some reps were delighted to be relieved of an onerous, detail-oriented task. Those who considered themselves expert configurers and had liked the task, however, grew increasingly negative toward the automated configuration software over several years.[18]

Specialization leads to expertise, of course, and therefore the availability of deep knowledge to apply to problems. However, the resulting distinct "thought worlds" rarely intersect, unless purposely driven to do so.[19] When Ceramics Process Systems Corporation was founded, its founders enunciated a principle so important to the company that the first president had a statement of it framed and hung on his wall: "Our most important technical breakthroughs will come from disciplines and literature outside our industry and scientific field."[20]

CERAMICS PROCESS SYSTEMS CORPORATION

Ceramics Process Systems Corporation produced highly pure compounds of metal with oxygen, carbon, nitrogen, or other elements. These compounds had remarkable properties. For instance, silicon nitride had a strength-to-weight ratio four times that of steel; it was chemically inert, was harder than any known material except diamond, and had an extremely high melting point. The scientific breakthrough leading to the company's formation was the creation of ceramic powder consisting of submicron, monosized particles. Ceramics made from such powders were both higher-quality and potentially lower-cost than those on the market.

The scientific team at CPS was deliberately constituted of individuals from very different backgrounds—physicists and mechanical, civil, and chemical engineers as well as ceramics engineers. This approach was especially unusual given that the people at this small start-up company were some of the world's acknowledged experts in ceramics. Moreover, they hired some of the world's top students in that field. With such pedigrees, one might expect these scientists to indulge in an arrogantly high degree of "not-invented-here." However, they were more interested in not *re*inventing whatever knowledge could be borrowed.

Source: Clay Christensen and Dorothy Leonard-Barton, "Ceramics Process Systems Corporation," case 691-028, Harvard Business School, Boston, 1992.

The open-minded philosophy at Ceramics Process Systems had important payoffs. Faced with the need to control very precisely the rheology, or viscosity, of its ceramic slurries being pumped through a forming machine, the scientists wondered, Who would have the best techniques for controlling slurries? After concluding that paint processing afforded similar challenges, since paint consists essentially of latex particles dispersed and suspended in an emulsion, they hired an award-winning polymer engineer from the paint industry. By applying the lessons learned in the paint-processing context, they were able to develop a system that pumped, poured, and molded the ceramic slurry at a variety of pressures without affecting the properties of the product.

Another challenge was the difficulty of removing ceramic forms from molds. Interested in the possibility of very rapidly cooling the forms to below-freezing temperatures to facilitate release, company managers again asked themselves, Where in the world resides the best knowledge about quick-freezing processes? They turned to the food industry for help. In fact, during their first few years, the ceramics engineers called upon experts from numerous fields besides their own. (See Figure 3-3.)

Figure 3-3 Innovation at the Intersection: Multidisciplinary Problem Solving at
CPS

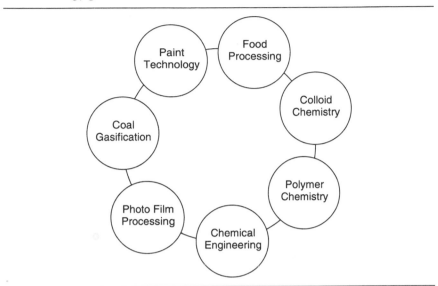

Source: Adapted from Clayton Christensen and Dorothy Leonard-Barton, "Ceramics Process
Systems Corporation," Harvard Business School Case 9-691-028 (1990), 14.

New products today are more likely than not to emerge through innovation
at the interface of different specialties (or sometimes at the interface of
existing products). As further discussed in Chapter 6, "technology fusion," or
the ability to combine knowledge bases housed in different core technological
capabilities, often distinguishes innovative companies.[21] For example, when
3M consumer research showed that people were unhappy with rusting steel-
wool pads, experts from 3M's adhesives, abrasives, coatings, and nonwoven
technologies divisions got together to create Never Rust plastic soap pads.
In the eighteen months between January 1993 and June 1994, Never Rust
and its spin-off, Never Scratch, captured 30 percent of the U.S. soap-pad
market.[22] Similarly, the creation of Hitachi's high-capacity computer disk
drive drew upon expertise from a number of different divisions. Nuclear
engineers at the Energy Research Laboratory were best equipped to simulate
the complex disk drive on their cutting-edge software. Chemical engineers
at the Research Lab invented new organic coatings for the disks. The tiny
precision motors powering the drives required miniaturization expertise from
manufacturing, and the complex microchip at the heart of the drive's re-
cording head came from the Device Development Center and Musashi
Works.[23] Hewlett-Packard's program in "MC²" (measurement plus comput-

ing and communications) is promoted by the head of HP corporate laboratories, Joel Birnbaum, as a unique capability that will yield a crossbred series of totally new products. Looking ahead to all the possibilities created by digitization, Birnbaum predicted in 1993: "HP's going to be an almost totally different company 10 years from now."[24]

These examples illustrate how companies find synergy across specialized knowledge bases that have been nurtured over the years. In contrast, some companies from inception set up shop at the intersection of technologies and disciplines. In some industries, *no products* can emerge without technology fusion. Survival depends on it. Consider the product development process at Vertex Pharmaceuticals, a company using structure-based rational drug design (SBRDD). This process combines the mature technology of synthesizing drugs with the nascent biotechnology techniques for reproducing the proteins and enzymes that human bodies produce. The ultimate aim of SBRDD is to produce orally deliverable drugs to treat major diseases. Large-protein drugs produced through traditional biotechnology methods usually have to be administered intravenously. Small, specific active molecules produced through SBRDD can potentially be taken in the form of self-administered pills or nasal sprays. Both production and administration of such synthetic compounds are much less costly than the protein drugs produced through biotechnology. As the term *rational* implies, SBRDD is also much more efficient in zeroing in on effective drugs than the more random searches typical of traditional pharmaceutical product development.

However, SBRDD drug production requires integrating numerous disciplines, including advanced biology, chemistry, and biophysics. Figure 3-4 displays just how many different disciplinary knowledge bases are needed. The process starts when a protein, usually an enzyme central to disease, is identified, purified, sequenced, and cloned to produce bulk quantities sufficient to grow crystals suitable for structural mapping by X-ray crystallography. Then, nuclear magnetic resonance adds information about the protein's structure in its more natural liquid state. This enables accurate documentation of both functional and anatomic dimensions of the areas of the enzyme, called active sites, that control function. The pooled data are then manipulated using 3-D computer modeling to enable the design of small-protein drugs that can specifically interact at the active sites to block disease-causing processes. Computer modeling effectively substitutes for much of the actual synthesis and screening in traditional drug design.

As these examples illustrate, specialization provides the deep reservoirs of knowledge necessary to solve extremely complex problems in new-product

Figure 3-4 Vertex Pharmaceuticals' Process Flow for Rational Drug Design

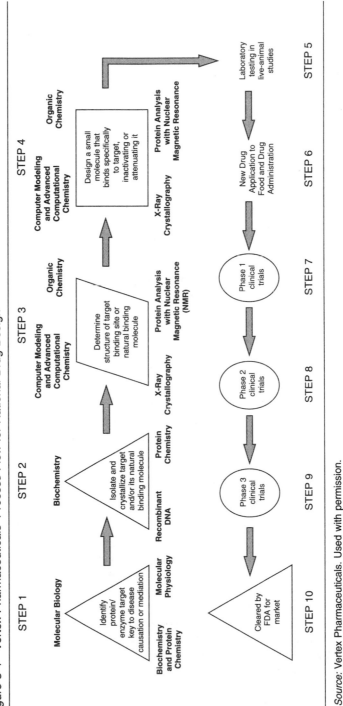

Source: Vertex Pharmaceuticals. Used with permission.

and new-process development, as long as the specialties can communicate with each other.

Cognitive Style Preferences

Differences in preferred cognitive styles (even within specialties) add another potentially jarring note to sessions in shared problem solving. Probably the most famous typology of personalities is the one captured by the Myers-Briggs Type Indicator, which employs four bivariate characteristics to describe people. Two of the four pairs of opposing descriptors are extremely relevant to how people approach tasks—sensation versus intuition, and judging versus perceiving. The difference between a preference for facts, history, and experience (sensation) versus a liking for metaphor, imagery, and speculation (intuition) has been suggested as "the source of the most miscommunication, misunderstanding, vilification, defamation, and denigration. *This difference places the widest gulf between people.*"[25]

Many task forces or teams throw together people who tend to problem-solve on opposite sides of this gulf. They hit misunderstandings because people preferring intuitive problem-solving approaches rely on imagination and hunches, whereas sensation-bound (sensible) individuals "tolerate no nonsense" in work and want down-to-earth, practical approaches.[26] These two groups also differ on the second dimension, judging versus perceiving. Judging-type people prefer "closure over open options" and push for decisions, whereas perceiving-type people look for more options, more data, and are willing to live with ambiguity longer. These cognitive preferences have significant implications for managers of creative projects.

MULTIMEDIA AT MICROSOFT

Tom Corddry, manager of family reference multimedia products at Microsoft, finds two very different mental processes essential to produce a product that combines computation and database management with user interfaces capable of engaging, pleasing, and informing the user: (1) option creation and (2) option reduction. He needs both people who can "think up" and those who can "shoot down."[27] Although people representing these two approaches can be found in any innovation team, two creative groups commonly involved in developing multimedia products typify the extremes: the most analytically inclined among software code developers—the same people who created Microsoft Excel spreadsheets—and the artistically oriented designers of the user interfaces, screens, icons, and background patterns.

The first group is excellent at logical argument, at finishing things, at getting things done efficiently. The analytical developers can "make decisions like Ninjas," calculating the probabilities of a particular course of action's being correct and immediately acting upon that analysis. At the other extreme of the continuum, the designers tend to be relatively indecisive and to relish ambiguity. "If you ask them to choose between A and B, they will ask: 'What about C?' " Analytical people who have traditionally added value and been rewarded on the basis of their ability to reason logically and swiftly to a conclusion may initially assume that people who operate at the opposite end of the mental continuum are not smart because they are often inarticulate about their ideas and both reluctant and slow to drive toward resolution. On the other hand, option creators may believe that highly analytical people are so impatient for closure that they spend too little time on the broad issues of scoping out product concept and that they move on quickly to details, thereby possibly settling for a suboptimal design.

Corddry humorously describes the superficial differences between the two groups at the extremes: developers work at night, wear rumpled T-shirts, and dine on pizza; designers work during the day, wear "found-object earrings," and prepare gourmet meals. Such lifestyle differences are merely surface indicators of very different worldviews. The concept of something as simple as a line drawn on the screen is totally different to the two groups. To very analytical software developers, a line is a mathematical formula expressing the shortest distance between two points. To artistic designers, a line has characteristics—weight, a variable edge, color, density. Whereas developers believe that a line is a line, designers believe that a line can convey messages about time and space that allow a user to infer function. Designers are skilled in the "art of the desirable" and developers in the "art of the possible." Designers may be relatively naive about what kind of computer power is required to construct and deliver a function. Would a feature require a supercomputer or a personal computer? They don't (initially) know.

As Corddry notes, "In a disposition-driven culture like Microsoft's, it is important to encourage the imaginative impulses of people who tend to resolve issues almost before they think about them and to attract and hold some people who tend to imagine alternatives faster than they resolve them."[28]

Corddry's observations are echoed by other managers of innovative groups. At Interval Research, a West Coast think tank set up to explore the future of media, President and CEO David Liddle talks about the need for both "nerds and hippies."

INTERVAL RESEARCH

According to Liddle: Hippies are people who care about doing the right thing, and once they have done the right thing, they kind of let getting it finished up be left to somebody else. Nerds are people who care about doing things right, and they don't worry too much about the big, broad, flexible outlook and all that sort of stuff. They are very, very proud of their execution and quantitative aspects of what they have gotten done and so on. The myth is that those two are completely distinct and that companies, or at least laboratories, consist of only one or the other and that individuals have only one or the other component in their character. . . . I know better than that. But there is a grain of truth in this set of ideas. It's very, very difficult to do . . . research that takes long strides and big risks and changes the complexion of an industry . . . in a very tight and nerdlike organization. In the same way, trying to execute a successful product with a 100 percent hippie organization is issuing rifles to the band.[29]

These organizations not only prize cognitive differences but regard them as essential to problem solving. Management very consciously designs hiring and staffing to maximize cognitive diversity. Nissan Design International hires in *pairs* of contrasting cognitive preferences. For example, a strongly rational, logical, and analytical designer is balanced by one whose enthusiasm centers on color, aesthetic rhythm, and pure form. If NDI hires only one person per year, the next year's hire is considered the second half of the pair.

At Xerox's Palo Alto Research Center, a special program called PARC Artist-in-Residence (PAIR for short) is similarly designed to introduce more cognitive diversity into this scientists' sanctuary. The program matches an artist with a scientist; the artists are screened for their interest in software technology (which constitutes somewhat of a common language with the scientists) and meet with various scientists to seek a match in interests. The program is young, and it is not clear how much benefit PARC will derive from the artists' presence. However, Rich Gold, who set up the program, notes a shift in vocabulary and perspective among the researchers. "You hear those postmodern words that you never heard around here before. You begin to see a broader take on what could be science or what would be interesting research . . . a deeper interest in aesthetic issues—which almost was none. . . . [Aesthetics] were considered kind of a user interface problem. [Now they are] moving deeper into the fundamental parts of the problem."

At Interval Research, managers have deliberately recreated the best of a research university atmosphere—the clash and mix of subcultures and cognitive styles—while avoiding the sterility associated with long-term hires. Management invites "sabbatical" visits from professors and visitors from varied backgrounds.

The assumption underlying all this effort to diversify approaches to problem solving is that cognitive diversity stimulates creativity. As explained later, the same managers expend considerable effort in consciously managing this intellectual variety.

Preferences in Tools and Methodologies

The third element in signature skills is a preference for certain methodological approaches—often embodied in particular tools. Such preferences are derived from, and interdependent with, the other two elements—task preference and preferred cognitive style. In the mid-1980s, a large electronics firm's research laboratories and engineering departments encountered a stark example of different problem-solving approaches based on preferred methodologies when they introduced computer-aided design (CAD) tools to members of the physical design group, who designed cabinets to hold the electronics equipment. Members of the group who had been trained as engineering technicians were accustomed to designing sequentially, each drawing being an incremental improvement over the last. The physical designers, who came from artistic backgrounds, created multiple but very rough freehand drawings, including close-ups of particular details, leaving multiple options open for as long as possible. They then laid out all these potential designs and selectively derived the best features from each to integrate into a still very conceptual organic whole.

Because the CAD systems accommodated their linear problem-solving methodology, the engineering-trained designers accepted them without difficulty. Each CAD image represented decisions made—concrete progress toward the final version. In contrast, the CAD systems forced the artists to alter their methodology, to construct one design at a time in considerable detail. In order to view all options, the designers had to print all the images out before making selections—a very time-consuming process. Although eventually all the designers used CAD, the artists were more hesitant to adopt it. And even after the switch, they continued to feel constrained by the new tool. Research suggests that the artists were pulling more on the right side of the brain, and the technicians more on the left, to accomplish the same task.[30] The artists were more intuitive and perceiving, the engineers more "sensible" and judging. The CAD tools were far more compatible with a methodology based on a left-brained, sensible, and judging approach.

Methodological preferences also derive from early training: we are most comfortable with the tools on which we learned—even if our choice is based on "nonobjective" merits. Thus, prosthodontists who learned to use gold in constructing bridges, caps, and crowns at dental school tend to be quite disdainful of "lesser" alloys.[31] Perhaps surprising to the layperson is the *fervor* with which dentists espouse their chosen material (gold over alloys or vice versa). Both groups produce persuasive arguments to bolster their preference, but it is difficult to argue based on scientific evidence that there is a "right" material. The choice depends on individual preferences—and strength of conviction. Obviously, the more a dentist uses one material in preference to the other, the more skilled he or she becomes in using that material and the more it becomes a part of the individual's signature skill.

Mechanisms for Managing Specialization, Cognitive Diversity, and Methodological Preferences

In all of the above examples, integrative activities are critical, whether the integration requires crossing long-established "stovepipes" of vertically organized expertise, creating a new company based on the assumption of technology fusion, or simply producing a complex new product. Even if we wanted to avoid the challenge of managing multiple signature skills, we have little choice today. Careful research confirms our everyday observation that products on the market are increasingly complex and draw upon diverse sources of expertise.[32] Instruments and pieces of equipment that used to be stand-alone tools are linked as more manufacturing processes are moved from single-task-oriented job shops to continuous-flow operations. More and more hardware tools have software components, from operating room equipment in hospitals to automobiles. Different types of software themselves are mingled to create whole new types of products. And even within the domain of software, which might be assumed to encompass a single mind-set, there are tremendous differences based on how "close to the silicon" the developers work—i.e., whether they design computer operating systems and compilers or create user interfaces and applications. And as we saw at Microsoft, even within the world of applications, those who produce spreadsheets have a very different set of signature skills than those who develop games.

Abrasion is guaranteed; it is management's task to ensure that the friction is creative. Members of product teams that succeed in the magic midwifery of technology fusion are often euphoric about the experience. "It was the hardest work and the most fun I've ever had," one engineer declared about a product development project that drew upon several different technology bases within the company. "I hardly knew those guys [other technical staff] existed. But we came up with more [new-product] ideas over one beer than I'd seen come out of our own shop in a year." So the conclusion is, The experience can be highly positive for the individual as well as the company. And the question is, What integrating mechanisms exist for managers to use in managing creative abrasion?

Managers who consciously address this challenge use a variety of strategies to ensure that the inevitable abrasion is in fact creative. In the following pages, we examine a few of the mechanisms that help, focusing in turn on the management of: (1) specialization, (2) preferred cognitive styles, and (3) preferred methodologies.

Managing Specialization

Groups comprising individuals who operate from a base of deeply specialized knowledge need mechanisms to translate across the different "languages" and encourage the depersonalization of conflicting perspectives. The translators can be members of the group or its managers.

People with T-Shaped skills. As individuals grow in experience, some begin to embody apparently opposing signature skills, especially a combination of both deep theoretical knowledge and practice. Such people are extremely valuable for managing the integration of very diverse knowledge sets because they speak two or more professional "languages" and can see the world from two or more different perspectives. They have T-shaped skill sets. The term *T-shaped* originated to describe the abilities of critical members of system-focused research and development teams:

> [T]hey are not only experts in specific technical areas but also intimately acquainted with the potential systemic impact of their particular tasks. On the one hand, they have a deep knowledge of a discipline like ceramic materials engineering, represented by the vertical stroke of the T. On the other hand, these ceramic specialists also know how their discipline interacts with others, such as polymer processing—the T's horizontal top stroke.[33]

The need for T-shaped skills surfaces anywhere problem solving is required across different deep functional knowledge bases or at the juncture of such deep knowledge with an application area. (See Figure 3-5.) People possessing these skills are able to shape their knowledge to fit the problem at hand rather than insist that the problem appear in a particular, recognizable form. Given their wide experience in applying functional knowledge, they are capable of convergent, synergistic thinking.

Figure 3-5 T-Shaped Skills

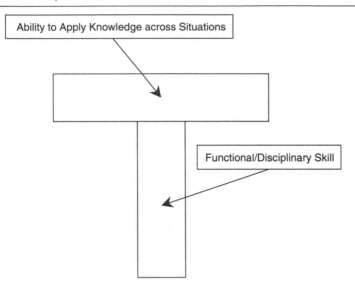

In the research cited above, Iansiti found that team members with T-shaped skills constituted the underpinnings of the systems-focused approach used by superior-performing companies. These companies needed fewer than one-third the engineers and completed their projects an average of 2.6 years sooner than competitors designing directly competing products in the same business.

If people with T-shaped skills are an integral part of such an important competitive advantage, where do we find them? In most organizations, T-shaped skills are not created as a deliberate policy but emerge because individuals have been willing to risk pursuing a somewhat marginal career.[34] Most formal organizational incentives encourage I-shaped skills—the deep functional expertise represented by the *T*'s stem. As a result, the individual is driven ever deeper into his or her expertise, which the organization continually draws on and rewards. At the same time, the organization provides no clear career path for those who want to top off the stem with a broad range of applications—i.e., the crossbar.

But creative problem solving requires us to manage the *balance* between rewarding only deep functional knowledge and rewarding only application or integration skills. Iansiti found that the system-focused companies deliberately created T-shaped skills by carefully shaping individual careers to provide exposure. Of course, a risk is creating a class of generalists with no deep knowledge of any particular specialty but possessing only the crossbar of the *T*. Managers in one company that has recently moved to cross-functional team structures for product development struggled with this possibility. Because teams were the latest and greatest innovation in new-product development, functional assignments were regarded as second-class. Employees were reluctant to return to their functional "homes" after serving on a development team because the activity there was not as highly regarded. Company managers decided that team members would periodically return to their functions specifically to refresh their functional skill base—lengthening the stem of the *T*. During that period, the team members would work on explicit benchmarking or skill-enhancing projects. Rather than regarding this time in the functional organization as banishment, employees began to see it as an opportunity to refurbish skills, thereby enhancing their own value for the next team assignment.

Perhaps the greater danger in trying to develop T-shaped skills in most companies, however, is that the press of urgent daily tasks will lead managers to pull the nearest available competent individual into a project, with little thought to the implications of that assignment for developing T-shaped skills. Given that such skills have proved to be very valuable, it behooves managers to think about an individual's assignments in terms of a balance between developing the shaft and developing the crossbar.

People with A-Shaped skills. Although rare, some individuals embody technology fusion. T-shaped skill implies deep know-how within one discipline (the stem) and more superficial knowledge about how it interacts with others (the crossbar). Some people actually learn more than one discipline (although more than two is unlikely) and so have two disciplinary "legs" on which to stand. Usually, such skills are acquired sequentially. In the creation of multimedia products, Microsoft manager Corddry looked for "crossovers"—i.e., people who had disciplinary roots in one knowledge base (e.g., music or art) and who had invested a lot of time in on-the-job training in another (e.g., computer science). However, in environments where technology fusion is the norm, some individuals may become bilingual. At Vertex Pharmaceuticals, one such individual says, "I am an immunologist by training, but I've sort of moved a little bit towards protein biochemistry, and I now do about 50 percent of each in terms of my interests and responsibilities here."

Multilingual Managers. Additional organizational glue in diverse creative groups is provided by managers, some of whom describe themselves as "schizophrenic" or "multilingual"—i.e., capable of operating in more than one specialized realm and perhaps utilizing more than one cognitive style. Nissan's Hirshberg was trained as an engineer as well as an artist; although his preferred mode is artist, he understands the engineering approach very well. John Seely Brown, head of Xerox's Palo Alto Research Center, was trained as a computer scientist but has tried very hard over the past few years to educate himself in the ways of anthropologists and historians. As he says, "It doesn't hurt to have the director of the place willing to appreciate the kind of elegance that each group brings to the table, because . . . the critical component here is the willingness to suspend disbelief . . . to engage in active listening."

Managers must be able and willing to intervene in the interactions among opposing groups—not to smooth over differences but to channel the energies in a positive direction. Groups that gloss over differences, applying a patina of accord and seeking superficial peace, are not likely to be creative. Yet disagreements have to be impersonalized or emotions will also interfere with creativity and leave bitterness in their wake. The multilingual managers handle their interventions differently, but always very self-consciously, encouraging participants to focus on *both* the process and the content of the discussion.[35]

Corddry of Microsoft promotes consciousness of potential creativity by reminding the disparate groups of software developers and screen designers that they actually have some deep underlying similarities. Both possess an unusual ability to "see things in their heads." They often recognize their particular gifts early in life. They are all "control freaks"—perfectionists who like to control the details to ensure that the outcome meets their demanding personal standards.

Hirshberg of Nissan Design calls attention to group process. He warns the groups going into a design negotiation session of difficult moments ahead; they will simply need to persevere, in both listening and explaining—without getting angry. Then, in meetings, when frustration peaks, he reminds them that "this is one of those times," like white-water rafting, when they are riding through the big ones.

Another manager who encourages creative confrontation in his work similarly draws overt attention to the conflict as a good process. "These are good issues for us to understand," he says when tension is high. "Let's be sure we have all the points of view represented." And he draws in other group members who may not have been engaged directly in the argument, legitimizing the disagreement as healthy and useful.

Managing Diversity of Cognitive Styles

Preferences for certain cognitive styles predispose individuals toward certain specialties,[36] but there is by no means an inevitable correspondence between discipline and preferred style. Nor are such cognitive preferences referenced in functional titles. Therefore, diversity of cognitive styles is usually not identified, discussed, or consciously managed. However, some managers have experimented with open acknowledgment of such differences, select employees according to their ability to collaborate, and even retain professionals to help mediate disputes.

Acknowledging Differences in Cognitive Style. At Nissan Design, early employees took a "personalysis" test, which divided cognitive preferences into four types, represented graphically by colors, so that individuals could see how their choices reflected different degrees of orientation toward decisive action versus the need for much information, for example, or inclination toward very rational reasoning versus more intuitive approaches, and so on. There are dozens of such diagnostic tests; Hirshberg is quick to point out that the one his employees took is "not an in-depth kind of psychoanalysis; it has its limits. . . . But . . . for us, it works beautifully in helping us to be open about the fact that each one of us is quite different, and there are some tremendous opportunities to alleviate some of the tensions we are experiencing by acknowledging openly those differences, . . . [which] are never deemed good or bad, better or worse." Using himself as an example, he explains that until the members of his organization identified their cognitive differences, he tended to misinterpret the responses he got from group members who were cautious about intuitive conclusions, thinking them "anticreative. I was wrong. They simply needed to come to the table with a different set of preparations and expectations." Hirshberg, like several other managers whose more "right-brained" style clashed with that of their more "left-brained" team members, found that the latter contributed importantly to problem solving if given a bit of time to mull over the options and reason their way to defensible conclusions.

Nissan Design took the unusual—but not unique—step of inviting individuals to announce their preferred cognitive styles by displaying a color chart of their "personalysis" on their desktop. There are obvious dangers in such declarations of cognitive diversity—the possibility that fellow employees will prejudge reactions and apply unjustified stereotypes or that such identifications could be used in some fashion to discriminate against people. However, managers who wish to stimulate creative abrasion argue that they can guard against such misuse and that open acknowledgment and acceptance of cognitive diversity legitimizes "out-of-the-box" thinking, often lending support to the more intuitive members of the group so that "the best arguments win—not just the best arguers."

In fact, formal declarations are often unnecessary because the way individuals use and decorate personal space tends to provide strong clues as to their preferred cognitive styles. A visitor wandering around Microsoft cannot help noticing the difference between the Spartan austerity of some developers' rooms, with orderly whiteboards and clean desktops, and the childlike clutter of some designers' rooms. At the extreme, one designer's office appears to be the inside of a toybox, with every conceivable space (including the ceiling) adorned with toys—enormous playing cards, a plastic brain, squirt guns and dolls, jack-in-the-boxes, and paper parasols. This office clearly belongs to someone who enjoys play and irreverence. Describing such individuals, Corddry says that their "imaginative capacities don't get quite so efficiently limited as they grow up, and . . . they tend to pop new things out."

Hiring and Selection. The ability to collaborate across specialties and different cognitive styles is not revealed on résumés, except perhaps in descriptions of prior jobs or as a propensity for certain leisure activities. Mostly, managers probe for this ability during intensive interviewing—often not conducted by a personnel department. In Chaparral Steel, workers were hired for their interpersonal communication skills as well as their interest in learning and their ability to learn. A manager at Vertex Pharmaceuticals notes: "We hire people who are, by the very way their brains are wired, collaborative and want to cross the boundaries that have traditionally separated scientific disciplines." Similarly, Interval Research's director, David Liddle, says of hirees that "one very important characteristic was . . . a very high capacity for collaboration and interaction."

At Intuit, the software company that blasted to the top of software charts with its personal financial planner, Quicken, software engineers had to like working directly with customers, since creative understanding of user needs is a competitive advantage of Intuit. Therefore, from the beginning, founder Scott Cook sought developers who enjoy seeing their product in the hands of users. Developers at Intuit are not buffered from customer foibles or complaints during the design process; they have to be willing to sit down, observe naive users interacting with a Quicken prototype for the first time, and come away with suggestions and ideas for making the program more user-friendly.

At Nissan Design International, designers and engineers are screened for their interest in working across cultures (Japanese and U.S.) as well as the degree to which they have a secure self-identity. Some individuals are comfortable only with the well known, and they are unlikely to be happy in an environment that encourages the ambiguity, uncertainty, and friction characteristic of creative abrasion. NDI's Hirshberg notes, "We tell people when they hire in, 'If you enjoy fences in your backyards, this is probably not going to be a happy place for you. We ask people to climb over the fence, to abuse the fence, to get into your turf, to step on your toes, and to come up with silly or stupid or outrageous—or sometimes very interesting—ideas about how you should do your business."[37]

Retaining Trained Facilitators from Outside. Managers who consciously initiate and manage creative abrasion often retain (sometimes on a rather casual basis) someone trained in facilitation who is also well acquainted with the organization. These people are available to staff members experiencing difficulty communicating with each other or with management. Because they are not regular employees, the facilitators are more likely to maintain objectivity, to be able to mediate disputes without prior or subsequent bias. Such individuals facilitate fractious meetings, consult with individuals or dyads, and sometimes lead open discussions on the state of the organization.

Managing "Religious Wars" about Tools and Methodologies

Because preferences for certain tools and methods are interdependent with preferred cognitive styles and specialized skills built up over time, individuals can defend their particular methodologies with near-religious fervor. As illustrated below, flexibility in approach can sometimes be encouraged by introducing "alien" methods from totally different specialties. Other times, managers have to make hard, Solomon-like choices, and in such cases, the best tactic is often to shift the ground of the argument, to change the criteria on which the methodological choice is being made.

Regarding Alien Methods as Herbs in the Dish. At Interval Research, manager David Liddle thinks of the infusion of alien methodologies into team projects as the herbs that make the dish.

> [O]ur ethnographers, our cognitive psychologists, our people that focus on product design and interaction design, the people who focus on or understand character and narrative, our research videographer, the people who do our mechanical and machine design and high-quality physical design, the people who do genetic algorithms and complexity and so on—those are seven or eight different people who are overstressed around here because of the number of different people who want at least to consult with them and often to tug them into another project altogether. Most of those people are the herb, not the entrée, in the particular project that's being baked, [but] the minor ingredients . . . are really very, very important. There is no chance of doing good, new work in these areas in a sterile environment where there are no herbs allowed.

At Xerox's Palo Alto Research Center, computer scientists working on some very esoteric topics include philosophers and anthropologists in their groups. Asked what a philosopher can contribute, manager Gregor Kiczales explains:

> A lot of people say that object-oriented computing is going to change the face of computing because objects are a more natural way of thinking about things and the world is made up of objects and if we just think that way it will all be more natural. . . . Now, of course, whether the world is made up of objects or not is very much an open question. If you sit in a world like my office, the world looks to be primarily made up of objects because things like pens and clipboards really have a primary carving up into objects. But if you look on an August evening in San Francisco . . . at the fog coming in over the bridge, and it makes different shapes and the bridge kind of disappears into it, then . . . I might see one set of objects where somebody else might see a different set of objects. . . . [C]omputer scientists who are talking about object-oriented programming [have] huge debates about what "the right" object structure is. . . . [O]ne of the things that this group takes as a given—in part, because we've been educated by our collaboration with our colleagues who are philosophers—is that . . . there can't be "the right" object structure. There can only be the right one for this purpose or the right one for that purpose because registration, which is what some philosophers call carving the world up into objects, is inherently about the perspective that you bring to it, and you can only do best for a certain task.[38]

Anthropologists play a similar role in another Xerox project, one focused on understanding how people will interact in "cyberspace"—i.e., in virtual space created by sharing common work space on computers, connected by video, voice, visuals, and data transmission capabilities. For example, how will people "bump into" each other to have the hallway conversations that are generally acknowledged to be important sources of creative problem solving? The methodologies of computer scientists do not help resolve such issues, but anthropologists are trained to consider human interaction under conditions that are novel to the dominant culture.

The introduction of totally different methodologies into a project thus ensures against being blindsided in problem solving. Individuals from an alien subculture serve as gadflies, pricking any unjustified balloons of complacency. However, the challenges of totally unfamiliar methodological approaches do not occasion the bloody methodological wars that erupt *within* a specialty. Which is the better metal for repairing teeth—gold or nickel alloy? Which is the better computer language for this task—C + + or some version of

LISP? What counseling technique results in the best response to treatment? Should a component part be molded or machined?

Shifting the Terms of the Debate. When differences of opinion (based on signature skills) threaten to slow or derail a project, the manager may have to make the unpopular decision to insist on a standard approach. One technique that appears to help resolve wars of opposing technical methodologies is to change the way the debate is framed. For example, after studying choices of information technology in fifty large organizations, Davenport, Hammer, and Metsisto[39] concluded that managers in the most effective companies articulated a few basic principles about how the companies would use information technology over the long term. By shifting the terms of the debate from technology-based ones to business strategy–based ones, the managers clarified the criteria to use in selecting technology. Similarly, by changing the criteria for choice of methodology from purely technical to ones dictated by the project objectives, managers can more likely defuse tensions and transform abrasion into creative energy.

Managing Signature Skills for Creative Abrasion

In addition to the mechanisms just described for addressing the different approaches occasioned by specialization and cognitive and tools preferences, two managerial levers—a prototype of the product or process and a clear project destination—aid in cutting across all the intellectual boundaries in a project team—whatever the origin of those barriers to communication. In Chapter 5, we return to the topic of prototyping as a form of experimental *activity* and consider different ways of carrying out that activity. Here we focus on the physical model or prototype itself, as a communication device enabling people possessed of different signature skills to cocreate.

Physical Prototypes as Boundary-Spanning Objects

One of the most neutral and yet evocative mechanisms for shared problem solving is a product model or prototype because it serves as a "boundary object."[40] Boundary objects "are both plastic enough to adapt to local needs and the constraints of the several parties employing them, yet robust enough to maintain a common identity across sites. . . . They have different meanings in different social worlds but their structure is common enough to more than one world to make them recognizable, a means of translation."[41] A model need not be a fully functional representation of the desired product or process. In the Sony Walkman development project, the engineer leading the team brought a small block of wood to his colleagues and challenged them to come up with a cassette player that size or smaller. The next-generation Walkman was represented by a smaller piece of wood; the ultimate aim was to produce a player only minimally larger than the cassette of music it played. However, the block of wood is a limited example of prototyping for several reasons. There is a very wide range of models or prototypes that developers can use as boundary-spanning objects, from two-dimensional sketches to fully functioning and apparently ready-to-use products. As a rough physical representation, the block of wood fell toward the primitive end of such options. (See Figure 3-6.)

A second, and more important, limitation was its use only as a tool within the engineering team, to stimulate *technical* problem solving. As Wheelwright and Clark note: "Prototyping cycles offer a wonderful opportunity to bring together the various functions, determine the degree of progress made to date, and consider how alternative solutions might play together, at an intermediate stage. In essence, prototyping can be an important vehicle for cross-functional discussion, problem solving, and integration."[42] Schrage further observes, "Within some innovation cultures, prototypes effectively become the *media franca* of the organization—*the* essential medium for information, interaction, integration and collaboration."[43] When prototypes are used only for testing technical concepts and not as communication vehicles for problem solving across boundaries, developers are overlooking enormous opportunities for creative abrasion—and integration. Moreover, because prototypes are physical or visual objects, they can communicate with people who have no special training but whose untutored eye may predict general public response much better than the judgment of the "experts."

Recalling his days as a designer at General Motors, Hirshberg comments that everything at GM revolved around the "car in the platform" as first priority. However, no one outside of the development team was ever allowed to see or comment on the clay prototype of the car. By contrast, when a new product has reached a prototype stage at Nissan Design International, anyone and everyone who is free and has an interest is invited to come and comment. "Secretaries, maintenance people, shop personnel—absolutely everyone in the building who has an interest to go outside" joins in the design critique. This egalitarian view of the validity of everyone's taste, even that of nonexperts, can result in painful—and useful—observations. Hirshberg tells of the time that a secretary, Cathy Woo, arrived, coffee cup in hand, at a new-car showing and observed candidly, "I think it's kind of stupid-looking." Members of the design team, who had been "yea saying" on the design, "looked at each other

Figure 3-6 Models and Prototypes

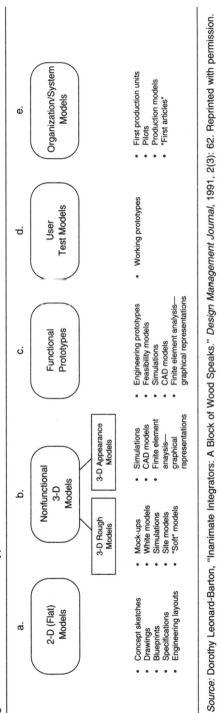

Source: Dorothy Leonard-Barton, "Inanimate Integrators: A Block of Wood Speaks." Design Management Journal, 1991, 2(3): 62. Reprinted with permission.

and knew that we were just kidding ourselves—we didn't have it yet." They retreated into the building, went back to the drawing boards, and three months later called Ms. Woo in to thank her—and invite her to celebrate with them the new design.

A Clear Destination

A manager's most powerful ally in focusing creative energies is a very clear project destination. Working with the designers and software code developers whose collective skills are required to create a multimedia product, Microsoft's Corddry directs the groups to work backward from a "vision of what the product will be when it is done. What is it? What value is it trying to offer? How will users engage with it?" Both form and function are essential. "If the machine is gorgeous but it is like a nice house with no one home, it is stupid. And if there is great code and functionality but you can't get at it or understand how to use it, the machine is useless," Corddry observes. The two skill sets are "locked in a business embrace."

Every new-product development project potentially has two, interdependent, destinations: the product itself and an improved new-product development process—product concept and project guiding vision. The product concept guides team members and coordinates their decisions with regard to the outcome of the project for the *customer*. The project vision guides team members and coordinates their decisions with regard to the outcome of the project for the *developing organization*. Keeping both in mind helps project members make hundreds of independent decisions about both the design as output and the design as process.

Product Concept. A formally agreed upon product concept "defines the character of the product from a customer's perspective."[44] Since the various subgroups developing a new product hold varying viewpoints about how the customer will experience the product, a common vision helps guide individual decisions about design details.[45] When the four hundred people on Ford's 1994 "Team Mustang" design team were charged with redesigning this best-selling car on a tight budget, they debated the image that would appeal to their customers. After considering "Rambo," a muscle-bound, hard-hitting image, and the more cultured "Bruce Jenner," the team reached an agreement: "Schwarzenegger"—"rugged but cultured."[46] Each member of this vast "team" would subsequently make tiny, daily decisions about a particular part of the car—the grill, the doors, the trunk, the windshield, and so on. Each detail would affect the look, feel, and sound of the finished product. As researchers Clark and Fujimoto observe, "Democracy without clear concept leadership is the archenemy of distinctive products."[47] If, for instance, the sound and power of the Mustang motor were being designed with "Rambo" in mind, it might not fit the interior that another group was developing with "Bruce Jenner" in mind. The product concept thus focuses design decisions and aids in integrating diverse viewpoints. When it is "owned" by the working-level technical staff who design the final product, it unifies and guides.

Project Guiding Vision. By offering opportunities for experimentation and innovation, development projects serve as engines of progress in managing the new-product development process. Yet such projects are usually conducted at a frenetic pace, often in an aura of crisis. Not surprisingly, project team members often lack any sense of linkage between their activities and the corporate or even line-of-business core capabilities.[48] The men and women on new-product and new-process development projects work with their heads down. Focused on delivering their innovation on schedule—or at least as soon as humanly possible—they have no time to consider what the corporation should be learning from it. As a consequence, they frequently end up feeling like Sisyphus in the Greek fable. For all eternity, Sisyphus was sentenced to haul an immense boulder painfully to the top of a hill only to see it repeatedly crash back down to the bottom. Too often, the researchers and engineers on development projects harness their mental and physical creative powers to achieve the almost impossible—often at considerable personal cost—only to wonder, at project's end, whether and why the corporation needed that particular boulder moved, or to speculate that they were climbing the wrong hill and the work was in vain. Each development project is another trip up a different hill, with little or no sense of cumulative achievement. Whatever knowledge is generated, is collected by individuals—not necessarily by the organization; there is little cross-project and cross-individual learning.

In a study of twenty projects in five companies, Bowen and colleagues discovered that more successful projects were likely to have a "project guiding vision."[49] This vision defines the output of the team in terms of both the *product* and what the project is *adding to the knowledge base of the firm.* In other words, a project guiding vision places the particular effort in relation to a clear business purpose (e.g., launching a certain product line) and to the critical capabilities the corporation is building. Thus, project team members know what immediate business purpose they serve *and* the streams of knowledge to which they are supposed to contribute. A clear project vision is "guiding" because, like a product concept, it helps individual project team members make dozens of decisions daily. These may involve seemingly inconsequential trade-offs—for instance, in placement of controls, choice of

Figure 3-7 Dual Purpose for Projects

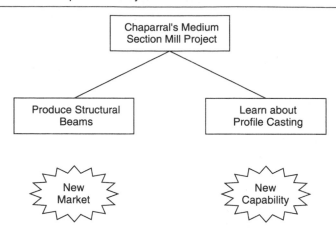

materials, or the number of features included. Yet in aggregate, such individual decisions not only have significant impacts on and limit designs of future products in the product line but also determine the degree to which the particular project adds to corporate intellectual capital. Guiding visions also help morale. Team members gain a sense of larger purpose, beyond the moment. A project vision, therefore, can help to ensure that all the effort expended in technology development is meaningful to both the individual and the corporation—i.e., that it results in an acknowledged contribution to existing or emerging capabilities.

So, for instance, when Chaparral management decided to construct a new mill to produce medium-size (12-inch to 14-inch) structural beams, the project vision had two parts. (See Figure 3-7.) First, the new beams would launch Chaparral into a different set of markets. Second, this project was the company's first attempt to do "profile casting"—i.e., to cast steel in a shape closer to the final rolled I-shaped configuration than the usual rectangle. An important objective in the project was to develop this new capability. The beams cast in this mill came out of the mold with already-indented sides, which obviated the need for a certain amount of energy-intensive rolling into the final structural shape. The experience gained in the project was essential when Chaparral launched its large structural beam products (18 inches to 24 inches). As described in Chapter 1, the large beams were cast in the revolutionary "near net-shape" so as to avoid a great deal more rolling and consequently meet the highly challenging cost goals the company set for itself.

Summary

Individual and organizational creativity is limited by background, training, and personal preferences in approach to problem solving. Creative abrasion is an antidote to core rigidities because it forces the constant reexamination of whatever perspective dominates at the time in the organization. However, creative abrasion does not happen automatically; it is designed into the organization. Managers in some organizations devoted to innovation stimulate creative abrasion by maintaining a diverse, eclectic mixture of different signature skills among their employees. In this chapter, we have considered three components of individuals' signature skills that serve as sources of intellectual diversity—specialization, cognitive style preferences, and preferences for particular tools or methodologies.

To ensure that the energy generated by the inevitable cognitive friction among individuals is channeled into creative knowledge-building actions rather than siphoned off into unproductive personal battles, managers need to encourage integrative skills among employees and develop those skills themselves. A number of mechanisms for integration were reviewed in the chapter, including both some that are especially beneficial in managing each source of intellectual diversity and a couple that cut across all sources—using physical prototypes of the intended product and constructing very clear, shared visions of the project outcome.

As we will see in the next chapter, boundaries around knowledge enclaves within a corporation must be breached in implementing new tools and methodologies as well. Companies compete not only on the basis of creativity in new-product development but also through superior process knowledge. We turn next to considering implementation as innovation.

CHAPTER FOUR

Implementing and Integrating New Technical Processes and Tools

A pilot who sees from afar will not make his boat a wreck.
—Amen-em-apt (700 B.C.)
  Egyptian Philosopher

The reasonable man adapts himself to the world: the unreasonable one persists in trying to adapt the world to himself. Therefore all progress depends on the unreasonable man.
—George Bernard Shaw
  Man and Superman (1903)

Knowledge is the only instrument of production that is not subject to diminishing returns.
—J. M. Clark[1] (1927)
  Economics Professor, Columbia University

The preceding chapter suggested that shared problem solving leaps to a new level of creativity when managed for creative abrasion. In this chapter, we examine how implementation of new technical processes can move beyond merely increasing efficiency when managed for learning. (See Figure 4-1.) Examples herein focus more on internally generated processes and tools than purchased ones since the former embody proprietary information and potentially contribute more to core technological capabilities. (The contribution is *potential* because core rigidities can also embody much proprietary know-how; the uniqueness of knowledge is no guarantee of worth.) Moreover, when implementation is seen as an act of innovation rather than the mere execution of a plan, integration of even those tools and processes available on the open market can constitute a competitive advantage.

Implementation as Innovation

The story in Chapter 2 of the ill-fated jumping ring circulator's introduction into an aluminum mill encompassed many of the problems that implementation of new tools often encounters—from immature technical design to incompatibility with operator incentives. The single biggest underlying cause for the demise of this initially promising innovation was the quite understandable but simplistic assumption that physical installation was the sole project objective and criterion for success. Implementation of the JRC was not regarded as an exercise in knowledge creation or management.

In a study of thirty-four projects that developed software tools to enhance internal productivity in four large U.S.-based electronics firms, Leonard-Barton and Sinha[2] found that, in addition to the quality and cost of the technology, and its initial compatibility with the user environment, two managerial processes were important in explaining different levels and types of successful implementation. The first of these was the degree and type of user involvement in the design and delivery of the system, and the second was the degree to which project participants deliberately altered the technology and also adjusted the user environment in a process of mutual adaptation.[3]

Both of these processes essentially involve managing the creation and channeling of knowledge. They are very similar to the management tasks involved in new-product development, except that the market is internal to the organization. However, implementation is not usually managed as if it were an exercise in innovation, and that is the key point in this chapter.

User Involvement

Two generic reasons are typically cited for involving users in the development of a new technical system: (1) implementation implies some level of change in the users' work, and research on change suggests that people are more receptive when they have contributed to its design; and (2) involving users

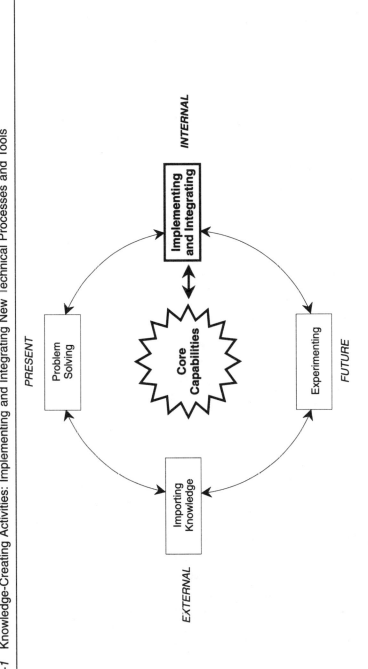

Figure 4-1 Knowledge-Creating Activities: Implementing and Integrating New Technical Processes and Tools

in the design of their tools results in superior designs since users have specialized knowledge about the environment in which the tools will be utilized, and that knowledge should be embodied in the design.

Creating "Buy-In"

For almost a generation, managers have realized that people participating in the design of their environment appreciate the sense of control that such participation provides.[4] By involving users in the design of their tools, managers create "buy-in" to the implementation process—i.e., some receptivity to the change the new tools imply. The obverse is also true: leaving users out of the development process may generate dissatisfaction with the new tools. A developer in a highly controversial and unsuccessful project to build a proprietary computer-aided engineering tool observed of the engineers in the department designated to use the innovation: "We could have given them the most wonderful system in the world and they would not have been happy because they were totally excluded from its design."

Embodying Knowledge

The second motive for involving users in process development projects is more germane to this book, however. As noted in the discussion in Chapter 1 about the four dimensions of core capabilities, technical systems embody accumulated knowledge, aggregated from multiple sources inside and outside the organization. Developers rarely possess all that knowledge themselves but must interact with users to create, or capture and structure, and then embody the requisite knowledge. Tool developers understand the principles and scientific knowledge that underlie the new process tool: the technical engineering or scientific knowledge required to build the tool itself—for example, software, hardware, chemical, or biotechnology engineering principles. However, it is the proprietary know-how about specific tasks in the organization's particular work environment that is critical: such know-how adds the potential for a tool to become part of a core technological capability. Highly skilled users who understand their own work processes are usually the source for such know-how.[5]

Merits of User Involvement. Involving users in the design of a new process tool does not automatically lead to a successful project outcome. In fact, there has been much debate in academic literature about this issue since different studies have found relationships between user involvement and project outcome that range from positive to neutral to negative.[6] Confusion about the benefits of user involvement has arisen in large part, however, because so many studies have treated the topic simplistically. They usually fail to take into account the selection of users, the timing of their involvement, the nature of the involvement required by the relative novelty of the system being built, the users' ability and willingness to provide the right kind of knowledge, the expectations of users and developers about the nature and extent of the knowledge to be embodied, and so forth. Yet as the examples in this chapter illustrate, such factors explain why user involvement sometimes seems integral to success and at other times is inimical to it.

User Selection. If the objective for involving users in the development of new process capabilities is to integrate their knowledge about operations into the design of the new tools, then selecting those users is a critical managerial task. The criteria for selection are often far from clear. The question is, What kinds of knowledge should users possess in order to guide problem solving and the creation of the system? For instance, is it more important that users *be expert in the task* to be aided, so they can provide critical comments on the functionality of the tool, or that they *typify the user population* in their ability to manipulate the user interface? As the following example suggests, the two different kinds of knowledge do not always come in the same human package.

Differing Forms of Expertise. A corporation that manufactures large air-conditioning systems for commercial and apartment buildings employs a sizable field staff to maintain and service equipment. In designing the expert system "HELPER" to use on-site to check maintenance and service tasks, the developers searched for the most experienced maintenance people they could find. They finally identified and enlisted the help of a union pipe fitter, "Bill James," with over twenty-five years of experience and a reputation as an excellent diagnostician. However, after moving James and his family over 1,500 miles to be near the development effort, they discovered that he did not possess the requisite knowledge. Although James knew how to diagnose and service the chillers, he responded to symptoms with very little understanding of the inner workings of the chillers—i.e., the *causes* of problems. To construct the expert system rules, the software engineers enlisted an instructor in maintenance from a local vocational technical school who was deeply versed in the electronics and mechanics of the systems but who retained the perspective of a user—not an engineer/designer. On the other hand, James was an excellent choice to help developers design a system interface for use by "a hairy-chested pipe fitter who had never seen a computer before in his life." He had no prior experience with computers but was very familiar with the task.

The HELPER system was ultimately successful, paying for its development in less than a year because the contract base for service to chillers grew by

40 percent within the first six months after the system was installed. However, the developers were left wondering how they could have ascertained in advance that their expert maintenance man could not provide the needed domain knowledge.

Representativeness. The same dilemma exists with the first site that tests a new tool. If the tool is to be customized for only one set of internal customers, the selection issue is relatively simple. However, if the new technical systems will be distributed to multiple offices or factories throughout the corporation, then the choice of the user site to help develop and test prototypes becomes crucial. A comparative study of three plants implementing a software package uncovered significant hazards associated with the unwitting selection of an atypical user site to guide design.[7]

The plant site selected as the first recipient of the package designed by corporate services to automate and monitor purchasing functions within manufacturing differed from other sites in several important ways. The most critical was its atypically low number of long-lead-time purchased parts. Based on its experience with this nonrepresentative plant, the corporate team programmed the software to order this category of parts to arrive only once in six months.

When the software was implemented in the other plants' purchasing departments, where as much as 40 percent of the orders fell into the long-lead-time category, the receiving departments were quite literally buried under incoming components on a given day every six months. This apparently simple miscalculation, with its attendant complications, was very difficult to correct locally at the individual plants, for they did not own or have access to the centrally controlled software code that had to be reprogrammed. The needed adjustments took well over one year to complete and caused considerable friction between software developers and users.

User Willingness. Regardless of the knowledge sought from users, another critical criterion for selection is users' willingness to participate—to take the time to provide feedback and suggestions. The task of soliciting and convincing users to become involved usually falls to the development manager, who is likely to value "know-who" above know-how and fall back on interpersonal contacts—a plant manager who was a college chum or a production supervisor with whom the development manager has worked before. Willing users may not be representative, of course, and representative users may not be willing. In fact, in a study of end-user computing in forty-four firms, Doll and Torkzadeh found that users who were involved more than they desired in the development of a system were less satisfied with the end result than were users involved less than, or just about as much as, desired.[8] User "codevelopers" must be willing to venture far beyond their job descriptions and often outside the boundaries of any reward or incentive system. Reflecting on participating in such a project, one manager of such a user group said, "We take some very large risks. This was one of them. I had people come to me and say, 'You're jeopardizing your career. Why do you think this will pay off?' "

Modes of User Involvement

User involvement is a broad term, covering a multiplicity of possible interactions. In the above-mentioned research on thirty-four software tools developed within four large electronics firms, four different modes of user involvement were observed.[9] (See Figure 4-2.) On average, the projects in which users were consistently and heavily involved from first to last were completed more quickly (mean of 20.8 months, as opposed to an overall average of 28.9 months across all thirty-four projects). However, the importance of user involvement to project success, as measured by increased productivity and other benefits, varied. Projects in which the developers already

Figure 4-2 Multidimensional Scaling Map of Modes of User Involvement

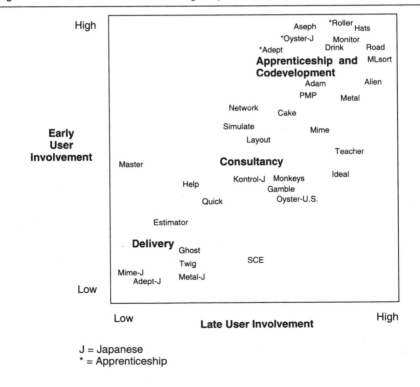

J = Japanese
* = Apprenticeship

had a lot of information about the user environment could succeed without user input. Projects in which developers had inadequate knowledge, either because of their own mind-set or because the tools were revolutionary and the interaction of those tools with the user workplace was uncertain, required shared problem solving, and hence user involvement, in order to succeed. These points are best explored via concrete examples.

Delivery Mode, or "Over-the-Wall". Among the thirty-four projects, some development teams conceived of a tool in the absence of any user specifications—or even expressed user need. Developers acted as vendors, delivering a completed tool to users, sometimes without training or manuals. It was simply "tossed over the wall" between the two groups, with the expectation that (1) it was completely ready for use or (2) users were capable of figuring out and customizing the new process themselves. If feedback from users was solicited, the impact more likely would be felt on the next generation of the tool or process than on the current one.

In this approach, developers often designed a tool that they themselves would like, so their product concept was drawn from an understanding of their own needs and desires. From the users' point of view, the over-the-wall interaction with developers was satisfactory only to the extent that one of two conditions existed: (1) the new tool or process was in fact totally self-explanatory, and the users did not need any understanding of its internal workings; or (2) the users themselves were as technically skilled as the developers and needed no help. In either case, there was no expectation that knowledge integration was necessary.

"TWIG": SUCCESSFUL OVER-THE-WALL

Users receiving a new artificial intelligence program called "Twig" from internal corporate developers said, "[The developers] tossed us a [software] tape, and off we went." These users were totally unconcerned that the new tool they received had no specific accompanying documentation because a number of them had technical backgrounds equivalent to those of the developers. "We all have advanced degrees in computer science and artificial intelligence; we can read [generic AI] manuals, and there's no difficulty." In this case, the users could fill in any gaps in knowledge transfer not accomplished by the tossing of the tape over the wall to them.

Obviously, such a close match between developer and user mind-sets and skill sets is rather rare. Since there is no user feedback during development, delivery mode presents multiple hazards. Developers may fail to anticipate user needs accurately. Users may not have the skills to integrate the tool into their work environment. They may desire more knowledge than provided; without more explanation and demonstration, they may not understand the potential of the new tool to change their work. Since the delivery mode is a one-way flow of information, no mechanism for knowledge integration exists. In sum, the effort devoted to creating a new technical capability can be partially, if not totally, wasted.

"CACTUS": UNSUCCESSFUL OVER-THE-WALL

"Cactus" was a proprietary software environment used by programmers in various sites around the world to create country-specific operating interfaces for the equipment the corporation manufactured. Although Cactus was highly successful within U.S. sites, when it was transferred to a Japanese partner, the users were highly dissatisfied. The developers sent over the software application—but not the source code that underlay the application. Nor did the developers offer access to any additional technical knowledge. From the Japanese perspective, the interaction was incomplete; no transfer of technology had occurred. "We think that *transfer* means that we understand the new technology and have an ability to modify the function of some tools by using that new technology," the Japanese explained. "We learned from [the developers] how to *use* Cactus—but not how to change it. [The developers'] image of this project was to *install* Cactus, not to transfer the technology [embodied] in Cactus."

For Japanese users, the implementation of Cactus did not augment their capabilities enough to warrant investment in learning its operation. More than the incremental improvement to programming productivity, they wanted the capability to improve Cactus, adapt it to their needs—and to absorb underlying technological principles so that they could construct their own software. The U.S. corporate laboratory in this case had never expected to deliver those kinds of benefits; as the Japanese users correctly observed, the developers interpreted their role more narrowly than the users desired. Although the resources devoted to developing Cactus paid back in the United States, those expended on transferring the system were wasted.

Consultancy Mode. Developers in a number of the study's projects believed that periodic consulting with users about features and functions provided adequate opportunity for feedback and user input. When work processes in the user environment (the factory, the engineering department, the office) were relatively well established, and therefore "domain knowledge" was already structured and codified, developers did not believe that users needed to be part of the development team. This mode of interaction seemed to work for upgrades of existing tools or when the corporate objective was to standardize a work process as well as further automate or computerize it. The greatest need for new user knowledge in these situations lay in designing the user interface. The more potential user groups there were, the more difficult the task, of course, and internal vendors were often unfamiliar with the kind of trade-offs external vendors constantly make when designing products for a diverse market. As one internal developer lamented, "We felt we had something that was applicable to a lot of laboratories [in the corporation]. So we tended to listen to everyone and promise everybody everything." The most successful "consultancy" projects were very large, highly structured endeavors in which user groups were treated like customers with diverse needs and a right to influence, but not totally direct, development.

Codevelopment. In codevelopment projects, users were part of the development team. Continuously involved in the project, from inception to implementation, they strongly influenced the design of the new tool. Although codevelopment projects were not appropriate *only* for radically new technical systems, the obverse did seem to be true: the successful development of entirely novel production systems (new technical systems and redesigned work processes) *required* heavy user involvement. One reason for this was the obviously greater need for user "buy-in" when a new technical system would radically alter the production processes. Even more important was that such projects represented explorations into unknown territory. "We were flying without parachutes," one team member observed. Other research also suggests that, in general, more interaction between team members exists in the presence of uncertainty. Codevelopment is therefore the preferred mode when (1) developers are not quite certain how their new system will interact with work processes, and (2) users are not initially certain how they can best redesign work so as to exploit the full potential of the new technical system. Unlike the consultancy situation, in which users help codify knowledge by reacting to prototypes or prior models of the technical systems, in codevelopment, users are helping to create knowledge from a ground base of almost zero.

One of the primary hazards associated with extensive user involvement (quite apart from the obvious possibility that a revolutionary "stretch" project may fail) is users' having insufficient "forward vision" to provide good guidance. As a developer commented, "There's a tendency for users to be fixated on what they're using today instead of thinking about features they'll need in three years." Users can lead the development team into automating history.

"MONITOR": UNSUCCESSFUL CODEVELOPMENT

The users involved in the design of "Monitor," a software package developed to monitor and control the flow of work in process on a factory floor, were extremely conservative in their demands. They took as their model an existing control system at General Motors, applied it to their current operations, and insisted that the developers fulfill those specifications as closely as possible—which the developers did very well. However, unbeknownst to the operators on the factory floor who were heavily involved in drawing up these specifications, the corporation was moving away from traditional work-in-process monitoring toward just-in-time inventory control. The basic principle underlying this new, mostly visual and manual system was to have as little work-in-process inventory as possible. Rather than a software system that could tell them exactly where a given lot of components was in the huge piles of inventory making their way slowly through the factory, they now needed a system that could handle lot sizes of one—if they needed the software at all. "We would have been way ahead of where we are now with Monitor," a developer commented ruefully after the project had gone through several major redesigns, "if we had gone to just-in-time at the start."

On the other hand, when users are innovative and can envision where their organization should be headed, codevelopment projects may succeed beyond the expectations of either the users or the developers. At its best, codevelopment creates an *esprit de corps* like that of the Chaparral Steel product development teams. Everyone takes responsibility for pushing the boundaries of knowledge and for treating problems as minor delays rather than major deterrents.

"CONSTRUCT": SUCCESSFUL CODEVELOPMENT

When first suggested by a research group, "Construct," a computer-aided system for designing the operator interface on copier machines, captured the imagination of several different groups of users, including industrial designers and software programmers. These different user groups saw the potential of the simulation system not only to help them design on the screen instead of with physical models but also to help them communicate with each other. Through Construct, software designers, industrial designers, and product designers for the first time had a common medium of expression. Far from pushing the Construct developer to duplicate functionality that they currently had, they kept trying to use the tool for new and previously unconsidered tasks, such as simulating a color screen rather than a black-and-white one. "I gave them a screwdriver," the Construct developer commented in admiration, "and when I came back, they were using it to build the Golden Gate Bridge [across San Francisco Bay]."

The interaction of the developers and users in this project was an act of creative extension, with each group pushing the other to think beyond current capabilities.

Apprenticeship Mode. In a few of the thirty-four projects, users assumed total responsibility for integrating the technical expertise required for building a new tool, drawing upon their knowledge of their own work situation. They traveled to the developer site and apprenticed themselves to the tool designer in order to develop and build a system, which they then took back to their own work site.[10] Users wanting their own capabilities and independence from developers employed this apprenticeship mode. Developers had to be willing to play the role of tutors rather than providers, and users had to be willing to invest enough time and resources both to become expert in the underlying technology and to implement all the needed changes when they returned to their home territory. The few projects falling into this category succeeded to the degree that those conditions held.

"ADEPT": SUCCESSFUL APPRENTICESHIP

"Adept," an expert system that identifies and diagnoses problems in circuit boards during manufacture, was built by users in a California factory—a manufacturing test engineer with a long history of troubleshooting in circuit board manufacture and a technician in charge of the work position where most flaws were to be caught. Neither had any software-programming experience. The software developers expert in artificial intelligence taught the two how to run a proprietary expert system shell and then stood by as mentors and advisers as the two manufacturing people wrote "99 percent of the code themselves." The developers were eager in this case to turn responsibility over to the users. "We took the lumberjack approach: it's your ax—you keep it sharp."

Adept was a great success. Before it was instituted, 38 percent of the circuit boards that failed during the final "burn-in" test could not be diagnosed and were labeled a "no trouble found" component. Because the unknown problem might recur in the field, such circuit boards were discarded, at great cost to the company. Adept reduced that proportion to 19 percent within six weeks. Moreover, the project also succeeded in transferring much technical software-programming capability to the users. "Education became an additional objective," one of the developers who mentored the project noted. After implementing their new system, the technicians took over the program and continued to fine-tune and develop it. Within a year, they had the "no trouble found" proportion down to 3 percent—at which point, such boards did not even go through a retest as it was cheaper to discard them. Perhaps even more important, manufacturing now possessed a capability it had not had before—to create small expert systems to help control processes. The manufacturing test engineer went on to build a number of other such programs for use in the factory.

Although all four types of user involvement can succeed if certain conditions are met, only the codevelopment and apprenticeship modes really integrated knowledge from the two very disparate groups—software developers and software users. Moreover, the apprenticeship mode had comparatively limited impact on the user organizations. User apprentices integrated knowledge in their own heads and therefore broadened their personal abilities; they often went on to assume the role of developers. However, the developer group was little altered by having an apprentice work with them for some months, and the user group to which the apprentice returned sometimes rejected the innovative knowledge developed. As a result, the corporation added only minimally to its process capabilities.

In contrast, codevelopment projects *forced* the developer and user groups to share problem-solving activities, to create and integrate knowledge, and that shared responsibility educated both groups to a better understanding of each other's worlds. (See Figure 4-3.) Integration occurred at a group rather than an individual level. The developers came to understand the demands of the production process, and the production personnel began to see the potential inherent in the technologies offered them. In a number of cases, the codevelopment teams proceeded to conduct a series of projects together, as their collaboration revealed more opportunities for improving processes. In aggregate, these projects significantly enhanced the corporation's production capabilities. Not only were advanced proprietary tools created, but some corporate barriers to knowledge integration had been considerably truncated. Codevelopment, in short, had much more effect on the organization's learning process than the other modes.

Figure 4-3 Responsibility for Knowledge Creation in the Four Modes of Tool
Implementation

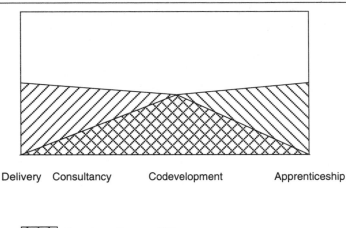

Delivery   Consultancy   Codevelopment   Apprenticeship

⬚ Developer Responsibility
⬚ User Responsibility
⬚ Shared Responsibility

Mutual Adaptation

One of the major reasons that codevelopment more strongly affected organizational capabilities in the study described above was that the shared development process offered an opportunity for the mutual adaptation of *both* technology and user work environment. (The essence of the current push for "reengineering" in many companies is the notion that organizational redesign and technology design should proceed simultaneously, each informing the other.) Mutual adaptation is the reinvention of the technology to conform to the work environment and the simultaneous adaptation of the organization to use the new technical system. It requires that managers in charge of implementing new technical systems recognize and assume responsibility for both technical and organizational change.

Two major aspects of mutual adaptation are: (1) it occurs in small and large recursive spirals of change, and (2) it often requires attention to all four dimensions of capabilities. Recognizing these aspects suggests management levers that can be used to improve the contribution of new technical systems to technological capabilities.

Adaptive Spirals of Change—Small to Large

The process of adaptation requires a revisiting of prior decision points—reopening issues of technical design that the developers had assumed were resolved and also "unfreezing" organizational routine.[11] These are spirals rather than cycles because the decision to be reconsidered is never exactly the same one made earlier. The decision context has altered, given the passage of time, external events, learning effects, and so on. The adaptive spirals vary in magnitude, depending on how fundamental is the change to be made. In the case of technology adaptation, a small spiral entails fine-tuning the new technical system; a large one may entail the developers' returning to the drawing boards and perhaps even redefining the problem to be addressed. Similarly, a small adaptive cycle in organizational redesign may require merely altering a particular role or task. In contrast, a large one implies a strategic shift for the plant, the office, perhaps the whole division since it means rethinking the critical success factors by which performance is judged.

A significant challenge managers face is detecting when a large spiral is masquerading as a small one; that is, when a series of small adaptive spirals is inadequate to create or support an important technological capability and a large spiral of change is required—in either the technical system, the work environment, or both. In such cases, the manager is, perhaps unwittingly, thrust into the role of revolutionary organizational redesigner.

This role is particularly tricky if most people in the organization at least tacitly assume that only incremental changes are required. Recall that the jumping ring circulator described in Chapter 2 appeared to be a rather minor upgrading of current melting capabilities. The project apparently required merely installing an additional piece of equipment within an existing furnace and slightly retraining operators to use it—small spirals of change. Yet, in fact, in order to successfully implement this new capability, the equipment developers would have had to undertake large spirals of change, including redesigning the JRC for use in aluminum foundries as opposed to steel. Moreover, factory managers would have had to rethink the way they were producing aluminum, including the incentive system under which their operators worked and the use downstream of molten aluminum that contained the "contaminants" of recycled can stock. Relatively greater changes on the technology side would have lessened the need for changes in the work environment and vice versa. However, no one involved recognized the magnitude of the changes that would be required to make this project succeed; otherwise, they either would not have undertaken it or would have assigned more resources to its implementation.

In the case of CONFIG, described below, the designers had quite a few resources. Although they were told repeatedly that the basic design of the system was flawed, they applied those resources of time and software-engineering skill to incremental, small-spiral improvements in the belief that such changes would eventually add up to a successful system. They struggled along with enough funding and support to make steady incremental improvements but without the influence, the vision, or the resources to make the large-spiral changes required.

CONFIG

CONFIG was a software system designed to help salespeople select from literally thousands of possible combinations those component parts of a complex computer system that would satisfy their customers' needs. CONFIG promised to enhance the completeness and accuracy of the sales orders and thereby avoid costly configuration errors. For instance, sales representatives often forgot to include in the order cables or connectors—which then had to be included at no cost to the customer. Or the representatives inadvertently suggested to the customer a particular linkage of systems that were actually incompatible or redundant; when the mistake was discovered in the assembly plant, the order had to be completely revised. So CONFIG offered considerable potential financial benefit to the corporation. However, the system offered little direct benefit to the sales representatives. They were not paid on the basis of the accuracy of their orders—only on their sales volume. Nor did it aid them in their configuration task as they conducted it. They needed to be able to cite cost information to the customers along with the description of component parts and often reworked the configuration several times during negotiations. CONFIG offered no cost information, and because it was designed for a linear, sequential transaction, it was not well suited to the highly iterative way the sales representatives worked to converge upon an acceptable design.

The developers of CONFIG spent a total of eight years improving it incrementally. However, they were never able to address either of its most fundamental flaws: (1) it did not fit the configuration task as actually performed by sales representatives, and (2) the sales representatives' performance criteria did not include any reward for accuracy and completeness. An application support specialist for the program observed: "The people responsible for developing CONFIG are trying to breathe life into something that should be allowed to die. They have to start fresh—instead of building on top of what they have now. . . . CONFIG . . . has failed miserably. The problem is, nobody wants to shoot it in the head."[12]

The developers of CONFIG might have profited from diagnosing the misalignment between their system and the organization, considering all four dimensions of a capability. For CONFIG to succeed, managers should have revisited some very basic design decisions underlying the software architecture; the system did not tie into other *physical systems* critical to the sales representatives but was modeled on, and intimately linked to, a manufacturing system. Second, the managers would have had to influence the sales organization's *managerial systems*, changing incentive schemes to reward the completeness of orders—not just their quantity.

Either of these two changes represented a large undertaking since, in many physical systems and organizations, there is a design hierarchy;[13] once certain basic design decisions are made, all other, more minor decisions flow from, and are subordinate to, them. The CONFIG system was to be used for verifying the configuration (a function more critical to assembly than to sales): that was the design decision. All subsequent design decisions flowed logically from it. To revisit the system's basic concept and rethink it from the sales perspective—as a tool to aid the selling process—would have required a large-spiral adaptation: cycling back to revisit and revise basic assumptions. Similarly, order accuracy was not central to the sales organization's mission, and to convince that body that it should be meant enlarging the scope of responsibility that sales assumed.

The other two dimensions of a capability were somewhat less affected. However, although providing sales representatives with the *skills and knowledge* to use the system posed little difficulty, the apparent irrelevance of configuration to sales work meant that there was a definite conflict between the *values* embodied by CONFIG and those of the sales force. Implementing the kind of large-spiral organizational adaptation required to make CONFIG successful was impossible from outside the sales organization, and the CONFIG developers had no powerful advocate within it.

In the eight-year life of CONFIG, several opportunities occurred to reconsider its design and its misalignment with the sales operations—e.g., during budgeting cycles and large-scale organizational restructuring. Research on implementation suggests that such opportunities occur more than once in the life of most new technical systems, not just at the point of initial introduction.[14] However, to start over so visibly would be tantamount to admitting monumental failure. Instead, the managers continued to tinker with the user interface, with user support—investing in all manner of seemingly significant improvements that nevertheless avoided the central flaws. The CONFIG managers were not unusual in their escalating commitment to a flawed process "improvement" and their inability to distinguish the character of large-spiral adaptation from an aggregation of small spirals.

Pacing and Celebration: Refilling the Bank

One of the challenges of managing implementation and learning is the extra effort required, which draws upon people's energy levels and their self-esteem. This process resembles the gradual depletion of a bank of energy and self-esteem. Every time we are asked to learn something new, we challenge our old bases of self-esteem, especially if the innovation threatens our signature skills (as described in the previous chapter). Because implementation of new processes and tools involves a high degree of uncertainty, it is energy-sapping almost no matter what the outcome. Therefore, we draw down that bank. (See Figure 4-4.) Eventually, if we continue to withdraw yet make no deposits, the bank runs dry.[15] In such situations, we see people depressed at the thought of more innovation. "I'm not opposed to change," an engineer beleaguered by a series of process innovations within a few months once commented.

Figure 4-4 Bank of Energy and Self-Esteem

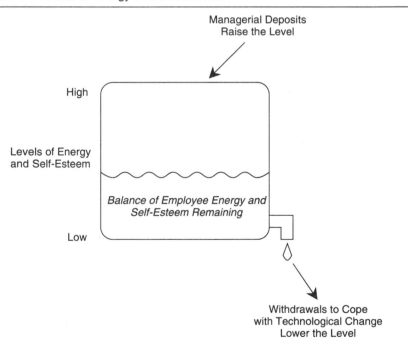

"I just can't figure out how to handle this much change—and still maintain my sanity."

To combat experimentation burnout, managers need to slow the outflow and replenish the bank. They can: (1) pace the changes insofar as possible and (2) celebrate small successes and milestones along the way. Owens-Illinois managers were puzzled when they studied two plants implementing the same new high-speed, highly automated bottle-forming equipment. Their Atlanta plant seemed to absorb the innovation much more readily than their Streator plant. Atlanta not only had the new "ten-quad" machine up and running sooner but achieved higher productivity with it. Although there were a number of differences between the two plants, one significant variation was the way that the innovation champion at Atlanta controlled the pace of introduction. Instead of acquiescing to the pace dictated by the corporate engineering center, he delayed acceptance of the new equipment until he felt that the workers were sufficiently comfortable with the last wave of new equipment.[16] Of course, such pacing may be viewed as a luxury not to be contemplated in these days of hectic innovation. However, if the price of speed is burnout of key employees, managers may have to learn to pace innovation.

The second lever managers can pull to replenish the bank is the celebration of small successes along the way. In 1986, when Beth Reuthe took over Digital Equipment's Augusta plant as manager, she found people "walking around bent over as if they had been hammered down with a croquet mallet." They had just undergone a very traumatic reengineering project driven mostly by the need to switch to a new manufacturing resource planning process (MRPII). A number of signature skills had been challenged and jobs altered. The Augusta plant was no stranger to innovation; more than 70 percent of the products being manufactured had been introduced within the past twelve months. However, Reuthe needed to introduce yet more drastic change in order to significantly reduce the time that a product spent as work in process. She conducted a number of participatory exercises to gain commitment and to include everyone in the planning process. Then a just-in-time system was introduced, with all departments asked to innovate and experiment toward the ultimate goal of bringing down inventory. For six months, people experimented, even coming in on their own time to brainstorm or tinker. Some of the innovations significantly reduced inventory; others had little effect, despite people's best efforts. However, Reuthe decided to close the plant for a half-day to "recharge everyone's batteries." It was like a plant fair—a celebration of progress. Everyone presented to peers the experiments he or she had conducted. No matter how small the improvement, it was recognized. The plant went on to exceed the goals set for cycle time, reducing it to five days rather than the initial target of fifteen. Even more important to Reuthe was employees' experiencing change as a positive factor in their work.

Summary

Integrating proprietary knowledge into process tools and methods potentially offers a competitive edge. However, the implementation of such tools must be managed as an innovation project—not just the execution of plans, however carefully made. Nor is all the requisite knowledge likely to be held in one location or one set of heads. Users of process tools provide critical information to be integrated during design. However, user involvement must be carefully managed, as extracting knowledge from atypical, disinterested, or very near-term-oriented users can damage rather than enhance the design of a new process tool. A study of thirty-four development projects suggests that active codevelopment of tools with users is not only more efficient but far more effective. Moreover, the greatest competitive advantage likely comes from a process of mutual adaptation—adapting both the technology to the user environment and the user environment to the technology so as to exploit its full potential. Managers who attend to these two activities of user involvement and mutual adaptation are more likely to reap significant and lasting benefits from process innovation. Managers also need to avoid "burning out" their employees with uncontrolled change.

The managers' challenge is, in the midst of the whirlwind of daily activities, to keep in mind the potential effect of their every action and behavior upon the growth of technological capabilities in the firm. In this chapter, we have examined in depth the way that the development of new tools and processes can be managed to maximize learning and to counter the unconscious accretion of core rigidities. In the next chapter, we look at another pair of activities, deliberate experimentation and prototyping, that create knowledge assets.

CHAPTER FIVE

Experimenting and Prototyping

[A] man's reach should exceed his grasp, or what's a heaven for?
—Robert Browning
  "Andrea del Sarto"

Intelligent failure is an acceptable mode of operation.
—Frank Carrubba
  Former Director, Hewlett Packard Laboratories[1]

I don't want any yes-men in this organization. I want people to speak their minds—even if it does cost them their jobs.
—Samuel Goldwyn[2]
  President, Goldwyn Pictures

Del Sarto was an optimist. As suggested in the preceding chapter, constantly reaching beyond one's grasp is an uncomfortable task, and there is little certainty that it is heaven that awaits the outstretched hand. Today's managers are constantly abjured to "stretch the envelope," manage the "cutting edge," or face down "unprecedented" competition. The future for which they reach is far from clear, however. Crystal balls may be an obsolete forecasting technology, but our current tools are little better. Moreover, in a number of industries, the growth that propelled sales figures into an upward trajectory has slowed or stopped. Managers therefore confront the task of restarting the organizations' engines in midflight. They must create forward momentum from inside the companies rather than rely on the energy that expanding markets provide. Although this constant reaching beyond current grasp implies risk, there is no safety in trying to maintain the status quo either, as Chapter 2's description of core rigidities suggests. In fact, core capabilities that become core rigidities are a much greater threat to company survival than well-managed and modest—but continuous—explorations into new territory.

This chapter discusses the organizational learning that moves companies purposefully forward in their quest for improved capabilities.[3] The primary activities spawning this learning are experimentation and prototyping. (See Figure 5-1.) In the following pages, we first consider why experimentation and prototyping are so important.[4] We then turn to an examination of the manager's three major tasks relative to these activities: first, and most critical, to create a climate that tolerates and even encourages experimentation; next, to see that a lot of experimentation and prototyping actually occurs; and last, to set in place mechanisms to ensure that the organization learns from those activities.

Experimentation and Corporate Resilience

Managers know that every decision they make today affects their organizations' ability to compete tomorrow. Strategic planning used to be touted as the essential exercise guiding those decisions. As traditionally implemented, such planning exercises emphasized setting very specific end goals and constructing detailed descriptions of steps to reach them. Yet planning ahead is difficult in a maelstrom of uncertainty. Technological, economic, and social winds are constantly shifting and changing the outlook, making it difficult to choose a direction, let alone chart a certain course. For this reason, strategic planning has been attacked as unrealistic and unhelpful in most current circumstances.[5] Detailed strategic plans can be outdated by the time they are approved, rendering them useless as guidance and perhaps even dangerous:[6] today's core capabilities can become tomorrow's core rigidities.

What, then, can managers do? They are increasingly pushed to create a portfolio of choices, a menu of thrusts into alternative futures.[7] Experimental endeavors—even failed ones—create new options for a company in the face of enormous uncertainty. In the past, large companies such as IBM and Fujitsu had the resources to pursue parallel technological paths for some time, deliberately setting up competing teams for new-product development so as to increase the chances for a breakthrough. As such parallel efforts

Figure 5-1 Knowledge-Creating Activities: Innovating and Experimenting

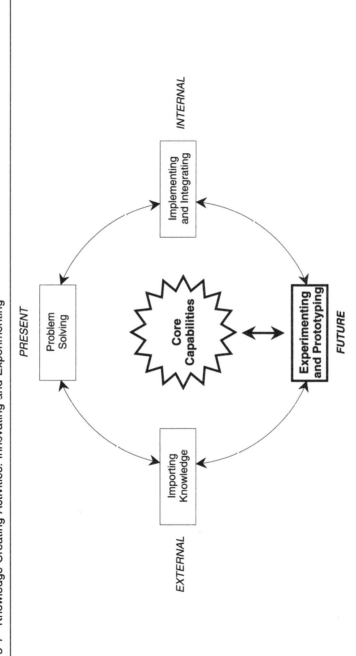

become too expensive, we need to find other ways to maintain a variety of options, better ways to experiment quickly, voluminously, and relatively inexpensively. The temptation, instead, is to cut back on experimentation. However, experience and history suggest that any short-term gains from such economies will be more than offset by the loss of long-term flexibility.

Interaction of Experimenting and Core Capabilities

The activities of experimentation and prototyping create two kinds of new capabilities. First, experimentation creates what has been termed "requisite variety" in products and processes—i.e., a diverse portfolio of technological options. Second, the act of experimenting sets up a virtuous cycle of innovation; this cycle can constitute such a dominant characteristic of the organization that the ability to experiment and prototype efficiently and competently itself constitutes a competitively advantageous capability.

At the extreme, two formulas exist for creating new strategic directions— the "great leader" formula (top-down) and the "hands-on champion" formula (bottom-up), as discussed in the following subsections.

Strategic Intent as Grand Experiment

An example of the top-down formula is the dramatic project initiated to support a new strategic direction—a new corporate "strategic intent"[8] that potentially remakes the business. Top executives may foster such projects as the only way they see to break the stranglehold of core rigidities. Exciting new technologies trumpeted in the popular press tend to motivate spates of such executive-championed grand experiments. Recently, the allure of multimedia technologies has inspired formerly staid telecommunication companies to set up costly video-on-demand service ventures, for instance, or even video production houses. When biotechnology first hove over the horizon, some equally unexpected investors set up expensive experiments, as the following vignette about Monsanto indicates.

MONSANTO'S CHARGE INTO BIOTECHNOLOGY

In 1979, Jack Hanley, then CEO of Monsanto Corporation, lured eminent scientist Howard Schneiderman away from his academic post as dean of biological sciences at the University of California, Irvine, by promising to build a $150 million Life Science Center for biotechnology research. Hanley and Schneiderman's vision was for Monsanto to "become a world force in biotechnology in applying molecular biology to industry in five or ten years."[9] At the time, Monsanto's only biotechnology capability was a small "skunk works" operation in the midst of conventional chemical projects in the Agriculture Company. Within a couple of months of his arrival, Schneiderman had licensed a growth hormone from Genentech to launch the company's research into animal husbandry products. Monsanto invested millions more to recruit and reward the top talent available, competing successfully with universities and small, potentially lucrative start-ups to build one of the strongest biotechnology capabilities in the country. By 1990, CEO Richard Mahoney said, "There has never been a time since I've been with the company, when we've had this array of things coming [from research]."[10] Among the multiple product lines emerging were animal growth hormones to increase dairy cattle's milk production (bovine somatotropin, or BST); genetically altered seed for herbicide-resistant crops, so that Monsanto's herbicides could be used more widely; and therapeutic drugs. Monsanto ran into strong public opposition to BST because of fear that its use would contaminate milk supplies as well as industry opposition on the grounds that milk was in oversupply in the United States.[11] However, there was little question in the early 1990s that Monsanto had built a very impressive biotechnology capability. In 1992, the corporation reported thirteen potential products in three arenas—pesticide-resistant crops, crops with enhanced quality (e.g., a high-starch potato), and insect- or virus-resistant crops. Of these, five were expected to be on the market by the mid-1990s.[12]

Hanley launched this new technological direction for Monsanto because, looking ahead, he could see profits from the traditional chemicals business shrinking; he needed to renew the company's technological base. The chemical industry had come under fire in recent years for its contribution to air and water pollution.[13] A number of laws passed in the 1970s and the creation of the Environmental Protection Agency suggested that public pressure would only increase and, with it, a squeeze on profits.[14] With ample cash reserves, he considered several alternative investments, including electronics, before settling on the then just-emerging biotechnology field. The objective to become a world force in biotechnology was very ambitious, given that the company had only about thirty-five scientists working in the cell biology skunk works at the outset.

Strategic Improvisation as Modest Experiment

Dramatic new technological directions can also arise from "strategic improvisation."[15] Single, initially unremarkable, projects can eventually shift the

strategic direction of a company or initiate the growth of totally new technological capabilities. (See Figure 5-2.) Many new experimental technology
thrusts originate far from the boardroom. The scope of technological experimentation depends in large part on the culture of the industry, which, in
turn, is influenced by capital requirements of the underlying technology.[16]
The chemical industry's propensity for "lumpy" capital investments set the
stage for Monsanto's expensive experimental venture, whereas, except for
semiconductors, innovation in the electronics industry has not historically
required large capital investment. Thus, the concept of growing an important
strategic capability from small beginnings has been quite acceptable in
electronics.

Still headed in the 1980s by their original founders, companies such as
Digital Equipment Corporation and Hewlett-Packard prided themselves on
maintaining an entrepreneurial culture. The founders valued a maverick
mentality because they had built the companies from an audacious idea.
Recognizing that clever, technologically talented employees could create
whole new businesses for the corporations, starting with an experimental
project to develop a particular product or process, such leaders tried to foster
an atmosphere in which a thousand flowers could bloom—at least initially.[17]
Top management concentrated on strategic recognition rather than strategic
foresight,[18] that is, on the ability to identify and support high-potential ideas
rather than on the ability to plan out future moves in detail. Stories of
individual product development projects that altered the course of the corporate ship abound at such companies.

Figure 5-2 Development Projects and Core Technological Capabilities

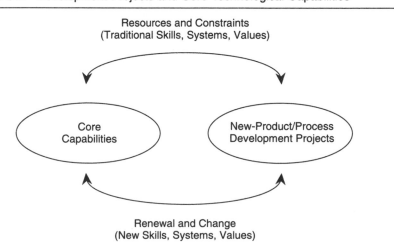

Resources and Constraints
(Traditional Skills, Systems, Values)

Core
Capabilities

New-Product/Process
Development Projects

Renewal and Change
(New Skills, Systems, Values)

Hewlett-Packard has an especially enviable record in strategic recognition of opportunities.[19] By 1989, the calculator business worldwide totaled $2.23 billion, and HP was one of two leaders in the United States for the professional segment.[20] What launched HP into this business was the development and advent in 1972 of its highly successful HP-35 scientific calculator—the first portable calculator to perform trigonometric, logarithmic, and exponential functions. Founder Bill Hewlett had personally championed the project because he wanted an "electronic slide rule" for his own use. Initial marketing reports suggested that five thousand could be sold, but within the first three years, HP sold more than three hundred thousand.[21]

Corning Glass similarly benefited from strategic improvisation. In the late 1960s, researchers tackled a problem being explored at other laboratories around the world—how to create optical fibers capable of transmitting data. Corning developers sought a technical solution in the opposite direction from that pursued by other researchers, however. Rather than make the glass more pure, they introduced an impurity (a "dopant") that rendered the core of the fiber more refractive than its outer layer and, hence, able to transmit light.[22] Their managers indulged this heresy—and launched a new business for the company.

Intel's ultimate exit from the DRAM business and concentration on the new core capability of memory chips started when Intel created the microprocessor while developing a new semiconductor chip set for Busicom, a Japanese calculator company. With a team of designers, chip architect Ted Hoff eschewed special-purpose, custom-designed semiconductors in favor of a few general-purpose chips that could be programmed to perform calculator functions. Recognizing that this design could be readily applied to many other situations, Hoff then successfully lobbied top Intel management to buy back from Busicom the rights for all noncalculator applications. By the mid-1980s, Intel had "moved from a silicon-based distinctive competence in memory products to a distinctive competence in implementing design architectures in logic products."[23]

Creating a Climate for Experimentation

So, top-down or bottom-up, experimental ideas create the future. If, as argued in this chapter, experimentation is an important activity for creating capabilities, it is clear that managers must create an organizational climate that accepts and encourages that activity. An idea becomes a reality when espoused by someone unafraid to turn heretic against predominate technology or company culture. There are excellent books and articles on the topic of championing[24] as well as on the topic of "organic" organizations versus "mechanistic ones."[25] Rather than review that literature here, I suggest a few simple actions within the reach of managers at multiple levels in the organization that make a difference in how much people are willing to experiment and risk failing. The ultimate objective of such managerial actions is to be able, like Chaparral, to weave a certain amount of experimentation into the fabric of the organization as a whole rather than isolate it into a research function. The more uncertain the future, the more essential becomes an environment in which *everyone* in the company is primed for experimentation and learning and in which prototyping is not a specialized, technical activity relegated to the engineers but *a way of thinking.*

How does one create such a climate? Two essentially conceptual yet intensely practical tasks are critical: (1) to separate intelligent failure from unnecessary failure, in both language and managerial response, and (2) to recognize the role of failure in building knowledge.

Intelligent Failure

Organizations are adept at ignoring negative news. In their extensive exploration of a biomedical innovation (therapeutic apheresis, or TAP) in several companies from 1983 to 1988, Van de Ven and Polley documented many instances of hiding failure. They identified four sources of "learning disabilities": (1) impression management through overly optimistic presentations; (2) setbacks not detected as errors that could provide learning; (3) proliferation of interdependent activities that distracted from a real evaluation of the core idea; and (4) transitory project membership, leading to organizational forgetting.[26] Note that the first two "disabilities" involved an inability or unwillingness to take an optimistic look at the downside—i.e., to view negative information as valuable. Knowing that any sign of failure could be interpreted as fatal to innovation, the project members consistently presented the bright side of every event, even when it would have been to their advantage to remove the rose-tinted glasses. Of course, one of the reasons for putting a positive "spin" on negative news is that individuals are promoted for succeeding—not for failing.[27]

We should distinguish between failures that result from inherently doomed enterprises and failures that result from creative experiments. Humorist John Cleese distinguishes between "true copper-bottomed mistakes like wearing a black bra under a white blouse, or, to take a more masculine example, starting a land war in Asia" and "mistakes that at the time they were committed did have a chance."[28] Obviously, we do not wish to encourage the former type of mistakes, which offer little possibility of benefit. The latter types of failure, however, are "intelligent,"[29] and they are not only beneficial but absolutely necessary. Intelligent mistakes result from risk taking. If people can't take the risk of saying or doing something wrong, there is no room for creativity.[30] Employees carefully watch what happens to people in the organization who take risks that result in intelligent failures.

At Chaparral, Medium Section Mill Superintendent Dave Fournie took a risk when he championed a $1.5 million arc saw for trimming finished beams. Originally prototyped at the vendor's site, the saw was brought back to Midlothian when it became evident that it was impossible to conduct realistic tests outside of the mill. Production pieces could be routed either to the experimental saw or to parallel processing by traditional band saws. The arc saw was a spectacular failure. The magnetic fields attracted small, unattached pieces of metal (including watches and pens), transforming them into projectiles, and the engineers were never able to refine the equipment to the point of effective operation. After a year of unsuccessful tinkering, the saw was replaced. Subsequently promoted to vice president of operations, Fournie is somewhat amused to find that outsiders "can't believe you can make a mistake like that and not get crucified."[31]

This incident exemplifies "intelligent failure," in that everyone involved acknowledged the possibility of failure inherent in the risk. Yet some managers seem unable to distinguish these from the "copper-bottomed mistakes" of which Cleese spoke. Failure is not popular. As the quote from Samuel Goldwyn at the start of this chapter suggests, even when top executives beckon their employees toward risk taking with one hand, they may be holding a large club in the other, behind their backs, in case the venture fails. In U.S. organizations, failure carries an unmitigated negative connotation.[32] Our usual organizational response to failure is to bury it quickly—and without a headstone. One reason may be that we generally underestimate the role of failure in building knowledge essential to success.

The Role of Failure in Knowledge Building

The scientific research community has provided the most familiar stories of failing forward—i.e., creating forward momentum with the learning derived from failures. Unsuccessful explorations in one direction have serendipitously revealed totally unanticipated promising leads in another—as, for example, in the famous discovery of penicillin. Alexander Fleming was grumpily sorting through plates containing staphylococci cultures he had been growing when an unusual mold caught his eye. Already deciding that the plates contained only useless information, he had stacked a number of them in a shallow tray of Lysol for disinfecting prior to cleaning. When a former research associate dropped in for a visit, Fleming seized at random one of the plates that was stacked high enough above the Lysol to remain dry as an example of the work under way. Only then did he spot the inhibiting effect the mold had on the growth of the infectious cultures in the dish and begin to speculate about its potential medicinal value.[33] He literally rescued invaluable information from the mass of failed experiments.

Penicillin is not the only "miracle" drug that metamorphosed from failure into success. Drugs that proved ineffective in their first target applications have proved potent in others. The recently approved Betaseron (a brand name for beta interferon) had "kicked around for years in Cetus's labs." Although it failed in at least seventy clinical trials as a treatment for cancers and viruses, it turned out to be a highly effective treatment for relapsing/remitting multiple sclerosis—so much so that Cetus initially had a great deal of trouble manufacturing enough to meet demand.[34]

Outside of research laboratories, experimentation is less understood or tolerated, and we tend to hide the explorations of blind alleys. Except for the well-publicized example of 3M's invention of Post-it Notes, which stemmed from a failed search for an adhesive for use in automobile ceiling covers, knowledge applied from failed new-product or new-process development is not well documented. Failed product development projects are considered best forgotten. Therefore, the contribution of prior development attempts or prior projects that provided critical knowledge usually goes unheralded.

One reason why it is so difficult to acknowledge failing forward, even when it occurs in new-product development, is our current preoccupation with speed to market.[35] Although this emphasis is both necessary and beneficial in causing organizations to focus more on strategic technology desired by a market, at the same time, it has spawned several undesirable side effects. One is the tendency to overstate the achieved rate of speed by ignoring all knowledge-gathering activities prior to the official start of a project, including the time spent on unsuccessful projects. In burying prior failures, organizations unintentionally lie to themselves—and others—about the length of time required to bring a product to market. Antecedent knowledge-gathering efforts are devalued if not totally ignored. IBM's famous 360 computer drew heavily on knowledge developed in a "failed" prior project, and Digital Equipment's first workstation, the 3100, used software and hardware design concepts from the canceled "Foxfire" project and at least one other. Nevertheless, in most organizations, because previous projects were "unsuccessful," they become invisible, and managers delude both themselves and others about the debt owed to failures. Only development team members know how much they individually gained from previous unsuccessful explorations.

In a study of 158 new-product successes and failures in the electronics industry, Maidique and Zirger found that "the knowledge gained from failures was often instrumental in achieving subsequent successes. . . ."[36] These researchers discovered that in order to understand how corporations failed forward, they needed to examine product families rather than single products—"the development of new market approaches, new product concepts, and new technological alternatives based on the failure of one or more earlier attempts."[37] Although, with hindsight, it could be argued that some of this experimental thrashing around should have been avoidable, in practice, some kinds of learning *are* heavily experiential.

Experiments and Prototypes: Quick and Dirty or Long and Clean—but Lots of Them

The more that companies practice continuous, widespread experimentation, the better they become at it and the more tolerant the organization and its employees become of the concomitant shocks.[38] The very thought of experimentation sometimes conjures up visions of complex matrices, mathematical formulations of probability, and expensive equipment. Experiments need not be highly formal to yield a lot of useful knowledge, however.

Experimenting

A Ph.D. in genetic engineering was once assigned to visit a seed company in order to interview a man famous for breeding the very best corn seeds in the United States. The objective was to investigate the opportunity for the scientist's company to venture into the seed business. Genetic engineering ostensibly offered the potential for vastly improved seed development, but traditional methods were lengthy and required much trial and error. Experimenters iterated toward the desired characteristics by raising plants and harvesting the seed from the best specimens, replanting that seed, and harvesting again. The Ph.D. was surprised to find how fragmented the seed business was. Each geographic location had different soil and climate conditions, meaning it was hard to know in advance which among several candidate plants would work—and considerable fine-tuning of seeds was necessary in order to satisfy the different conditions. This would take time, regardless of how the seeds were developed. In other words, the ultimate experiments would have to take place in the field. Even more enlightening, however, was discovering how the cross-breeding expert did his work. He had only a high school education, but his simple methodology was potent. When testing for a plant's ability to withstand minerals and organics native to that soil, he took a board with a nail in the end, stuck the nail in the ground beside each plant, and pierced the plant with it—to inject the plant with an extra dose of the local conditions. The surviving plants were harvested for their seed. His test for drought resistance was similar. Instead of providing the usual 4-foot space between the plants, he planted them in clumps 1 foot apart—and deprived them of water. Whichever plants survived, he bred. The geneticist felt humbled by the simple elegance of the experiments.

As this example and the Chapter 1 description of Chaparral's experiments with plywood to simulate splashboards illustrate, simple, inexpensive experiments can yield potent information. Not all cut-and-try experiments work so well, of course, and sophisticated experimental methodologies are often much more efficient. However, we are frequently deterred from experimentation and prototyping because we think of these activities as confined to research laboratories. Certainly, that is where experimentation is best accepted. Wherever experiments are conducted, however, the level of managers' tolerance for failure on the way to success can make a huge difference.

Forcing Experimentation. James E. Burke, CEO of Johnson & Johnson during the years 1976–1989, is fond of recalling when he introduced a chest rub for colds in 1954. It failed. However, General Robert Wood Johnson, chairman of the corporation at the time, congratulated Burke for taking the risk. Throughout his time at J&J, Burke urged employees to take risks, and although the message was often diluted by the time it reached the troops, a number of people in the company took it to heart.

In 1986, then vice president of operations for J&J's Ethicon, Inc., Robert Baker was asked to rethink the company's manufacturing strategy. Ethicon produced surgical sutures, which comprise needles attached to various kinds of sutures, encased in sterile packages. Part of the vision was to change the manufacturing process to a continuous flow, and Baker set up a new plant to try out a number of new technologies, including high-speed equipment. The new processes would require reformulating the product itself with a 20 percent stronger alloy, but Baker's marketing colleagues were supportive; such a needle could be advertised as the strongest in the world. Baker challenged a senior metallurgist in central engineering to come up with a new, 20 percent stronger alloy, and the scientist responded enthusiastically, "I thought no one would ever ask!" Baker then imposed an interesting condition: for every three heats of metal, two *must* be thrown away. This mandate had several effects: it forced purposeful failure; it rewarded volume in experiments;

it forced critical choices to be made with each batch of metal. Within one year, the metallurgist delivered the alloy.[39]

"Natural" Experiments.   Experiments often occur naturally in large companies when a new tool, methodology, or process is adopted by different sites simultaneously. Too often, however, such spontaneous experiments are regarded solely as an opportunity to learn about the technical aspects of innovation. The technical part of the innovation is carefully assessed in each locale, but no one takes responsibility for observing the differential effects of implementation on the organization, across sites. For instance, in a company introducing computer-aided design to automate engineering drawings, two corporate pilot sites identified the logical users of the system differently. In one site, the design engineers themselves were designated the users. Many costly errors could be avoided, it was argued, if the design went directly from the engineer's head into the software, and designating the engineers as the users placed the responsibility for quality where it should be. In another site, a special cadre of technicians was set up as a central support group for the engineers. The arguments for this system were that the task needed to be performed relatively infrequently—a few times a year at most; therefore, it did not make sense for the engineers to have to learn the system. Moreover, the technicians could serve as inspectors of the engineers' work.

The implications of these two structures were quite profound, both for the design of the next generation of CAD tools and for the conduct of a quality program in engineering design. Since the CAD system was not scheduled to be rolled out to the rest of the corporation for several months, these two different managerial systems could have been observed and evaluated for their effect on the organization and on the process of engineering design. However, the purpose of the pilot experiments was narrowly interpreted as providing feedback about the software features to its designers—not providing feedback to the corporation about the interaction between the software and the way it was implemented. No one thought of these differing sites as experiments (or as prototypes of differing conditions). Therefore, no one in management seized the opportunity to gather information to guide corporate decisions.

Prototyping

There are striking differences among the types of models considered prototypes by various professions and individuals. As noted in Chapter 3 (Figure 3-6), they range from a two-dimensional sketch to a fully functioning product, demonstrated in a real working environment. The best representation of an idea in prototype form depends on the information gap to be filled when communicating with possible users and/or other information needed from the prototyping exercise. When Hewlett-Packard engineers conceived of a continuous frequency counter, customers could not grasp the concept from a mere description. Even analogy with a familiar tool (the voltage oscilloscope) was not enough. A two-dimensional sketch would not help because it was the new functionality that the customers failed to grasp—not the physical shape of the invention. Only when users saw a three-dimensional, fully functioning prototype did they understand the instrument's potential to meet their current needs. On the other hand, HP researchers could (and did) ask their current customers about a vastly cheaper and better gas chromatograph because customers had a very clear concept of this instrument—what it looks like, what it does. A simple description of the proposed new chromatograph, combined with a two-dimensional sketch, conveyed enough information to the users, who could extrapolate mentally to a three-dimensional, functioning instrument. As these stories illustrate, each type of prototype elicits a different response and therefore different information from the market.

The Thermos Company Lifestyle team, challenged to design a totally new outdoor grill, made two models of its new electric grill—"an ugly one that worked and a stunning plastic foam dummy." The team dubbed these the Monitor and the Merrimack (after the Civil War ships) and used them to obtain feedback on both function and appearance from retailers and consumers. Producing a single prototype that was both good-looking and operational would have taken six months longer. The feedback gathered on the two prototypes allowed the company to go straight into production.[40]

Exercises in prototyping are often handicapped by the same preconceptions as those visited on experimenting—that "quick and dirty" reflects poorly on the designer or that it will be mistakenly interpreted by the viewer. Both are real dangers. Product and process developers relate cautionary tales about two types of encounters with managers—times when managers could not extrapolate from the prototype to the finished product and times when they did so prematurely. Designers themselves are accustomed to developing ideas through "a kind of reflective conversation with the materials of a design situation."[41] They are able to fill in the missing information—or use what is present to suggest what is possible. Many people, however, seem unable to tolerate incompleteness, to fill in missing details, to see the potential in the prototype—and they are the bane of designers' lives. They will take every presentation of line, shape, and color as absolute and final. Consequently, designers soon learn that some clients cannot be shown preliminary ideas at all. In companies where such people predominate, prototypes are treated as "an end product of thought, not as a vehicle for it."[42] Unsurprisingly, interaction about the prototype in these situations is much less likely to stimulate new ideas or allow client and designer to explore, back and forth, the most creative matching of need and solution.

Other developers describe the unfortunate experience of carefully warning managers that what they were about to see was a prototype, only to have the latter consider the product almost ready to launch. At Digital Equipment, a prototype of an expert system (software) productivity tool was shown to a vice president of marketing and sales in September 1982. Although proud of their accomplishments to date, members of the development team were keenly aware that at least a full year's work lay ahead of them before launch. Yet the vice president was so impressed with the demonstration that he insisted they should be able to have the software tool in the hands of every sales representative by Christmas.[43] The team began to call the incident their "Christmas goose," believing the early demonstration had "cooked their goose."

Despite the perils, however, prototyping is an essential exercise in both outbound communication and elicitation of information. Organizations conduct rapid prototyping cycles in order to learn quickly. The climate required for prototyping is the same as that required for experimentation—an emphasis on learning rather than blame. "We had a hard time convincing our engineers not to take the prototype all the way to a functioning model before showing it to people; quick meant entirely too dirty to them," recalled a manager in a company striving to shorten product development cycles. "But once they saw that we really understood the concept of a prototype, they started turning them out much faster."

Internal Wrecking Crews

Companies gain an inherent advantage in learning when employees can simulate an outside market—in effect, prototyping the conditions that the new product will face when launched. "Internal wrecking crews" serve a function similar to the user groups described in the preceding chapter, feeding reactions back to product developers. Gillette's male employees for decades routinely came to work unshaven so they could try out new razors and blades—one on each side of their face. Kodak had a standing policy that any employees could have film if they would report back on their use of it. (Among the many payoffs from this policy was the waterproof "Weekender" camera, inspired by the misadventures of an engineer who took film on a weekend kayaking trip and ended up in, rather than on, the water.) Digital Equipment engineers set up an internal wrecking crew to test their prototypes for the workstation 3100. The crews that succeeded in identifying the most bugs got to keep the new equipment as a reward. When the United Kingdom–based firm Amstrad was developing its "personal digital assistant" (some eight months ahead of Apple Computer's famous—or infamous—Newton), management passed out several hundred prototype devices to see how the company's own employees would use them. The Thermos team designing a new electric grill gave out the first production run to fellow employees—with instructions to use the product hard. These internal wrecking crews apparently obliged, as they reported back that the plastic shelving on the side of the grill could not support heavy dishes—feedback that resulted in a change to a stronger plastic.

Even when wrecking crew members are not current users of the product category, if they have deep prior experience with the user environment, they can significantly aid the prototyping process. Jay Forrester attributes the remarkable reliability of even very new radar products produced by Raytheon during World War II to the tough, experience-based attitude of the head of the power equipment division:

> Bertram had been a submarine man in World War I. Living in a submarine generates a keen appreciation for why one wants reliable equipment. He passionately insisted that he would not produce equipment that he would not be willing to receive if he were still in the military. He created incidents to demonstrate his values. For example, a new radar set was ready for production; the production prototype had been built; it had been approved by the Navy. Nothing remained except a check of final details before release for production. A conference for final clearance was scheduled, with the production prototype displayed in a corner of the conference room. Everybody but Bertram had taken their places at the table. He entered, sat down, and looked at the prototype as he pondered. He then walked to the prototype, used some collapsing parts on the front for a ladder, and climbed to the top. Other parts he used as a ladder to descend also failed. Then he reached over and broke off two pieces on the front of it and said, "Take it away! This won't last in the organization for ten years." He was on absolutely solid ground; he knew the Navy boys would use it for a ladder if they had to fix something in the overhead. . . . He also probably assumed correctly that if it were poorly designed on the outside, it was shoddy on the inside.[44]

Of course, internal wrecking crews cannot pretest the products and processes of many companies. Nuclear reactors come to mind or turbine engines. Moreover, employees who do not represent the targeted consumers can mislead the product developers. Hewlett-Packard's practice of designing for the "next bench"—i.e., for the engineer at the next workstation—worked well when the primary product lines were calculators and measurement equipment. When HP branched out into medical products, even into computers initially, the company had to seek other ways of representing its primary customers' needs. However, when the HP engineers began to use computers and printers at home, it was again feasible to ask employees to design the products they—or the people at the next bench—would like and to test them internally. In Chapter 7, we explore in much greater depth various kinds of market experimentation.

Organizational Prototyping

There are many opportunities to learn through prototyping beyond those offered by technical feasibility tests for new products. During the incorporation of new methodologies or process tools, *organizational* prototyping stimulates critical learning. The purpose of organizational prototyping is the same as for technical prototyping—to execute a design on a small scale as a knowledge-generating experiment. As noted in the previous chapter, process tools interact with the skills and customary organizational activities in ways that are often unpredictable. Yet even when pilot projects are set up as experiments, the learning generated is almost always limited to technical knowledge. One reason is that technical staff are accustomed to thinking about experimenting and prototyping. Managers in general are not. Therefore, the managers in charge of "testing" the new process tools often fail to take advantage even of opportunities that may arise for conducting organizational prototyping at very little expense.[45]

Creating local expert users is one relatively inexpensive form of organizational prototyping when introducing a new process to a site. These advance scouts serve two purposes: they anticipate organizational changes likely to be needed, and they become readily available, customized, local resources to support implementation. When drawn from the ranks of those actually affected by the proposed new system or procedures, such representatives integrate expertise about their own tasks and work environments with acquired knowledge about the innovation—and understand the interaction of the two. Although such individuals are therefore valuable guides in the mutual adaptation process described in the last chapter, managers are often reluctant to invest people's time specifically to experiment, to learn, before the full-scale implementation. Returns on such investments sometimes appear questionable to supervisors. Therefore, even if individuals are designated as corporate "guinea pigs," they are usually not relieved from enough other responsibilities to have the free time to kick all of the tires and identify potential pitfalls in use.

A study of software implementation in a matched pair of companies suggests that investing in such modest organizational prototyping in fact pays off generously.

SOFTWARE IMPLEMENTATION AT ALPHA AND BETA CORPORATIONS

In 1967–1968, two competing computer companies disseminated among their manufacturing plants software packages to control purchasing of materials and components. Six sites studied (three in each company) varied extensively as to resources expended, duration of disruption, length of time before productivity gains, and amount of trauma experienced. In Alpha company, site B was relatively unsuccessful. As Table 5-1 shows, site B was in a state of disruption longer than the other two sites, both in absolute terms (twelve months as opposed to zero and seven) and as a proportion (67 percent) of total implementation time. This disruption delayed realization of productivity gains about 50 percent longer than at the other two Alpha sites and cost many more person-days (per buyer) of effort devoted to training and learning.

In Beta company, sites X and Y similarly experienced higher cost than site Z. Site Y expended more than twice as many person-days on planning, training, and learning as did site Z, although the two plants were roughly the same size. At site X, over a nine-month period, approximately $2 million was spent for temporary help, consultants' fees, and the costs associated with a large inventory buildup, including rental fees for off-site storage.

Analysis revealed that these differences among sites could not be attributed solely to such variables as their rank ordering in the sequence of plant implementations worldwide. Merely waiting to implement a new system until others have "worked out all the bugs" did not always guarantee a smooth implementation. Nor did being among the first to implement the new system automatically mean that the site would experience greater difficulties than later sites. Therefore, pioneering could not totally explain high-cost implementation. More up-front planning failed to explain the difference between lower- and higher-cost sites. Sites Y and Z spent about the same proportion of the total person-hours devoted to implementation on preinstallation planning. And site B spent *more* hours on such planning than the relatively lower-cost site A.

The principal difference among the sites, common to both companies, was investment in organizational prototyping. (See Figure 5-3 for a comparison of sites Y and Z.) Managers in the more successful sites did two things: (1) they invested in building very site-specific knowledge about the likely interaction of the new system with their plant operations before installation; and (2) they provided easily accessible, abundant help throughout the peak periods of need during installation. In sites A, C, and Z, the managers designated local user-experts to experiment with the new system well in advance of its introduction. For instance, in site C, one buyer's usual assignment of parts was cut 75 percent so that he could spend three months simulating and then trying out the new system on his own allocation of parts, well in advance of the other fourteen buyers.[46]

Table 5-1 Software Implementation at Alpha and Beta Corporations

	Rank Order of Implementation Sequence	Disruption Period (months)[a]	Time to Productivity Gains (months)[b]	Total Person-Days of Effort[c]
ALPHA				
Site A	7	0	14	67
Site B	18	12	18	126
Site C	29	7	10	89
BETA				
Site X	2	9	13	N/A[d]
Site Y	4 (1 in U.S.)	20	21	5915
Site Z	20	2	4	2576

[a] Measured from cutover time when purchasing department regained preimplementation level of efficiency.

[b] Measured from cutover time when purchasing department realized gains in productivity.

[c] Number includes time spent by implementation team and purchasing department in planning and training for implementation. It does not include time spent by the Information Systems Department on programming. For ALPHA sites, the number is normalized as effort per buyer to allow comparison between sites of different sizes. The effort is measured in total person-days for BETA sites, since these two sites are about the same size.

[d] Completely comparable figures could not be obtained for site X. However, because many contract workers and consultants were hired, the figure is known to be larger than that for site Y.

Source: Adapted from Dorothy Leonard-Barton, "Implementing New Production Technologies: Exercises in Corporate Learning," in *Managing Complexity in High Technology Organizations,* ed. Mary Ann Von Glinow and Susan Mohrman (New York: Oxford University Press, 1990), 171.

The managers in the three sites that invested in creating expert users were confident the investment paid off—and the outcome figures support their conclusion. The managers who believed that they could not spare the resources to prototype actually spent much more time and money cleaning up the mess incurred by the haste, the confusion, the anger. Moreover, the

Figure 5-3 Software Implementation at Beta Corporation: Sites Y and Z

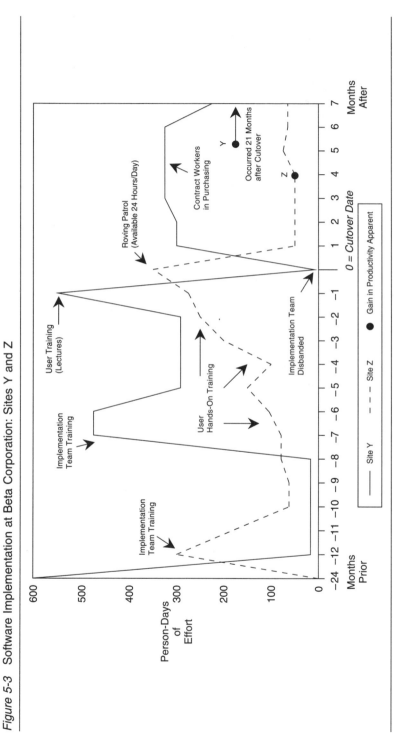

Source: Adapted from Dorothy Leonard-Barton, "Implementing New Production Technologies: Exercises in Corporate Learning," in *Managing Complexity in High Technology,* ed. Mary Ann Von Glinow and Susan Mohrman (New York: Oxford University Press, 1990), 181.

user-experts served as on-site consultants long after the initial implementation and advised on the design of the next-generation tools. So the original investment in organizational prototyping continued to pay off long after the innovation had become routine.

Learning from Prototypes and Experimentation

There would seem to be little point in setting up experiments or in prototyping unless managers ensured that the organization in fact learned from the exercises. As every parent, manager, or teacher knows, a crucial tool for learning is feedback on action and behavior. "If the action-outcome-feedback links are *short* and *frequent*, the individual is in a good position to learn about, and thus comprehend, the probable effects of actions on outcomes: short links enhance the ability to improve decision making by taking corrective actions. The opposite is true when the links are infrequent, long (in time), and subject to distortion."[47] Research has documented that when feedback loops are long or feedback is not readily interpretable by the individual, all sorts of biases influence the individual's actions.[48] Yet once again, the temptation is to shortchange investment in learning.

Systematic Learning: Project Audits

If anecdotal assessments by individuals are likely to be faulty, then a more systematic approach to learning is required. One mechanism designed to derive learning from projects is a postproject audit—i.e., team-conducted reviews at the end of development projects, for the explicit purpose of identifying what could be done better the next time around.[49] The more experimental the project, the more critical such audits become. Managers in many companies *say* that such audits are conducted. However, there are three crucial questions that ascertain the actual *usefulness* of such audits: (1) Who conducted them? If a few of the team members have moved on to other development assignments and therefore not all team members are present, the audit is incomplete. (2) How inclusive of all projects are the audits? Have all projects (including ones that did not result in marketable product) been audited? Although auditing even a single project is extremely useful, patterns of chronic problems show up across projects, for different types of products. Multiple project audits are a valuable tool for uncovering core rigidities. (3) What happened to the information gathered? Most managers can answer this question confidently: someone wrote up a report. If one inquires, What happened to the report? or What changed on the next project? the response is usually a sheepish admission that the report is securely buried in a filing cabinet somewhere. At best, the team may have made a list (usually a very long one) of possible improvements. Rarely is the list ranked by priority, with the top three or five problems used to generate specific action items assigned to particular people—plus implementation dates or names of specific projects in which the new procedure is to be tried. In short, the major challenge in conducting project audits is to act *systematically* upon the information gathered.

For example, developers of a local area network in a computer company recognized that marketing information had entered the process late and the launch date had slipped because the development team belatedly incorporated features critical to important customers. In a postproject audit, team members diagnosed why the desired features had been identified so late. They discovered that in fact the young marketing person on the team had noted the need for these features early in the design process. Discounting this person's observations because of her youth and inexperience (and marketing background), the team members ignored those recommendations. However, when two engineers visited some key customers two months before the product was to be launched, they heard the need from the customers' own mouths—and hastened back to revise the design. When the same pattern—ignoring marketing information until it was validated by engineers—was noted in several projects, the managers concluded that they had tripped over a core rigidity.

Process Overhaul

Until very recently, companies were unlikely to systematically review whole process streams in their operations. Hewlett-Packard was ahead of the reengineering trend when, a few years ago, engineering management decided to rethink its new-product development process. One interesting aspect of HP's approach was that by selecting "successful" and "unsuccessful" projects across a number of its divisions to study, the managers, in effect, simulated a quasi experiment. This kind of frank assessment of "failure" as well as success requires a dispassionate interest in generating knowledge for the purpose of process improvement.

HEWLETT-PACKARD REDESIGNS ITS PRODUCT DEFINITION PROCESS

In the late 1980s, Hewlett-Packard faced a major shift in market focus from test and measurement to computers. Top management issued a challenge to each of its businesses: halve the time to breakeven (when cumulative product profits equal development costs) by simultaneously reducing product development time, increasing revenue streams, and controlling expenses. The challenge generated much thought about the sources of overly long break-even times. Senior managers identified a number of recurring problems traceable to an underlying weakness in the product definition phase of new-product development. Because product definitions were unstable during the course of the development projects, resources and time were wasted when the definitions shifted. Corporate engineering at HP therefore decided to develop a product definition process that would address these issues.[50]

Its model for studying current processes was academic research that had contrasted commercially successful with unsuccessful new-product projects and identified five factors distinguishing the two groups, principal among which was the degree to which the innovators understood user need.[51] The Hewlett-Packard study systematically examined case studies of nineteen successful and unsuccessful projects in nine of HP's fourteen business groups. All the projects had been completed and the products introduced to the marketplace.[52] Despite the difference in geographic settings and the intervening years, the HP findings duplicated the primary findings of the academic research: the major cause of difficulties in the marketplace was a failure to understand user needs. This failure was not always, or even usually, attributable to a lack of effort. Some teams spent months and millions of dollars in a vain attempt to answer some fundamental questions about their customers. They faced problems in identifying the target user, the actual buyer who controlled the financial decision, and other stakeholders who affected the buying decision. The less successful teams were unable to determine exactly what problems had to be solved to satisfy each link in the set of customers, from the factory to the end users. They could not translate user needs into product.[53]

We will return to the topic of determining user needs in Chapter 7. However, at least as interesting as the findings from the HP study are two other aspects of this process audit: (1) the quasi-experimental conditions managers set up, with careful inclusion of "failures" as well as "successes," and (2) the extensive use to which HP put the study results. On the basis of this very systematic review, HP redesigned its new-product development process and took study results on the road to far-flung divisions. Company managers also joined forces with academics to extend their study into other companies.[54]

Summary

Experimental activities draw upon core technological capabilities, but more important, they create new ones. The experiments that build a rich repertoire of technology may result from top management's strong vision of the future, or they may be driven by a much less visible champion deep within the company. Whatever the impetus, these innovative activities are critical guards against core rigidities because they introduce new sources of knowledge, new channels of information, new methods for solving problems. However, some percentage of experiments must fail, and unfortunately, organizations tend to bury failures rather than learn from them.

As has been discussed in this chapter, there is a big difference between avoidable and intelligent failures. If companies are to "fail forward," managers must create an environment in which both types of failure are openly examined for their learning potential—and the latter type is actually encouraged. People do not automatically learn from experiments, however. Managers therefore face another management task associated with experimentation and innovation—designing and setting up deliberate learning mechanisms to wring actionable knowledge out of the experience. Many companies conduct audits of new-product development projects. Most do so in name only. Their reports molder away in filing cabinets while the organizations continue to make the same mistakes because the projects are not viewed as opportunities to learn about the development *process*. Failures that may have been intelligent the first time should be avoidable the second and third times around.

We have also seen examples of managers who view development projects as experiments and who ensure that organizational learning ensues. They establish strong feedback channels for the flow of knowledge back to product developers and project managers. They prototype organizational forms of interaction for the same learning purpose as that served by physical prototypes. Constant innovation feeds the wellsprings of knowledge. And innovation is born of both formal and informal experimentation.

However, not even the most extensive experimentation is likely to create *all* the knowledge required to sustain a core capability. The most internally creative of firms nevertheless seek knowledge outside their boundaries to augment (or supplant) internally grown intellectual assets. Therefore, the ability to absorb externally generated know-how is another key activity, which the next chapter is devoted to exploring.

CHAPTER SIX

Importing and Absorbing Technological Knowledge from outside of the Firm

Technology has become so sophisticated, broad, and expensive that even the largest companies can't afford to do it all themselves.
—Robert Z. Gussin
  Former Vice President for Science and Technology, Johnson & Johnson[1]

The role of the Technology Manager is [to] see to it that the corporation has available and uses the technologies it needs from whatever source they may be procured.
—James F. Mathis
  Technology Vice President, Exxon[2]

As suggested in the previous chapter, experimentation and rapid, prolific prototyping create many technological options for a company. However, very few, if any, companies can build core capabilities without importing some knowledge from beyond their boundaries. Therefore, successfully absorbing technological knowledge from beyond the periphery of the firm is as important a managerial activity as integrating it across internal boundaries—and no less difficult. (See Figure 6-1.) The "ability of a firm to recognize the value of new, external information, assimilate it, and apply it to commercial ends is critical to its innovative capabilities."[3] This ability, a firm's absorptive capacity,[4] is the focus of this chapter. An absorptive capacity has become increasingly important as the world's economic borders dissolve and the market for knowledge expands. If threads were drawn among all the recipients of technology around the world and all their sources, the globe would appear encased in fabric, so numerous are the connections and so diverse. Japanese firms ally with small universities in the U.S. Midwest; Swedish firms find African partners; Chinese firms seek German allies; U.S. firms work with Russian factories. Knowledge *benefits* flow along such lines unequally, depending not only on the sagacity of the technology source but, even more important, on the absorptive capacity of the recipient. Although, in empirical studies, a firm's investment in research has been used as a proxy for this capacity, it actually involves much more—and different types of—investment. As we will see in this chapter, firms differ considerably in their ability to develop outside wellsprings of knowledge—i.e., to identify, access, and assimilate knowledge from external sources.

Companies usually create a technology alliance for one of two reasons: to forestall a competitor's partnership with the targeted ally or to plug a hole in their own technological capabilities. The first reason is of little direct relevance within the context of this book; when the motive for seeking partnership is a race to possess knowledge ahead of a competitor, companies often have little time to assess its value. Therefore, such alliances may measure their life spans in months rather than years or prove excessively costly (or both). For example, Intel allied with VLSI to develop a chip set to supply the handheld personal digital assistant market, in large part to preempt archrival AMD from acquiring VLSI. When the PDA market failed to take off as rapidly as anticipated and the acquisition threat faded, Intel dissolved the alliance.[5] Such hastily created technological insurance alliances may protect capabilities temporarily, but they do not precipitate knowledge development. In contrast, alliances to shore up weaknesses in current capabilities affect the long-term growth of technological expertise.

Not all capability-enhancing alliances offer equal opportunities for importing knowledge, however. Gomes-Casseres notes three types of alliances—learning, supply, and positioning.[6] The latter two are essentially "arm's-length" agreements. Supply alliances are formed to minimize the transaction costs of trade and product exchanges. Positioning alliances are part of a marketing strategy, helping firms create or overcome market entry barriers. Both supply and positioning alliances may allow knowledge spillover, but they are not

Figure 6-1 Knowledge-Creating Activities: Importing Knowledge from External Technology Sources

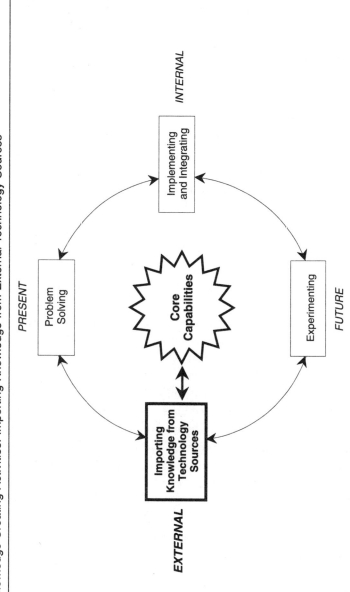

motivated by an effort to integrate capabilities.[7] Learning alliances, however, are intended from the beginning to augment internal knowledge. They are therefore more likely to occur early in the development of new products and new capabilities, as the data from early entrants into the PDA market, presented in Figure 6-2, suggest. The learning alliances began several years before the PDA products hit the market, but positioning alliances were almost an afterthought. Companies started worrying about distribution once they knew they would have a product to market.

This chapter focuses on learning alliances—early, knowledge-exchange-intensive agreements, some of which scarcely earn the name of alliance but rather are informal linkages between technology source and receiver. The major topics we shall explore are: the nature of capability gaps that lead companies to seek out external technology; the variety of sources from which knowledge may be acquired; the menu of mechanisms for acquisition; and finally, some of the important managerial issues in building an absorptive capacity.

The Nature of Capability Gaps

Companies seek to acquire knowledge from outside when there is a capability gap—that is, when strategically important technical expertise is unavailable or inadequate internally. The degree to which a company experiences a capability gap thus depends on at least two considerations: (1) the relevance or strategic complementarity of the necessary technology to the core technological capabilities of the firm and (2) the firm's existing degree of familiarity with the requisite technical knowledge. As noted in Chapter 1, technology may *support* or *enable* a core capability without itself being the source of competitive advantage. *Core* capabilities involve technological knowledge and activities that distinguish the company from its competitors and are essential to achieving the strategic intent of the firm. The lack of an enabling technological capability is less critical to the firm's survival than the absence of one that is core. In order to identify a capability gap, then, managers must first understand the link between strategy and technology in their business and then assess the degree of familiarity with that technology that currently exists within the company. The following sections discuss the strategy-technology link and the issue of familiarity.

Linking Technology to Strategy

As discussed in Chapter 5, top managers are increasingly disillusioned with the notion that they can put forth detailed strategic plans to guide their corporations. There is too little *déjà* in the *vu*. Yet because employees require

Figure 6-2 Growth of Alliance Clusters during Product Development (Average for Six Companies' PDAs)

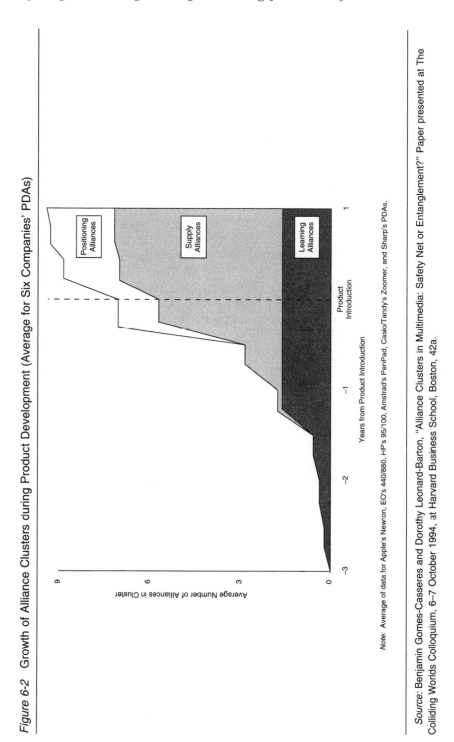

Note: Average of data for Apple's Newton, EO's 440/880, HP's 95/100, Amstrad's PenPad, Casio/Tandy's Zoomer, and Sharp's PDAs.

Source: Benjamin Gomes-Casseres and Dorothy Leonard-Barton, "Alliance Clusters in Multimedia: Safety Net or Entanglement?" Paper presented at The Colliding Worlds Colloquium, 6–7 October 1994, at Harvard Business School, Boston, 42a.

guidance to be productive, managers in many innovative companies set out a "strategic intent"—a word picture of a desired future state. Useful strategic intents are simple, general enough to encompass a variety of specific technologies, and imply the potential for dynamic responses to the unexpected. The strategic intent may or may not include an element of technology. Although most U.S.-based companies today are technology-*intensive* (possible exceptions being very small restaurants or "mom-and-pop" services such as western dude ranches, which use only faxes or photocopying), not all are technology-*based*.

As the case of Chaparral Steel suggested, the strategic intent of technology-based companies necessarily includes technology as an important element. Monsanto's charge into uncharted territory was led by the intent to be a world force in biotechnology. Kodak's strategic intent is to be the "world leader in imaging"—and very specifically, "pictorial imaging." This term encompasses all kinds of images, delivered by means of a variety of technologies such as photography, electrophotography, and electronics.[8] In such companies, the strategic intent cannot be achieved without the requisite technical knowledge, and the link between business strategy and technological capabilities would seem clear.

Yet the link between strategy and technology is often weak or missing, and the deficiency may exist at either end of the desired connection. At the strategy end, the strategic intent may be either poorly understood and communicated or else nonexistent. In the late 1980s at Digital Equipment Corporation, a product development team was asked how its product fit into the strategic intent of the firm. The answer? There was no single strategic direction for the company—no strategic intent of which team members were aware. The team members, including an experienced and senior vice president, explained that the best way to infer a strategic intent for the company was to consider all the current projects and identify the direction in which they seemed to be headed. For that particular group of people, a strategic intent was undesirable as it suggested top-down direction in a company that highly prized entrepreneurship. However, the lack of such an overarching strategic direction also left the team adrift about the contribution its particular development project was to make to the corporate weal.

The link between strategy and technological knowledge development may be broken at the other end—i.e., the technology being fostered has no obvious relevance to a core capability, no apparent connection to competitive advantage. Technologists often consider their particular interest to be strategically indispensable, whether it is in fact or not. At 3M, one of the most technically innovative companies in the United States, a technologist was startled by the bluntness of an executive explaining his impatience with a presentation on artificial intelligence: "I can't hear you because you aren't addressing my list of needs. The list is short, and if you don't talk to it, I can't hear you."[9] The technologist had not linked artificial intelligence to a business need. Proprietary technologies can also lose their strategic importance if the outside market catches up to or surpasses the internal capability. When "Shield Electronics" first invested in computer-aided engineering software, its systems were way ahead of anything available on the market, and having a swift and integrated design capability provided a strategic advantage over competitors. However, as the years passed and the technology matured, the massive internal software development group that grew up to service CAE trailed behind cutting-edge technology available on the open market from dedicated firms. Maintaining internal CAE development capabilities no longer made financial or strategic sense.[10]

When the strategic intent is clear, managers can identify the technological capabilities—both core and enabling—necessary to achieve it.[11] The Imaging Group at Kodak has explicitly articulated the link between strategy and technical expertise. In support of Kodak's strategic intent to be the world leader in imaging, the group has identified ten core competencies, six of which are technical: silver halide imaging materials, non–silver halide imaging materials, precision thin-film coatings and finishing, optomechatronics, imaging electronics, and imaging science.[12] Two of these technologies are ones in which Kodak has long invested: silver halide imaging can be traced to the origins of the company in 1881, and imaging science research started when the Kodak Research Laboratories were established, in 1913. Imaging electronics is a much newer field, and Kodak—like Polaroid, Fuji, Xerox, and others in the imaging business—is scrambling to develop the requisite knowledge. The company's strategic intent, however, provides clear direction for those efforts.

To help it decide which technological capabilities to pursue, Ethicon Endo-surgery has created the model presented in Figure 6-3. The key surgical activities fundamental to most surgical procedures, and potentially covered by company products, are listed on the vertical axis. These traditional activities are carried out in a wide variety of therapeutic procedures (the "specialties and procedures" horizontal axis). The critical choice for Ethicon Endo is to select a few intersections between those two dimensions and match the selected intersections with a third (the "technologies" horizontal axis)—the best technology to support that activity for that medical specialty. Choosing foci for development of technological capabilities this way helps managers avoid the potential trap of a core rigidity. That is, reasoning from the potential customer need back to the choice of technology rather than vice versa keeps open a wide variety of technology

Figure 6-3 Business Development Model

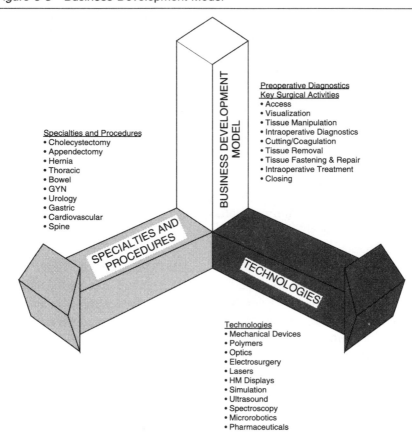

Specialties and Procedures
• Cholecystectomy
• Appendectomy
• Hernia
• Thoracic
• Bowel
• GYN
• Urology
• Gastric
• Cardiovascular
• Spine

BUSINESS DEVELOPMENT MODEL

Preoperative Diagnostics
Key Surgical Activities
• Access
• Visualization
• Tissue Manipulation
• Intraoperative Diagnostics
• Cutting/Coagulation
• Tissue Removal
• Tissue Fastening & Repair
• Intraoperative Treatment
• Closing

SPECIALTIES AND PROCEDURES

TECHNOLOGIES

Technologies
• Mechanical Devices
• Polymers
• Optics
• Electrosurgery
• Lasers
• HM Displays
• Simulation
• Ultrasound
• Spectroscopy
• Microrobotics
• Pharmaceuticals

Source: Ethicon Endo-surgery; used with permission.

options. There is less danger that deep familiarity with one technology (for example, suturing to fasten or repair tissue) will blind the company to a potentially different solution for the basic surgical need. This approach also does not presuppose the origins of the requisite technological expertise; it may be found inside or outside of the company.

Familiarity: The Role of Internal Development

Assuming that a particular technological capability is clearly essential in order to fulfill the corporate strategy, we next need to assess the degree to which the requisite supporting physical systems, the skills and knowledge, the managerial systems, and the supporting norms already exist within the corporation or its close affiliates. This assessment essentially consists of asking two questions: Is our knowledge current? Is it complete? The more current and complete the knowledge, the more "familiar" the technology. Since such an assessment requires placing existing capabilities under the harsh light of competitive realities, it is not easy and not always pleasant. Benchmarking against best-of-class in other industries helps managers calibrate a core technological capability, especially the physical and managerial systems dimensions.

Xerox was one of the first companies to use benchmarking extensively, when it struggled to retake the copier market from Japanese competition. The firm benchmarked American Hospital Supply and Caterpillar for ideas on how to improve the logistics of distribution, IBM to improve data processing, and American Express to improve telephone responses to queries. Xerox also examined L. L. Bean's computerized system; the Maine mail-order merchandiser picked and packed goods three and a half times faster than Xerox could its spare parts. And of course, Xerox continuously compared the performance of its equipment to that of its competitors. All this information was used to determine where internal capabilities fell short.[13]

Determining the level of technical knowledge and internal expertise relative to that of direct competitors is much more difficult; yet, as discussed below, technology-scanning is critical to keeping managers apprised of the company's competitive standing in key technologies.

Juxtaposing the two dimensions of strategic importance and degree of familiarity with the technology yields the set of four potential technology-sourcing situations pictured in Figure 6-4. Starting in the lower left-hand corner and moving clockwise, we see that there is little reason to invest in a technology that is not at all strategically important (not even enabling) and with which the firm has little experience. Technologies that the firm is both familiar with and capable in but that are extremely low in strategic importance may be outsourced to specialist firms. Technologies falling into the upper right-hand quadrant, are probably important elements of current core capabilities, and the firm will invest in enhancing these. The greatest need for external acquisition, of course, falls in the lower right-hand quadrant, where there are capability gaps. Strategic importance is high, but the company's internal knowledge is incomplete or out of date.

Causes for Capability Gaps

Capability gaps grow, like fissures in the earth, from slow erosion or sudden tremors. Alternatively, they may always have existed but suddenly become important given a new market opportunity that requires a technological

Figure 6-4 Need for External Sourcing of Technology

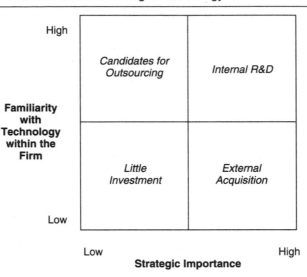

foundation where none currently exists. Although there are many potential reasons for such gaps, three are of particular significance. First, the United States has experienced a decline in the rate of investment in "basic" research. At the same time and at a frenetic pace, we have been mining our existing base of scientific knowledge for new products, rapidly making technology and technical expertise obsolete. Finally, advances in technology have also created huge opportunities for innovation where none existed a mere decade ago. We will look briefly at each of these three possible causes for capability gaps.

The Decline of "Basic" Research in Industry

In the 1940s through the 1960s, vertically integrated firms established large central laboratories on universitylike "campuses" where scientists pursued knowledge—AT&T's Bell Labs, RCA's Sarnoff Laboratory, Kodak's Central Laboratory, Xerox's Palo Alto Research Center, Du Pont's Research Laboratories. As one researcher characterized the period: "Management deposited large bags of cash on the doorstep and tiptoed away." Unable to recover enough direct financial returns on their investments, many of these companies have cut back on their laboratories.[14] They have also redirected research toward more immediately commercializable results, a trend that has researchers worried.[15] Some have pointed to the demise of large corporate research laboratories as a case of slow erosion in the scientific underpinnings that give rise to innovation. Moreover, the late 1980s were characterized by a slowing in the *growth* of both research and development overall in the United States, leaving the United States on some measures behind countries such as Germany and Japan. Japan spends about 3 percent of gross domestic product on nondefense research and development compared to just under 2 percent in the United States.[16]

Does this trend foretell capability gaps in our foremost technology-based companies? Not necessarily. First, large investments in R&D do not always imply technological prowess. In 1993, General Motors was the biggest of U.S.-based big spenders on research (at over $6 billion) yet seemed unable to recapture a lead in the car market.[17] Second, simplistic, bifurcated categories (basic research versus applied) are misleading guides for deciding what kinds of technical inquiry yield scientific progress. Even scientists are quick to point out that some very important inventions have been driven by "applied" research.[18] And although definitely "basic research is *not* a luxury, [it] will constitute a competitive advantage if, but only if, it is coupled with world-class performance in [a] much more extensive set of skills, institutions, and investments. . . ."[19] Therefore, in and of itself, the decline of central corporate laboratories may not presage weaknesses in the internal capabilities of these leading companies. It does, however, create stronger incentives for sourcing some technology from outside the firm.[20]

Technology Maturity and Obsolescence

An ocean of scientific invention poses a constant threat to the shores of every technology-based company.[21] The waves of innovation may merely deposit new possibilities to be combined into current and future products—or they may wash away the technical foundations of the company. Technical innovations are thus competence-enhancing or competence-destroying. Researchers and consultants have attempted to predict competence-destroying tidal waves by describing technology life cycles as progression along an S-shaped curve. (See Figure 6-5.) At the bottom of the curve, the technology is new and untried. Over time, or with the application of effort (authors vary as to which the bottom axis represents), the technology gains in performance at an increasing rate. Then, as the technology matures, growth and innovation slow and level off as the curve reaches performance limitations imposed by nature. So steel replaced iron, steam propulsion outpaced wind power in shipping, and polyurethane foam proved latex foam cushioning out of date. The implications of S curves are clear: continuing to ride a technology wave when a new S curve is starting—a wave that will render obsolete the firm's technological foundations—is suicidal.

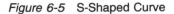

Figure 6-5 S-Shaped Curve

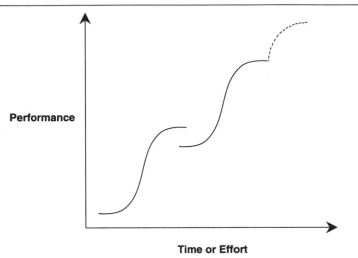

The biggest managerial challenge is understanding at any particular moment where one is on the ultimate curve—near the bottom, in the nearly vertical stretch of swift innovation, or approaching the asymptote at the top—and therefore knowing how much more to invest in this technology. The dangers of complacency, of believing that the particular technological wave one is riding will never peak and level off, are obvious. We saw in Chapter 2 the hazards faced by companies whose core capabilities have become core rigidities.

However, managers also face the opposite problem—consigning a technology to a premature grave. This danger, albeit less discussed, is nonetheless important in identifying real capability gaps. Technologies have not always proved subject to the "natural" limits originally imposed on them, as suggested by the dotted-line extension of the S curve in Figure 6-5. In her research on step-and-repeat photolithographic equipment, Henderson found that in the early 1980s, a minimum possible line resolution was predicted because of the physical limits of the wavelength of light; yet that supposedly inviolable limit was in fact exceeded by 1986.[22] Christensen observed that by the time Hitachi and Fujitsu finally switched to thin-film technology for the production of computer disks, the two companies had ridden the ferrite oxide "S-curve far longer and had achieved . . . over eight times the performance IBM seemed to have identified as the limit of the ferrite-oxide approach. . . ."[23]

Apparently, companies sometimes prematurely thrust a technology into the nursing home—not because it is reaching the natural limits of its "life" but because infatuation with a new technology heaving into view causes managers to reduce or cease investment in the "old." In the disk drive industry, from 1976 to 1988, the efforts of both Fujitsu and Control Data Corporation to wring more performance out of ferrite oxide technology are best described by *two* S curves—-not one. The performance of the old technology plateaued in each company when engineering resources were switched to the new thin-film technology for a while. When managers discovered that this new process would be harder to conquer than originally believed, engineers were redeployed back to improving ferrite oxide, and that technology caught a "second wind."[24]

The natural excitement and "hype" surrounding new technologies may also mislead managers into considering them a substitute for current technology (competency-destroying) when in fact they could be integrated into current capabilities (competency-enhancing). Managers in large companies absorbing the impact of such new technologies as artificial intelligence and biotechnology tended initially to overestimate their radicalness. Artificial intelligence found its most practical initial commercial application in expert systems—i.e., software programs intended to mimic the judgments of human decision makers with a series of nonlinear, linked sets of rules. Expert systems were—and are—used to diagnose everything from flaws in computer disks to human diseases.[25] Because expert systems looked so different from conventional software programs, traditional information systems developers disparaged the new software as undisciplined, whereas other observers heralded a new age of machine intelligence rendering everything in its path obsolete. Companies such as Digital Equipment built up artificial intelligence centers, employing hundreds of knowledge engineers. Over time, however, traditional technology merged with and absorbed the innovative development techniques and design features of expert systems. They became a much less distinct class of software applications, as the rapid prototyping and strong user influence that characterized them have gone mainstream and as rule-based systems have been absorbed into hybrid systems.

Biotechnology has undergone a similar process of integration into standard pharmaceutical company processes. Initially, the pharmaceutical companies used these capabilities as a competitive means for creating protein-based drugs, which were too complex to be synthesized through traditional chemical means. Over time, however, the established firms began to absorb biotechnology techniques into their traditional core capabilities of drug design and delivery.[26] Increasingly, such companies employ biotechnology in complementary processes, to create proteins used in "rational" drug design such as the process used by Vertex Pharmaceuticals, described in Chapter 3.

In identifying capability gaps, managers thus confront the potential not only for erring on the side of complacency but also for overreacting to new technology and underestimating its complementarity with existing capabilities. Of the two errors, complacency is more likely to be fatal to the firm. However, assuming that a new technology is competency-destroying when it could be enhancing—that is, failing to seek the synergies between the new technological knowledge and current capabilities—is also very costly.

Technology Fusion Opportunities

A capability gap may emerge simply because no potential existed previously to bridge the chasm between different technologies. Technological discoveries create opportunities for technology fusion. Such opportunities occur with increasing frequency, creating new classes of products and processes all along the traditional stream of value-creating activities in an industry. As Figure 6-6 suggests, the advent of biotechnology has affected the value chain in pharmaceuticals less than digital signals' replacing analog has altered the value chain in many media-related industries: digitization affects more activities in the translation of raw materials into products, reducing visual, numeric, and voice information, hitherto regarded as distinct forms of communication, to a common unit, the byte, that can be manipulated in countless ways. Because of digitization, the potential for competency destruction exists even in such organizations as museums or corporate training departments. Innovation in the emerging multimedia industry is thus an example of technology fusion on a bewildering scale.

As noted in Chapter 3, the fusion of formerly distinct technologies into new ones is as important a source of innovation as is more traditional scientific invention. HP's "MC²" program combining measurement, computing, and communications; Hitachi's magnetic-levitation train; NEC's multimedia delivery to the home—all are examples of technology fusion that require extensive, varied, and deep pockets of expertise. Yet even such large and innovative companies are significantly challenged to locate all the requisite knowledge in-house—and integrate it successfully into complex products.

Table 6-1 presents the alliances of one company, IBM, at one point in time, mid-1993, in the area of multimedia products. The value-chain categories across the top of the table represent all the competencies required to develop a complete multimedia product. Some partners (e.g., Time Warner) are competent in creating the content desired by users and have built up

Figure 6-6   Effect of Revolutionary Technology on the Value Chain in Different Industries

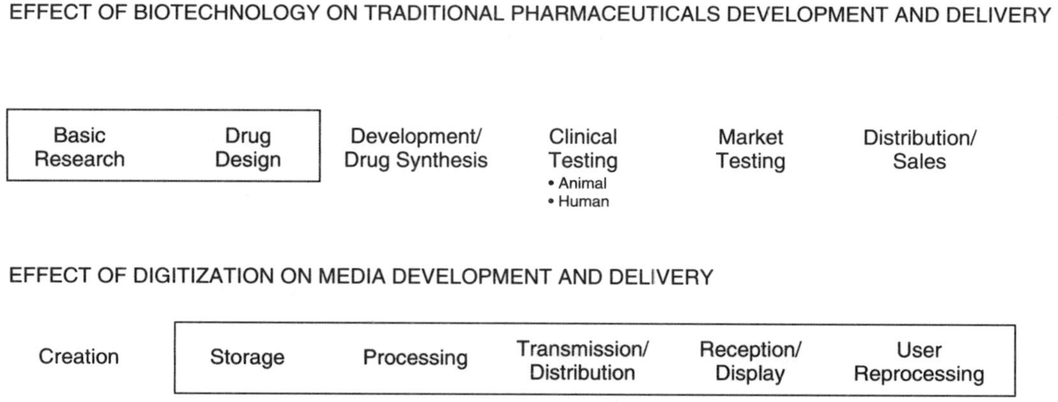

EFFECT OF BIOTECHNOLOGY ON TRADITIONAL PHARMACEUTICALS DEVELOPMENT AND DELIVERY

| Basic Research | Drug Design | Development/ Drug Synthesis | Clinical Testing • Animal • Human | Market Testing | Distribution/ Sales |

EFFECT OF DIGITIZATION ON MEDIA DEVELOPMENT AND DELIVERY

| Creation | Storage | Processing | Transmission/ Distribution | Reception/ Display | User Reprocessing |

Table 6-1 IBM Multimedia Partners and Products as of Mid-1993—Technology Capabilities

Value Chain of Information	Creation/Providing Content (a)	Processing (b)	Transmission (c)	Storage (d)	Reception (e)	Reuse (f)
Multimedia Delivery Mechanisms						
Set top (Television)	Time Warner	Time Warner Media Lab	Bell South Media Lab Bell Atlantic Rogers Cable Motorola/ Scientific Atlanta	Time Warner Media Lab	Time Warner Media Lab	
Kiosk	Blockbuster Home View	Fairway Blockbuster Home View		Fairway Bockbuster	Fairway TSS Blockbuster	NewLeaf
Desk top (Computers)	Home View Integration Media CNBC/Numedia Videologic Digital Domain Prodigy	Media Lab Taligent Digital Domain First Cities Micrografx Prodigy Red Shark Kaleida Labs Interactive Media Tech Advantis	TI/Spectrum Pacific Bell/ Northern Telecom Media Lab Rogers Cable TV Bell South Advantis	Microsoft Media Lab Kaleida Advantis	Creative Labs Gain Technology TI/Intermetrics First Cities Media Lab Altec Tecmar Kaleida	Media Lab

(a) Creation refers to companies which mainly provide content (i.e., data, news, graphics) to the alliance.
(b) Processing includes companies which focus on creating tools to build items necessary for multimedia, such as compression algorithms, tools to build software, etc.
(c) Transmission incorporates companies creating and having the means to transmit data, whether through cable or phone lines or laying down fiber optic lines, etc.
(d) Companies in storage provide companies creating systems to store data.
(e) Reception refers to companies which build the machine that receives and plays the multimedia software.
(f) Reuse refers to companies that make a product where the user can manipulate data to create something (i.e., create a compact disc or a personalized newspaper).

Source: Compiled by Allegra Young with the help of Langer and Company.

over time a reservoir of such content (databases, movies, books). Other partners (e.g., Digital Domain) have created tools to manipulate such content—to rearrange it, compress it, process it. Some partners specialize in creating the means of transmitting that content (notably, the telephone and cable companies). Still other partners are creating ever more capacious optical or magnetic storage forms. The content must be received and played for the end user, in a kiosk, on a television, on a computer, or by a personal appliance; and numerous partners are creating the software and hardware to receive the transmitted content. Finally, at the end-user site, that same content may be rearranged and transformed into new, personal forms by the user. Thus, for instance, NewLeaf proposes to deliver music to stores so consumers can select favorite songs and create their own CDs.

Because the information in Table 6-1 was collected from public sources, all possible technologies under internal development at IBM are not included. Moreover, some of these alliances predate the organizational restructuring that created a Personal Systems Division and therefore were likely made with objectives beyond creating a multimedia capability. Nonetheless, the table does illustrate an implicit, emerging strategy. It also presents one method for targeting desired capabilities: first determine the necessary total set of competencies to be covered; then map current external and internal sources of those competencies.

External Sources for Technological Knowledge

Once a capability gap has been recognized, managers face a choice among multifarious potential sources of technological knowledge. If history is a predictor of the future, many alliances created to obtain knowledge from such sources will be relatively short-lived. For instance, one study of 895 strategic alliances competing in three industries during the years 1924 to 1985 found that 86 percent lasted less than 10 years; average duration was 3.5 years.[27] However, brevity is not always equivalent to failure. Many alliances accomplish important objectives before dissolving.[28]

As Figure 6-7 suggests, potential technology allies range from institutions with a research mission, such as universities and national laboratories, to consortia comprising competitors or noncompeting companies, to customers. We will not inventory all possible technology sources here but briefly consider a few examples.

United States–based universities, as reasonably prolific knowledge producers, are becoming more aggressive in extracting financial value for their scientific knowledge through patents and licensing agreements.[29] The Massa-

Figure 6-7 External Sources of Technological Knowledge

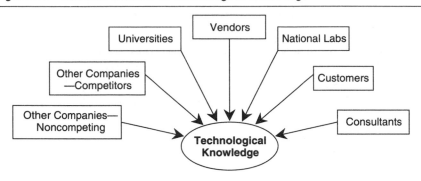

chusetts Institute of Technology reports licensing technology at an annual rate of eighty to one hundred licenses.[30] The commercial value of such knowledge output is indicated by the fact that even a partial listing of companies wholly or partially based on MIT technology shows twenty-seven start-ups between 1990 and 1993.[31]

At the same time, national laboratories in the United States are becoming more ambitious in peddling their knowledge wares to industry. So, for instance, the company U.S. Alcohol Testing of America has licensed exclusive rights to manufacture and sell a new drug-detection technology known as flow immunosensor, developed by the Naval Research Laboratory. This desktop computer system can detect a few *billionths* of a gram of cocaine—roughly equivalent to a teaspoon of the drug dissolved in a swimming pool—*in less than a minute.*[32]

After the National Cooperative Research Act was passed in the United States in 1984, consortia mushroomed. By the end of 1992, 325 research and development consortia had registered with the Department of Justice.[33] Many were learning alliances with potential competitors. The PowerPC chip was developed by IBM, Motorola, and Apple Computer. General Motors, Ford Motor Company, and Chrysler have formed a dozen consortia on everything from improved crash dummies to electric-vehicle batteries.[34] At least one study found a rate of return for cooperative research to be nearly 150 percent greater than that for internal research among noncooperative firms.[35] However, as discussed later in the chapter, one of the oldest of research consortia, the Microelectronics and Computer Technology Corporation (MCC), has experienced, and demonstrated for others, many difficulties inherent in managing such technology-based "precompetitive" agreements.

The transfer of knowledge across organizational boundaries may be somewhat easier when stakeholders are not direct competitors. Like IBM, many companies today are assembling jigsaw puzzles of capabilities drawn from multiple, noncompeting sources. For example, GM's Electronic Data Systems Corporation is experimenting with interactive media by allying itself with a wide variety of partners—an in-room, hotel-movie venture with Spectradyne; a gambling venture with Video Lottery Technologies; an agreement with USTravel to explore automated machines dispensing tickets for airline or Broadway show seats; a CD-ROM home-shopping experiment with Apple; and a home-banking service with USWest and France Telecom. Each of these partners is expected to provide some expertise that EDS neither has in-house nor intends to develop.[36]

Mechanisms for Sourcing

Technology from external sources may be accessed through a multiplicity of relationships, ranging from industrial theft (neither recommended nor discussed herein) to the mergers and acquisitions that so intrigue business school graduates. These relationships may be arrayed along a continuum expressing the extent of mutual commitment between the parties (and to a lesser degree, knowledge integration) implied by the particular form of agreement. (See Figure 6-8.) The degree of commitment and integration cannot be precisely correlated with particular forms of interaction. An R&D contractor may be so well integrated into a firm that she is treated

Figure 6-8   Mechanisms for Sourcing Technology

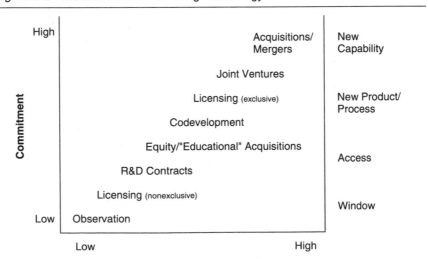

like an employee, whereas a "merger" may result in two quite separate organizations with little integration. In short, much depends on the relationship between the actual people involved in the knowledge-acquisition arrangement. However, in general, there is a progression in commitment from short-term, usually low-cost technology-observation privileges shown at the lower left-hand corner of Figure 6-8 to the long-term, sometimes "bet-the-farm" expensive mergers shown at the top right-hand corner of the figure.[37]

Mechanisms for accessing external technological knowledge also differ according to their potential for acquiring an entire new technological capability comprising deep expertise and know-how as well as supporting physical equipment, training and reward systems, and values that encourage the necessary types of knowledge. As Figure 6-8 suggests (right-hand axis), technology observation, nonexclusive licenses, and R&D contracts generally cannot be expected to provide new capabilities; they provide windows onto the technology and perhaps samples of its potential.[38] Equity in a venture or "educational" acquisitions provide an opportunity to investigate a technology in depth. Codevelopment inevitably results in knowledge "bleedthroughs"[39] from one company to another and thereby potentially launches a new capability. However, acquisition of a new core capability is likely only through joint ventures, company purchases, or mergers, which potentially transfer a technology in its full business context, with all four dimensions of the capability represented.

Building a Capability over Time from External Sources

Companies may grow a new capability over time, using outside sources in an incremental path from low-cost, low-involvement explorations of a technology to an acquisition or multiple acquisitions—that is, using a number of the mechanisms described above in roughly sequential order of increasing commitment (from the lower left to the upper right of Figure 6-8). In the early 1970s, for instance, Corning Glass made a small investment in MetPath, an emerging leader in nationwide clinical testing of biological specimens such as blood and urine. After observing the company for some time, Corning acquired MetPath. Corning then closely studied the way that MetPath segmented its market, handled the logistics of gathering and processing the specimens, analyzed the test results, referred the data back to physicians, and billed clients and Medicare. Corning next invested resources (human and financial) in expanding MetPath. In 1987, Corning acquired Hazelton, a leader in toxicological testing services. Corning thus parlayed its initial expertise in laboratory glassware to knowledge about producing analytical instruments; it next progressed to clinical and diagnostic instruments, then became expert in reagents, and ended up possessing a full capability in clinical and toxicological testing services.[40]

Similarly, Harris Corporation grew from a traditional mechanical printing press company into an electronics power by a careful strategy of acquisition and digestion.[41] In 1956, Harris acquired Airtronics, a contract research house for defense. Two years later, the company bought Gates Radio, a manufacturer of radio broadcast equipment and transmitters; in 1959, it bought Polytechnic Research and Development, a producer of microwave and highly sophisticated electronic instruments. In 1967, another critical acquisition, Radiation, Inc., introduced essential expertise in advanced digital communications to the company. Harris president Richard Tullis noted of the latter merger that "[we managers] did not impose ourselves. . . . For the first year, we had a hands-off policy while we learned how we could make both halves fit." In 1969, the purchase of RF Communications added knowledge of two-way radio technology, and in 1971, GE's broadcast equipment division was acquired. The acquisition of Datamation in 1972 added knowledge of minicomputers.

Managing the Absorption of Knowledge

Even if the technological knowledge can be accessed from outside, however, tremendous management effort is required to nurture that initial outlay into an enabling or core capability. Harris's Tullis observed in 1977, "We spent 20 years evolving into a different kind of business. . . ."[42] To use an analogy, companies may grow a new capability by purchasing seeds, seedlings, or a whole orchard—but the technological capability will not flourish unless the ground has been prepared before planting and assiduously tended afterward. Companies vary as much in their ability to absorb new technology as they do in their skills at building technological capabilities from scratch. As we will see, the managerial behaviors that build a true absorptive capacity are common across a variety of technology sources and alliance mechanisms.

Create Porous Boundaries

Managers need to expose their companies to a bombardment of new ideas from outside in order to challenge core rigidities, encourage inventive serendipity, and check technological trajectories for vector and speed versus competitors. An amazing amount of knowledge exists in the public domain. If a company has antennae out into the world community and encourages employees to collect and disseminate that information internally, that knowledge is a treasure trove.

Scan Broadly. Because technological knowledge comes from a very diverse set of sources, the wider managers cast the net, the more likely a prize will be caught within it. A study of Japanese, Swedish, and U.S. firms found technology scanning considered second only to internal research as the most important technology-acquisition strategy.[43]

Despite the formidable language and cultural differences they must overcome to obtain insight into new technologies, Japanese researchers are remarkably tenacious technology scanners. It is difficult to think of a technology conference *unattended* by representatives from Japanese companies, and more than one presenter has been startled to find an audience member from that country assiduously snapping photographs of each overhead slide from a front-row vantage point. This is not to say that top U.S. and European companies do not also invest in observation, however. Technological conferences are well attended by U.S. researchers, and U.S. industries provide many research grants to universities. Moreover, some U.S.-based companies use their far-flung sales offices as sensors for technological advances. As a vice president of research at a major diversified medical supplies company explained, "If I hear of a scientific advance presented in a conference in Germany that might be even remotely interesting, I get on the phone and ask [my colleagues] to track it down for me." Programs such as MIT's Industrial Liaison Program encourage visitors from member companies to meet periodically with faculty to catch up on the latest technical thinking, and many of the national laboratories are increasingly encouraging corporate visitors.

More than U.S.-based firms, though, large Japanese firms invest in knowledge gathering by posting researchers abroad for years at a time. Japanese researchers work at university laboratories from MIT's Media Lab to the Chester Carlson Center for Imaging Science at Rochester Polytechnic Institute in New York. A provost at Cornell, investigating where in the institution industry visitors were located, discovered five in biotechnology—all from Japan: "They were not junior scientists here for a little trimming up before they started their industrial jobs; most of them had been with their corporations for more than a few years. Two of them had quite responsible positions in their companies but they were at Cornell spending two years to find out what was going on in genetic engineering, in one of the best laboratories in the country."[44] Japanese companies have also set up corporate research laboratories in close proximity to U.S. universities. Hitachi Chemical Research Center financed the construction of a new biochemical research center at the University of California at Irvine. The bottom floor is used by UC scientists, the second and third floors by Hitachi scientists.[45] Although physical proximity does not ensure knowledge flow, it certainly increases its probability.

Provide for Continuous Interaction. A characteristic of companies skillful in importing knowledge is that they do not check the state of their technical understanding only once, at the beginning of a project, and then work, heads down, to achieve their objective. When Chaparral decided to invest in horizontal casting, for instance, managers revisited their knowledge sources a year after project initiation to make sure the approach was not already out of date. Studies on information flows in research laboratories provide some empirical evidence that such continuous monitoring benefits performance. Comparing high- and low-performance teams, Allen found that low performers were much more variable in how much information they sought—either a lot or none. Moreover, they spent most of their outside exploration time in two lumps—at the beginning and just after the midway point. In contrast, high performers kept up a consistent, continuous relationship with information sources of all types during the project.[46] Such constant attention to outside information sources is difficult because it takes time, and time is often the resource in shortest supply during a project. Nonetheless, this attention is essential because competitors or information sources may have made progress since the last contact.

A small ceramics firm set itself a price and performance target for substrates to be used in producing a new circuit board, which managers were confident would wipe out competition because it was so far ahead in quality and price. Unfortunately, by the time the company was ready to manufacture, competitors had cut the performance gap by so much that the small firm could not charge the premium essential for profitability. With hindsight, the managers realized their prospective customers could have provided them with information suggesting the gains their competitors were making. Instead, the managers had unwisely assumed that while they ran the race, competitors were lounging on the sidelines.

Nurture Technological Gatekeepers. The sourcing, flow, and direction of information into research laboratories is heavily controlled by technological gatekeepers. Such self-selected individuals expose themselves to more outside sources than do their colleagues; they are also critically important nodes for sifting and disseminating technical knowledge. As extensive studies of such individuals have shown, gatekeepers are not at all like information officers, who might direct people to information sources. Rather, gatekeepers are outstanding technical performers who keep their colleagues apprised of the latest happenings in their field. In recent years, information technology has automated part of the gatekeeper's job. Many companies have clipping services, routine patent searches, and continuous electronic scanning through databases, using "keywords" as guides. The information produced, however, still needs to be screened by a human gatekeeper for relevance. Therefore, managers continue to identify and reward such individuals as important conduits for knowledge importation.[47]

Nurture Boundary Spanners. The role technological gatekeepers play in a company's absorptive capacity is augmented by that of boundary spanners— people who understand the world of the source and the world of the receiver and translate as well as disseminate knowledge. (Such individuals are also needed within corporations to translate among disciplines, as discussed in Chapter 3.) Boundary spanners must be selected with care. They have to be entrepreneurial since working at the interface between two organizations requires the skill and risk-taking aplomb of Odysseus sailing between the twin threats of Scylla and Charybdis. Researchers studying interfirm alliances have remarked that a weak liaison (young, inexperienced, or an outsider) is likely to doom the alliance.[48]

Moreover, however skillful, a single interface between technology source and receiver is inadequate.[49] One boundary spanner can become a bottleneck in the flow of knowledge. The more the knowledge to be transferred approximates a full capability, the more important are multiple points of contact and multiple conduits for information flow, managed over time. Some companies therefore lay out in explicit detail exactly how contacts are to take place, between whom, and with what frequency. For example, a contract between the small biotechnology firm Immunex and the large pharmaceutical company SmithKline included a list of the principal scientists who would be responsible for the companies' joint project, a detailed schedule of at least weekly telephone conferences, and a provision for at least quarterly joint meetings.[50]

Continuity among personnel is another factor greatly affecting the success of knowledge absorption; as noted above, a large portion of knowledge (and often the most valuable part) may be tacit—i.e., still in people's heads.[51] When boundary spanners move on to other jobs, their role may not be adequately assumed by others. Niederkofler recounts the deterioration of a relationship between a large pharmaceutical company and a small biotech firm. Initially, two boundary spanners successfully translated the research developments at the small firm into the language of the large company. They were especially skillful at framing the uncertainty and risk of the small company's technology in terms of the structured, formal analysis familiar to managers in the large firm. However, once the two went on to other projects, the managers in the large company decided that they were dealing with "a bunch of long-haired scientists who [knew] nothing about business. . . ."[52] The degree of uncertainty had not changed—only the way that the risk was presented.

Fight Not-Invented-Here. When the attempt to implant knowledge from outside into the body of an organization is rejected, it is often characterized as "not-invented-here" (NIH) syndrome. The term covers a multitude of common reactions, from a general distaste for adopting someone else's idea rather than birthing one's own to a (possibly correct) conviction that the new technology is flawed. Most companies have few incentives for borrowing and using knowledge grown outside. Writing about the difficulties experienced by MCC in transferring output to its shareholder companies, Gibson and Rogers conclude: "Knowledge creators, not users, are the ones celebrated in the technology transfer process."[53] Resistance shows up in various subtle and nonsubtle ways, undermining the relationship. For instance, researchers at a small computer company were highly offended by the apparent NIH of their colleagues when their much larger partner retested a communications product that had already passed inspection and received certification.[54] Evidence of NIH abounds. Observing patterns of behavior across hundreds of relationships, a researcher found that managers in some U.S. firms regarded the suggestion that they could learn from their partners through sharing facilities "heretical . . . because they already believed that outsiders' ideas were inferior. . . ."[55]

Yet the 1990s' rebound of U.S. automobile makers from their slough of despond in the 1980s proves that NIH can be overcome. A study of the automobile industry in the 1980s (mentioned in Chapter 2) revealed a strong Japanese advantage in quality, development productivity (measured in engineering hours), and lead time.[56] By the late 1980s, that advantage had begun to shrink, and a 1994 replicative study found that the "average U.S. projects virtually eliminated the performance differences in development lead time and productivity."[57] How was that gap closed? Ford learned from Mazda and Toyota; Chrysler mimicked Honda and Mitsubishi.[58] U.S. automakers were able to take advantage of all the capabilities that Japanese automakers accumulated throughout the postwar years in Japan in response to fierce domestic competition at home and resource scarcities.[59]

In fact, U.S. producers not only successfully emulated their Japanese competitors; they also articulated and systematized management practices that the Japanese themselves did not initially recognize as coherent systems. They were able to leapfrog Japanese practice in some areas. For instance, U.S. managers coined the terms *simultaneous* or *concurrent* engineering to describe the overlapping and integrated problem-solving practices that the

Japanese followed as a matter of routine, thus making implicit management systems and values explicit enough to transfer; moreover, some U.S. companies went beyond Japanese practice by setting up dedicated, colocated development teams to further reduce product development lead times. The U.S. managers saw such teams as a logical extension of concurrent engineering; the Japanese did not engage in the practice regularly.[60]

The threat of extinction tends to focus the mind. U.S. auto companies overcame not-invented-here because they had to. How can managers in less dire straits persuade their employees to welcome ideas from the outside? Some combat NIH by forcing joint responsibility between source and receiver. A recently merged company gave product concept responsibility to a joint marketing team and then presented that concept for manufacture to the whole organization. The shared focus on a specific task and then joint responsibility for its delivery to customers (under a stiff deadline) encouraged team members to meld the best ideas from both organizations. Managers in other companies have experimented with awards for the best examples of "stealing" ideas—e.g., the "Golden Thief Award." However, the most successful antidote to NIH is an organizational culture that embodies a sense of urgency for innovation, encourages interactions with outside sources of expertise, and helps employees understand the wellsprings of creativity—which are almost never filled in isolation.

Close the Readiness Gap

Technology acquired from outside is often incomplete from the viewpoint of the recipient firm. That is, a sizable gap exists between the technology as licensed or acquired and the form in which it will be deployed as part of a product or an improved internal process. The gap has to be closed by someone—the source, the recipient, or through the cooperative efforts of both. Laboratory-sourced technologies are notorious for being closer to science than to market; laboratories are, after all, institutions devoted to the development of *public* knowledge. Yet some very important inventions have emerged from laboratories in this century, and many were pushed by their inventors to prototype form because of the exigencies of war. A famous example is "Project Whirlwind" at MIT during World War II, an R&D contract that resulted in the first high-speed, real-time digital computer and spawned a whole new capability in digital computing for the Defense Department.[61]

PROJECT WHIRLWIND

Project Whirlwind started in 1944 with a $75,000 grant to MIT to conduct a feasibility study of an airplane stability and control analyzer—a flight trainer and a calculating machine for determining flight characteristics. ASCA was actually never built; Whirlwind emerged in its place. By early 1946, Project Director Jay Forrester proposed that the team switch attention to the emerging digital techniques instead of analog, promising "more reliable performance, higher accuracy, lower cost, smaller size and more flexible operation."[62] As Forrester recalled years later, funding for such applied research was scarce. "There was no . . . private industry interest at that time . . . on the part of a company like IBM. I would say that it's unlikely that [the computer] would have happened [without government funding]. There wasn't any visible private-sector interest."[63]

Forrester sought the best engineers, reasoning that "producing a satisfactory working system often requires greater technical contribution than producing the basic components of that system."[64] The Whirlwind team comprised a number of MIT graduate students as well as project engineers such as Kenneth Olsen (founder of Digital Equipment), comanager Robert Everett, and Forrester. In the fall of 1949, Forrester himself was responsible for one of the most substantial inventions in the project—random-access, magnetic-core data storage. He recalled:

> It was a shot in the dark. . . . I was doing lots of other things, but I was spending enough time to get a personal feel for the technology, which is the only way I believe that the chief executive officer is able to have the confidence for a major change of direction. I was fairly insistent that a patent application be filed. MIT hesitated over this for a period of time and then turned it over to the Research Corporation, which is an outfit that handles patents for universities . . . and asked the Research Corporation to file the patent. They came back with the written opinion that they saw no commercial use for such an idea and that the military had a royalty-free license anyway and that it wasn't worth the cost of filing, which was $1,000 or so. MIT exercised the option of saying, "well, we will pay the cost of filing; go ahead anyway."

Everett and Forrester's approach has been contrasted to that of their contemporary John von Neumann at the Institute for Advanced Study, who was also building a computer. Forrester, quoted at the time, opined that the von Neumann team was

> engaged in what is essentially an experiment, [so] they are not particularly interested in reporting on the construction of their experimental equipment, nor in integrating that equipment with other existing equip-

ment nor in training people for the use of machines. . . . . MIT. is building what can more correctly be called a prototype. . . . The intention is that the prototype should embody as many as possible of the desired features and characteristics. To be sure, the MIT. approach is . . . more expensive, but it should be faster. Speed in the attainment of usable computers seems of great importance under present conditions.[65]

Project Whirlwind was unusual for university research in the degree to which a practical, immediate, real-world problem drove the project and, hence, the degree to which the project output was designed for ease of absorption by the military. Forrester was convinced that responding to the military's urgent need was a great advantage. "R&D, done without a specific objective, can waste resources by working on issues without reason. However, one must be ready to revise the objectives as the situation changes. Research may show that the original objectives are not possible, or that tasks are easier than anticipated and the goals can be set higher. Available financing may decrease or increase, thus altering the realistic future of the program."[66]

However, the gap need not always be filled primarily by the technology source. Researchers are often ill equipped to serve as product developers. Moreover, in some situations, the inexorable pressure on researchers in technology sources to shape their output into near-final product form has subverted the original purpose of their organization.

The Microelectronics and Computer Technology Corporation (MCC) and SEMATECH in Austin, Texas, were established to foster precompetitive research cooperation among companies in the same industry. Summing up a detailed history of MCC over its first ten years, researchers Gibson and Rogers concluded that MCC had not met its founders' expectations—that the consortium would help the U.S. computer and electronics industries compete with Japan in computer architecture, design tools, software, and technology cooperation. Packaging/interconnect technologies had been successfully transferred, but output in computer architecture, design tools, and software was disappointing.[67] It turned out that MCC's main contribution was to serve "as an important real-life laboratory to study the barriers [to] and facilitators of collaborative R&D leading to technology application and commercialization."[68]

MCC suffered from a problem typical of many types of alliances: the high-level managers (CEOs in the case of MCC) who set up the original partnership were not responsible for making it actually work. The lofty objective of creating a common pool of precompetitive knowledge was not shared by the researchers and product developers within the stakeholder firms, driven as they were by competitive market pressures to get products out the door. The deputy director of MCC's artificial intelligence program in 1987 noted of his program that because the MCC software technology was precompetitive, in-company developers could not see how to apply it in productive applications and did not have the financial resources to do so even if they wanted. They were not prepared to close the readiness gap. Moreover, because MCC researchers and in-company developers were mismatched in education and training, their use of different computer architectures and languages made communication difficult and collaboration to close the gap unlikely.

Thus, MCC's failure to reach the original objectives was managerial, not technical. The technology was available; several companies based on MCC technology have been spun off. The problem was getting the technology across the *organizational* boundaries. It was not in MCC's original charter to take the technology to the level of readiness desired by the member companies, and the individuals within those companies could see little advantage to devoting part of their internal product development budget to technology that was still far from commercialization.

Another characteristic of the readiness gap is that its scope and type depend on the needs of the recipient firm. MCC had so many different constituent firms that trying to tailor the technology to the needs of one member might well have rendered it less desirable to another. Almost any consortium tends to encounter this problem since having multiple investors confuses the knowledge-generation process. Not only does each investor try to influence the technology development, but each has built a different level of internal expertise and, hence, a different receptive capacity for the technology. A spin-off from Carnegie-Mellon University, for example, was almost drawn and quartered by its powerful, well-intentioned investors.

CARNEGIE GROUP

The Carnegie Group (CGI) was founded in 1984 by four widely respected computer scientists from Carnegie-Mellon University. From the beginning, it was financed by a group of its largest customers, which purchased equity in the company in return for access to new artificial intelligence research, products, and tools. One of the original investors, an aerospace firm, quickly became disillusioned with the prospects of obtaining useful knowledge and switched to the passive role of financial investor. Each of the remaining companies had a different idea of what it would obtain from the partnership.

Digital Equipment Corporation managers had provided funding from CGI's inception. DEC's pioneering XCON project, from which the company had built its sizable internal artificial intelligence capability, had been conducted with one of the CGI founders. DEC managers viewed CGI as a continuous source of applied research knowledge that could be transferred to the internal group for transformation into productivity tools in operations.

Texas Instruments, which also had an internal AI group, sought technology to incorporate into future products.

USWest viewed its partnership with CGI as a way to obtain proprietary knowledge-based software for its internal operations *and* for products while building the technical capabilities of its fledgling research and development organization.

Ford Motor Company, with few internal capabilities in artificial intelligence, regarded CGI as a vendor that could provide turnkey, cutting-edge engineering design, manufacturing, and diagnostics applications for internal Ford operations. For instance, the first joint effort was a Service Bay Diagnostics System project that employed expert systems technology to help technicians diagnose service problems in Ford automobiles.

CGI was thus faced with providing knowledge products to financiers whose demands varied from new research results at one extreme to fully functional, tested systems at the other.

Source: This case is derived from Paul Sagawa and Dorothy Leonard-Barton, "The Carnegie Group," case 690-033, Harvard Business School, Boston, 1990.

On a much smaller scale, CGI faced many of the same management challenges as those confronting MCC. CGI's solution was much simpler, however—split the business into two separate divisions—one that concentrated on research and one that delivered ready-to-use, customized systems. The former half delivered cutting-edge research to Digital, for example, where the in-house experts took over the technology and built it into processes. The latter half served as a vendor to companies such as Ford. But even then, only the enormous amount of goodwill built up over the years among the individuals involved in the alliance saw the company through the problems of figuring out intellectual property rights among the equity owners. The degree to which various equity-holding companies received knowledge payback (not just financial payback) varied, depending on the individuals involved at the time and the aggressiveness of the companies in addressing the readiness gap.

Understand the Trade-Off: Transferability versus Desirability

One of the great paradoxes inherent in accessing external technology is that the more desirable it is from a competitive viewpoint, the less inherently transferable it is, and vice versa. (See Figure 6-9.) Technical systems are more likely to convey a competitive advantage and be part of a core capability if they embody some of the latest technology available in the world. Therefore, state-of-the-art technical systems are likely to be more desirable objects of transfer than old models. Yet their very newness means they may not be fully documented; they may be "hot" off the designer's table. Because of their newness and lack of tested documentation, they are more likely to be operator-dependent: operator skills are often an important component of cutting-edge equipment. Thus, Chaparral sent operators to Germany to help design the proprietary casting mold that gave the company an advantage in near-net-shape casting. Managers have to make a trade-off between desirability and transferability. If the operator knowledge comes with the equipment, fine. If not—is the system operator-independent? If it is not, transferring the equipment may not transfer any portion of a capability.

Forward-looking, new managerial systems are more desirable (assuming they are working well) than standard systems used throughout the industry. For instance, mimicking Chaparral's apprenticeship systems, incentive systems, and "vicing," as they were described in Chapter 1, could give any company a boost in productivity. But not every important practice at Chaparral is codified. In fact, merely transferring rule books might not capture the essence of the managerial systems at all since practices such as "vicing" are informal. The more codified the managerial practices, the more easily they are imitated—but that doesn't mean they are desirable.

Similarly, the scarcer the skills and knowledge embedded in the technological capability being acquired, the more competitively valuable they are since they cannot be purchased on the open market. However, market-scarce skills may be firm-specific and based in the experience of longtime employees. These characteristics make such skills difficult to transfer. As the experience of ELP recounted later in this chapter will show, the tacit knowledge of people even quite far down the organizational ladder, and not explicitly recognized as experts, may be an essential part of the technological capability being acquired. Such individuals may not be identified as key employees and therefore may not transfer. If the people themselves do not move, it is difficult to transfer the tacit knowledge they carry in their heads.

Finally, enacted values—the values and norms actually used to guide decisions and behavior—are more desirable than sterile lists of guidelines

Figure 6-9 Capabilities Audit—Evaluating the Desirability and Transferability of a Potential Technological Acquisition

Rate Targeted Capabilities:
Mark position along continuum that best represents your assessment of each of the ten descriptors.
(D = Desirability; T = Transferability).

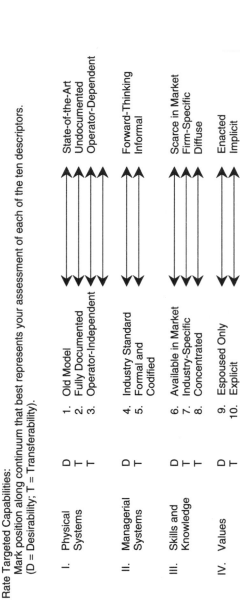

I. Physical Systems	D	1.	Old Model	⟷	State-of-the-Art
	T	2.	Fully Documented	⟷	Undocumented
	T	3.	Operator-Independent	⟷	Operator-Dependent
II. Managerial Systems	D	4.	Industry Standard	⟷	Forward-Thinking
	T	5.	Formal and Codified	⟷	Informal
III. Skills and Knowledge	D	6.	Available in Market	⟷	Scarce in Market
	T	7.	Industry-Specific	⟷	Firm-Specific
	T	8.	Concentrated	⟷	Diffuse
IV. Values	D	9.	Espoused Only	⟷	Enacted
	T	10.	Explicit	⟷	Implicit

and decorative mottoes, which may be espoused (i.e., embraced in theory) but not followed.[69] As noted in Chapter 1, firms such as HP and J&J have very explicit norms of interpersonal behavior. The "HP Way" and the J&J "Credo" are posted on company walls and do guide behavior. Explicitness does not necessarily preclude enactment. However, these are generic, big values that influence interpersonal behavior. The kinds of little values that determine the screening and rewarding of different types of knowledge tend to be implicit. Companies do not post explicit norms valuing the import of knowledge over its re-creation, assigning greater status to electronic than to mechanical engineering, for example, or promoting the influence of design in new-product decisions. Therefore, some of the values and norms that most influence a technological capability are likely to be implicit and possibly difficult to identify—much less to transfer.

Develop the Ability to Evaluate Technology

Managers who skimp on their homework when evaluating technology acquisition are unwise. One needs to understand the potential of the technology itself, be able to assess the expertise of the source in that technology, and identify the true location of that expertise—which may not reside in the most obvious human or system repository.

Assess Technology Potential. How can potential be evaluated unless someone understands both the new technology and the business it would support—in depth? Consultants with no stake in the outcome of the decision can help since they may understand the technology very well. But unless they have had a long-term relationship with the firm, they are unlikely to understand whether and how a new technological import could be incorporated and absorbed. Usually, some relevant expertise inside the firm is required. A major study of joint ventures found that the best technological ones were formed by partners that had each done considerable R&D work on the problem in question prior to their collaboration. Some companies set up parallel research experiments in their wholly owned labs to learn more about their partner's technological approaches; they might rotate scientists and other technical people through both the joint venture and wholly owned labs.[70] Similarly, researchers who analyzed R&D investment in 318 U.S. manufacturing firms argued that "the ability to evaluate and utilize outside knowledge is largely a function of the level of prior related knowledge."[71] Therefore, paradoxically, firms that already do some research in a field are best positioned to import related knowledge. At the same time, owing to the selection biases described in Chapter 2, managers should be encouraged to consider technologies that are not already a core competency.

Evaluate the Expertise of the Source.   Joint ventures became very popular in the 1990s as a means (at least ostensibly) of creating whole new competencies out of the various pieces held by venture partners. As noted above, opportunities (some would say, mandates) for technology fusion in multimedia set off a scramble to "do JV deals" in the early 1990s reminiscent of the acquisition and merger mania of the 1980s. Some of the Romeo and Juliet partnerships between such traditional enemies as IBM and Apple amazed observers.

Joint ventures often begin in a glow worthy of a Hollywood set. Uninvolved onlookers declare it a lovely couple; top management throws rice and mumbles vague admonitions to the kids to work out any problems; shareholders, like would-be grandparents, impatiently await offspring. Meanwhile, a group of real people have to get up in the morning and make this marriage work.

Viewed from the perspective of knowledge management, a critical issue that can derail the marriage before it really gets started is a misapprehension of the capabilities each of the parties brings to the joint venture. A joint venture is set up to create a set of complementary capabilities, with each parent company providing essential but very different knowledge bases. What happens when the complementarity turns out to be illusory is illustrated by GE Plastics' experience with a new venture.

GE PLASTICS AND THE POLYMER SOLUTIONS JOINT VENTURE

In 1989, GE Plastics, a $4.8 billion group within General Electric Company, developed, manufactured, and marketed engineering plastics to durable goods industries. GEP's polymer pellets were transformed by its customers into a wide variety of heavy-duty products such as computer casings, telephones, and even automobile bumpers. In addition to competing on the basis of the properties of these highly engineered plastics, GEP provided technical services to corporate clients, helping them apply GEP materials optimally. Industrial designers helped customers visualize how plastics could be used in new products. Applications engineers understood polymer and resin characteristics so well that they could determine the feasibility of using each material in proposed products. After analyzing and modeling the behavior of a given material in a mold to take into account the material's flow properties, computer-aided engineering specialists advised customers how to design molds and parts. GEP designers and engineers did not follow their customers' designs into full manufacturing; their involvement often ended quite early in the customers' product development projects. However, the design and applications engineering services were important to GEP because customers often had no idea what could or could not be done with the highly engineered plastics. Only by influencing clients to use polymers instead of metal, or to include particular polymers as part of product specifications, could GEP continue to grow the market for its materials.

By 1989, it was clear that providing such services to customers without charge was costing the company more overhead than could be sustained. Therefore, the group decided to set up a joint venture with an outside partner to serve customers from "art to part"—that is, helping clients develop product designs and then following the products right through manufacturing—at a profitable price.

GEP managers debated between allying with a design house or an engineering firm. The design house might have access to different sets of clients than GEP's usual set; moreover, designers could influence customers very early in the product development cycle, thereby locking in GEP materials to product specifications. On the other hand, GEP already had some industrial designers but had no experience with manufacturing. Since the joint venture would need that capability to provide full services to customers, perhaps the engineering house would be a better partner.

In the fall of 1989, GEP decided to set up the joint venture Polymer Solutions with a prominent design house that had in-house engineers—a seemingly perfect solution. However, the very first totally new product development project undertaken by the new joint venture, development of an automatic teapot, revealed a gap in the marriage contract. Both parties had cadres of engineers. Neither had manufacturing engineers. This lack turned out to be critical: the plans that designers drew up for the new automatic teapot were inadequate to guide construction of the tools needed to mold the plastic parts. The consequent confusion, delays, and recriminations rendered the product more costly than anticipated, and the joint venture reorganized several times as the partners tried to figure out just what their combined skills enabled them to do.

Sources: Karen Freeze and Dorothy Leonard-Barton, "GE Plastics: Selecting a Partner" and "Polymer Solutions: Tempest about a Teapot," case studies, Design Management Institute, Boston, 1991 and 1992, respectively.

GEP's decision to partner with the design house was driven as much by the personal chemistry between the decision makers as by any systematic assessment of current and needed capabilities to provide an "art-to-part" solution. GEP managers were pleasantly impressed by the business sense evinced by the design house; the designers liked GEP managers' sensitivity to the importance of good design. Each side brought largely unexplored assumptions about the competencies with which they were partnering. They did not systematically assess whether or not their combined competencies added up to a whole capability—in this case, the ability to develop a totally new product.

The GEP side of the alliance knew that the design house had done engineering jobs; therefore, GEP managers assumed that Polymer Solutions would benefit from the designers' manufacturing experience. However, the engineers in the design house were in Ohio, not Massachusetts, where GE Plastics was located. The design house side of the partnership knew that GEP had designed many products requiring complex engineering; what its management failed to realize was that GEP *customers* were the ones who had always taken the product clear to manufacturing. Therefore, the joint venture was still missing a critical piece of the capability to deliver a product "art-to-part"—the manufacturing expertise.

With hindsight, one can speculate about the gaps in equipment and knowledge that a careful mental simulation of the development process might have revealed. Because knowledge is difficult to assess, we tend to equate role or title with know-how. That is, rather than consider the skills and knowledge needed, we tend to evaluate a capability by checking off, say, the number of engineers. That may work, but an engineer is not an engineer is not necessarily an engineer, to paraphrase Gertrude Stein. Not only do individuals differ, but design engineers bring to product development a very different set of skills than do manufacturing engineers.

Each partner in this joint venture knew at least enough about product development to enumerate the steps necessary for taking a product concept through manufacturing. At each step in the development process, they might have asked: What does our capability look like at this point? Do we have all four dimensions covered? Such a conscientious comparison of the knowledge possessed by the joint venture with the knowledge required in order to perform effectively at each step might have revealed, for instance, the lack of computer-aided-engineering equipment and skills to deliver tooling plans—all of which became painfully obvious when the project was already committed to an exhibition at a critical appliance show. When such gaps are uncovered, fingers start pointing in every direction except toward self.

Pinpoint the Location of Knowledge. Even if the targeted acquisition has demonstrated the desired capability in past projects, the challenge remains to determine just where the know-how resides. In equipment? Software? Procedures? The heads of a few key individuals? Failure to commit resources to "due diligence" exploration of an acquisition in a financial sense would be highly unusual. Acquisitions usually involve hordes of lawyers examining the legal and financial status of the proposed acquisition with enormous care. Who is capable of conducting an equivalent due diligence examination of the technical capabilities being acquired? Certainly not the lawyers. In fact, technical due diligence usually requires a detailed understanding of operations, including equipment and processes. Further, the really important knowledge may not be physically embodied at all. Consider the case of E-L Products.

E-L PRODUCTS

E-L Products (ELP), a division of Astronics, was by 1986 one of four leading manufacturers of electroluminescent lamps. The flat, lightweight, pliable, and almost heatless lamps, which could conform to any curved surface, were used in special applications such as airplane cockpits and automobile dashboards. In 1988, ELP was offered the opportunity to acquire a competitor, Grimes, which sold into the same market segments. After a two-day visit to the Grimes site, the managers of research and development, engineering, and sales and marketing returned highly impressed with what they had seen. Grimes had many more formally educated engineers than ELP, newer coating equipment, and a very sophisticated computer-aided design system. Its lead times were shorter, its work-in-process inventories appeared much lower, its lamination area produced dust-free lamps (no spots), and Grimes was successfully using a GE-patented coating suspension that ELP had abandoned five years earlier in favor of its own chemistry; ELP technicians could not make the GE formulation work reliably.

After the acquisition, Grimes operations were moved to ELP, the purchased equipment was set up, and a series of unfortunate discoveries followed. The "new" machinery actually had secondhand parts inside. Moreover, the Grimes equipment worked fine while under the supervision of the Grimes lamination operator, who came for a couple of months to train ELP employees, but once she left, they started producing defective lamps. When ELP employees opened boxes of finished goods inventory from Grimes, they found that 80 percent had delamination problems. Finally, the GE-patented chemicals proved too expensive to use.

ELP managers realized to their chagrin that they had not investigated below the surface of the apparently superior Grimes capabilities. Their most knowledgeable equipment engineer did not go on the two-day visit to Grimes. They assumed that finished goods were salable, so they did not inspect any. Finally, impressed by the formal education of Grimes engineers, ELP managers had not noticed that some of the most critical operating knowledge was in the heads of line employees—whom they had not moved to the new site.

Sources: Johanna M. Hurstak and Oscar Hauptman, "E-L Products (A)," "E-L Products (B)," and "E-L Products (C)," cases 691-013, 691-014, and 691-015, Harvard Business School, Boston, 1990.

The sad saga of E-L Products should be highly unusual—but it is not. Often the haste to "do the deal," the excitement surrounding the impending marriage, the preoccupation with the financial details—all occupy the time and resources that should be devoted to some up-front planning and design for implementation.[72] Planning for stock exchanges and staging the event for Wall Street take precedence over factory tours. Operating expertise is relegated to a back-row seat as the financial wizards do their magic center stage. However, after the show is over and someone has to merge the disparate capabilities, gaps are recognized and incompatibilities identified. As ELP also illustrates, there is a tendency to underestimate the importance of knowledge held by key people in an operation, especially if they are not of visibly high status.[73]

Manage *Learning* Investments

Having looked at two situations in which the partners did *not* in fact have all the complementary knowledge sets expected or needed, let us now turn to a case in which the parts of the capability *did* exist. The marriage was still initially rocky, but both sides persisted, with the expectation that their investment in learning would pay off.

PLUS DEVELOPMENT CORPORATION

Plus Development Corporation was set up in 1984 as a joint venture between computer disk drive maker Quantum Corporation and VCR manufacturer Matsushita Kotobuki Electronics. The JV product was a "hard card," a small, easily installed disk drive that IBM PC owners could use to convert their machines to the storage capacity of the PC-XT introduced by IBM in 1983—at a fraction of the cost. As an OEM supplier to computer makers, Quantum had strong design capabilities but lacked expertise in volume manufacturing for a retail market. MKE's volume production of VCRs demonstrated tremendous capabilities in electromechanics and manufacturing.

The partners soon discovered that although sets of knowledge may be complementary, it does not mean they fit together as effortlessly as pieces in a jigsaw puzzle. The Japanese required seemingly endless design details of their partners, at a level of specificity to which Quantum engineers were totally unaccustomed. "Less than 10 millimeters" was not good enough; the Japanese needed to see "9.8 millimeters." Moreover, the MKE engineers required design changes to enhance manufacturability, even when the changes did not significantly impact the cost goals. An important market window (Christmas and end-of-year) was imperiled as the MKE engineers focused on getting the specifications perfect. The Quantum engineers in

---

charge of Plus Development despaired as they saw the schedule slip; some questioned the value of this quest for perfect manufacturability, given the time pressures. However, both sides persevered.

The first payoff from the tremendous effort both sides had put into knowledge exchange came when the Hardcard hit the market on time; the up-front design for manufacturability had shaved weeks off the usual problem fixing at the end and enabled instant ramp-up to full-volume production. Moreover, the Hardcard was a market success, being both reliable and low-cost. The second payoff arrived when the basic product concept turned out to be so easily imitated with cheaper, much less elegant designs that within twelve months of launch, the product was challenged by forty-five competitors! The Hardcard's advantage turned out to be that it used only one of the limited number of expansion slots available in PCs, whereas the competitive products required two. This superior design was the product of Quantum's design skill and MKE's abilities to produce miniaturized electromechanical parts—a joint capability that none of the competitors could imitate.

A third very important payoff appeared when MKE helped launch the parent company into a new generation of disk drives. By 1987, Hardcards were contributing 54 percent of Quantum's sales and all of its profits; the company had lost all but two of its customers when the standard shifted from 5¼-inch to 3½-inch disks in disk drives and Quantum was late into the market. The managers who had run the JV switched attention back to the parent company. They brought in MKE to revamp Quantum's whole design process so that the small disks could be assembled by robots. Once again, MKE's attention to manufacturability brought new meaning to the term *painstaking.* After four months, the Quantum engineers "were ready to quit." But they once more persevered, and MKE invested about $150 million in an automated line. Of the disks assembled at MKE, 97 percent needed no rework, compared to 90 percent for most competitors. By 1991, Quantum had "among the highest gross margins in the industry, even after MKE's cut."[74] Although Quantum went on to produce its highest-performance disk drives itself in California, it retained its relationship with MKE, which produces all disk drives below a certain (constantly increasing) capacity.

Sources: Nan S. Langowitz and Steven C. Wheelwright, "Plus Development Corporation (A)" and "Plus Development Corporation (B)," cases 687-001 and 689-073, Harvard Business School, Boston, 1986. Joint copyright with Stanford University.

MKE's obsession with manufacturability imposed a discipline on the knowledge exchange that most joint ventures do not possess. Moreover, the company was willing to have its engineers invest months away from home in educating the U.S. designers about the requirements for manufacturability in a high-volume market. However, Quantum's managers also deserve credit for recognizing the complementarity of MKE's expertise and for their faith—in the face of tremendous competitive pressures—that a superior product and production process would win in the marketplace, even if it took a bit more time to factor in high quality.

Both GE Plastics and Quantum selected noncompetitive partners, thus avoiding the problem of overlapping capabilities. The closer the joint activities are to the partners' strategic cores, the more likely managers are to opt instead for licensing, cross-marketing, or other more easily controlled relationships.[75] Ultimately, joint ventures cannot depend on written agreements, however well constructed. A researcher who studied 492 joint ventures observed: "Firms could be as crafty as they pleased in writing clauses to protect technology rights, but the joint venture's success depended on trust."[76] Since knowledge leakage is inevitable when technical personnel from both firms are working together, joint ventures are obviously easier to manage if the partners' capabilities are complementary rather than competing.

The GE Plastics and Quantum cases illustrate the findings of researchers: managers initially entering joint ventures tend to be somewhat naive about the partnerships. They expect few minimal conflicts and believe the JVs are "forever." In both examples, the managers really worked at the relationships. The fact that Quantum's knowledge investment repaid the parent organization much more than did GEP's was probably attributable to the fact that the complementarity of capabilities was much stronger to begin with—and that it was a very much larger investment by the parent company.

Managers in firms with extensive experience in alliances learn to expect changes in their relationships.[77] The more extensive the knowledge swap, the more difficult it is to outline every contingency and detail of interaction in advance. Although most alliances are temporary, "cooperative partnerships often have unpredictable ways of succeeding."[78] These observations mesh with findings about implementation in general. As emphasized in Chapters 4 and 5, detailed planning is fine unless the terrain ahead is uncertain—and when is it not? Road maps are useless if the destination turns out to be undesirable. On the other hand, as we have learned, simply trusting that benefits will blossom from a relationship started for unclear reasons is also foolish. Managers who have overseen many knowledge-importing relationships steer a middle ground, striving from the beginning for clarity of objectives, roles, time frames, and capabilities. At the same time, they constantly revisit the relationships to make certain that the assumptions underlying the original objectives still hold in an evolving environment. Selecting, managing, and exiting technological alliances are skills improved by experience—if managers deliberately set out to improve them.[79]

Summary

Even companies with extensive internal research capabilities need to tap into complementary external sources of technology. This chapter has focused on companies' absorptive capacity—the ability to identify, access, and use technology from a wide variety of sources. The activity of importing knowledge starts with identifying gaps in core capabilities—i.e., technological knowledge that is strategically important but unfamiliar within the company. Such gaps may arise for many reasons, three of the most important of which are: (1) a deliberate corporate policy to lessen internal research, (2) sizable advances or discontinuities in a given technology, or (3) newly identified opportunities for technology fusion. Sources of technology to plug such gaps mentioned in this chapter include universities, national laboratories, and other companies. Herein we have also reviewed a variety of sourcing mechanisms available to managers, ranging from the relatively low commitment of a research contract at one extreme to the major investment of a merger or an acquisition at the other. All of these mechanisms can be problematic under some circumstances, and none is invariably more successful than the others.

All require attention to a common set of critical managerial issues. Firms cannot access knowledge from outside sources passively; importing technology requires enormous effort. Building a capability with the help of such sources requires a set of skilled activities, including rendering the organizational boundaries porous by scanning broadly and continuously for technological opportunity, identifying and effectively using those employees who serve as technological gatekeepers and boundary spanners, and combating the not-invented-here syndrome. Managers also need to close the gap between the technology as it exists at the source and the form needed to augment internal capabilities, trade off desirability against transferability, and evaluate the technology. This last activity includes assessing the technology's potential and the level of expertise that the source possesses in that technology as well as identifying the location of the actual knowledge required—be it in people's heads or in systems. The chapter concluded with an example of a case in which two partners deliberately managed a joint venture for cross-boundary learning, with very positive results.

Today's managers are better trained in competitive behavior than in cooperation. Cooperative situations require different skills and perspectives. Managers must therefore continuously probe their organizational boundaries to determine how porous they are to admitting the influx of external knowledge—how adequately their firms can access external wellsprings of technological knowledge. In the next chapter, we will consider the market as an equally important source of product inspiration and knowledge.

CHAPTER SEVEN

Learning from the Market

Market research just hasn't delivered. It has been an embarrassment.
—Jim Figura
  Vice President, Colgate-Palmolive Company[1]

Meno . . . see what a tiresome dispute you are introducing. You argue that a man cannot enquire either about that which he knows, or about that which he does not know; for if he knows, he has no need to enquire; and if not, he cannot; for he does not know the very subject about which he is to enquire.
—*Dialogues of Plato*[2]

The growth and nurturing of core technological capabilities require constant fertilizing by streams of information. Of these, none is more important to a technology-based firm than knowledge flowing in from the market, for this information shapes science into commercial product or service. (See Figure 7-1.) Although new-product development projects serve as the channels through which market information irrigates technological capabilities, many innovations fail in the market. In fact, statistics on new-product development in the United States are grim. On average, as much as 46 percent of all resources devoted to product development and commercialization is spent on products that are canceled or fail to yield adequate financial returns.[3] One report estimates that for every one hundred projects that enter development, sixty-three are canceled, twenty-

Figure 7-1 Knowledge-Creating Activities: Importing Knowledge from the Market

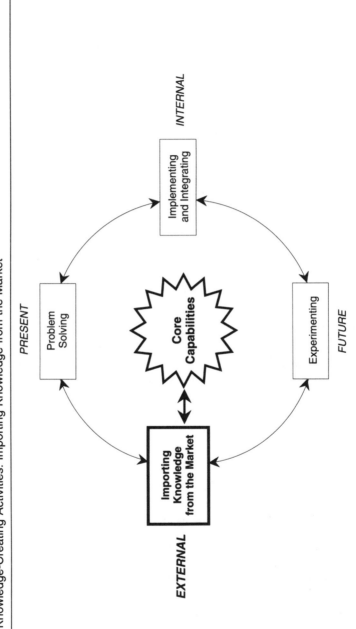

five become commercial successes, and twelve are commercial failures.[4] At the same time, some companies boast a success rate of 70 percent to 80 percent in new-product launches[5]——which suggests it is possible to beat the averages through a superior product development process. A principal component of that process is the ability to import knowledge from the market.

A study of 252 product development projects in 123 firms discovered that preliminary market assessments were conducted in successful product development projects; however, formal market studies, done in only a quarter of the projects, were usually rated as "poorly handled." Moreover, the studies tended to be reactive competitive comparisons in over a fourth of those projects. There were almost no concept tests—i.e., studies of customer reactions to a proposed new product in concept form. Less than a fifth of the project teams studied what customers actually wanted or needed, to generate product specifications. Finally, at least as much detailed market research was done for the failed projects as for the successful ones.[6] It would appear that merely increasing emphasis on market research in itself does not lead to better understanding of user needs and a higher probability of product success.

In the numerous studies of product success and failure over the years, consensus has developed that understanding user needs is a key factor leading to commercialization success.[7] Yet that observation is not easily translated into action.

This chapter addresses the question, What sources and channels can be developed to feed market information into new-product development projects? Companies differ as to the variety and number of mechanisms they are capable of deploying to anticipate customers' needs and desires. Well-established market research techniques, and especially quantitative ones, will receive relatively little attention here, because they are well understood, widely taught in marketing curricula, and generally available to everyone who can afford to pay for them. They are therefore less likely to be part of a core technological capability—i.e., to confer a unique, sustainable competitive advantage. Hence, although cutting-edge market research techniques in the traditional mold are mentioned, the discussion in the following pages emphasizes importing knowledge from the market under conditions of considerable uncertainty and using nontraditional techniques. More art than science, these techniques are a powerful addition to a company's market intelligence activities. They also avoid some of the hazards associated with listening closely to the market.

New-Product Definition Situations

Most companies are faced with a variety of new-product definition situations—each requiring a different range of information to be imported from the market. Figure 7-2 suggests that two basic factors shape these situations—the maturity of the technological design underlying the product line and the degree of alignment between the proposed product line and the current customer base. Variance along these two dimensions determines the level and types of uncertainty that new-product developers face and consequently the types of information needed.

Technological Design Maturity within a Firm

The translating of science into technology and the subsequent embedding of that technology in products follow a kind of life cycle. When science is being first harnessed to practical purposes of work or play, and the proposed product is completely novel to the world (top of the vertical axis in Figure 7-2), the developer's primary concern is, Can I make it work? Can I invent solutions to the problems intervening between understanding the technology's potential and realizing it in a commercially viable product or service? Once

Figure 7-2 Technology and Market Factors Shaping the New-Product Definition Situation

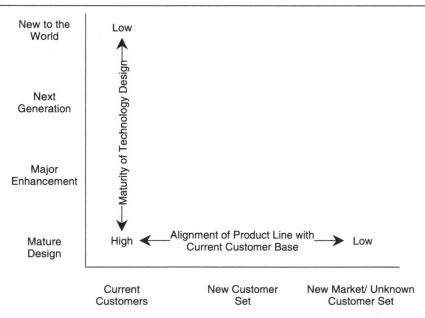

technical feasibility is proved at some level of benefit for customers, the challenge is always to produce the next generation, the next leap in performance. However, while one team of developers focuses on that innovation, usually another team simultaneously seeks enhancements and refinements to the basic design embodied in the first line of products. Therefore, redesigns emerge with increasing frequency as one moves down the axis toward mature design, where "new and improved" usually entails a change that is more cosmetic than fundamental. That is, at the bottom of this vertical axis, the development question has become, What minimal technological innovation will maintain or improve our status?

In established firms, the pressure of competition influences movement up the vertical axis, but the pressures of internal organizational routines (and as discussed later, of current customer sets) push developers down the vertical, toward incremental improvements on basic and mature designs. Once a firm commits to producing a given product for a given set of customers, the engineering, design, and manufacturing capabilities around production of products conform to or are complementary with that design. All organizational functions invest in developing specialized capabilities. Furthermore, there is a sequential logic to design decisions. Once a "dominant design" is established in an industry, overall architecture prescribes and constrains the design of parts and components.[8] This architecture has been called the "design hierarchy" in recognition of the fact that early basic design choices drive innumerable subsequent, more detailed ones. Drawing upon the development of the automobile engine as an example, Clark notes that "the choice of a core concept creates a set of given conditions with which other parameters must deal."[9] For example, because the gasoline engine predominated over both steam- and electricity-powered vehicles by 1902, that dominant design then affected the way the engine was started and fired, how valves and camshafts were placed, and so forth. Automobile companies then invested in accumulating expertise about those parts—expertise that would have been quite different had electric cars emerged as dominant instead. Once again, as we have seen throughout the book, it is this investment in knowledge building that makes a switch to a totally different skill base so difficult and resource-intensive.

Of course, the life of a dominant design can be long or short, and eventually, it is likely to be challenged. For example, the long-anticipated electric engine for cars is finally beginning to emerge, driven by regulation.[10] The life cycle has restarted, and the major U.S. car companies have gone back to the top of the design hierarchy to reopen technological questions not asked for decades. Some of their solutions will be new to the world, and companies will find themselves in the unaccustomed position of being at the top of the vertical axis in Figure 7-2. Neither their current technology development routines nor their current market information techniques prepare them well for that exploration. Indeed, their current development capabilities are, to some degree, rigidities in producing a car that is new to the world.[11]

Market Alignment

The second dimension of Figure 7-2 is the degree to which the proposed product aligns with the desires and needs of the current customer base. Assuming that a product's performance in the market is satisfactory enough to warrant further investment, reasonably simple product enhancements for current customers can be highly profitable. The left-hand side of the axis is therefore likely to be the easiest to manage. The major question guiding the import of knowledge from the market is simply, What features do our current customers need and want in our product line? At this side of the spectrum, we know our customers quite well. Our channels of information from the market are well established and our sources clearly identified.

Again, this well-developed capability can constitute somewhat of a rigidity, in that information imported from current customers about their immediate needs is not always a good guide for nurturing capabilities that will serve the corporation in the future. In an extensive study of the computer disk drive industry, Christensen researched four architectural transitions represented by the reduction in disk diameter from 14 inches to 8 inches, 5.25 inches, 3.5 inches, and 2.5 inches. Each reduction entailed not only "shrinking" individual components but rearchitecting the relationships of components within the system, and each reduction was most attractive to producers of different types of computers (minis, micros, laptops, and palmtops).

These architectural changes tended to be introduced by new firms entering the market rather than by established firms, Christensen noted. A primary reason was the disinterest of *existing* firms' customers in the smaller disks: "The sluggishness or failure of established disk drive manufacturers faced with architectural changes seems rooted . . . in the inability of their *marketing and administrative* organizations to find customers who valued the attributes of the new-architecture drives . . . not . . . because their architecture-related *engineering* knowledge was rendered obsolete. . . . Rather, the changes in product architecture seem to have rendered obsolete the established firm's knowledge of *market*. . . ."[12] That is, the very intensity with which firms served their current users' needs led those firms to be blindsided by a new generation of technology that served a different market. In the very few cases in which the new technological architectures did appeal to the firms' current customers, existing rather than entrant firms dominated. For example, Conner Corporation was able to make a "very smooth transition into 2.5–inch drives" [from 3.5–inch] because the smaller disks appealed to current customers.[13] Such observations suggest that technology-based companies will always have to move to the right on this horizontal axis, seeking new customers and perhaps even new markets.

In his book *Mobilizing Invisible Assets,* Hiroyuki Itami[14] notes that there are three different kinds of customers, each contributing differently to a firm: (1) customers who generate profit, (2) customers who will generate sales growth, and (3) customers who allow the accumulation of invisible assets. Itami suggests that every company would wish to have a balanced mix of customers, so that the revenue-generating ones may tide the company over financially while other less profitable markets generate important knowledge for the future. The choice of customer can therefore lock a firm into undesired paths—or open up opportunities. Hunger for profit alone can obscure the need to consider the long-range implications of the choice. On the other hand, considering *only* the potential long-term benefits of working with a particular set of customers can obviously cause a company to miss payrolls. Although there is no one-to-one correspondence between Itami's three categories and the customer sets suggested across the horizontal axis of Figure 7-2, Christensen's observations in the disk drive industry suggest that development of *new* "invisible" knowledge assets—new technological capabilities—will be stimulated by customer sets falling toward the right-hand side of the figure, not current customers.

The concomitant observation is that market uncertainty increases as one moves to the right, climaxing in the frontiers of new-market creation, where new-product developers cannot be certain they have even identified the correct set of users as they undertake design. At this end of the axis, the major questions facing new-product development often are: Who will benefit from using this technology? Who is the customer? As we shall see, the activities in which a firm engages to import knowledge from the market vary tremendously depending on where the product under consideration lies on this horizontal axis.

New-Product Development at the Extremes

At the extreme corners of the matrix formed by these two axes, the new-product development situation looks very different. Figure 7-3 suggests five generic situations: (1) user-driven enhancement; (2) developer-driven

Figure 7-3 New-Product Development Processes at the Extremes

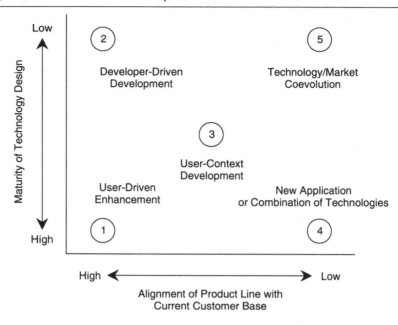

development; (3) development inspired by the user context or user environment; (4) technology transfer from another application or combination of technologies into a system; and (5) technology and market coevolution—i.e., market creation. Each of these archetypal situations is described below, with examples.

User-Driven Enhancement (An Improved Solution to a Known Need). Competition or explicit customer demands often drive technological improvements along known performance parameters for current products. In such cases, with or without extensive market research, developers know that lower costs, more features, or better quality are likely to win in the marketplace. HP's Signal Analysis Division, which produces spectrum analysis devices for testing and analyzing radio-frequency and microwave signals, had traditionally competed on product quality and performance rather than price. However, in the mid-1980s, the commercial market expanded, particularly at the low end, where Japanese offerings threatened HP products. Although a low-cost spectrum analyzer existed in the laboratory, there was little interest in commercializing it until an R&D manager returned from a plant visit with a customer in Italy; the customer pointed out that the Japanese had produced a "low-cost" product with features comparable to HP's "high-priced" spectrum analyzer. HP then embarked on its "Hornet" project. Intent on bringing it to market within eighteen months, the team nonetheless took time to conduct what was then a totally unprecedented price study. Moreover, marketing personnel accompanied engineers on customer visits to assess user needs, although R&D maintained responsibility for product definition. The "Hornet" met both cost and schedule goals and was a marketplace success.[15]

Less successful was the Hewlett-Packard 150, an early attempt to produce a personal computer. The day after HP introduced the HP120, a terminal for use with the HP3000 minicomputer, IBM introduced its first PC. HP responded by changing the project charter for the HP150, a follow-on to the 120. Rather than simply being a terminal, the 150 was now expected to have enough computing power to stand alone and be capable of supporting MS-DOS, the operating system for the IBM PC. One of the problems the development team faced was that the targeted customer set was new (farther to the right on the horizontal axis of Figures 7-2 and 7-3). However, the original marketing plan for the HP150, which viewed the product solely as a terminal for the HP3000, was not altered. Thus, the product development team continued to optimize the performance characteristics suitable for the customers originally envisioned. As a terminal, the HP150 was quite successful; as a personal computer it was never profitable.[16]

In both these HP cases, the developers established user needs in reactive mode: the competition defined the meaningful parameters on which the development team then attempted to achieve parity if not superiority. There were definite benchmarks against which to design. The challenge lay in identifying the right set of users to interview. This process was much easier for the spectrum analyzer than for the personal computer because the analyzer customers were very clear about what they needed in the next HP product. In contrast, at the dawn of personal computing, terminal users were still wedded to powerful centralized systems. They were very clear about their needs for the next machine connecting them to mainframes; they were not prescient enough to guide HP into distributed processing or aid in making design trade-offs.

Developer-Driven Development (A New Solution to a Known Need). Potential users' ability to translate their felt needs into a request for a particular solution decreases from bottom to top of Figure 7-3 because the relationship between their needs and the potential for a given technology to satisfy them becomes increasingly obscure. Users may have a need for which they cannot imagine a solution if they don't know about a particular technological advance. Users cannot see their world through the eyes of the technologist and therefore cannot know what solutions, functions, enhanced features, or capabilities a technology may offer. They could not ask for the solution because they do not know that the technological potential exists. However, a current need in the marketplace can be obvious to developers—even in the absence of direct competition or customer demand—just from their knowledge of current cost or functionality barriers to usage. The developers may know the users' work practices so well they can anticipate an unspoken need.

Developers may proactively decide to "delight" their customers with leaps in performance that no competitors have attempted and no users have directly requested. The challenges of pushing beyond current technical barriers can be very significant. In the early 1980s, HP was the leader in gas chromatography, an old, mature market. In about 1983, managers in the analytical business decided on a bold target: a chromatograph with one-third the components of the current model and three times the quality—for one-third the price. Such a product was not just a logical enhancement of the current chromatograph. The design required a tremendous leap in performance. In fact, it "wasn't even on the same price/performance curve," yet the developers "knew in their hearts" that the customers would want it.[17] Customer forums and site visits to observe user practices helped developers identify critical features. As expected, the product was highly successful, not only in its traditional market but, because of its lower cost, in new application areas. It reached the current customer set but also extended into a new one.

User-Context Development (A New Solution to an Unexpressed Need). User needs may exist for years before a technological solution is presented, of course. For instance, a secretary who had always followed the traditional practice of using paper clips to attach notes to sheets of paper once argued passionately that had anyone watched her frustration with this highly unsatisfactory way to interact with others, the critical need for the famous 3–M Post-it Notes would have been obvious. However, she admitted that she herself would never have been able to conceive of an adhesive with just the right amount of stickiness to adhere temporarily and without leaving a residue—and therefore could never have offered guidance for product specification. In this case, the user need was so pent-up that Post-it notes met with success way beyond any expectations. But users had little ability to communicate that need in a form that could guide product development since they did not know what *could* be done. Before the technical system exists, people have a hard time imagining either its form or its function. The general public never demanded computers and even a decade ago could say little about what shape and function should characterize a mouse to move a cursor around on a screen.

In such cases, the two kinds of knowledge that, combined, would result in a new product are held in separate domains by individuals who are unlikely to interact on their own. When developers immerse themselves in a user environment, the possibilities inherent in the user context drive product development.

New Application or Combination of Technologies (A Novel Solution to an Identified Need). This fourth situation is akin to the second: technology potential rather than market demand drives product development. However, in the second situation, the target was current users. In the present situation, developers take an application of technology that is mature and well understood in one domain and apply it to an entirely different one—for a totally new set of users. This often involves technology transfer across industries.

Consider the case of polyurethane-based casts for setting broken bones. The technology originated with a company producing polyurethane coatings for roofs. Once hardened, the foam constituted a lightweight but very durable and insulating covering to protect roofs from the elements and was especially popular for flat roofs in temperate climates. Managers seeking more applications for their patented material could see its medical potential; however, the company had no entry into the market, no distribution   and no interest in getting into this totally foreign business. It therefore licensed the technology to a major medical supplies company, for which the light weight and initially extreme flexibility of the material offered tremendous advantages over traditional plaster-of-paris settings.

An example of a transfer of technology from military to commercial applications is the fish locator used by sport fishermen to identify the location of schools of fish in lakes and oceans. The underlying technology, underwater sonics, was developed for military applications such as pinpointing the location of submarines. The first fish locators were available as Heath kits for depth sounders, but they were not easy to assemble or operate. In 1971, Techsonic Industries, maker of the Humminbird depth sounders, introduced its first model to the American fishing public and netted an immediate market success. This initially very simple product has spawned a line of now highly sophisticated pieces of equipment, including liquid crystal displays, produced by several competing companies.

Technology/Market Coevolution (An Evolving Solution to an Uncertain Need). At times, technologists run far ahead of consumers by developing an application for which they initially target the wrong market. Although such an ad hoc process of invention or discovery is obviously expensive and inefficient, it has also resulted in some of the most revolutionary and arguably the most beneficial products the world has experienced, such as xerography. Technology always offers more possibilities than can be recognized and commercialized. Examples range from establishing paternity through DNA tests of blood samples (not the most obvious application of the discovery of DNA) to holographic greeting cards (not the most profound application of holograms).

Such cases are often called (disparagingly) "technology push," in recognition of the fact that technical possibility preceded any known user need. Laboratories and the basements of home inventors are full of failed solutions to unknown problems. However, the negative connotation of the phrase is misleading in two ways. First, there are many products on the market for which no user felt or expressed a need but that embody no technology. The notorious "Pet Rock" sold in the 1970s perhaps exemplifies "sellers' push." Second, of course, there are many extremely well known inventions for which there was initially no user demand but that many people today would insist they need, such as xerography or Post-it pads.

Sometimes need and solution evolve together. Two widely used technologies that started life in quite different forms at IBM were shaped by trial and error and through the brutal help of internal corporate selection processes and the marketplace. The voice mail systems so ubiquitous today originated at IBM when a remote dictation system was designed so that traveling managers could relay their correspondence back over telephone lines to a pool of specially skilled typists in a manuscript center. The so-called Advanced Dictation System was not used as expected. Both managers and documentation preparation people disliked it. However, people started sending messages back to their secretaries using the system, which was consequently retitled the Audio Distribution System. In the early 1970s, this system became the Speech Filing System—the prototype of current voice mail.[18]

The reduced instruction set chip (RISC), also widely used today, similarly started life in a very different form. In the early 1970s, when the eventual intersection of telephones and computers was foreseen, researchers at IBM saw a clear need to apply digital computing technology to digital switching for telephones. Since such switches have extremely long lives, the computer software that underlay their design needed to be structured so as to evolve. Moreover, the hardware needed to be scalable. The computer architecture invented to meet this need was not used for this original purpose because of IBM business decisions but was generalized and extended for less specialized uses. It became the basis, in the mid-1970s, for what is known today as RISC architecture. Thus, a project originally aimed at helping IBM get into the telephony business was the origin for the architecture that evolved into RISC.[19]

In this fifth situation pictured in Figure 7-3, there is a strong element of serendipity.[20] Technological potential and market need have to coincide in both time and place for the necessary synergy to occur. Companies may try to force that coincidence—that is, they may create the market when they present totally new products—but it is a risky business. In the emerging world of personal digital assistants, Apple's "Newton" burst upon the market with more fanfare than fans. Only 80,000 to 90,000 of the initial model were sold in the twelve months after its introduction in early August 1993; the company had expected to sell at least 250,000 the first year.[21] However, Apple helped create a market for other companies by raising public awareness that such appliances were technically feasible. Tomorrow had arrived. When Apple was criticized and satirized for pushing a product that was technically imperfect and fell far short of market projections, managers pointed out that in the mid-1980s, some of the first of Apple's extremely popular Macintosh computers had also "failed" in the marketplace. The "Lisa" failed despite attempts to redesign it into the Macintosh product line, and the Apple III had to be pulled from the market because of persistent hardware failures.

Importing Knowledge from the Market

At the same time that "listening to the customer" has become an important management mantra in many companies, the mechanisms for interacting with the market, and especially for obtaining guidance for new-product development, have come under fire. After growing at an annual average rate of 8 percent during the 1980s, inflation-adjusted revenues for the $2.4 billion market research industry declined starting in 1990.[22] Industry experts attributed the stall in growth to a number of trends. First was Americans' increasing reluctance to answer even "five minutes" of survey questions as supper congeals on the dinner table. More alarming was the inability of some amazingly esoteric computerized methods to deliver actionable information. However, importing knowledge from the marketplace is absolutely essential, whether the product concept is an apparently minor extension of a product already in store windows or the new-to-the world bonanza of an accidental discovery in the laboratory.

The different new-product development situations described above require different interactions with the market. The basic underlying information-gathering activity differs in emphasis. Communication of the product concept and elicitation of user reactions become progressively more difficult and potentially more expensive as the commercialization situation departs from market alignment (the lower-left quadrant of Figure 7-3) and moves toward market creation (the upper-right quadrant of the figure). In the following subsections, I first describe those interactions when the product line is well established and the customer base well known (situation 1 in Figure 7-3). Next, I turn to situations 2 and 4, when either technology *or* market is uncertain, and 3, when there is moderate uncertainty about *both*. Finally, I examine situation 5, market creation, when the customer base is uncertain and the technology still very immature.

Market Research Techniques: Inquiry

When the current customer set is targeted for an extension of a well-established product line (situation 1 in Figure 7-3), the major activity is *inquiry.* This is the province and strength of traditional market research tools—especially surveys and focus groups. (As I will note later, such traditional market tools *can* be employed in other situations, but as Figure 7-4 suggests, these apply best where market knowledge is most structured.)

Surveys, Focus Groups, and Mall Studies. When customers can refer to a known product, they can answer most questions about their preferences, and their responses are reasonably reliable guides to new-product development; therefore, surveys and focus groups can yield useful information. The so-called mall study, whereby a new product or prototype is taken to a shopping

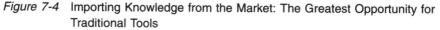

Figure 7-4 Importing Knowledge from the Market: The Greatest Opportunity for Traditional Tools

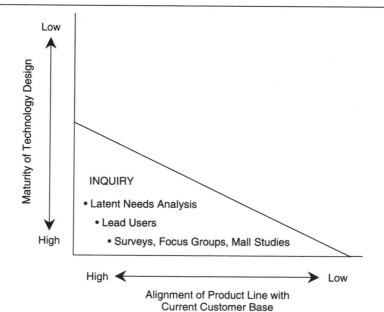

mall for testing and soliciting shoppers' reactions, exemplifies a more ambitious but widely used technique.

Because the product already exists in the market and users are familiar with its function, they are easily able to recognize some of their own needs and suggest improvements. For instance, drivers know what they like and dislike in cars and can be quite articulate in expressing preferences. Therefore, car companies are expert at very sophisticated market research on exactly what different market segments such as yuppies versus retirees desire. Such market research builds upon decades of experience. Consumers can be queried about everything from the obvious preferences in size and cost to such subtleties as engine sound, tightness of steering, and ability to "feel" the road. Designers at Nissan Design International even tested consumers' preferences for the smell of various kinds of leather in order to design for the olfactory preferences of Americans versus Japanese. In Nissan's search for the right leather smell for the Infiniti J30, the designers sniffed their way through some fairly offensive leathers—and discovered that they could articulate the responses of their nasal passages. "There are bitter leather smells," explains Gerald Hirshberg of Nissan Design International. "There are sweet leather smells. There are leather smells that should better have been left underneath a cow."[23]

Taking advantage of cutting-edge computer simulation capabilities, market researchers have even managed to compress within less than two hours an extensive consumer search for information about a desired car—collecting a huge amount of data about an individual consumer's preferences in the process. The "information accelerator" presents advertising, enables the prospective customer to "interview" by computer a selection of people who offer their opinions about the car, "visit" a showroom and look at the car from all angles with the click of a mouse—including close-up views of the dashboard or other features. The only thing a customer *can't* do is take an actual test drive! This interactive computer program collects information on everything the consumer does, from time spent reading or viewing different types of advertising, to choice of informants about the car.[24]

Despite the tremendous sophistication of such interviewing techniques, they can only uncover those needs and desires about which the informants are aware and can articulate. This is not to say, of course, that expert designers cannot conceive of improvements in ergonomics or function that would not occur to the average user and therefore contribute their expertise even at the lower-left segment of Figures 7-2 through 7-4. The point is rather that the *relative* ability of the users to guide product specification is greater when a product category already exists.[25]

Lead Users. Careful choice of customer representatives to query (through whatever techniques) can carry developers a step further into the future. Von Hippel suggests that for new products being introduced into the fast-moving high-technology industries, where new models may differ quite radically from old, so-called lead users may help guide development. Lead users have two characteristics: (1) they "face needs that will be general in a marketplace, but they face them months or years before the bulk of that marketplace encounters them; *and* 2) they are positioned to benefit significantly by obtaining a solution to those needs."[26] Von Hippel applied this concept to foretelling the needs of computer-aided design for designing high-density printed circuit boards. After developing a description of such a system based on lead users' preferences, von Hippel sent this description along with three others (including the "best commercial" system available at the time) to 173 users. Respondents strongly preferred the design generated by the lead-user group—even when it was priced higher than competing concepts.

Dialogue with lead users operates within one of the boundaries characteristic of the other techniques mentioned so far. At least the first generation of the product must already exist in the market—i.e., a referent product must exist. Lead users must be *users* of the existing technology in a practical form. They make their suggestions for improvements based on their experience with the current products in the market. Moreover, the needs of these lead users cannot be totally idiosyncratic but must be somewhat representative of future buyers. For instance, when solar water-heating panels first became available again in California, after a hiatus of many years when fuel was plentiful and cheap, the first few people to purchase were either extreme environmentalists who were committed to a life of "voluntary simplicity"—i.e., a lifestyle based on minimal resource consumption[27]—or individuals who had very particular needs, such as a health requirement to swim daily and, hence, the need to heat a private swimming pool. Neither of these initial adopter groups represented a large potential market and would not have served as good lead users.

Latent Needs Analysis. Some techniques are designed to probe users' desires less directly and thereby uncover latent and less readily articulated needs. An example is the "K-J" analysis, a highly structured brainstorming process for gathering and analyzing qualitative data. First developed by a noted Japanese anthropologist, Jiro Kawakita, it has been applied to quality improvement programs in Japan and the United States with the help of Professor Shoji Shiba of Tsukuba University and to "concept engineering" at the Center for Quality Management in Cambridge, Massachusetts.[28] Another example of systematic need elicitation is the proprietary Value Matrix used by a group of design houses, the Design Consortium, to uncover the often latent desires of a wide spectrum of user-stakeholders in a client firm.[29]

Current customers are often unable to articulate some desirable product attributes since they are unaware of their own psychological and cultural responses to symbols and forms. Recently, university researcher Gerald Zaltman has devised a technique that uncovers unarticulated, perhaps even unconscious, preferences among customers. The "Zaltman Metaphor Elicitation Technique" identifies the metaphors, constructs, and mental models that drive customers' thinking and behavior, allowing people to express feelings, thoughts, and intentions through visual images as well as words. This tool "brings to the surface ideas and information that customers are not always aware that they have or that they may find difficult to express."[30] Such techniques carry inquiry to the edges of the subconscious.

Market Research Techniques: Empathic Design

Situations located on the diagonal from upper left to lower right in Figure 7-3 (developer-driven development, user-context development, and a new application or combination of technologies) require techniques not usually taught in marketing courses. Often decried as "technology push" when they result in unacceptable products (and as "lucky" when they succeed), these situations offer the greatest opportunity to exploit existing technological knowledge in novel ways. Products developed with new technologies for old markets and familiar customers (developer-driven), the application of moderately mature technologies to new or evolving customer sets (user-context development), and old technologies renewed through their embodiment in different products (new applications)—all three can contribute significantly to the development of core technological capabilities and to the bottom line.

In all three of these situations, no directly analogous product is yet on the market—but potential users can be identified. The various techniques that match known technological potential with market need I have lumped together under the rubric *empathic design* (defined below). As suggested by the bulge in Figure 7-5 and by the discussion below, empathic design can be deployed to augment the development of product enhancements, but the major opportunities lie in those situations in which a technology can be shaped to meet an unarticulated but observable need. Empathic design is less applicable when either the target market is very well known (in which case, the users can be queried directly) or the user population is not yet identified (in which case, the observers do not know for certain with whom

Figure 7-5 Importing Knowledge from the Market—The Greatest Opportunity for Empathic Design

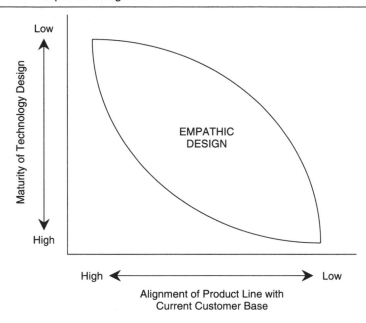

they should be developing empathy); however, even at these extremes, there are occasions when empathy is critical. On the other hand, as I will discuss later, the traditional market research tools already described are used to augment empathic design. Product concepts developed through empathic design must be tested and refined through customer feedback. The boundaries, in other words, are not as distinct as Figures 7-4 and 7-5 suggest.

Empathic design is the creation of product or service concepts based on a deep (empathic) understanding of unarticulated user needs.[31] The deep understanding may be created a number of ways, some of which are described below, but there are three important characteristics that set empathic design apart from other forms of market "research":

1. The product concept is based on *actual observed customer behavior* (versus espoused behavior, self-reported behavior, or opinions). The market research is thus totally behavioral rather than attitudinal. Because the user is observed *in situ*, the whole user "system" is directly observable. That is, both the context in which the user operates and the user's interdependencies with other people, equipment, or climate or physical surroundings can be determined. Moreover, even when customers are subject to inquiry, this kind of

intervention into the customers' behavior is instigated only *after* a period of observation.

2. Empathic design is usually conducted through *direct interaction* between those who have a deep understanding of the firm's technological capabilities (product developers such as engineers and designers) and the product users. As the examples below will illustrate, occasionally individuals other than the product developers collect behavioral observations about the customers, but these are communicated in qualitative rather than quantitative form and are often presented as raw data—not predigested by a specialized marketing function. The important point is that the user environment is absorbed by people who also have a deep understanding of the *potential* of a set of technologies.

3. Empathic design tends to draw on existing *technological capabilities* that can be somewhat redirected or imaginatively deployed in the service of new products or markets. It is possible, of course, that the observers of potential users will conceive of solutions requiring invention, but because at least some of the observers have technical knowledge, they know whether the new solution concept is "blue sky" or within the realm of possibility, given the firm's technological capabilities.

The mechanisms through which product developers induce empathy with users range from the serendipitous to the deliberate. The effort here is to identify ways of increasing the frequency of the latter. As Figure 7-6 shows, there are three major types of empathy-inducing mechanisms, each of which is discussed below.

Developer's "Market Intuition". Technologists who have developed a fine "intuition" for what the market wants now and will need in the future (top left of Figure 7-6) are responsible for some of our most successful businesses today (and some that have gone through a boom-and-bust cycle as well.) The myriad spin-offs from technology-based universities such as the Massachusetts Institute of Technology testify to technologists' optimism that such intuition can be either possessed or developed.[32]

USER-DEVELOPERS. A technologist's empathy with a user is obviously at its height when the two are one. Technologists who also happen to be potential customers of the products they build can integrate technological potential with user needs in a single head. Those who have experienced a problem apply technology to solve it.[33] Von Hippel has documented hundreds of cases in which users of industrial products were the primary inventors of a new tool or process.[34] Within companies in which professionals design for the market the same tools that they themselves use, there is less need for market research since the developers are twin to their customers. Historically,

Figure 7-6 Importing Knowledge from the Market—Empathic Design

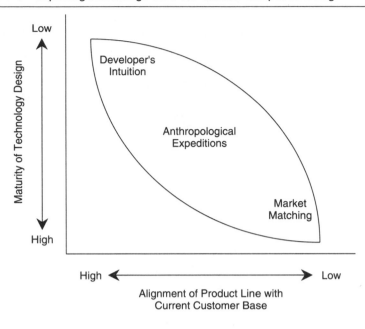

in both Hewlett-Packard and Digital Equipment Corporation, new-product ideas originated with the engineers who wanted such equipment for themselves. As we saw, HP's famous original calculator (HP 35, introduced in 1972) was born of Hewlett's desire to have an "electronic slide rule."[35] DEC's 3100 computer, the first workstation the company ever put on the market to challenge Sun's dominance, was built by a team that designed what team members themselves would like to use. At these companies, designing for the engineers on the "next bench" produced a strong stream of engineering tools that fattened the bottom line for years.[36]

Microsoft founders Bill Gates and Paul Allen started to immerse themselves in computers so early in life—and so intensely—that they were effectively born into the computer industry. Playing (and working) with computers from early high school days on, they were the quintessential nocturnal "hackers," who slept curled up under computer tables and emerged into the real world only when forced to by a lack of equipment, food, or hygiene (usually in that order of importance). Describing the phenomenal success that Microsoft experienced from the outset, early employee Steve Wood said, "One of the real keys, and this has always been true of Microsoft, was we were able to anticipate the markets pretty effectively. . . . We were always a year or two ahead of where the demand was really going to be. But we were generally guessing right. A lot of it was Bill's and Paul's ability to see where some of the stuff was going to go."[37] Gates and Allen knew what kinds of features and functions would place their software ahead in the market because they knew all the producers, the competitive products—and the users—so well.

What can companies do to stimulate such innovation? As suggested in Chapter 5, one way is to encourage their technologists to serve as internal markets, continually seeking the intersection of their needs as consumers with their knowledge as technologists. Kodak's popular inexpensive underwater camera was stimulated by a kayaking accident experienced by an engineer employee on a weekend trip. Had he not been provided with free film by the company in return for his feedback as a user, and had he not returned from the trip with wet film in a plastic sack, the idea might never have been born.

INDUSTRY EXPERTS. Industry experts serve as another lens into the user world. When the market shifts or the company moves into a market not represented by its development community, there arises the need to bring in former users to represent potential customers. For instance, at Hewlett-Packard, the product line manager for Mass Spectrometry and Infrared Spectroscopy Systems has a Ph.D. in organic chemistry, with a specialty in mass spectrometry. As he noted, "Most of our senior managers have been born and raised in the [analytical chemistry] business. . . . When we speak with customers, the full implications of every word are immediately relevant to us. . . . We can feel the pulse of the customer."[38]

A potential problem with experts hired in from the user world is that they can become so enmeshed in daily business activities that they eventually lose touch with the cutting edge of the environment from which they came. Their crystal ball clouds over.[39] However, if, as in the HP case, the users-turned-developers maintain their ties with the old environment, they are valuable integrators of need and solution. They have a natural empathy with users.

In other cases, companies create industry experts deliberately. A highly profitable steel company (not Chaparral) has a market development group whose task is to entrench itself in the personal networks of the customer base it serves. Each member of the group is a walking compendium of several vital kinds of information—intense technical knowledge about certain alloys and their application; widespread personal contacts among industry experts and customer companies; deep knowledge about standard setting and regulation in his or her industry.

Such rich personal databases are the foundation of the experts' "intuition." They collect information about competitors' capabilities and technical advances in the scientific world. Their ability to sense where the market is headed is based on immersion in the user world. Their limitations as guides to capability development are therefore similar to those of the users whom they represent. They can lose their forward vision, become too narrowly focused, and adopt the same myopic view of the world that their users have. In short, they may "go native."

Another major management dilemma in creating industry experts is that their expertise is largely tacit and undocumented. Such tacit knowledge is difficult to evaluate financially since commercialization ideas planted in one year may not yield sales for five or ten; moreover, it is not easily codified or transferred. Selling activities tend to drive out marketing; the need to bring in dollars supersedes the need to import market knowledge. The impact of a current sale on the bottom line is much more visible and immediate than that of a *potential* sale. Therefore, unless the experts prove their immediate value by helping close sales in the customer realm with which they are familiar, they tend to be discounted as overhead. Yet if they are busy with sales, they have no time to develop the forward vision needed.

Market Matching.   Companies leverage their core technological capabilities by identifying applications for which users have a need but for which they would be incapable of imagining a solution because they do not know the technological potential exists (bottom right of Figure 7-6). The technologist's awareness of a market opportunity can arise from a deep familiarity with a given user environment (as in the case of the fish locator, described above) or from partnering with those who possess such familiarity (as in the case of the polyurethane casts). However, most companies are relatively passive in seeking such opportunities for leverage. Market matching occurs only if the organization is set up to encourage and reward active searching.

TECHNOLOGY TRANSFER.   Consulting companies have long understood that knowledge developed for one client constitutes a reservoir to be tapped in serving another, although not all are equally adept at institutionalizing the process of transfer. American Management Systems, a custom software house based in Virginia, routinely applies know-how, and often some portion of actual software code, developed for one market, to another. Of course, its technical expertise in software development, especially for the new client-server technology, can be used in a number of vertical markets, from telecommunications to pharmaceuticals. However, the technology transferred goes beyond the software languages and understanding of software architecture—which fall into the category of *public* knowledge mentioned in Chapter 1. Rather, the company develops the other two types of knowledge mentioned—*firm-specific* knowledge in one *industry*—encapsulates that expertise in software, and then extracts general principles, concepts, and some software routines for transfer to an application for a different client. So, for example, a lot of the expertise embodied in software systems developed to increase the effectiveness of financial institutions' credit-card collection systems turned out to apply very well to the needs of California's state tax-collection agency, the Franchise Tax Board.

This kind of awareness of the value of transferring knowledge between market domains is more rare in manufacturing firms. Harris Corporation is a remarkably resilient organization that has transformed itself over the years from an old-line printing press manufacturer into an electronics firm.[40] One of the powerful sources for growth in electronics capabilities, especially during the late 1970s and early 1980s, was technology developed for defense—and transferred into commercial product. In fact, Harris undertook government work only if it was related to existing product lines—or to a targeted future market. Examples abound.

Harris's first electronic newsroom terminals were spin-offs from an army battlefield message sender developed during the Vietnam War. Harris's laser facsimile machines profited from technology developed under a navy contract for satellite-to-ship communications. When Harris was expanding the electronic newsroom set up for the *New York Times*, the government systems group was called in to solve some intractable problems. John Hartley Jr., president during the heyday of defense contracting (1978–1986), was as clear as his predecessors about the need to set up managerial systems that supported such knowledge transfers. "Technology transfer is an unnatural process. Once you have divisions, you have barriers—people who follow their own interests. Unless you tell the managers of your business that part of their promotions, salaries and punishments will depend on technology transfer, nothing will happen."[41] Harris management emphasized that understanding the application of military technology to commercial markets was the route to the top by placing its best hirees in the government systems division and then each year transferring the top twenty or so of those into commercial divisions. The company's leaders have generally originated in that pool of talent. As a consequence of such clear management signals, technology has flowed across divisional boundaries, creating new products and sometimes new markets.

PARTNERING WITH CUSTOMERS. Another technique for matching technological capabilities to market needs is to partner with the market. Rather than bringing customers in-house to represent the user world, some companies have pursued a policy of commercializing their basic technologies through partnerships with customers. ALZA Corporation is noted for its nontraditional drug-delivery systems—that is, ways to deliver drugs into the blood-stream over time at a continuous rate. The corporation has patented transdermal patches and slow-release capsules that can deliver dosages of a wide variety of therapeutics. ALZA partners with specific customers to design customized delivery systems for a particular drug. For example, Janssen Pharmaceutical sells transdermal patches, for which ALZA tailored its membranes, to deliver a painkiller, Duragesic, for cancer patients. Similarly, ALZA partnered with Pfizer to deliver medicine for the treatment of angina; the medicine may be taken just once a day instead of three times. Such partnering with customers runs some risks (as suggested in Chapters 2 and 6): the partners can direct technology commercialization into narrow, self-serving niches. However, if a variety of customers are selected, partnering enables the widespread leverage of a base technology in diverse markets.

Anthropological Expeditions. The most unusual, and perhaps most promising, option for creating the deep understanding of the user world necessary for empathic design is for developers to immerse themselves in the user environment, much as anthropologists do when they inhabit villages in unfamiliar parts of the world. Next to converting users into developers, such anthropological expeditions (middle of Figure 7-6) are the most powerful aid to empathic design. Designers or developers with a thorough knowledge of technological potential live in the user environment long enough and absorb enough understanding of that environment to empathize with user needs. They see how users cope with unnecessarily inconvenient, uncomfortable, inefficient, or inaccurate tools and consider how to solve the unspoken problems. Product concepts derived through this process present users with functionality, ease of use, and other benefits for which they themselves would not have thought to ask. Several different types of anthropological expeditions are described below.

OBSERVING USERS' PRACTICES. Sandvik, a leading Swedish toolmaking firm, annually sends its R&D personnel to spend a few weeks with customers, to explore future problems with specialists in product and process development as well as in production.[42] One of the most famous industrial designers in U.S. history, Henry Dreyfuss, used to require his designers to live with whatever tool they were designing. They rode corn pickers and prowled factories. Similarly, today, Hewlett-Packard product developers in the medical division spend time in intensive-care units and hospital clinics. It was on such a visit that a product developer noticed the way that nurses, in the course of their duties, inadvertently blocked the surgeons' view of the television screen, which physicians used to guide their intricate work. The physicians had accepted the temporarily blocked view as an inevitable part of the surgery routine and did not even question its necessity—or recognize it as a problem. In an application of empathic design, the developer combined her observation with her knowledge of computer technology to originate a solution that would not have occurred to the physicians. The product designer conceived of a tiny screen mounted on a surgeon's helmet, to keep the image directly and constantly in view.

The anthropological expedition is the empathic design technique with the widest potential application. As the shape of the empathic design zone pictured in Figures 7-5 and 7-6 suggests, although empathic design is less applicable when markets are either very familiar or totally unknown, the techniques can still help develop product concepts at the extremes.

The creation of Thermos's new electric grill demonstrates how such expeditions can yield insights even in the design of new products within an existing category. The Lifestyle team not only set up the traditional focus groups, but team members visited people's homes and videotaped barbecues. To their surprise, it wasn't always Dad slaving over the grill; increasingly, it was Mom. Moreover, many cooks were getting very weary of the mess, smell, and smoke associated with charcoal, and they wanted something attractive (not just functional) to put on their expensive patio decks. When the team returned to Thermos headquarters, its product concept was very different from the products the company currently had on the market. Team members' observations of real people in real usage environments caused them to focus on the customer instead of the product—and that focus made the difference between another me-too black iron box with a gas grill built in and a very novel, handsome electric product. This example also exhibits another characteristic of empathic design: the cross-functional observation team included engineers who recognized an opportunity to draw upon in-house core technological capabilities to solve a previously intractable technical problem. Prior electric grills never got hot enough and therefore tended to bake rather than sear meat, thus defeating the whole purpose of an outside grill. The design imperative was to raise the temperature within the grill enough and sustain it long enough to sear the food and thus deliver a grilled taste. Thermos engineers accomplished this objective in two ways. First, they built the electric heating rod directly into the surface of the grill itself. Second, they drew upon a core technological capability of Thermos—its knowledge of vacuum technology—to create a domed vacuum top that traps heat within the grill.[43]

In a different type of anthropological expedition, Xerox has employed trained anthropologists and other behaviorists to investigate exactly how people actually interact with sophisticated copier machines and report their findings to the corporation as a whole. Such social scientists did not have to divide their time between observation and product development but served as the developers' eyes and ears. The market knowledge fed back to the product development teams differed radically from that obtainable through traditional market surveys. The behaviorists camped out in user territory with the mentality of zoologists observing animal behavior in the wild: they watched what people *did*—without intervening—and only afterward asked *why.* The anthropologists discovered that there were communities of practice—i.e., shared routines and approaches that grew up around the use and servicing of the machines. These explorations resulted in knowledge about users' assumptions and mental models that was very pertinent to machine design but had never before been systematically gathered.[44]

CAPTURING PRACTICE ON FILM (OR VIDEO). The lens through which user behavior is observed can be in a camera. The advantage here is twofold: (1) the images and behaviors can be stored, retrieved, and displayed; and (2) they can be played back to the users, for exploration and verification. Designers at Nissan Design International were overwhelmed by the visual information presented to them when a professional photographer displayed at a New York gallery his hugely enlarged candid shots of people in their cars around the United States. The photographs chronicled people's behaviors and, through the magnified camera eye, detailed the detritus left behind from prior actions—magazines, blankets, toys, and containers of every size and imaginable use, from coffee cups to chicken crates. NDI commissioned the photographer to travel throughout several large cities, capturing raw data for the designers—glimpses into the way people were using their cars and trucks. When he returned, the designers put the pictures up on the walls and began to absorb the meaning of what they saw. One thing they noticed was the number of people eating whole dinners in the car—even spaghetti![45]

In a medical instrumentation company, the development team designing a portable operating room for the military took this kind of observation a step further. Desiring to approximate real battlefield conditions, they approached a local trauma unit, whose members respond to emergency calls, seeking permission to accompany them and film their operations. At first, the paramedics were skeptical, explaining to the designers that they rigidly adhered to set procedures, which they could just as well describe and demonstrate without actual patients present. However, they allowed the filming. The film, as reviewed by both the trauma unit members and the designers, was extraordinarily revealing. In the emergency situations, with lives at stake, the paramedics in fact violated a number of their own rules of behavior. When standard procedures or certain use of equipment would have delayed treatment, the paramedics took shortcuts. By studying the shortcuts, the designers were able to identify barriers that might be removed through the application of technology. The trauma unit members themselves were amazed to see the difference between their actual behavior under stress and their espoused behavior—what they told others (and themselves) that they did.

ROLE-PLAYING THE FUTURE.   Some developers are using quasi-anthropological techniques to peer into the future, combining observation of behavior with subsequent role-playing. Developers designing equipment for a nursing home in the distant future improvised—and recorded—their own behavior, as they imagined it, were they the senior citizen clients in such a home. Through this empathic exercise, they combined their insights into client needs with their understanding of how technologies might make that future less bleak. At Interval Research, product designers spend days observing insurance salespeople in their offices, retirees in a nursing home, or a hairstylist in a salon. They take pages of notes and videotape the participants' activities. When they return to Interval, they role-play the participants' day to "try to live the electronic future" in the participants' shoes. When the participants to be recreated are much older, the researchers wear weights to slow their own younger reactions or thick-lensed glasses that simulate possible fogged vision. Researchers ask questions during these "informances" (meaning "information performances"). They try to imagine the hairstylist using a digital communicator or a retiree having a relative "visit" over interactive video.[46] This is an example of how empathic design can reach into the uppermost right-hand corner of the matrix in Figures 7-2 through 7-6. In such applications, however, *part* of the direct observation is necessarily of actors, of people playing the part of users in the future—not actual users today.

Combining Empathic Design with Traditional Market Research

As noted above, empathic design techniques are most useful in the process of creating new-product concepts—not in testing those concepts. Common to all the modes of empathic design described above is an attempt to maintain an open mind about how *unarticulated* user needs can be met. A key activity is observation, unfettered by direct inquiry—a pause for creative reflection before the product developer begins to ask for customer input. However, once a concept has been identified, potential customer feedback is important. That is, once empathic design techniques have identified possibilities that the users themselves would not have requested, more traditional techniques are employed to refine and test the concept. Prototypes are almost certainly essential in this process since the concepts may be so novel as to have no parallel in the current market. Such prototypes may need to include videos of simulated use or other techniques for displaying to customers the way that they might interact with the innovation in the future.

Market Research Techniques: Creating a New Market

Where neither technologies *nor* customers are certain, inquiry and user observation are impossible. Inquiry is impossible because even the technologists are not sure what product form the technology should take; for the same reason, and because no viable analogies exist, the very identity of the customers is in doubt. Therefore, information from the market must be sought through extrapolating from today to imagine a possible future or else seeking information through trial, error, and (ideally) success. (See Figure 7-7.)

Extrapolation of Trends.   By extrapolating societal, technological, environmental, economic, or political trends, developers attempt to foresee what users in a current market will need in the future when those trends mature, to anticipate a world none can confidently predict. To someone who understands both industry and societal trends, the needs themselves may be fairly obvious. Timing, however, is often extremely unclear. When will there be enough users or complementary technology or adequate infrastructure to justify development? Moreover, of course, the trends interact. For instance, society's

Figure 7-7   Importing Knowledge from the Market—Creating New Markets

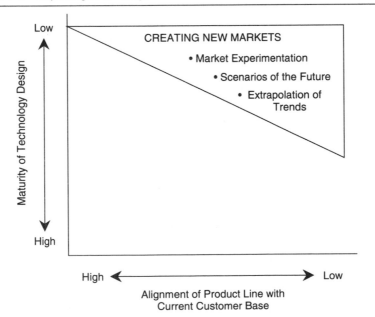

demand for faster, more proximate means of communication interacts with the technological trends that are driving computers to become commodities and communications to become wireless.

Researchers at Hewlett-Packard track a number of trends that may be harbingers of future markets. Long before fiber optics were a reality, or optical signaling technologies were on the market, HP was designing optical signal measurement equipment to be ready when its customers needed it. Three years before impending national heat-efficiency laws went into effect, specialty steel producer Allegheny Ludlum had a corrosion-resistant alloy on the market for its heating-equipment customers. The alloy, which was already used in power plants, reduced heat loss and thus helped heat-equipment producers meet national standards.[47]

Scenarios of the Future. Formal scenario-construction techniques extrapolate political, social, and environmental trends in different directions, to create pictures of alternative futures.[48] The intent of such scenarios is less to predict a future state exactly than to stimulate consideration of nonobvious futures, to force "out-of-the-box" thinking—to divorce thought from a straight, unwavering trend line. The limitation of market scenarios, however, is that they are intended only to provoke possibilities—not to predict the future with any assurance.

Yet they can still be useful to stimulate thinking about product design. Schwartz tells how Smith & Hawken, a mail-order garden tool business, sharpened its focus when the company decided, in the late 1970s, to consider possible futures. It constructed three scenarios: (1) "more of the same but better," (2) "worse" (decay and depression), and (3) "different but better" (fundamental change). The company determined that the first two scenarios both suggested direct mail as the best approach, since either people would be wealthy enough to buy but too busy to get to the store, or the market would disappear and capital-intensive retail operations would be highly risky. Scenario 3, fundamental change, implied a concern for the environment and distrust of throwaway tools. The 1980s turned out to be a mixture of the three scenarios, with both yuppie wealth and homelessness in the United States and a growth in concern for the environment. Although none of the scenarios exactly played out, the company was better positioned because its managers had thought through which steps to take under the various conditions.[49]

Market Experimentation. For short-lead-time items that can be quickly manufactured, many companies simply do not invest in crystal balls. Rather, as in the (admittedly messy) test for whether spaghetti is cooked, they throw the pasta against the wall and see what sticks. The great value of testing a fully functioning product in the real marketplace is, of course, the validity of the information received. Real users responding in real time to the real thing—what better guidance could one get for future promotions, advertising, and product improvements?[50] For companies with relatively inexpensive product lines, test marketing in a limited geographic area has always been an important weapon in the marketers' arsenal. Recently, however, some companies have begun to perceive such limited testing as dangerous: competitors are afforded time to imitate, and market feedback may be distorted. For instance, if a competitor blitzes the region with promotions or coupons at the same time that a company is conducting a market test, initial consumer response to the new product may not predict actual buying intentions over the long term. General Mills addressed this kind of problem by introducing Multi-Grain Cheerios in a portion of the Unites States too large to distort. Increasingly, consumer companies are rolling a product out either in a whole national region or in a foreign country. "You just go out and find out what happens," explains a researcher of this kind of market experimentation.[51] "Today, the bias is toward immediate action."[52]

The emerging personal digital assistant market exemplifies the necessity for market experimentation. In 1993, when John Sculley (CEO of Apple Computer at the time) announced the Newton architecture underlying Apple's MessagePad as "the defining technology of the digital age . . . a focal point for the coming convergence of . . . computers, communications and consumer electronics,"[53] there were already a number of competitive products on the market—and many more on the way. Each of the vendors attempted to convince consumers that it was offering the *true* blue-blooded PDA. However, the initial product offerings differed widely in both price and features. Some, like AT&T's EO 440 and 880, which differed chiefly in price and speed of performance, emphasized communication. A built-in microphone and speaker allowed voice annotation of documents; a built-in modem permitted both sending and receiving data; and an optional cellular telephone module made it a "complete wireless communications system."[54] Other PDAs, like Hewlett-Packard's 95LX and 100LX, were more like supercalculators, with the Lotus 1–2–3 spreadsheet built in; HP advertised its product as the "road warrior's weapon of choice." No one was certain what features would define the market. Who would use a PDA? For what? How much would a user pay?

Market uncertainty was confounded by technological uncertainty. Some of the underlying technologies were very immature, such as handwriting recognition, judged by industry experts to be only 70 percent reliable. Moreover, no one could be certain what operating system would win the standards battle: Apple's Newton? GeoWork's GEOS? Microsoft's much-delayed Winpad? Different semiconductor chip sets were possible, from AT&T's new Hobbit to off-the-shelf standards. Then there was the question of communication standards. It was all very confusing, and market research was of limited help. Before any product was actually available, researchers could only extrapolate from current uses of cellular telephones, computers, calculators, and personal organizers to predict enormous markets.[55]

Firms attempting to create, or at least influence, this emerging market adopted very different experimentation strategies, which may be grouped into three major ones. Each of these three—Darwinian selection, product morphing, and vicarious experimentation—is schematically represented in separate panels in Figure 7-8. Over time (represented on the vertical axis for the entire figure), companies tried out products that were variously positioned along a given design feature (represented by the arrow at the top of each of the three panels). This horizontal axis could measure any one of a number of design features or functions, such as the degree of portability, the type of operating system, or the richness of communications capability. The first two panels (Darwinian selection and product morphing) represent a single company trying out products that vary along one or more design dimensions, whereas the third pictures the strategy of several different companies.

DARWINIAN SELECTION. Companies employing the Darwinian selection strategy experimented with multiple models in the market simultaneously, to see which ones the market appeared to value. In 1993–1994, Sharp Corporation fielded PDAs based on its proprietary operating system, sold in Japan as part of the Zaurus product line. Sharp also licensed Newton architecture from Apple (for which it was manufacturing the MessagePad) to produce Expert Pad, a direct competitor with Apple, and it put out a PDA based on GEOS from GeoWorks. Plans for the future include trying out Microsoft's Winpad and any other operating system with a chance of ultimately dominating.[56]

PRODUCT MORPHING. Although they differed enormously in the degree of risk represented by their initial market entry, Hewlett-Packard and Apple's experimentation strategies were similar. That is, their starting points were different, but both firms used market feedback from the launch of their first product to alter the next model, to incrementally "morph" toward a commercially viable product. Apple's second MessagePad placed greater emphasis on communications; HP's 200LX placed greater emphasis on personal organizing capabilities.

VICARIOUS EXPERIMENTATION. A third strategy is vicarious experimentation: wait and let the pioneers get the arrows in their backs and learn from their mistakes. Although IBM showed a functioning prototype of its PDA at the fall 1992 Comdex Show, even two years later, Simon was still not on

Figure 7-8 Three Different Market Experimentation Strategies

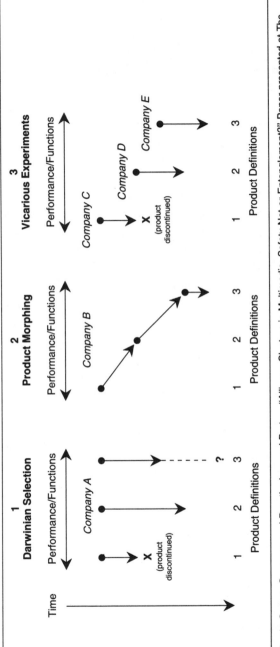

Source: Benjamin Gomes-Casseres and Dorothy Leonard-Barton, "Alliance Clusters in Multimedia: Safety Net or Entanglement?" Paper presented at The Colliding Worlds Colloquium, 6–7 October 1994, at Harvard Business School, Boston, 22a.

the market. Motorola and Compaq likewise delayed entry even after product announcements.

Of these three generic experimentation strategies, Sharp's Darwinian selection seems stereotypically Japanese.[57] The Japanese are well known for their "product churning"—i.e., turning out dozens of possible versions of a product to home in on the one preferred by most customers. About a thousand new soft drinks are brought out annually in Japan, although almost all of them fail within a year.[58] Sony has tried out numerous models of its Walkman, many of which never made it past an initial test run of a few thousand units. An example was a Walkman in the bottom of a purse—for teenagers. (It didn't sell.) Sharp was the first to bring out a compact-disc player with slots for two CDs, despite apparent uncertainty as to who would use them for what. The answer turned out to be that teenagers created their own music recordings by mixing tracks from two CDs.

U.S. companies are uncomfortable with this "throw-it-against-the-wall-and-see-what-sticks" attitude. However, U.S. companies are not particularly patient with the product-morphing approach either. An early entrant into the PDA market, EO, expected to iterate several times before getting its product just right. CEO Bob Evans, brought in just as AT&T was closing the purse strings in the spring of 1994, noted: "If you hit it right and succeed with the first product, it's wonderful, but you need the customer experience."[59] EO was closed down just as its managers felt they knew exactly who their market was and what the market needed.[60]

Vicarious is surely the cheapest kind of market experimentation—unless the early birds succeed in creating standards that dominate. Standards battles can take years, but as the dwindling number of third-party software developers creating for Macintosh computers suggests, dominance in standards can override technology advantages.

Obviously, the first two kinds of experimentation are impossibly costly for companies producing very costly consumer items (the Edsel was not really intended to be an experiment!) or high-ticket industrial products such as power plants or even turbines. However, for companies that can transform market feedback immediately into improved product, this is a cost-effective way to gather information.

Using Prototypes to Coevolve Product Concept

Real products in the market are the ultimate prototypes for gathering market intelligence, but models and prototypes that fall far short of the ultimate product can serve many different purposes. As noted in Chapter 3, they help elicit responses from disparate groups and integrate perspectives during problem solving. Chapter 5 mentioned the potential for organizational prototyping. Prototypes play an equally important role in importing market knowledge, from guiding design at one extreme (product enhancements) to stimulating product evolution at the other (market creation), since the developers' ability to communicate the exact potential of their technology as a product increases only as the technology design matures.

For instance, the HP continuous frequency counter, first introduced in 1986, originated when developers saw an opportunity to extend sales to current customers. Traditional frequency counters for monitoring various types of waves gradually became outdated as transmitters generating frequencies increased in accuracy. One HP engineer envisioned a counter analogous to an oscilloscope: it could read frequencies continuously as a series of digits, which could then be plotted on an X/Y display and could track drift in frequency signals. However, even this analogy did not help communicate with prospective users, who responded very unenthusiastically when marketing described the new concept. Convinced that a current (if nonobvious) need did in fact exist, the engineers constructed a functional prototype, which they persuaded marketing to take to the field. Somewhat to everyone's amazement, customers seized upon the prototype with such enthusiasm that marketing sometimes had a hard time retrieving the models. Users saw immediate applications—including many the engineers had not anticipated. One customer wanted to hook the counter up to his radar system to check its functioning. The product became a great commercial success, representing approximately 15 percent of the division's sales and, most important to HP, reinvigorating the product line.

One reason why prototypes are so important for soliciting information from the market is that users often try to understand a new-product concept by analogy. But their imaginations tend to be conscribed by the analogies they draw to current products; at first, they will mentally lump even radically new product concepts in with items familiar to them. Researchers have long known that "an individual will behave toward a new thing in a manner that is similar to the way he behaves toward other things he sees the new thing as similar to."[61] Such analogies are often misleading. For example, when Microsoft first brought out new multimedia educational products for children, it found that the children tended to compare them to video games and find them lacking in the constant stimulation and instantaneous feedback characteristic of such games. The children were therefore dissatisfied. Yet were the educational programs to match the fast-moving, act-and-react play of the games, there would be no time for reflection and learning. In order to get helpful feedback from the targeted users in such cases, the product developers have to redirect the users to appropriate analogies. As this example suggests, prototypes help alter customer perspectives, but reeducation may still be necessary.

Another use for prototypes is stimulating market demand: getting consumers started thinking about a future product, without going to the ultimate step of putting an actual product on the market. As noted before, when the markets are yet to be created, users have a difficult time thinking ahead to assess whether they will want the technology and, if so, in what form. In order to stimulate interest in recycled plastics and prove that products based on these materials can be attractive, GE Plastics built a "house of the future" in Pittsfield, Massachusetts, using recycled plastics in such applications as countertops and faux slate shingles on the roof. Although the investment is considerable, such three-dimensional, functioning demonstrations of technologies *in situ,* as they would actually be used, are necessary to help customers understand the commercial potential.[62]

Increasingly, technological tools such as virtual-reality software may help developers present alternative potential futures without actually building products. Currently, prospective clients can "walk through" simulated buildings of the future; advanced computer-aided design tools allow viewers to revolve a three-dimensional object on the screen and view it from different perspectives; stereolithography enables immediate transformation of design specifications into three-dimensional (but of course, nonfunctioning), solid models. However, none of these tools allows prospective users to actually experience the object being developed, and until that happens, physical prototyping skills will still be needed.

Summary

One of the most critical engines of renewal for companies is new-product development. Development projects not only draw upon and enhance existing technological capabilities but also motivate the creation of new ones. Importing knowledge from the market is clearly an essential activity in the design of a range of product lines—including some that meet current demand and others that anticipate future customer needs.

Traditional tools for importing market knowledge are valuable but limited in situations in which technological potential outstrips user understanding. That is, users have needs for which they cannot imagine a solution because they do not know about an applicable technology. In such situations, the traditional tools of market research, which emphasize very carefully structured inquiry, are less valuable channels of market information for developing novel product concepts because inquiry will elicit only such needs as the users are capable of articulating.

This chapter has introduced a set of qualitative tools for identifying new-product opportunities. This set of tools, which I term *empathic design,* has three characteristics that distinguish it from other qualitative methods: (1) the design is based on *actual observed customer behavior;* (2) it is usually conducted through *direct interaction* between those who have deep under-standing of the firm's technological capabilities and potential users; (3) it draws upon existing *technological capabilities* that can be somewhat redirected or imaginatively deployed in the service of new products or markets. Various types of empathic design, which do not replace traditional techniques but augment them, were explored and illustrated with examples.

When the technology is evolving *and* the set of potential users is at least somewhat uncertain, companies are forced to employ market experimenta-tion. This is not the same as limited market testing but involves putting real products out for consumption, in order both to educate consumers as to the potential of the technology and to observe how the new products will be used in real life. Some companies put many test products out at once, in an exercise of Darwinian selection. Others select a particular product concept and then iteratively "morph" toward a more acceptable product as directed by market feedback. Still other companies simply wait until the pioneers have scouted out the territory and then move in. The strategies of companies competing in the emerging personal digital assistant market illus-trate the different types of market experimentation.

Whether the products being developed are slight enhancements to existing lines or radically new additions, prototypes are very useful mechanisms for eliciting user feedback. However, they are most evocative when product developers cannot communicate the full potential of a new product because no exact analogy exists in the marketplace.

The more that a company exploits core technological capabilities to *create* new markets, rather than relying on a "me-too" strategy for product develop-ment, the more important it is that managers be able to draw upon a full range of tools for importing knowledge from the marketplace. Market creation does not relieve the firm from the responsibility of responding to real user needs; however, probing the market may require very different sets of skills than those currently available in many firms and currently taught in marketing curricula.

P A R T   T H R E E

GROWTH AND RENEWAL

CHAPTER EIGHT

Transferring Product Development Capabilities into Developing Nations

The global company of the 90's . . . makes use of all the world's resources . . . intellectual, technological, and physical . . . to the benefit of the corporation, its shareholders, and its employees.

—Donald K. Peterson
   Group Vice President of Meridian Business Systems, Northern Telecom[1]

[T]here is a conceptual change among major multinationals [entering China]. Now they are looking at an integrated approach that involves manufacturing, sales, and research and development.

—John Frisbie
   Director, U.S.-China Business Council, Beijing[2]

[I]t is hard to transfer the full complexity of a technology. . . . If the receptor knows very little, he can do very little even with the simple idea, because he cannot generate the mass of detail that is required to put it into execution. On the other hand, if he knows a great deal and is capable of generating the necessary details, then from just a few sentences or pieces of technology he will fill in all the rest. That is why it is hard to transfer technology to the Third World and very hard not to transfer it to Japan.

—Ralph Gomory
   Former Vice President and Director of Research, IBM[3]

In a global economy, the boundaries of a firm are not geographically determined. On corporate location maps, symbols of the widespread offices of even relatively small firms freckle the face of the earth. Prior chapters of this book have suggested how core technological capabilities are built and sustained at the home site of a corporation. This chapter addresses the question, How is the capability to develop new technology-based products transferred to a new site? As we will see, managers' approach to capabilities transfer is heavily influenced by their expectations about the foreign sites' potential to become alternative wellsprings of knowledge for the corporation.

The flow of technological capabilities across political borders is as old as history itself. One thousand years ago, Japan was flooded with Chinese educators and scientists who brought the Chinese written language, education, and religion. A few centuries later in Europe, the Renaissance joined together islands of knowledge previously isolated by the so-called Dark Ages, creating a body of information of such force that it revolutionized society. In the more recent 1800s, young women in Massachusetts worked in hundreds of woolen mills on imported British looms using borrowed British know-how.

Transferers of technological knowledge have been driven by multiple motives. For the better part of this century, U.S.-based managers were impelled by a search for more favorable economics in production—lower-cost labor, lower-cost land. Or they followed their markets, expanding into geographies relatively uncrowded by competitors. "Our reason for being here," said President Verlyn Landuyt of Sino-American Shanghai Squibb Pharmaceuticals, "is not to exploit low cost labor, but to attack the Chinese market for our products."[4] However, in the future, a new imperative may drive at least some of our most innovative companies—the quest to harness the skills of the world, wherever they may be found. New information technologies make this increasingly possible. For example, the tiny firm Black Box, headquartered in Hong Kong, creates its CD-ROM titles using writers and materials from around the world, skilled programmers in China, marketing representatives in the United States—all tied together electronically. Increasingly, managers transfer capabilities to developing nations not just to off-load capacity or to lower costs but to invest early in future sources of intellectual capital. Such investments, however, are neither cheap nor swift to mature.

Asia today presents an inclusive portrait of different levels of development. The fifty-year history of the rise of Japan from the ashes of World War II to become partner with and competitor to the rest of the developed world demonstrates the ultimate potential for investment in transferring capabilities. The emergence of the "little tigers" (Taiwan, Hong Kong, Singapore, and Korea) over the past twenty-five years offers more recent testimony to developing nations' ability to absorb, build upon, and ultimately challenge foreign knowledge. And the reopening of China to the outside world represents the latest entry-level opportunity for the transfer of technological capabilities.

In fact, the decline of communism in China in the 1980s opened a whole new territory and set off a dash for markets reminiscent of the contest for land on the U.S. frontier. In 1889, when the Oklahoma Territory was opened to all takers, would-be landowners literally raced each other at breakneck speed across the plains to claim available plots of land. When communism gave way to capitalism in Eastern Europe and China, the view of all that unexploited and uncrowded market space jolted company executives into similar frenzied activity. They envisioned 1.2 billion customers in China alone, waiting with savings in hand—to buy. Eyeglass makers counted 2.4 billion eyes as possible candidates for contact lenses; makers of adhesive bandages added up the 12 billion digits that might need covering. The vast country lacked power, transportation, and information infrastructure. Even a tiny portion of the market implied rivers of cash. If the opportunities in China seem more compelling than in other regions of the world, however, the realities of operating there are not unique. "Operating in China is not that much different from some of the other developing countries I've been in," observed Landuyt of Shanghai Squibb.[5]

From the relatively unsophisticated and chaotic deals in China to the much more knowledge-laden relationships in Singapore to the equal partnerships ultimately achieved in Japan, examples of companies operating in the Asian region richly illustrate the transfer of technological capabilities. This chapter therefore concentrates on descriptions of company activities in this geographic region to illustrate the managerial challenges of transferring technological knowledge.[6]

The Perils and Promise of Transferring Capabilities

For generations, cross-border flows of knowledge were characterized as *technology transfer*. The term connoted a one-time, one-way expenditure of knowledge and hence denoted an uncomplicated transaction. The term was, and continues to be, applied to everything from the sale of a piece of equipment in up-country Thailand to the establishment of research institutes in Korea. Although practitioners have grown increasingly sophisticated in understanding the enormous differences in commitment and behavior implied within the range of activities encompassed by "technology transfer," misunderstandings continue. Returning from a trip to China in 1991, China scholar Denis Fred Simon remarked, "[E]ven though in 1981 when the

'Interim Regulations on the Administration of Technology Introduction and Equipment Import' were adopted by the [Chinese] State Council, a formal distinction was made between import of 'technology' versus import of equipment, the reality is that confusion continues to persist regarding just what is considered to be 'jishu yinjin' [technology transfer]."[7]

Conceiving of technology movement from one company to another and across international boundaries as the flow of technological *capabilities* rather than technology transfer helps to highlight the inadequacies of the old managerial mind-set and to suggest the kinds of activities essential to success. (See Figure 8-1.) However, implicit in this newer term is the assumption that the technology transferer in fact *desires* to establish knowledge-creating activities in a foreign location. This assumption does not always hold. The story of Japan's evolution into a preferred and powerful manufacturing source is both inspiring and, to some, frightening; so is the role of U.S. companies in promoting that development through joint ventures, as the following statement suggests:

> As more and more production moves to Japan, our work force will lose the capacity to make valuable contributions to production processes. . . . U.S. companies are selling themselves too cheaply; in letting their Japanese partners undertake product manufacturing, they are giving away valuable production experience. . . . Over the long term, U.S. companies that enter joint ventures with Japan cannot maintain high profitability by providing services, such as assembly and distribution, which add very little value to the product being sold. The resulting interplay, while superficially promising, could really be just an extended dance of death.[8]

According to this view, managers should be alert to losing the vital knowledge engendered during manufacturing that is needed to feed the next round of new-product development. Arguments to support this contention include the points raised in Chapter 5 about the critical knowledge generated during prototyping. If prototyping is outsourced, that knowledge is lost to the company. However, a counterargument is that, as suggested in Chapters 3 and 6, the technology fusion required to produce many of today's complex products necessitates partnerships. A number of U.S. companies have drawn upon the proven capability in many Asian countries for miniaturization of parts; and, they contend, they could not have reached the market in any timely fashion without having done so. As we have seen, in the mid-1980s, Quantum Corporation produced the first "hard cards" to expand personal computer memory with the help of Matsushita Kotobuki Electronics; in 1993, Apple sought the help of Sharp to manufacture the now-famous

Figure 8-1 Transfer of Technological Capabilities from Technnology Source to Technology Recipient

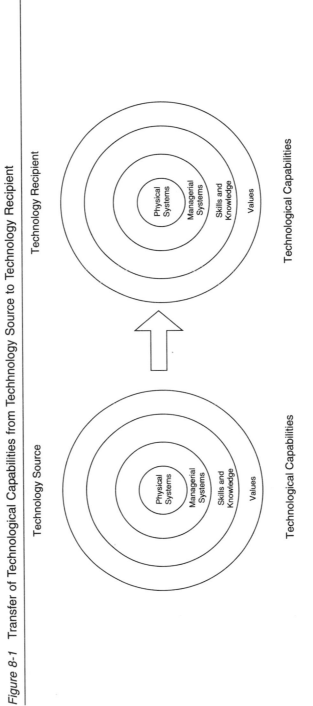

MessagePad, with Newton architecture. The fears of losing all competitive advantage to Japan by helping to create a manufacturing powerhouse seem overblown today. One can debate the merits of individual ventures (we will see some unsatisfactory ones in this chapter), and it is true that companies often create their own future competition by transferring capabilities overseas. However, many companies will choose to selectively transplant some portion of their knowledge nearer to new markets or needed resources, and managers will have to manage that challenge without giving away critical core capabilities. Their initial assumptions about what and how much to transfer obviously affect the entire transfer process.

The following discussion does not distinguish between joint ventures and wholly owned subsidiaries, since the presence or absence of restrictions on the transfer of product development capabilities is determined less by the legal structure of the relationship than by the intent and implementation of the partnership. Some managers consider even wholly owned subsidiaries as foreign entities, to be treated with caution, whereas others regard their joint venture partners as an extended arm of the corporation, to be fully informed. Obviously, the legal relationship reflects the motives and objectives of the two parties involved and sets some boundaries on the opportunities for transfer, but a wide range of transfer options can be embedded in any type of partnership.

Four Levels in the Transfer of Product Development Capability

A theoretical continuum of transfer situations stretches from the simple sale of equipment by source to receiver to, at the other extreme, the final absorption of so much knowledge that the receiver becomes product design source, capable of reversing the flow of knowledge. Underlying this continuum is a conceptual learning model, with the relationship moving from that of teacher-pupil to cocreators. This progression from left to right in Figure 8-2—from dependence to reverse transfer—is neither ubiquitous nor inevitable. Not all agreements between the original technology source and the originally designated receiver are set up with any intention to transverse this continuum, and even if they are, many agreements fade before the recipient has achieved a full product development capability.

A continuum, by definition, contains no discrete boundaries between stages along its course. However, numerous scholars have found it useful for purposes of analysis and discussion to identify levels of technology transfer characterizing very different management situations.[9] Austin's four-level

Figure 8-2 Interdependency of Technology Recipient and Technology Source in the Transfer of Technological Capabilities

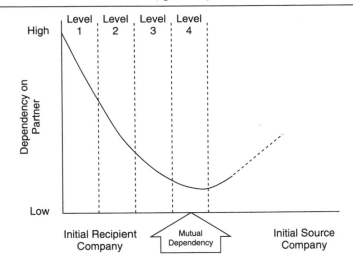

"technological capability ladder"[10] accords most closely with the levels used in this chapter: (1) assembly or turnkey operations, (2) adaptation and localization of components, (3) product redesign, and (4) independent design of products.[11]

The four levels, or points along the continuum, tend to represent not only levels of transfer but also contrasting philosophies about entering a developing nation. Managers in firms setting up factories in developing nations such as China only to take advantage of an inexpensive labor source seem to assume that the knowledge will, at least for the foreseeable future, flow in one direction—from the home headquarters in a developed country to divisions in a developing nation—and that the technology to be transferred is mostly self-contained process machinery or software. Managers will therefore aim for a level 1 or 2 transfer. At the other extreme, managers in some multinationals anticipate from the beginning that their divisions in developing nations will become equal partners in the design and production of new technology and therefore structure their agreements with an eye to eventually achieving levels 3 and 4. They are making *knowledge* investments as opposed to purely financial investments. Many agreements have passed, over time, through all four levels of transfer described below, as employees of the recipient companies exerted pressure to achieve innovation capabilities or the source companies learned that the progression toward level 4 was predictable, if not totally inevitable.

The purchase of equipment by operations in the developing country, the establishment of a *turnkey* factory (i.e., a complete working plant) by a foreign company, or the establishment of an *assembly* plant by a multinational company—all have some characteristics in common. To the degree that this first level is the ultimate and only aim of the technology source, it represents the old notion of one-way, one-time technology transfer. The assumption is that, insofar as any new skills or managerial systems or norms of behavior are required or desired for use of the technology, they are embodied within the transferred equipment, software, or other physical systems. Both the source and recipient of the technology expect that the equipment or software can "plug in" to current production or service operations at the recipient site and be used without any alteration. Operators at the recipient site need to build skill in using the equipment and enough understanding of the underlying operating principles to maintain and perhaps repair it—but not enough to significantly alter it. In assembly operations, this level usually entails importing "kits" that include all materials necessary for production.

The second level, *adaptation and localization of components*, requires managers in the technology source company to expend more time, money, and energy to ensure that the recipient can not only utilize the technology transferred but also fine-tune both it and the local operations system into which it fits. Not only must the recipient workforce know how to operate, maintain, and repair the equipment, but local professionals must also understand the principles on which the technology is based. The most significant alteration in product is usually switching the sourcing of componentry to local firms. Since such local suppliers also need to develop the requisite technological capability, achieving level 2 usually requires the technology source to broaden the target of its transfer activities beyond the initial recipient to encompass an entire network of firms.

The third level, *product redesign*, moves the recipient organization closer to an independent ability to innovate. Rather than adapting components, the recipient now redesigns the whole product as a system. Recipients, however, are still dependent on the technology source for basic know-how and know-why—i.e., for the scientific knowledge underlying the original product design. Even if the two parties codevelop a product, major segments of the design activities are still carried out by the technology source. The receiver would not yet be ready to conduct all the innovative activities itself. However, the receiver may still create products competitive with those of the source by layering its own expertise on top of licensed technology.

In the fourth level, *independent design of products*, advanced technological knowledge possessed by both the original source and the original recipient flows bidirectionally. (See Figure 8-3.) The source has become a recipient, and the recipient has become a source.[12] In these cases, the two are equivalent in technological capability; new-product development may occur at either site. The challenge for the parties in such cases is to overturn historical roles and work as equals.

Success in transferring technological capabilities depends on, at a minimum, agreement between source and recipient about the level of development transfer to be achieved and also on both sides' understanding of that goal's managerial implications—i.e., the effort and resources necessary. Of course, many companies in developed nations have a long history of transferring capabilities from their home base to developing nations—i.e., passing through all four stages. However, reports of eventual "success" stories tend to bury the details of problems experienced along the way—especially those that, with hindsight, are seen to have been avoidable. The more that managers understand the classes of problems that occur and develop the ability to anticipate issues through preagreement diagnosis, the greater the likelihood of success. This chapter is therefore devoted to discussing the *managerial challenges* inherent in capabilities transfer at each level.

In the following pages, each of the stages of transfer is illustrated by the experiences of various companies and also through the history of a single facility (Hewlett-Packard, Singapore), which we will observe moving over time from assembly to new-product design. The four levels of capabilities transfer interact with the dimensions of a capability; each level is characterized by particular challenges in each of the four dimensions (physical systems, skills, managerial systems, and values), and therefore, much of the commentary on each transfer level is organized according to the dimensions. Critical success factors are suggested for achieving each of the four levels (assembly, localization, product redesign, and product design). The chapter concludes

Figure 8-3 Flows of Knowledge During Capabilities Transfer

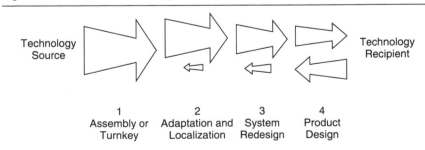

Levels of Capabilities Transfer

with general observations about the transfer of development capabilities, regardless of the stage to be achieved.

Level 1 Transfer: Assembly or Turnkey Operations

HEWLETT-PACKARD IN SINGAPORE: THE EARLY DAYS

In the late 1960s, a high-level team of managers from Hewlett-Packard investigated potential manufacturing sites in Asia. According to trip leader John Doyle, Singapore appealed because "the government was stable, understanding, responsive, reliable, and honest. Potential employees seemed to be energetic, educated, honest, creative—and they spoke English, which would help build team cohesion." Taking advantage of the low cost of labor in the region at the time, HP started operations with the extremely labor-intensive stringing of computer core memories. In 1973, the company switched Singapore operations to the assembly of the HP-35 calculators, and by 1977, the facility was also producing computer keyboards, solid-state displays, integrated circuits, and isolators. All of these products were designed, developed, and initially manufactured in the United States before being transferred to Singapore for production.

Sources: Details in this and other descriptions of HP's activities in Singapore in this chapter are taken from George Thill and Dorothy Leonard-Barton, "Hewlett-Packard: Singapore (A)," "Hewlett-Packard: Singapore (B)," and "Hewlett-Packard: Singapore (C)," cases 694-035, 694-036, and 694-037, Harvard Business School, Boston, 1993.

As noted, Western companies have historically transferred assembly operations to developing nations for one of two reasons—to lower costs or to follow the market. Managers in these companies have not traditionally felt responsible for how their investment might evolve in the future—i.e., for knowledge growth beyond the initial transfer. For their part, developing nations have always been vulnerable to a similarly simplistic hope—that purchase of new equipment would catapult them over an inadequate infrastructure and lack of managerial experience into modernity. Both parties at this level of transfer define success simply as the profitable production of the intended product.

Physical Systems. As Figure 8-4 suggests, the capability being transferred in adoption or assembly situations is almost entirely confined to the physical system itself. Such a transfer might seem simple, but it often runs afoul of an inadequate fit either with other, existing production equipment or with local infrastructure. The assumption that equipment can be plunked down and used in a foreign environment with little or no adjustment either to it

Figure 8-4 Level 1 of Capabilities Transfer: Assembly or Turnkey Operations

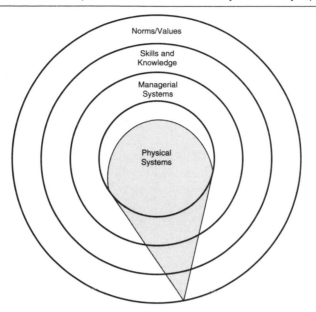

or to the surrounding physical systems places a tremendous burden of self-sufficiency, flexibility, and endless reliability on equipment design. Even within developed nations, physical equipment or software is rarely so self-contained and so malleable.[13] It is not surprising, therefore, that the biggest challenge to level 1 capabilities transfer usually arises from the assumption that the surrounding physical systems into which the new technology is introduced are compatible and adequate to support productive use.

One of the most striking examples of a miscalculation about the adequacy of the existing basic infrastructure I have observed was actually made by the government of a developing nation. In the early 1970s, the Indonesian government shipped about $1 million worth of extremely complex oceanographic equipment to a tiny university at the northern tip of Sumatra. The intention was to recompense the local population for the drilling that a government-owned oil production company was conducting off its coast. Unfortunately, the equipment arrived in water-vulnerable wooden crates a few weeks before the seasonal monsoons. The university had no building in which to house it, no electricity source adequate to run it, and the most qualified local engineer had a master's degree—in chemistry.

Although this may be an extreme example, companies venturing into southern China in the early 1990s have confronted similarly inadequate infrastructure—primitive roads, inadequate electricity and water, few standardized supplies. The ASTEC factory, which produces computer power supplies and was one of the first to set up operations in the Boa'an area, constructed its own water purification plant and installed a generator to supplement local electricity supplies. The plant manager of another relatively simple electronics assembly operation in the south China area commented, "We had to bring everything—and I mean *everything.* Screwdrivers, bolts, sandpaper, paint—you name it."

Imported equipment is also very frequently incompatible with a local partner's existing operations. Everything from hose fittings to power supplies to computer software (where it exists) is likely to be different. Although inventiveness can go a long way toward the mission impossible of combining incompatible machinery, many times the imported equipment just sits inactive for months while the technical staff scrambles to source and import a critical coupler, a cable, a different power supply.

Skills and Knowledge. Transfer of skills is not a big priority in the adoption/assembly situation. Nevertheless, the frequent mismatch between the physical system and the skills of the operators can be even more challenging than the lack of fit between equipment and surrounding physical systems. Although the major skills required may be manual, machine operation and particularly maintenance draw upon mental capabilities as well. Moreover, in order to function as designed, even the best equipment is likely to require some adjustment for local conditions or the particular characteristics of the product being produced. In a bottling plant in China, when Japanese-produced automatic filling equipment malfunctions and the bottles are filled unevenly, no one knows how to adjust it. A German automatic pump for agricultural chemicals stands unused in a Chinese factory while workers fill the barrels by hand. Why? Because the pump is set for chemicals of a lower viscosity, and no one has the skill to determine whether and how it can be adjusted. Nor does the machinery itself embody the intelligence to adjust automatically to different levels of viscosity, as it theoretically could if equipped with the right sensors and software.[14]

Occasionally, the mismatch between technology and worker skills is traceable to superior, rather than inadequate, worker skills. In a Philips joint venture set up in China to produce television tubes, more than 90 percent of the employees had been recruited from colleges and universities; primary school graduates ran the same types of production lines for Philips in Europe. In 1992, after the second year of production, two hundred of the sixteen hundred Chinese plant workers resigned, frustrated by the monotony of the highly automated and regulated advanced production lines. Since Philips spent about three months training new operators, the 12 percent turnover rate was very costly. One Philips executive complained that Hua Fei (the plant) would be "better off with farmers." A large U.S.-based computer company saw an expert system used for diagnostics in its California plant meet with complete rejection in its sister Japanese plant. The reason? The Japanese technicians worked one station for about six years, accumulating considerable expertise in problem recognition and solution, whereas the California technicians tended to move on after six months. As a consequence, the Japanese technicians could outperform the expert system and had no use for it.

Usually, the biggest challenge in transferring equipment or lines into a developing nation is lack of maintenance skills. The inability or unwillingness of local technicians to service imported machinery translates into long periods of costly machine downtime and inefficiency.

YUNNAN TOBACCO

In the early 1980s, the Yunnan Tobacco state enterprise imported a new type of tobacco leaf curing line that could potentially increase productivity greatly. However, the efficiency of the imported equipment fell below not only U.S. and European standards but those of equipment made in China. A number of problems contributed to this low performance. First, Chinese workers reportedly felt less comfortable with the imported equipment and consequently would not service it. Second, Yunnan lacked high-quality service technicians. Third, service parts were not readily available. Consequently, the line could not be adequately maintained and was underutilized. In 1991, Denis Simon, professor of International Business at the Fletcher School of Law and Diplomacy, calculated the economic implications of that failure by observing, "[I]f Yunnan could raise its effective utilization rate of the imported cigarette-making and packaging equipment by 10 percent over the next year or two, it could reduce future outlays of foreign exchange by US$12.6 million and add 64.33 million yuan in taxable profits to the state."

Source: This case is drawn from Denis Fred Simon, "China's Acquisition and Assimilation of Foreign Technology: Beijing's Search for Excellence," testimony to Joint Economic Committee, U.S. Congress, 1 January 1991.

Managerial Systems. Only minimal managerial systems are usually involved in a level 1 transfer (see Figure 8-4). Because of its communist history and the mixture of Soviet-type central planning with the attempt to make communes totally self-sufficient, China particularly lacks a heritage of managerial systems. For example, a Chinese government official in the Ministry of

Machinery Industry explained that an advertisement for machine tools in the *People's Daily* newspaper caused enormous confusion. Accustomed to having the government assign new technology to selected factories and then announce the assignment, readers wondered how machines could be advertised in advance of their official dispersal. The frustration of an expatriate manager of a joint venture in agricultural chemicals was similarly traceable to China's communist heritage. He was unable to convince his Chinese partners that they should not produce to inventory but try to track demand. This logic contradicted the partners' long experience with producing to government-decreed quotas, and they feared being responsible for shortages more than accumulating excess inventory. Another manager echoed these sentiments: the Chinese "are used to making their quota, regardless of quality," he observed. The president and vice chairman of Sino-American Shanghai Squibb, Verlyn Landuyt, explained, "There is a basic mismatch between the things that motivate us and the incentive system that our partner operates under. He doesn't get any reward if our joint venture is more successful than we forecast in any year, but he is reprimanded if we don't achieve our plan."[15]

Moreover, under prior communist regimes, there was no system for rewarding individuals for superior performance or skills; if one person deserved an increase in compensation, the whole group had to receive it. Because of such problems, the expatriates who set up an operation usually *are* the managerial systems for assembly operations. For example, Roland Filloy, the manager for a new Emerson Electric Therm-o-Disc line in southern China, had set up the identical line before in Mexico and ran it for a number of years. His Chinese assistant was positioned to take over the management as the facility matured. Managers in Philips' joint venture in television tubes finally resorted to a different tactic to ensconce managerial practices—extensive, highly specific documents controlling every detail. The following account suggests that this was a last resort—and not a very satisfactory solution.

PHILIPS HUA FEI

Philips, the Dutch electronics firm, has established ten joint ventures in China since 1986, producing everything from semiconductors to clothes irons, and has assembled some of the most advanced production facilities in the country.

The contract for Philips' joint venture with the Hua Fei television tube factory was signed in 1987, and production began in 1990. The first factory produced 1.3 million television tubes in 1992, which were sold to approximately fifty television makers.

When the company was in its start-up phase, Philips wrote up loose jobdescriptions, leaving room for individual initiative. Company executives found that workers were unwilling to do more than was specified. Moreover, work left incomplete by one factory shift would not be finished by another, leading to serious "production gaps." Philips' remedy was to write out job descriptions to the most minute detail, including even "how the tea boy does his rounds." The company ran into a similar problem with operating procedures, and Technical Manager F. D. Zeh's advice to other companies with comprehensive operating manuals is to set them down "as bibles."[16]

Values. Although setting up an assembly plant or selling a turnkey operation involves very little conscious transfer of values, the experience of Yunnan Tobacco suggests that a respect for the need to service equipment can make the difference between ineffective and effective operations. As Austin notes, in developing nations, "[p]roduction supervisors and workers may disdain or deem unimportant the rather mundane 'hands-on' imperative of routine maintenance. The lack of a 'maintenance ethic' is not uncommon."[17]

Another value often lacking is an emphasis on worker safety. For instance, in China, most state-owned enterprises and many Asian joint ventures pay little heed to what would be considered current standard safety procedures in U.S. or European-based factories. One sees workers thrusting an arm in between the rollers in a wool-knitting factory, walking sandal-footed in puddles of chemicals in a chemicals plant, shoving by hand pieces of sheet metal into a mammoth, multiton stamping machine in an automobile factory. It is possible to embody values in the design of the machinery and the line, however, and imported equipment may have safety features built in. In the Emerson Electric Therm-o-Disc line at its Chinese Boa'an facility, the woman operating a small punch machine must push two, widely separated buttons in order to activate it—a design that forces the operator's arms safely away from the moving mechanism and precludes any possibility of her getting her fingers caught.

In summary, companies setting up assembly operations or turnkey plants cope with the problems of level 1 transfer by attempting to embody the entire capability within the equipment and procedures. They select technology that will match the local infrastructure. The equipment is often older technology, but at least both it and the operating procedures are well proved because the operations have been "debugged" elsewhere. (The Therm-o-Disc equipment for the Emerson Electric line had been around the world—from South Carolina to Canada to Mexico to China; Hewlett-Packard transferred production from the United States; Conner Peripherals, which produces disk drives for computers in Shenzen, China, sets up new lines in Singapore first.) If the operations are not labor-intensive but involve high technology, then they are usually designed to be absolutely "foolproof." Conner Peripherals' clean rooms and automated equipment are world-class; similar ones could be seen in developed nations, for instance.

However, whether the line is labor- or capital-intensive, a level 1 transfer of technology does not involve any real conveyance of capability. The English word *technology* derives from the Greek word *techne*, meaning a "skill" or an "art," and therefore implies that its transfer involves the flow of knowledge. If all the knowledge transferred is embodied in some physical form but is invisible to the users, those users develop little new capability because, unlike the activities described in earlier chapters, these essentially reactive activities create very little new knowledge.

Level 2 Transfer: Adaptation and Localization

HEWLETT-PACKARD IN SINGAPORE: THE 1980s

In 1981, when Hewlett-Packard moved some production of the sophisticated HP41C handheld programmable calculators to Computer Products Singapore, CPS proposed conducting a cost-reduction program on this product line. Since one of the opportunities for lowering cost lay in reducing the number of integrated circuits, CPS set up a center to work on designing application-specific integrated circuits (ASICs). As a Chinese manager recalled, "Without the design capability and the ability to do chip integration, whatever cost-reduction plan we had might not have happened." A group of twenty CPS engineers and technicians went to the United States for more than a year to learn ASIC design and succeeded, on their return, in reducing the number of ICs in the calculator.

In 1983, HP's first ink-jet printer (the "ThinkJet") was transferred to Singapore for production. When it was manufactured in the United States, 80 percent of the parts came from U.S. or European vendors. After transfer to Singapore, 80 percent were sourced in Asia. The assembly was highly automated. Engineering Manager Lim Kok Khoon recalled, "Line processes now became critical. Before, when we produced at low volume, stopping the line was no big deal. But now inventory would pile up fast. Quality became a significant issue, and logistics were critical." CPS implemented statistical quality control and went to a just-in-time inventory pull system. In the period from 1984 to 1985, the manufacturing costs for the ThinkJet were driven down by 30 percent. One-third of the savings were attributable to line efficiencies and the rest to lower Singapore overhead, quality improvements, and lower-cost materials sourcing.

Success at level 2 is defined as the ability to adapt product and to produce it using mostly local components. Both the technology source and the technology recipient stand to gain from product adaptation and localization. The source gains in cost economies and the recipient in knowledge. The recipient must understand the technology itself, however—not just its use. Only if some knowledge of underlying engineering and scientific principles is transferred can local engineers alter the process or product to accommodate local needs and select local components. Therefore, achieving a level 2 transfer does involve more learning, more transfer of actual development capability, than level 1. (See Figure 8-5.) As joint ventures draw more advanced technological capabili-

Figure 8-5 Level 2 of Capabilities Transfer: Adaptation and Localization of Components

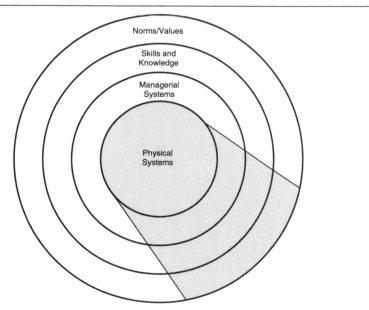

ties into a developing area, local sourcing becomes easier. The manager of a Du Pont joint venture in Shanghai observed that four years after setting up operations, he could have sourced about 50 percent more of the equipment needed because so many other joint ventures had been established in the area.

Physical Systems. Good financial reasons can be presented for and against localization. Foreign firms reap profits from sale of parts into the developing country. Of course, local sourcing is more economical for the local venture in that no (often precious) foreign exchange must be expended for parts. However, even if localization is desirable, it is difficult to achieve. HP's Tommy Lau recalled, "Re-sourcing for the ThinkJet was very eye-opening for us; whereas calculators had a pretty simple structure with a couple of ICs, the printers were a completely different animal. They had gears, mechanism, metal parts, and complicated plastic parts. We had never before explored the potential in this part of the world for sourcing these parts."[18]

In China, where suppliers are at an earlier stage of development, localization is especially challenging. An AT&T joint venture obtained local metal cabinetry constituting about 20 percent of the value of a switching product, yet even these relatively simple components were initially unacceptable: when the surface was baked, the paint came out differing shades. Chinese recipients of technology have tried to force greater knowledge transfer by setting ambitious localization schedules. However, these optimistic schedules have almost never been met, as Table 8-1 suggests. Degree of localization appears to

Table 8-1 Expected and Actual Localization Rates

JVs/Production Type	Year (December) Local Content %						
	85	86	87	88	89	90	91
Hua Fei (Philips) color TV tube							
expected						6.0	24.0
actual						5.0	8.0
Shanghai Volkswagen Santana							
expected	3.6	3.6	10.6	25.0	50.0	68.0	85.0
actual	3.6	3.6	12.6	17.1	30.0	60.09	70.0
Beijing Jeep (XJ)							
expected	1.7	5.2	10.0	20.0	42.0	84.0	100.0
actual	1.7	5.2	18.7	30.0	38.0	43.0	47.0

Source: Erik de Bruin and Xianfeng Jia, "Managing Sino-Western Joint Ventures: Product Selection Strategy," *Management International Review* 33, no. 4 (1993): 358. Reprinted by permission.

depend in large part on the level of capabilities transfer the technology source intends and on its willingness to invest heavily to reach that level. Beijing Jeep Corporation, a joint venture between the Beijing Automotive Works (BAW) and Chrysler Corporation (formerly AMC, which was bought by Chrysler in 1987), was scheduled to reach 80 percent local sourcing by 1990. The company had reached about 40 percent by that year.[19] Shanghai Volkswagen took five years to reach 30 percent of local content,[20] and its experience is not uncommon.

SHANGHAI VOLKSWAGEN

In 1978, although Beijing Jeep had been in China for many years, there were no passenger car joint ventures in the country, and local producers turned out a mere 3,000 vehicles a year. However, demand was rapidly rising, and the government forecast a need for 160,000 passenger vehicles a year by 1990. In the absence of domestic sources, this dramatic increase would have to be met through costly imports.

The Chinese Sixth and Seventh Five-Year Plans (1981–1990) supported building a domestic car industry. With investment backing from the Shanghai Automobile Industries Corporation and the Bank of China, the Shanghai Tractor Factory (STF) sought a foreign automobile manufacturer partner. After meeting with six different firms from Japan, the United States, Germany, and France, and after thirty-six rounds of negotiations in a six-year process, STF finally signed a contract with Volkswagen in the spring of 1985. The joint venture began operations in September of that year.

Volkswagen selected the "'Santana," a small four-door model, as the best car to compete in Asia with Toyota and Nissan. Although Shanghai wanted to manufacture a larger car and the Santana had failed in Europe, Volkswagen was confident that the car would do well in China. (Analysts have contended that Volkswagen saw operations in China as an attractive way to defray the high costs of developing the Santana.)

Shanghai lacked local suppliers to support an automobile industry, and items as minor as batteries had to be imported. However, seeking to balance their foreign exchange, the Chinese set an ambitious localization schedule (see Table 8-1), to which Volkswagen agreed on the condition that all local components meet German quality standards—a requirement that clashed with Shanghai's equally adamant stance on localization. Zhu Rongji, the mayor-designate of Shanghai at the time, complained bitterly to the press about the Germans' insistence on such high quality standards for the joint venture. Other public officials were also dismayed by what they saw as Volkswagen's inability to wean the joint venture off costly foreign components. Volkswagen contended that it could not risk its reputation on poorly designed local products, citing as an example the case in which local suppliers that were offered the job of developing a horn for the Santana took ten months to come up with a design. Similarly, a local manufacturer supplied the joint venture with headlights that turned off as the cars approached an object.

Such problems stemmed in part from the fact that Volkswagen did not offer technical assistance or formal technology transfer to local suppliers, and Shanghai did not request it. By 1991, the local content of the Santana reached only 70 percent, well below the joint venture's expectations. In 1993, local content reached about 80 percent.

Sources: This case was drawn from the following materials: Erik J. de Bruijn and Xianfeng Jia, "Managing Sino-Western Joint Ventures: Product Selection Strategy," *Management International Review* 33, no. 4 (1993): 335–60; Stuart Rock, "VolksChairman," *Director* (October 1990): 69–72; "Don't Get Off Yer Bike," *The Economist,* 16 April 1988, 81–82; "Big Expansion at VW's Shanghai Plant," *Motor Report International,* 3 February 1992, 3.

Skills and Knowledge. Transferring an adaptive capability implies a commitment to considerable training and willingness to release proprietary information; adapting a production line for local components, adapting the product design itself, or altering standard corporate tools all require some degree of understanding of the underlying technology. As the Volkswagen story indicated, the foreign firm may not be highly motivated to encourage local adaptation or sourcing. Another difficulty in reaching level 2 transfer is that training must extend beyond the manufacturing or assembly plant to local suppliers. Quality breakdowns in small components threaten the finished product's performance. Therefore, quality training programs must reach back to second- or even third-tier suppliers. As the manager of a communications company operating in China explained, "The first batch [of components] you get from a supplier may be fine, but after trial production, the second batch is terrible. They just don't know how to ramp up to high volumes."

Managerial Systems. Setting up logistics and working with a network of suppliers are hardly trivial tasks, especially for managers with little or no previous experience. In China, because of the communes' self-sufficiency, many industries are still very vertically integrated. For instance, the half-dozen air-conditioning producers in the country, as of 1993, were accustomed to producing everything from switches to chassis and compressors. These same companies distribute the air-conditioning units retail. They have no history of working with suppliers outside their own vertical chain.

A level 2 capability also implies that operations within the plant are under control. Volkswagen's start-up pains were not confined to its interactions with suppliers. Martin Posth, deputy managing director of the Shanghai car assembly plant, commented that the "thirty-person West German staff—only one of whom spoke Chinese—must train the local employees to accept unfamiliar western notions about product quality, responsibility and team cooperation." After the right training, the proportion of lazy or incompetent people could probably be cut to 20 percent or 30 percent of the total, Posth said. However, there were no accepted managerial systems for weeding out unproductive workers, "even guys who are doing nothing," Posth noted. In spite of the Joint Venture law in China, which did lay out procedures for firing people, local authorities blocked attempts to remove workers.[21]

Values. The two values that continuously crop up in any discussion of localization are discipline and quality—which are, of course, related. Seemingly ordinary disciplines such as keeping and adhering to a schedule may be novel. The expatriate general manager of a communications hardware company who asked his local staff whether they kept appointments calendars was nonplussed when he found that only one out of fifteen did, and that one used the calendar as a diary—i.e., to record events, not to anticipate them. It was therefore not surprising that his employees were also unaccustomed to standardizing and documenting processes. Like a number of other firms operating in China that have pursued ISO9000 certification[22] in order to shepherd production facilities along the road to quality output, this manager consolidated all his quality-related efforts under the successful bid for certification. His staff, he recalled, "got really enthusiastic [about the effort to achieve ISO9000 standards]. There was a tremendous change in the company as they saw how their performance resulted in high-quality product, better delivery, and customer satisfaction."

The major prerequisite for success at level 2 is an ability to reach down into second- and third-tier supplier operations to instill the discipline needed to produce quality output. Managers who want to source a higher proportion of their product components locally (or are forced by local government regulations to increase local content) have to conceive of the recipient of capabilities as a broad network of firms and individuals—not just their partner.

Level 3 Transfer: Product Redesign

HEWLETT-PACKARD IN SINGAPORE: REDESIGNING THE THINKJET AND THE JAPANESE PRINTER PROJECTS

In the latter half of the 1980s, Computer Products Singapore proposed to Hewlett-Packard's Vancouver division, which had product design responsibility for the ThinkJet, that CPS redesign the product for the lowest possible manufacturing cost and higher quality. Its specific plan called for an integration of two circuit boards into one, moving the power supply to outside the printer, changing the mechanical design, and making two levels of print quality available to the customer by rendering the bidirectional print head capable of either repeating the same line, for double-dot resolution, or proceeding to the next line to print in the lighter-color single-dot mode. This redesign was carried out by Singapore engineers physically located in Vancouver, where they could consult with the original designers of the printer. Project Manager Lim Kok Khoon explained: "[T]here is always an evolution of design—a reason *why* people have changed things along the way. In redesign, you have to understand the considerations the original designers made, so you can avoid replicating some of the problems they encountered." Many of those considerations were not recorded, even in the laboratory notebooks kept by the engineers, so as Lim noted, "it is inevitable that you have to talk to the designers." With help from the Vancouver engineers, the Singapore team successfully redesigned the ThinkJet. Then team members returned home to replicate their success on two other printers in the same family, with different PC interfaces.

In late 1990, after a two-year, abortive attempt to codevelop a product with Vancouver, Singapore managers proposed that they produce a Japanese-language printer entirely in Singapore. The expatriate manager in charge of research in Singapore, Frank Cloutier, noted, "The logical thing for us to do in Asia was build printers for Asia." General Manager Tommy Lau added: "We felt that we could do more. Our goal had always been to eventually do a finished product in Singapore." The development would be greatly simplified by use of the mechanical design and chassis of the U.S. product, the DeskJet printer. Only software and firmware had to be adapted for the Japanese market. Nine months later, the DeskJet 500J was launched. Initial sales were disappointing, as Japanese customers disliked the traditional Hewlett-Packard boxy appearance and faulted the printer for being too big. Lau summarized the performance of the 500J: "It certainly was no home run, but HP loaded a base in this tough market." The Singapore team believed it needed to persevere to crack the Japanese market, which did not yet recognize the HP name and tended to penalize companies not offering the market a continuous stream of new products. In 1992, the advent in the United States of the first HP ink-jet color printer, the DeskJet 500C, provided a model for CPS's second try. This machine, redesigned for the Japanese market as the DeskJet 505J, was quite a bit more successful, in large part because of the added capability to access a library of images and print in color. Using these features, Japanese customers could tailor-make the postcard greetings they traditionally sent twice a year to friends and family.

Success at level 3 is defined as the ability to redesign an entire product rather than just components. The intended result is not merely a product that can be locally produced but a *superior* product. The HP engineers in Singapore moved beyond their concentration on designing better integrated circuitry to tackle the redesign of a whole product as a system. It is only at a level 3 transfer that managers are truly engaged in transferring and recreating a new-product development capability. The recipients of the equipment, tools, and operating procedures must not only thoroughly understand the equipment itself but also comprehend the underlying technology so that they can modify the entire product or process for local production and/or for the local market. Therefore, at level 3, the knowledge transferred moves beyond know-how to know-why.[23]

Hewlett-Packard's Singapore facility took nearly twenty years to reach that capability. In today's environment of much faster paced change, companies in China are attempting to truncate the traditional time span from level 1 to 3—in part, because the Asian market has expanded so rapidly and there is such demand for innovative products. For instance, Emerson Electric set up an Asian Engineering Center at its Boa'an facility in southern China so that divisions could get help in redesigning products and processes for the Asian market. Both Xerox and Motorola have announced (and are implementing) ambitious attempts to bring their Chinese partners up to speed very quickly.

XEROX SHANGHAI

In 1987, Xerox Corporation entered a partnership with the Shanghai Movie and Photo Industries Company (SMPIC) to manufacture Xerox copiers in China. The production of a new product in China was planned from the beginning; Xerox stressed the need for funding new-product development to ensure that Xerox Shanghai could export world-class products. With that as a firmly defined goal, Xerox recognized the need to establish a receptive environment for the transfer of "high technology."

However, local suppliers were inexperienced and lacked the technology to manufacture parts for the Xerox machines. Concerned that total localization would take too long, Xerox designed and implemented a three-plant system in the Minhang economic zone. Xerox Shanghai began by establishing a plant to manufacture the 1027 copier, a midrange, older model that Xerox believed "was very suitable for China" because of its "reliable, sturdy operation." One year later, Xerox constructed a toner plant and then a low-capacity photoreceptor plant, which provided experience with the complex photoreceptor technology without the pressure of a high-volume production schedule. Before the plants were up and running, six Chinese engineers visited America for one year to learn fully the fundamentals of copier technology.

The three-plant system reduced the joint venture's dependence on imported components. Xerox also transferred technology and provided technical assistance to approximately sixty local suppliers, mostly in Shanghai, educating them in materials management and accounting as well as quality control so that locally engineered products could meet the company's high standards. Xerox diffused its "LUTI"—learn, use, teach, and inspect—system throughout the plant network, with each level of management teaching the level below. Only a small portion of the several million dollars spent in training, supporting, and monitoring Chinese suppliers was paid by them; the rest had to be absorbed by Xerox.

The joint venture's first postinstallation survey, conducted in 1990, showed that 90 percent of customers were satisfied with their products. In less than five years, Xerox Shanghai captured 50 percent of the Chinese mainland copier market. In 1993, the company unveiled the codeveloped Xerox 5416, the latest and smallest of Xerox's machines, which Joseph Donaro, general manager of Xerox Shanghai, said represented the "crystallization of cooperation between Chinese and American engineers and designers."[24] Xerox Shanghai has also received several awards for outstanding quality.

Sources: This case was drawn from the following sources: Kelly Nelson, "A High Tech Success," *China Business Review* (January–February 1992): 36–38; James Shapiro, Jack Behrmann, William Fischer, and Simon Powell, *Direct Investment and Joint Ventures in China* (New York: Quorum Books, 1991: 246–57); "Networking: Sourcing Goods and Parts," *Business China,* 5 April 1993: 3–4; "Chinese, U.S. Managers Sell Xerox Products in Shanghai," *Xinhua General Overseas News Service,* 23 November 1990.

Physical Systems. In contrast to level 1 and even level 2 transfers, physical systems are the least important part of the interaction for level 3. (See Figure 8-6.) That is, although a level 3 transfer of capabilities certainly requires adequate infrastructure, tools, and local suppliers, the transfer effort requires a proportionately much larger effort to convey managerial systems and operational values, as both the Xerox and Hewlett-Packard stories suggest. Level 3 therefore constitutes a real leap over level 2 in the transfer of unembodied knowledge. The challenge is not just to find local sources for componentry and improve parts of the product but to consider the product as a whole.

Skills and Knowledge. Redesigning a product requires engineering and design skills of quite high order and can be extremely difficult to achieve unless a basis of scientific knowledge already exists in the recipient organization. Of the dozen joint venture managers that I interviewed in China in 1994, at

Figure 8-6 Level 3 of Capabilities Transfer: Product Redesign

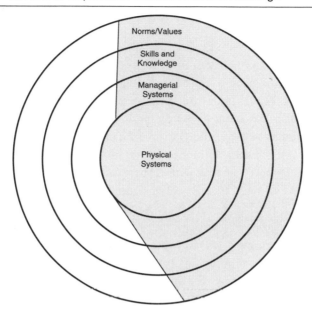

least half specifically mentioned the fact that Chinese engineers (both software and hardware) had an excellent grounding in mathematics and the theory of engineering principles—but they lacked practical experience. One software development manager pointed out that since the very few computers available in Chinese schools had been shared among hundreds of students while the engineers trained, they had little hands-on experience with real machines. Noting that the Chinese educational system does not equip them well to transform fundamental principles into product innovation, Ko Ching-wen, personnel director in Motorola's Tianjin plant, says: "Their knowledge of basic science is very strong, but they don't know how to apply it."[25]

The difficulties of redesigning products developed elsewhere are compounded when the original designers did not have a global market in mind to begin with. Software applications for Asia must be able to carry Chinese-type characters since not only Chinese but Japanese and Korean people use them. However, unless the software is designed to accommodate double-byte character sets, the redesign for the Asian market is likely to be awkward. Managers in three large, well-known U.S. companies described similar problems in transferring products to Asia. Programs redesigned for a Chinese character interface will run, but they occasionally crash and are slow; had they originally been designed to accommodate the characters, they would run more quickly. U.S.-based software engineers are not accustomed to considering the eventual destination of their creations during the development dash for the market.

Managerial Systems. In developing nations, technicians may be easier to identify and hire than managers. Individuals can develop impressive technical skills through reading and technical schooling but usually have little opportunity to learn managerial skills through professional schooling and/or international experience. In China, software production companies find it relatively easy to hire competent programmers, since the major Chinese universities have computer science departments (although new hires may need additional practical training). "Finding someone with six to seven years' experience is not difficult," explained an Intel manager. "But people with ten years' experience or more are really scarce." Therefore, locating project managers is extremely difficult. Moreover, people in China who have held positions of responsibility do not necessarily understand even the rudiments of management since they had little independent decision-making power under the previous communist system and almost no incentive to work hard at management.

A foreign manager in a communications equipment facility speculated as to why problem-solving skills seemed so lacking in his staff initially. "They tend to ask for all possible information—not just whatever might be needed to solve the problem. They say, 'Give me everything,' because they don't know what they may need, and they are accustomed to unlimited people resources. People were basically free of charge, so they had no need to analyze. If they had a problem, they just threw lots of people at it," he concluded.

Companies desiring to transfer capabilities into China often need to build understanding of management practices, including basic problem-solving skills and the kind of appreciation for quality that has reawakened in the West over the last decade. Walking through the Xerox copier factory in Shanghai, one is struck by the number of charts and graphs depicting the current state of quality in production. A prominent bulletin board at the entrance to the factory displays test results and Pareto analysis of problems encountered in production for the prior month; it is labeled "Leadership through Quality" and contains such reminders as "In the race for quality, there is no finish line." On the walls of the major conference room hang a series of framed operational principles—in matched pairs of English and Chinese. One details Xerox's nine-step procedure for working from desired output, through the translation of customer requirements into specifications and an analysis of process capabilities to meet those specifications, to an evaluation of results. Included in this set of procedures is direction to a problem-solving process at those points where a problem is identified. This problem-solving process is also outlined in a schematic. Arranged in a circle and linked by arrows are the phrases: "identify and select problem; analyze; generate potential solutions; select and plan solution; implement solution; execute solution." Yet another plaque reminds the people gathered in the room that Xerox is pursuing its Mission/Vision/Goal/Strategy and Objectives.

These plaques and the numerous charts on the factory floor illustrate Xerox's very conscious attempt to transfer not only the physical product and production equipment to Shanghai, and not only the skills to build machines, but also the managerial systems and the values supporting them—all of which constitute the company's core technological capability. Of course, merely posting plaques and even having workers chart their progress in quality control do not ensure that the meaning of the words and exercises will be absorbed. However, by making the desired management systems very visible and by emphasizing the desired norms of behavior, company management greatly increases the probability that a depth of knowledge not even attempted in many plants will in fact be transferred here.

Values. A major reason for setting out problem-solving procedures in such detail is to reinforce the point that the employees are responsible for operations. Producing quality output is everyone's task. Moreover, if the facility itself is to take responsibility for redesigning whole products, local management needs control over the entire process. Therefore, *initiative* in both operators and technical staff is highly valued. In a number of Asian cultures in which education has emphasized rote learning, respect for the opinions of people of higher rank, and conformity with the group, the risk taking and confrontation implied by redesign require a shift in values. When Larry Brown, a manager in the Hewlett-Packard peripherals division with over ten years' experience in research and manufacturing, first took on the task of setting up research in the Singapore facility, he had to learn how to formulate questions so as to leave his authority-conscious engineers options on how to respond: "If I suggested answers to my engineers, to them this became the only possible solution."[26]

Level 4 Transfer: Independent Design of Products

HEWLETT-PACKARD IN SINGAPORE: DESIGNING A PORTABLE PRINTER

The success of the DeskJet 505J won HP Singapore the right to design a printer for Japan—from scratch. This time, General Manager Tommy Lau wanted "a home run." Clearly, the printer had to be much smaller and more portable than the previous two DeskJet models produced for the Japanese market. Space was at a premium in tiny, crowded Tokyo offices. Moreover, a truly portable printer could be a winner in the U.S. market, as competitors Canon and Kodak were proving with the success of their compact machines. With the help of Jim Girard, an industrial designer from HP's Boise, Idaho, division, the Singapore team turned out a notebook-size printer in August 1992. The DeskJet Portable rapidly acquired about 6 percent of the ink-jet printer market in Japan. It also won a number of design awards for its unusual modular, sleek, and highly functional design, including the 1993 U.S. Industrial Design Excellence Award in the computer peripherals category. By November 1992, Singapore was given the worldwide charter (full R&D, manufacturing, and marketing responsibilities) for Hewlett-Packard's portable printer product line.

Success at level 4 is the *independent* design and production of a viable new product and the existence of potential for *reverse transfer*, although the step from level 3 codevelopment to level 4 is neither huge nor clear-cut. Perhaps the biggest difference between levels 3 and 4 is the shift in power and technological dependency. Whereas in level 3, the original transferer still possesses the lion's share of the knowledge, in level 4, the two partners are equals. (See Figure 8-7.) As the story of the portable printer suggests, Hewlett-Packard Singapore is just reaching that point. Some necessary new-product design skills are still transient, embodied in expatriates such as Jim Girard.

The best examples of foreign partners that have equaled or surpassed the original source of much of their new-product development capability come from Japan. From the time of its founding in 1962, Fuji Xerox invested in its own technological capabilities, gradually weaning the company away from scientific dependence on Xerox.[27] The company went through roughly the same stages as Hewlett-Packard Singapore and Xerox Shanghai, starting with copier sales, then assembly of kitted products, then domestic production, then new-product development. In less than ten years, Fuji Xerox reached level 3, redesigning Xerox products. Seeing a need in Japan for very small copiers, in 1970, the Fuji Xerox engineers presented Rank Xerox (in England) with working prototypes of a much smaller, lighter copier than anything Xerox had. The world's smallest copier, the FX2200, was introduced in Japan in 1973 with the slogan "It's small, but it's a Xerox." In 1978, Fuji Xerox reached level 4 with the production of the FX3500 copier, characterized by President Kobayashi as "the first . . . copier based on our own design

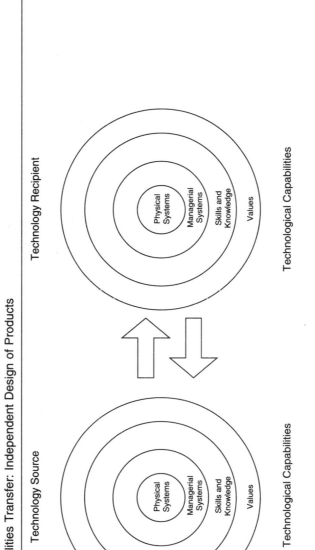

Figure 8-7 Level 4 of Capabilities Transfer: Independent Design of Products

concept."[28] The FX3500 was labeled by some as Fuji Xerox's "declaration of independence."

At level 4, the receiver has become the source—and the source can become the receiver. When parent company Xerox was attacked by unanticipated competition in its U.S. home base, it turned for help in lowering manufacturing costs to Fuji Xerox, which had won the coveted Deming Award for quality in 1981. In fact, in the early 1980s, Xerox borrowed from Fuji Xerox the quality management processes described above as being transferred into Xerox Shanghai operations in 1994. In a clear case of reverse transfer, Fuji Xerox taught its parent about benchmarking, just-in-time manufacturing, and faster product development. Fuji Xerox also gradually took over responsibility for product line parts. In 1980, only 30 percent of the low-volume copiers sold by Xerox and Rank Xerox were designed by Fuji Xerox; by 1987, 94 percent were. As Xerox CEO Paul Allaire observed, "Fuji Xerox is a critical asset of Xerox."[29]

Similarly, IBM's Fujisawa plant provided guidance in the design of a module for IBM's Communication Oriented Production Information Control System (COPICS) for controlling medium and large manufacturing facilities. Fujisawa had developed a module to support its highly successful just-in-time inventory management and continuous-flow manufacturing process, which had reduced parts inventory by 32 percent in 1988.[30] Worldwide IBM customers increasingly needed such a feature as more manufacturing operations adopted just-in-time. Although no actual software code went back to the United States, a number of groups visited Japan and picked up many design ideas.

As Figure 8-7 suggests, the new-product development capability looks similar at both sites when level 4 has been achieved; the four dimensions of the capability are the same ones reviewed in Chapter 1. When both parties have a real development capability, the challenge is to make the relationship synergistic. Typically, both make a huge investment in building the interpersonal relationships that serve as a web of support for technology flows. By 1989, Xerox managers estimated that 1,000 young Fuji Xerox personnel had spent three years apiece in residence at Xerox, and at least 150 Xerox employees had similarly resided at Fuji Xerox.

The transition to equality in power between partners is not easy. Over the years, Xerox and Fuji Xerox have periodically revised their relationship to reflect the gradual balancing of power between them. In 1988, managers at another long-term Japanese-American partnership, Yamatake-Honeywell, commented that although the technology flow from the United States to

Japan was still at least 60 percent one-way, part of the reason was that United States managers regarded products designed in Japan as regional rather than international. After the first big oil crisis in the 1970s, the Yamatake-Honeywell Component Products Division (producing microswitches and industrial controllers) was forced to design new controls to meet stringent local Japanese requirements for energy conservation. Yet as of the late 1980s, none of the adaptations had traveled back to the United States.

Companies' strategies will clearly differ as to whether pursuing a level 4 transfer of capabilities makes sense. For some companies, it is anathema; for many more, it is imperative. By 1990, Applied Materials was the only non-Japanese company among the top five semiconductor equipment providers, worldwide. Starting with a sales organization in 1979, the company grew local capabilities and, by the mid-1980s, had a very active research and development as well as manufacturing facility at its Narita Technology Center. In its 1990 annual report, Applied Materials managers explained their rationale: "This global strategy . . . has . . . exposed our products and organization to the toughest customers and competitors the world has to offer. This experience has tested us in ways not yet understood by most organizations."[31] As Bartmess and Cerny note in their discussion of this decision, "The goal . . . is to build a network of *capabilities*, rather than just a network of facilities."[32] For companies desiring to produce product internationally, the progression from level 1 to level 4 is inevitable.

In China, Motorola is one of the most aggressive U.S.-based investors and, like Xerox, has announced its intention of eventually developing new products in that country.

MOTOROLA IN CHINA

China plans to add seventy million phone lines by the year 2000, a figure that implies ten million lines of switching equipment every year at an estimated cost of $1.2 billion annually. Wireless communications are also an important part of the planned telecommunications infrastructure. In 1992, Motorola built a plant in the northern port city of Tianjin to produce paging devices. The company originally determined that local demand would be low to nonexistent and began searching for export markets. However, the demand for pagers rose from one million in 1991 to four million in 1993, and Motorola began building one of corporate America's largest manufacturing ventures in China. By the end of 1993, the company had completed its first phase of a $120 million plant in the Tianjin Economic and Technology Development Area to produce pagers along with simple integrated circuits and cellular phones. A plant that will produce automotive electronics, advanced microprocessors, and walkie-talkie systems is scheduled to become operational in 1996. The company also has tentative plans to build a plant to produce silicon wafers. All told, the investment could total more than $400 million.

Unlike past Motorola ventures, this one is set up to do much more than establish factories to take advantage of China's low-cost labor supply and penetrate China's vast market. Company executives imagine that, over time, the Chinese technicians will play a significant role in the design and engineering of products. Motorola hopes to replicate in China its past successes in Singapore and Malaysia, both of which have become product innovation centers.

Sources: This case was drawn primarily from the following sources: Peter Engardio, "Motorola in China: A Great Leap Forward," *Business Week,* 17 May 1993, 58–59; David Hamilton, "AT&T Steps Up Effort in Asia to Bolster Presence in Telecommunications Market," *Asian Wall Street Journal,* 28 June 1993, 3; Nick Ingelbrecht, "Busy Signals All over Asia," *Asian Business* 29 (September 1993): 57–59; Lin Sun, "China Follows the Long Road to Telecom Growth," *Telephony* (28 May 1990): 22–30.

Companies not having local capabilities in countries for which they are developing new products risk a very high failure rate. Nor is superficial localization always adequate. As examples of failures resulting from lack of local capabilities in new-product development, Bartlett and Ghoshal cite Kao's introduction of a liquid shampoo in Thailand, which gained a thin 7 percent market share after four years of intensive marketing, and NEC's original inadequate software for the U.S. market. By contrast, Philips "is the master of local innovations" and has a host of product lines developed in subsidiaries around the world to prove the point.[33]

Even companies like Philips still develop products primarily in other developed nations such as Australia, France, and Britain. Motorola and Xerox have taken on more challenging partnerships in places like China. If the past experiences of Xerox, Honeywell, and IBM in Japan are any indication of the potential in China, the companies that get in early may receive significant returns on their investment in transferring technological capabilities. However, such pioneers will have to take a long-term view, and the risks are significant.

Observations on the Transfer of New-Product Development Capability

The concept of transferring technological capabilities has evolved from the older notion of technology transfer. As we have seen from the examples in this chapter, "technology" has always encompassed much more than equipment. That fact was not always explicitly recognized in the way that technology transfer was managed, however. Today, both technology sources and technology recipients have become increasingly sophisticated in their understanding about transnational flows of knowledge, with the result that expectations on both sides about the potential for innovation are much higher than before. Managers in developing nations expect to create new-product development capabilities within their borders; managers in many multinational corporations expect to benefit from reverse flows of knowledge.

The examples presented in this chapter and the experiences of other companies that have engaged in the transfer of technological capabilities suggest some general observations about the factors affecting a company's relative level of success.

Long-Term Commitment

Perhaps the most obvious observation to make about transferring a new-product development capability is that it can take a long time and thus requires a long-term perspective. Hewlett-Packard spent over twenty years building up the Singapore division; the capabilities of the company grew as the region developed. Fuji Xerox developed faster, building on the more advanced Japanese infrastructure. The question for companies going into China today is whether that development process within the firm can be accelerated faster than the pace of change and development in the country as a whole. Motorola and Xerox are examples of the more ambitious companies in China; their managers are apparently determined to truncate the time involved in going from assembly capabilities to new-product design. One variable influencing the speed of capability growth is the intent of the technology source from the beginning—i.e., what level of transfer is the goal. Even if technology source managers do not intend to build a new-product development capability, the developing nation may well force such a transfer over time, but obviously, the process is accelerated if transferer and receiver share that objective from the outset.

Companies aiming at levels 3 and 4 of capability transfer are investing tremendous energy in training. Emerson Electric started funneling a few Chinese managers through its St. Louis headquarters a decade ago, anticipating the need for Asian personnel well acquainted with the corporate view. Motorola is spending millions on in-house training focused on product innovation. The company is preparing workers for its start-up design centers for integrated circuits and telecommunications products in China. For the

Chinese executives who will eventually head the Tianjin complex, Motorola initiated "Cadres 2000," a career management and leadership training program, in which Motorola places and rotates up to twenty top recruits through its operations around the world. Alcatel, Siemens, and Philips are also attempting to bring the Chinese workforce up to the level of world-class designer and producer by implementing programs similar to those started by Motorola.[34]

Two consultant observers of the China scene, after interviewing managers in multinational companies "regarded by their peers as 'doing China extremely well,' " noted that such companies "are not in China just to take temporary advantage of its low labor costs before hopscotching to another country when faster development inexorably drives those costs up. They are there for the long haul, have already figured out how to make profits and sustain them over time, and are working hard to lock out slower-moving competitors."[35]

Pull versus Push

In most cases, the *pull* of managers in the developing nations for new-product development capabilities exceeds the transfer *push* of managers in the developed nations. That is, the receivers want more capability than the transferers are willing or able to provide. The more advanced the recipient, the stronger the demand for transfer of deep technological knowledge. In interviews in four Japanese companies, recipients of a number of different engineering design tools from their U.S. corporate headquarters uniformly provided evidence of dissatisfaction with the technology-transfer process. The Japanese recipients were unhappy with their inability to adapt the tools and to learn about the underlying technology. The following comments are representative: "Even if we find bugs in the software, we can't change the code without corporate agreements. This makes development slow. . . . [W]e would like to be able to modify the code." "We want to be able to design future cathode-ray tubes and transfer in the knowledge—not just install a design tool." "Our ultimate objective is to improve our design techniques and ability to design." " *Transfer* should mean that we understand the new technology and have the ability to use it to modify products." There are many possible reasons for this inequality in desire, the most often mentioned being the transferer's need for various types of control.

In the case of disseminating corporate tools, headquarters must standardize across the globe so that widespread product development groups can communicate and products will be uniform. Thus, one sees headquarters taking an "installation" rather than a "transfer" approach to sending software tools abroad, to ensure standardization. A second, more serious conflict in priorities between technology source and receiver arises when the transfer of product development responsibility is involved. In the Hewlett-Packard case, Vancouver's product design control was tied very tightly to that division's profitability. Why should a division give away control of a profitable product line? The answer, of course, is that it may be in the best interests of the whole corporation to do so. Historically, as product lines have grown, HP has assigned various segments of them to certain divisions so that lines of responsibility were clear and duplication was avoided. As Singapore attained the status of a full-fledged division, its right to a product-line charter was recognized. However, it is not surprising if managers in a home country are somewhat reluctant to relinquish control over a product that their own employees have developed tremendous skill in producing. In the absence of appropriate corporate incentives, home-country managers are likely to balk at transferring critical capabilities.

A third type of control that the technology source exercises is protection of proprietary technology. Alarmed by the proven ability of Asian companies to copy product and, in the case of China, by the absence of readily enforced laws protecting intellectual property, home-country managers select older technologies for transfer or choose to supply particularly sensitive components from their home base for an indefinite period. A manager in one company noted that "sourcing the components [from the United States] is our only protection"; and an Emerson Electric manager explained that the company did "not want to risk loss of control" of a machining process in which the company had invested a lot of money—"which means we probably won't take it to China."[36]

However, developing nations are increasingly strident in their demands for the latest and best technology. Although, for the next several years, the very high purity of a few imported chemical components provides Du Pont a competitive advantage over local companies, Du Pont has agreed with its Chinese joint venture partner that it will increasingly backward-integrate until the Shanghai plant produces basic chemicals. Companies can exercise control over key components for financial rather than technological reasons, of course. As noted, some observers have attributed the fact that Volkswagen was slow to source parts locally as much to the profitability of importing parts as to local suppliers' inability to meet quality standards.

Even if the foreign company is willing to export technology, it can get caught in a tug-of-war between U.S. export restrictions and local demands. Technology gatekeepers in such developing nations as China are aware of the latest technical developments. A communications equipment company setting up business in China initially brought in technology that was current in Europe and that it thought would be good for at least seven years. By the second year of operations, the technology had progressed so rapidly that two of the ten products slated for local production were already obsolete. Moreover, engineers in the Chinese government were demanding product that had just come on the market in the United States and was still restricted for export. Since the Chinese venture was set up to produce the older product, the dilemma was what to produce until the newer technology could be brought in. The temporary solution was to sell the older product into more rural areas of China that were not yet requesting the latest technology. But the manager of the joint venture admitted ruefully that he was not sure how long it would be before even the most rural customers would be demanding the new technology. Managers of multinationals coming into China "should realize," he said, "that they are not insulated from technological change, even though China is a developing nation."

Design Biases

Product designers in developed nations do not necessarily have a global perspective. Equipment designed in developed nations sometimes suffers from a technocentric view—the belief that the system can only be used one way anywhere in the world.[37] Yet what seems obvious to technology producers may not be apparent to a potential recipient, and physical systems can be employed in many different ways in different cultures.[38] User interfaces can be variously interpreted. It is not self-evident that gauges read from left to right; symbols easily interpreted in some cultures are meaningless in others. Lotus software producers found that a crown icon on the computer screen did not trigger for Asian users, as it did for westerners, an automatic association with rules. We have already seen the difficulty of retrofitting software programs for an Asian language using Chinese characters when the software was not originally double-byte enabled. All IBM products were required to be double-byte enabled as of 1986; two years later, an IBM manager estimated that such design foresight would have saved about 40 percent of the effort engineers had just expended in retrofitting a piece of software designed without the double-byte enabling.[39] Software designers may not even know about such potential requirements when they labor along under the usual deadlines and market window constraints. However, as markets become increasingly global, considering the implications of original designs for later adaptation will become increasingly cost-effective.

Recipients of technology observe that U.S. designers in particular are quite profligate of resources in general and energy use in particular. Japanese consumer electronics developers note that U.S. applications use tremendous "overhead"—i.e., room on the operating system chip—and are therefore less cost-effective. Engineers in IBM's Fujisawa plant said that (as of 1988) their U.S.-based colleagues had "a large-system mentality" in designing software. When they wanted a shop floor control system based on personal computers, the Japanese designed their own rather than going to their sister plant in the United States. Similarly, in 1994, a manager in a food-processing company just opening in China noted that some of the difficulties experienced occurred because the corporation's U.S.-based engineers are "expert at building huge plants; they don't know how to build small ones" more appropriate for local conditions.

Technology Source as Educator

Transferring technological capabilities requires an extremely important managerial skill not always associated with technically skilled people—the ability to coach. Good coaching requires an appreciation for how knowledge is conveyed: that knowledge is often tacit—held in the head—and cannot be transferred through blueprints or documentation; that lectures are not effective communication devices; that a lack of understanding apparently due to inadequate skills may in fact be caused by language differences and vice versa—that apparent language difficulties may actually signal more serious gaps in comprehension. "It took me eighteen months and some major *faux pas* to become an insider," HP's Larry Brown said of his initial experience in Singapore. A process engineer responsible for a start-up of an Asian plant producing floppy disks for computers observed about his work with local engineers and technicians: "The hardest part is not doing it all for them. You want to get things working, get out of there, get home. But if you fix everything, they will be helpless when you leave. Some guys get their egos stroked by being Mr. Know-It-All. It's better to let [local workers] try things and fail and learn—help them think through why their solution didn't work. It takes a lot of patience." In Shanghai, the general manager of a major communications equipment company commented, "It's not that people aren't willing—but your request may seem impossible to them. I've never done in my entire life as much explaining as I have in the past three years." A manager of a chemicals joint venture put it more bluntly: "Retrofitting people is difficult."

Employees from developing nations value the opportunity to travel to the United States or Europe, and there are many advantages to conducting training at the home base. Instructors and students alike can concentrate on operations as they function under home-country conditions at the technology source. However, conducting pilot operations in the developing country also offers the great advantage of organizational prototyping.[40] For the purposes of creating local knowledge, local pilots are often preferable. In one Shanghai joint venture, the expatriate plant manager was forced by his Chinese partner to pilot a production process so that Chinese government officials could see some actual output before the end of the year. This initially onerous task proved beneficial, as many unanticipated problems with logistics were uncovered and the need for additional worker training was revealed. "I now advise anyone starting up operations to do this," the manager said. "It may be easier to pilot a line in Europe, but you don't learn nearly as much that way—and neither do the employees."

Multiple Levels of Cultural Influence

Transferring technological capabilities requires a sensitivity to at least three levels of culture: (1) national or ethnic, (2) company, and (3) function- or discipline-based. Managers tend to confuse the three in their diagnosis of problems when transferring capabilities and therefore do not always correctly identify the problem they think they are addressing.

Many managerial challenges occur because of the different ethnic and national histories people bring to a relationship.[41] Different languages are the first barrier nearly any manager mentions in working across cultures. However, the deeper problems have their roots in years of practicing different behaviors than those required by the new technological capability—i.e., in the core rigidities born of history. Communism in China deposited its residue on everything from attitudes toward work to comprehension of what constitutes a market. A number of difficulties mentioned in this chapter arose because the Chinese were accustomed to central planning, local self-sufficiency, production to quotas, and universal employment. However, the biggest culture-based difference that foreigners noted was the Chinese reliance on relationships for all sorts of business decisions—a characteristic traceable to a heritage older than communism.[42] To get anything done in China, from construction to travel, one must identify "the right person." Choice of personnel is thus based more on relationships than on skill base.

The balance between work and family life often differs in different cultures. Asian managers, from Japan to China, frequently mention the incomprehensible emphasis U.S.-based personnel seem to place on family obligations. In cultures in which dual careers are uncommon, male engineers are puzzled by their U.S. counterparts' explanations for absences or departures from long-distance conferences. "In the United States," concluded one Japanese engineer working long-distance with counterparts in California, "the top priority is family, not job. For example, sick children or vacation according to family schedule [takes precedence over] the business schedule. We may have to wait a week to get a response. A Japanese would do the job, regardless."

During interviews in Japanese-based firms conducted in 1988, one frequent complaint about U.S. engineers was that their job definition was "too narrow"; the Americans considered only their specialized piece of the design and were less concerned about the whole. So there do appear to be cultural differences whose boundaries can be somewhat loosely ascribed to nations. However, country-based cultural differences are relatively unimportant as long as the business is doing well. When the business falters, such differences are magnified and used as explanations for friction.[43]

The culture and structure within a *company* also profoundly influence the transfer of new-product development capabilities. Companies differ greatly in the levels of autonomy granted by corporate headquarters. Emerson Electric, which has grown mostly through acquisition, tends to give its divisions a good deal of autonomy, governing behavior almost entirely through financial goals and controls.[44] Decisions about where to locate capabilities are made by the individual companies. However, the corporation encouraged entry into China with a "silver platter approach."[45] The Boa'an "incubator" set up by the corporation to encourage individual Emerson Electric companies to transfer some operations into China comprised a physical plant, financial accounting support, and hiring of management and workers. Hewlett-Packard, which has grown less through acquisition and more through spinning off divisions when a new product line achieved sufficient market presence, is not as loose a federation as Emerson Electric. Although HP has always granted considerable autonomy to divisions, the latter tend to reflect a more homogenous corporate attitude toward capabilities development. Digital Equipment Corporation traditionally ruled its far-flung fiefdoms through networks of peer influence but maintained quite tight control over centrally designed products. IBM was known for relatively clear lines of authority and was referred to in some Asian quarters as "the Roman Empire."

The tighter the corporate control over product, the more difficult the power shift implied by moving to levels 3 and 4 of capabilities transfer. As we have seen, technology receivers often push for freedom from corporate constraints sooner than the headquarters might intend to move. Once Fuji Xerox gained more indigenous technological capability, it conducted rounds of renegotiations with Xerox at several points—and the relationship between the two companies in the Xerox group continues to evolve. In another company studied, in which the culture supported very tight central controls, the Japanese partners were scathing in their denunciation of corporate research's reluctance to release information about a particular software tool. "We couldn't wait for them to make up their minds to give it to us," the Japanese researcher explained. "We created our own [software tool]. Then they wanted us to use theirs. But it was too late." When asked if the locally created tool was superior, the Japanese developer just smiled.

Another way that company culture affects capabilities transfer has already been suggested by the discussion of values as a dimension of any new-product development capability. As described in Chapter 1, those values can be generic or knowledge-specific. Both forms are important. In the Shanghai Johnson & Johnson Band-Aid factory, a familiar-looking plaque adorns the wall at the reception desk. Even if she does not read Chinese, a visitor who is familiar with J&J can accurately guess that this is the famous "Credo" displayed in any J&J facility in the world. The "little values" get transferred also. Recall the plaques on the walls of Xerox Shanghai explaining standard problem-solving approaches and the corporate mission. Companies transferring capabilities overseas also export the same attitudes toward, and preferences for, specific kinds of knowledge that they have at home. Therefore, a company in the United States dominated by mechanical engineers will hire mechanical engineers abroad; a software-dominated culture will attract the best software programmers in a developing nation just as it does at its home base.

However, when new-product development tasks get subdivided among home-based and foreign facilities, the third type of culture—*discipline-based*—becomes especially relevant. Look closely at the following comment by HP's manager of research in Singapore, Larry Brown: in Singapore, "we had to work out an approach toward risk that would work culturally. We spent a lot of time on computer simulation, feasibility studies, and statistical design of experiments to decrease the actual risk of failure, because failure is unacceptable in Singapore. However, all this work had unexpected benefits in the end; we had the fastest, most trouble-free production ramp-up I ever experienced."[46] Is he observing Singapore-based differences in attitudes toward managing risk or the same attitudes that he would find in a good manufacturing operation anywhere in the world? Is the strong inclination to resolve any potential problems before starting high-volume production an example of national culture—or of manufacturing culture? Think back to the partnership between Quantum and Matsushita Kotobuki Electronics recounted at the end of Chapter 6. The design engineer in charge of mechanical design for the joint venture, Plus Development, observed of his new partners: "They live by specifications. The idea is that if every part meets specs, then every product assembled from those parts will work." The process the Japanese observed, he said, was: "One, prove the dimensions and tolerances that are required on each part up front. Two, create elaborate assembly tools. And three, check at every step of the process."[47] But of course, the manufacturers in this case were also Asian—Japanese instead of Singaporean.

In a number of companies, the attitudes, priorities, and skill sets born of a manufacturing orientation were combined in the minds of Americans and confused with "Asian culture." Similarly, some of the priorities and biases of the design engineers in the United States were attributed by their Asian counterparts to "U.S. culture." Yet those same sets of attitudinal differences and priorities can be observed *within* either Asian culture or U.S. culture. In a book about product design and manufacture written by and for westerners, we find the following observation: "Engineering's bias is to experiment with new technology because it is exciting and there are always fresh discoveries to be made. . . . Manufacturing operations thrive in a stable environment. For them bringing a new product into production means starting at the top of the learning curve. Manufacturing people are not rewarded for the headaches they incur by being involved in working the bugs out of a new product."[48]

Managers need to be capable of distinguishing national and historically based differences from ones grounded in discipline and education. Although we are still learning how best to deal with the more intractable variations caused by true ethnic and national "culture," we have evolved tools over the past decade or so to deal more effectively with discipline-based differences—including those suggested in Chapters 3, 5, and 7. Managers who expect to encounter, and strive to understand, cultural differences when they are responsible for transferring technological capabilities are likely to be better listeners and better coaches than managers who go in without those sensitivities. However, by recognizing different types of culture, the manager enhances his or her ability to respond appropriately.

Transferring Technological Capabilities—A Final Word

Few manufacturing companies today can afford to be totally regional. The market is becoming truly global. Therefore, managers are increasingly confronted with the issues not of *whether* to transfer technological capabilities but of when, where, and to whom—a partner or a wholly owned subsidiary? Developing nations such as China influence the last decision by setting up disincentives to total ownership. China has greatly softened its initial position, which insisted that joint ventures be 50–50 controlled. However, regulations still in place discourage 100 percent foreign ownership; in 1994, only 30 percent of a wholly owned subsidiary's output could be sold inside China, for instance. For their part, technology sources try to retain control over operations through majority ownership—the more uneven in their favor, the better. However, as Steven Sonnenberg, general manager of Emerson Electric's Branson Company, noted, "People tend to think that having 80–20 ownership gives them control. Having majority ownership in a joint venture does not guarantee control" over management decisions—including the transfer of technological knowledge. Especially in developing nations, where litigation is less important in settling disputes than it is in the West (and especially in the United States), managers must think beyond the legal arrangements to determine the flow of knowledge. Even 100 percent ownership does not make the organization immune to knowledge leakage: knowledgeable employees leave; competitors learn from suppliers and customers; partners learn process techniques and dissolve the partnerships. Various strategies protect the technology source. In this chapter, we have noted several. Some companies select sensitive proprietary components to be imported by the technology recipients rather than produced locally. Others may segment the market geographically, licensing technology to partners for use in products to be marketed only in a restricted area.

Two points emerge as especially important to understand in the transfer of capabilities. The first is that the more a company aims for a level 4 transfer (whether with a foreign partner or with a wholly owned subsidiary), the more deliberate and systematic the transfer of knowledge will need to be. The goal of level 4 assumes a learning perspective, a recognition from the beginning that the foreign site is a potential wellspring of knowledge. Since people are the major—and literal—embodiments of knowledge, a systematic transfer of capabilities implies much exchange of personnel, a lot of travel, and a great deal of thought given to designing incentive systems.

The second point is that U.S. companies seem better at transferring knowledge out than in. There are many reasons for this, starting with the obvious and deceptively simple one that English is a dominant language of business around the world, and therefore, recipient managers learn English more readily than U.S. engineers and managers learn other languages. However, the not-invented-here syndrome affecting many U.S. businesses extends far beyond a reluctance to learn another country's language. Innovation can be found in unexpected places. Chaparral discovered the best example—in fact, at the time, the *only* example—of a working hot link between furnace and steel rolling mill in Poland. The Sound Blaster card found extensively throughout the West for multimedia applications in personal computers came from a tiny Singapore company, Creative Technologies.

The creative spirit may flare most strongly around particular universities, companies, or geographic locations, but it is also visible throughout the world. Managers who recognize the potential for virtual development groups, organizations, or even corporations comprising creative individuals wherever they may be found ignite a knowledge source that can burn brightly for years.

Summary

Very few sizable companies today have strictly regional markets. In fact, in many industries, even start-ups are born with a global outlook. Although companies may set up subsidiaries abroad to serve local markets or to take advantage of low-cost labor or other resources, their managers must inevitably consider the transfer of technological capabilities, at some level, from the home site.

In this chapter, we have examined four different levels of capability transfer, using the capability to create new products independently (level 4) to calibrate the position of recipient companies. Each of the four levels of capability transfer involves different proportions of the four dimensions of a technological capability. Transferring capabilities at level 1 or 2 (assembly or adaptation) resembles technology transfer in the old sense of the term, requiring a lot of attention to transferring compatible physical systems and management systems but relatively less to transferring the deep knowledge that underlies the technology or the company culture. Transferring capabilities at level 3 (product redesign) necessitates much attention to teaching a recipient company about the science behind the technology and the values required for innovation as well as providing physical and managerial systems. A recipient company that reaches level 4 essentially duplicates the technological capabilities of the original technology source—not in the sense of possessing exactly the same science base but in the sense of being capable of interacting with the original source as an equal partner. Whereas technology flows mainly from source to receiver at the first three levels, at level 4, the flow is bidirectional. The relationship changes from parent-child to adult-adult.

Not all companies will choose to transfer their technological capabilities to this extent. Those that do will need to be aware of the necessity for a long-term commitment and the development of some new management skills. Transferring capabilities requires an awareness of inherent design biases in equipment and products, the selection of personnel who are capable of coaching, and a sensitivity to multiple types of cultural influences on the interactions between personnel at the home technology source and at the receiver.

C H A P T E R   N I N E

Continuous Wellsprings

[W]e . . . not only . . . think ourselves into a way of acting but also . . . act ourselves into a way of thinking.
—David G. Myers
Social Psychology[1]

The renewed emphasis in recent years on knowledge management and on organizations as organic repositories of skills, systems, and values has grown up in response to a turbulent environment, whose turbulence, as far as we can see into the future, is unlikely to diminish. Forecasts of social and technological change call for more "creative winds of destruction."[2] Managers seek some underlying stability in response to the uncertainty they face, and thus, the notion of core technological capabilities is appealing. It suggests some permanency in the midst of change—some deep current that flows more slowly and surely than the surface rapids and eddies roiling our organizations. And it is true that capabilities change more slowly than projects or management programs or product lines. Yet even capabilities must shift channels from time to time in response to other conditions. Research following the history of industries over generations has shown that there are *always* sharp discontinuities, often occasioned by new technologies and often competence-destroying.[3] Many firms founder, and a few survive. Survivors have been able to change their capabilities, totally renew themselves—more than once.

In the process of renewal, human minds are the most flexible assets a company has—and the most rigid. People are capable of making astounding leaps in intuition and, at the same time, of tenaciously clinging to the details of petty, unproductive routines. That is why this book has devoted so much attention to *behavior,* even though the focus is on *technological* capabilities. As we have seen, technological capabilities rest less upon technical information per se and more upon all the activities and systems that create that technical knowledge—and allow it to be *creatively* destroyed so as to adapt anew.

Organizations as Fractals

The remarkable aspect of vibrant and self-renewing organizations is the *consistency* of certain characteristics—no matter what level or unit of analysis one addresses. Talking to individuals, listening to project meetings, sitting in on a board of directors session—one hears certain themes over and over again. No organization is absolutely consistent, of course; individuals do differ, and pockets within the organization operate autonomously. I do not mean to suggest absolute conformity or homogeneity among individuals and groups. Rather, one finds a pattern of thought and behavior that is observable at all levels and that gives the organization its character.

The characteristics of this pattern permeate daily activities, and the pattern itself does not radically change whether one views the organization as a whole or the fragments within it. The mathematical geometry of fractals[4] provides a good metaphor here. "Fractals . . . offer an extremely compact method for describing objects and formations [with] an underlying geometric regularity, known as scale invariance or self-similarity. If one examines these objects at different size scales, one repeatedly encounters the same fundamental elements."[5] Seemingly chaotic forms in nature, observed at different levels of inquiry, have an underlying, regular rhythm and pattern that can be mathematically described and visually reproduced. A fern, a coastline, a bed of kelp—all are remarkably similar to forms mathematically derived from the repetition of very simple algorithms. Fractal forms are so complex, so intricate, that it is difficult to ascertain the pattern. Yet "*[t]he complexity of the behavior* arises from the iteration of simple rules."[6] The ultimate form of a fractal is highly sensitive to the initial starting point and conditions, but its apparent variation and sophistication grow from repeating a few mathematical procedures over and over.

So it is with organizations. Just as the piece of fern mirrors the whole frond, and as the twig mirrors the tree branch and the tree, so does the behavior of individuals and small groups reflect the attitudes toward knowledge-creating and -controlling activities of the organization. In this sense, the individual is responsible for the organization and vice versa.

The complexity we observe arises from the repetition of a few characteristic behaviors that cut across the knowledge management activities covered in this book. These life-giving characteristics and their opposites permeate all the positive and negative examples we have seen throughout and set learning organizations apart from stagnant ones. These characteristics separate firms that have created continuously renewing wellsprings from those that live—and die—by a single set of knowledge tools.

Characteristics of Continuously Renewing Organizations

In this book, we have examined in depth the nature of core technological capabilities (the four dimensions of physical systems, skills and knowledge, managerial systems, and values). We have explored four types of activities that create and sustain such capabilities (creative problem solving, implementation of innovative methodologies and operational tools, experimentation, and importing knowledge), and we have discussed some of the dysfunctional attitudes and behaviors that inhibit those activities. In this concluding chapter, we transverse those categories to extract and briefly review a few characteristics that, repeated throughout the organization and embedded in the actions of its managers, create an atmosphere for continuous renewal.

Enthusiasm for Knowledge

The first characteristic is an *enthusiasm for knowledge*—that is, for the knowledge content of every activity. The managers respect and encourage the accumulation of knowledge as a legitimate undertaking and one for which they are responsible. This love of learning is woven throughout the organization, whether the activity be problem solving across internal boundaries, creating knowledge through experimentation, importing it from outside, or transferring it to other sites and nations. People who are knowingly engaged in building core technological capabilities are *curious:* they are information seekers. There is a sense of enjoyment in the work—the lightness of step that suggests that building knowledge not only makes good business sense but is *fun.* The enthusiasm one senses among employees is a blend of professionalism and play. Of course, work is serious, but at the same time, one cannot take it or oneself too seriously—because tomorrow will bring change and will likely render current bases of skill obsolete. The only fundamentally important skill is the ability to learn.

We saw this enthusiasm in the line operators at Chaparral, continuously striving for better timing; we saw it at Nissan, where the American designers puzzled over the viewpoint of the Japanese and put the resulting answers to work in the design of other products. We saw it in the willingness of Hewlett-Packard engineers to place their entire new-product development project under the microscope in order to figure out how to improve the management process and again in Quantum's absorption of manufacturing expertise from Matsushita Kotobuki Electronics (MKE) through the Plus Development joint venture. And we saw how a *lack* of curiosity, a relatively passive assumption that they had the knowledge they needed, hampered the ability of E-L Products and of GE Plastics to recognize, ahead of time, the missing pieces in their acquisitions.

Drive to Stay Ahead in Knowledge

The second characteristic, and related to the first, is a *drive to stay ahead in knowledge*, to surf the waves of technological innovation. When people talk of "staying on top" of the knowledge in their profession, this is what they mean. Staying on top is not equivalent to being the first to commercialize a given technology, the first to enter the market. Rather, it means having the *capability* to enter the market if doing so is competitively essential. It means staying knowledgeable about the latest, best examples of experimenting, of stimulating creativity, of transferring technology. This desire impels the constant monitoring of the permeability of organizational boundaries discussed in Chapters 6 and 7. It motivates Sharp to license in technology from U.S. firms—despite its own significant lead in many aspects of the PDA market; it motivates Chaparral to send employees on technology searches around the world. Managers and companies with this characteristic strive to *anticipate* customer demands and extract from the market information that it didn't know it possessed, through empathic design. This drive to access the latest and best knowledge, wherever it originates, keeps people *listening*—another absolutely critical skill. The drive to stay ahead also gives managers forward vision. Just as in driving a car, keeping a lookout ahead, trying to discern the trends somewhat beyond the immediate vision, is the best safeguard against sudden disruptions in forward movement.

Tight Coupling of Complementary Skill Sets

A third characteristic is the *tight coupling among complementary skills,* a search for the interfaces among them—and then careful attention to managing those interfaces. Today's strong trend to tear down internal boundaries and operate in teams is healthy and desirable. At the same time, we should not drain the deep reservoirs of knowledge and skill providing sources of technological capabilities; we do not want to make everyone a generalist. We need enough boundary spanners, people with T-shaped and A-shaped skills, to manage across the interfaces, but we also want to retain the separate skill sets to be linked.

The nature of the knowledge reservoirs to be linked will undoubtedly change in the future. Centers of disciplinary and functional excellence that exist today as still-isolated stovepipes will give way to other specializations. The boundaries will become more fluid, and in many organizations, projects will drive daily business, as teams dissolve and regroup according to the dictates of business need. However, we will still need specialists and groups of people who concentrate on developing particular knowledge bases. In nurturing core technological capabilities, organizations will continue to need tight coordination among self-reliant, knowledge-rich groups and individuals. We need to maintain a balance between a coupling so tight as to erode specialized knowledge bases and so loose as to allow managers to overlook interactions and system effects. The desire and ability to manage interfaces enables specialized knowledge to flow from research organizations into product development, whether those researchers reside inside the company laboratories or in think tanks, national labs, universities, or the laboratories of partnering firms. Tight coupling enables product development based on technology fusion, but it requires a deep respect for knowledge bases other than one's own.

Iteration in Activities

The fourth characteristic is an appreciation for the *iterative, return-loop nature of all activities.* Whether the activity be problem solving, experimenting, importing knowledge from outside, or transferring knowledge, managers in the companies that successfully develop core capabilities know that they can never walk away from that activity with the assumption that it is now perfected. Managers in some companies seem to have the attitude about their job attributed to God by eighteenth-century Deists—that the world was set in motion and then abandoned to itself. Yet developing core capabilities is more like growing a garden than like building a brick wall. Activities and projects need watering with fresh insights, fertilizing with resources, the sunlight of management attention—along with an evening respite from constant management oversight. One cannot assume that a job done is a job finished.

So we see Hewlett-Packard testing the validity of its newly redesigned product development process by rediscovering the same guiding principles in other successful companies. We see Quantum retaining its relationship with MKE—yet changing it to allow manufacture in the United States, not just Japan. We see Nissan Design International experimenting with new ways of viewing its user world, never satisfied with the novel techniques discovered so far. And within individual product development processes, we see managers failing forward—one step back, two ahead. The realization that activities are nonlinear is very freeing: we can reexamine some of our assumptions; we can experiment and revise. The most obvious manifestation of this recognition of iteration is the prototyping of different kinds illustrated in this book—product prototypes, process prototypes, organizational prototypes. The "try-it-and-learn" attitude embodied in prototyping forestalls the arrogance that engenders core rigidities.

Higher-Order Learning

Closely related to this acknowledgment of nonlinearity is the emphasis on *higher-order learning* that one finds cutting across all the activities outlined in this book. If managers do not look for this higher-level learning, they will be absorbed by current problems. "Learning at the operating level of an organization substitutes for learning at higher levels."[7] As we saw in Christensen's study of the disk drive industry, listening too hard to current customers can blind one to important signs of needed change and the potential of totally new markets. We have seen that in some companies, project audits are used as mechanisms to force higher-level process learning, whereas in others, such audits either are not conducted or are perfunctory and pro forma. Ironically, the companies and the managers who most need to consider this higher order of learning are the ones most closed to self-examination.

Managers who successfully develop core capabilities look for organizational metaroutines that will lead the company into the future. So, for instance, when they sign a travel voucher for an employee to visit a customer site, they think about the use of the knowledge thus engendered. How will it be leveraged beyond the use by one individual? What mechanisms exist to share that information? How widespread is such travel? For every activity, the manager asks, What is the potential knowledge-building import of this action? Is it part of a larger pattern to which I should be devoting attention? If not, should it be? If it should not be, why am I doing it? Managers who look for the metaroutines are constantly asking, Why are we doing this? Why are we doing it *this way?* These simple questions are profound.[8] They also reach for the future; seeking answers to the "simple questions" will encourage long-term thinking rather than reflex action.

Leaders Who Listen and Learn

Finally, as the above comments suggest, *leadership* is essential in order to build, nurture, and sustain core technological capabilities. This does not mean only top management, although developing and sustaining core technological capabilities cannot happen without the support of top management. It means managers at every level in the organization are leaders. Whatever their sphere of influence and power, they are able to emphasize or minimize the importance of the knowledge-building content of decisions. Project audits can be either sterile and futile exercises or rich seminars on progress, depending on the managers' attitude. Interactions with the market can be either dull confirmations of existing biases or exciting explorations of new frontiers. Managers can be barriers to the import of knowledge—or open gates and active environmental scanners. It is no accident that in leading technology-based companies, the leaders *at all organization levels* are knowledgeable about the companies' technologies. These managers tend to embody the characteristics mentioned above—an enthusiasm for knowledge and an ambition to stay at the forefront, an appreciation for the iterative nature of their jobs, and significant personal skills in managing the interfaces. They are eager learners.

The same stream of research that documented the tremendous technological disruptions punctuating long interim periods of equilibrium in a number of industries uncovered another interesting fact. The firms that survived were those that reoriented and restructured. Often, the turnabout was directed by an entirely new management team, as we saw at NCR and as is occurring in IBM, Kodak, and Digital Equipment in the mid-1990s. Significantly, however, that same wrenching reorientation could be, and was directed by the *same* top management in a lot of firms—for instance, among half of the survivors in the minicomputer industry.[9]

Intel's exit from the memory chip business provides an interesting example of the difference leaders can make. Andy Grove, at the time the COO, remembered: "The fact is that we had become a non-factor in DRAMs, with 2–3 percent market share. . . . I recall going to see [CEO] Gordon [Moore] and asking him what a new management would do if we were replaced. The answer was clear: Get out of DRAMs. So, I suggested to Gordon that we go through the revolving door, come back in, and just do it ourselves."[10] To exit from the DRAM business, Grove and Moore had to overcome all the different kinds of resistance mentioned in Chapter 2 as associated with a core rigidity. DRAMs were the highest-volume product produced by Intel at the time, and many of Intel's key customers expected "one-stop semiconductor shopping"—i.e., to purchase memory chips as well as logic chips. Managers throughout the organization regarded the underlying technology as one of Intel's core competencies and were emotionally tied to DRAMs, as the product that had brought Intel to its pinnacle of success. Getting out of DRAMs, one middle manager said, was "kind of like Ford deciding to get out of cars."[11] However, Intel had, in effect, already relinquished that market to overseas producers. The future of the company clearly lay with logic chips, and fortunately, middle managers had engaged in strategic improvisation, investing heavily in the requisite technological capabilities to support logic technology. The wellsprings were in place, and top management was able to rechannel corporate energies to tap them.

Developing Core Technological Capabilities: A Continuous Process

None of the six characteristics described above implies the much-vaunted skills of "rocket science." Creating core technological capabilities instead implies incremental but steady investment in the future, with an occasional significant correction in the course of the organizational ship. Such corrections will be less drastic when managers are constantly making the small checks on position, direction, and proximity to competitors and scanning the coast for potential technical shoals suggested throughout this book. Among the largest U.S.-based companies, 3M, Motorola, Hewlett-Packard, General Electric, and others seem to be managing their capabilities so as to yield a constant flow of new products and processes. Others, such as AT&T and IBM, have undergone drastic surgery but have drawn on their underlying technological strengths to recover. Meanwhile, as the activities of these industrial giants dominate the sound bites, managers in hundreds of smaller companies like Chaparral, ALZA, Quantum, Thermos, and others mentioned in this book are building capabilities in areas less illuminated by the media.

Wellsprings of knowledge not only feed the corporation but are fed from many sources. If all employees conceive of their organization as a knowledge institution and care about nurturing it, they will continuously contribute to the capabilities that sustain it. No matter what the organization's current environment, management at every level has a role to play in encouraging the characteristics featured in this chapter. Moreover, as the intellectual assets of our firms become more complex, the ability to inspire employees to invest in knowledge will become more, not less, important.

Introduction

1. Morton 1971, 3.

Chapter One: Core Capabilities

1. Quoted in Stonham 1993, 152.
2. Hamel identifies three concepts critical to identifying core competencies (or capabilities). If the competence cannot be described in terms of (1) customer benefit, it is not core; identifying such competencies is not a matter of listing current activities but of creatively considering (2) a competitive advantage; once a company has identified a core competency, managers need to go back and (3) define the individual skills and technologies that constitute that competency (Stonham 1993).
3. Pryzbylowicz and Faulkner (1993) point to Kodak's deep knowledge of silver halide materials—that is, the technology by which such materials are sensitized to various regions of the spectrum—as a *core* capability. The tools and processes for measuring the tiny amounts of dye on silver halide grains are *enabling* capabilities, essential to control and manufacture the silver halide emulsions reliably but not in and of themselves constituting a competitive advantage.
4. Not all kinds of learning aid productivity and progression, of course. For instance, people in an organization can learn to hide the truth, to avoid decision making, to cheat their customers. However, here we are interested in learning as a continuous, positive form of exploration and knowledge accrual, resulting in better communication among organization members and improved organizational performance. I assume that learning occurs if "through its processing of information, the range of [an organization's] potential behaviors is changed" (Huber 1991, 89). That is, beyond contrib-

uting to an accumulation of formal knowledge bases, learning creates "capacities . . . for intelligent action" (Morgan and Ramirez 1983, 21).

5. The descriptions of Chaparral Steel in this chapter borrow heavily from Leonard-Barton 1991a.

6. Argyris and Schon 1978.

7. A growing literature on the topic emphasizes that organizational learning is more than an aggregation of individual learning (see, for instance, Hedberg 1981).

8. Senge (1990) argues persuasively that successful leaders are systems thinkers, able to see "Interrelationships, not Things, and Processes, Not Snapshots" (15). Other theorists similarly note how interrelated are strategy, structure, and culture in creating learning environments (see Fiol and Lyles 1985). Stalk, Evans, and Shulman (1992) maintain that an attribute of core capabilities is that "they are collective and cross-functional—a small part of many people's jobs, not a large part of a few. . . . Because a capability is 'everywhere and nowhere,' no one executive controls it entirely" (63).

9. Scholars theorize that a "certain amount of stress is a necessity if learning is to occur" (Fiol and Lyles 1985) and that complex, uncertain environments require decentralized, laterally linked organizations (Duncan and Weiss 1979).

10. Kantrow 1986, 96–97.

11. The utility of such stretch goals as stimuli for learning is implied by other researchers. Such goals may be thought of as "performance gaps" (Duncan and Weiss 1979), deliberately induced to motivate knowledge generation. Itami with Roehl (1987) suggest that "overextensions" and "dynamic imbalances" created to challenge the organization characterize the most successful Japanese manufacturing companies.

12. Each of the activities proposed here has been identified as characteristic of a learning organization: (1) problem identification and solving (e.g., Hutchins 1991), (2) integration of internal information (e.g., Duncan and Weiss 1979), (3) experimentation (e.g., Bohn 1988), and (4) acquisition and use of external information (e.g., Huber 1991).

13. Morgan and Ramirez (1983) suggest that a "holographic" organization (which epitomizes a learning organization for them) is designed so that "the nature of 'one's job' at any one time is defined by *problems facing the whole*" (4; italics in original). Similarly, from his study of knowledge creation in some of Japan's top firms, Nonaka (1992) concludes that "every single member of the organization should be able to suggest problems . . . and . . . solutions . . ." (44).

14. *Near net-shape* refers to the pouring of the steel through a mold configured so as to shape the red-hot metal into an approximation of the final product shape. Casting the steel into a near net-shape cuts down on the number of times the steel must be rolled.

15. A remarkably similar philosophy was observed by Basadur (1992) in four Japanese companies where "[e]mployees are trained from the first day on the job that 'R&D is everybody's business.'" Similarly, Itami with Roehl (1987) propose "'excessive' experimentation in production" since "[e]xperimentation and learning do not take place only in the lab" (95).

16. Thus, Chaparral takes advantage of both horizontal diffusion of innovations (from other manufacturers; see Leonard-Barton and Rogers 1981) and vertical diffusion (from research laboratories).

17. Von Glinow (1985) argues that the most effective organizational reward system to attract and retain highly skilled people is an "integrated culture" that combines a concern for people with very strong performance expectations. Chaparral's system appears to fit her description. See also Kerr 1975.

18. In a macroanalysis of sixteen studies using forty-two different data samples that estimated the effect of profit sharing on productivity, Weitzman and Kruse (1990) conclude that "these studies taken together provide the strongest evidence that profit sharing and productivity are positively related" (139).

19. Quoted by Dumaine 1992, 88.

20. See Snow and Hrebiniak 1980; Hitt and Ireland 1985; Prahalad and Hamel 1990; Hayes, Wheelwright, and Clark 1988; Pavitt 1991; Hofer and Schendel 1978; Itami with Roehl 1987.

21. 1974.

22. Hayes 1985, 118.

23. Hayes 1985; Quinn 1980.

24. Mintzberg 1990.

25. Quoted in Stonham 1993, 152.

26. Schumpeter 1942.

27. Henderson and Clark 1990.

28. As insisted by Prahalad and Hamel (1990).

29. Hof 1993, 72–75 passim.

30. Consultants Stalk, Evans, and Shulman (1992) draw a distinction between competencies as described by Prahalad and Hamel (1990) and capabilities. The consultants argue that competencies refer to a "combination of individual technologies and production skills that underlie a company's myriad product lines, whereas capabilities are cross-functional business processes . . . encompassing the entire value chain" (66). I believe that a real technological competitive advantage derives from a combination of reservoirs of skill and knowledge (competencies) *with* the managerial and technical systems (capabilities) that exploit those reservoirs in delivering value to customers. Moreover, although Stalk, Evans, and Shulman acknowledge the importance of reward systems that support the capabilities, they do not consider those systems to be part of a capability. I do. Reward systems that punish or inhibit activities generating particular kinds of knowledge undermine the organization's ability to grow a capability based on those

kinds of knowledge. Therefore, I find the definitions of both competencies and capabilities as reflected in this recent literature to be incomplete. The *whole system* of knowledge management is the core capability—not either the technical knowledge or the business process alone.

31. Companies that label a certain function, such as "manufacturing" or "marketing," as a core capability may be confusing the two types of capability. In many industries, having world-class manufacturing or marketing is the price of entry—not a particular advantage over competitors. Although they cannot afford to lose parity in such a function, these companies are unlikely to prevail in the marketplace unless that function is organized, structured, and staffed to deliver benefits that no competitor can match.

32. See Leonard-Barton 1992a and 1992b.

33. See, for example, Teece, Pisano, and Shuen 1990.

34. As Nelson (1982, 467) notes, the hybrid term *technology* refers both to technique (*tech*), which tends to be privately held information, and to science (*logy*), which is a public good.

35. Iansiti 1993.

36. A poignant example of how the loss of tacit, application-specific knowledge can render technical systems all but useless is the data collected over thirty years of spaceflight. More than three thousand images from the Viking mission to Mars, for instance, were never processed. The NASA documents describing data entry procedures (and hence, containing the keys to access) were written in technical jargon that was incomprehensible to the people trying to decipher it two decades later. (See Blakeslee 1990.)

37. Hopper 1990, 118.

38. See Bowen et al. 1994.

39. Kimberly 1987.

40. Schein 1984, 4. In an analysis of organizational culture, Schein maintains that there are three levels of culture: (1) artifacts and creations (a level I believe describes technical and managerial systems); (2) values, which are "debatable, overt, espoused"; and (3) basic assumptions about the nature of human nature, activity, and relationships.

41. See Aguilar and Bhambri 1983.

42. Company literature, courtesy of Hewlett-Packard.

43. Barney 1986.

44. For a discussion of vicious and virtuous cycles in general, see Wender 1968.

45. Brown 1992, 25.

46. Thiessen 1965.

47. Slutsker 1989.

Chapter Two: Core Rigidities

1. McDonnell 1994, 9.

2. Quoted in Tichy and Charan 1989, 118.

3. Quoted in Deutschman 1994, 90.
4. Quoted in Ohmae 1989, 132.
5. The term was coined by Leonard-Barton (1992a). However, other scholars have discussed similar phenomena; Levinthal and March (1993) discuss "traps of distinctive competence." See Argyris 1993 for a discussion of competency traps at an individual level.
6. Quoted in Loomis 1993, 40.
7. Quoted in Loomis 1993, 39; italics in original.
8. Mike Dore, quoted in Hays 1994, 8.
9. Quoted in Wilke 1991, B4.
10. Ohmae 1989, 126, 129.
11. Clark and Fujimoto 1991, 95.
12. Fujimoto 1994b, 50.
13. Fujimoto 1994b, 50.
14. Wheelwright and Clark 1992.
15. Ellison, Clark, Fujimoto and Hyun 1995.
16. Fujimoto 1994a, 21.
17. Clark and Fujimoto 1994, 304.
18. Fujimoto 1994a, 21.
19. Clark and Fujimoto 1994.
20. Miller 1990, 3.
21. Day 1994.
22. See Arrow 1962 and Breshnahan 1985.
23. See Pfeffer 1981.
24. Morison 1966.
25. Nelson and Winter 1982; Dougherty 1992; Day Forthcoming.
26. Boeker 1989.
27. Graham 1986.
28. Hannan and Freeman 1977; DiMaggio and Powell 1983.
29. Levinson with Hass 1994.
30. See Langer 1989 on the topic of mindlessness, and Sitkin 1992.
31. Morison 1966, 18.
32. See Christensen 1990.
33. Levitt and March 1988, 322.
34. Cohen and Levinthal 1990.
35. Wrubel 1992, 50.
36. Benioff and Rosenbloom 1990.
37. Replogle 1988.
38. For a discussion of different situations under which speedy product change constitutes a disadvantage for consumers, see Dhebar 1994.
39. For an empirical study of discontinuities, see Tushman and Anderson 1986.
40. Loomis 1993.
41. Quoted in Loomis 1993, 39.

42. Martin 1975.
43. Rosenbloom (1988) points out that even in the 1960s, research and development was still based in Dayton, where skills in mechanical machinery dominated.
44. Anderson with Truax 1991, 174.
45. Anderson with Truax 1991, 186.
46. Anderson with Truax 1991, 206–8.
47. Anderson with Truax 1991, 204.
48. Quoted in Anderson with Truax 1991, 183.
49. Anderson with Truax 1991, 198.
50. Anderson with Truax 1991, 176.
51. For a description of Project Whirlwind, in which magnetic-core memory was invented, see Chapter 6.
52. Anderson with Truax 1991, 199.
53. Schumpeter 1942.
54. Quoted in Lohr 1994, 1.
55. Quoted in Holusha 1994, D1.
56. Quoted in Kehoe 1992, 30.
57. Quoted in Cafasso 1994, 8.
58. Cohen and Levinthal 1990.
59. Chew, Leonard-Barton, and Bohn 1991.
60. Ohmae 1989.
61. Leonard-Barton 1992a; Leonard-Barton, Braithwaite, Bowan, Hanson, Titelbaum, and Preuss 1994.
62. Quoted in Wilke 1991, B4.
63. Zachary 1993.
64. Wilke 1992.
65. See Rogers and Larsen 1984.
66. Von Hippel 1987, 293.
67. Kimberly 1987.
68. Communication with Russell Boss, president of Cross, 16 July 1993.
69. Anderson with Truax 1991, 261.
70. Sherrid 1983, 45.
71. Grady 1992.
72. McClelland, Joseph, and Bolander 1993.
73. Ohmae 1989, 129.
74. Morone 1993.

Chapter Three: Shared Problem Solving

1. Koestler 1964, 121.
2. Interview, December 10, 1993.
3. Cyert and March (1963) describe problemistic and local search in problem solving, when people define their problems on the basis of past experience.

4. Duncker 1945.
5. Birch and Rabinowitz 1951; Adamson 1952.
6. Birch and Rabinowitz 1951, 125.
7. Simon 1969; Howard 1987; Rumelhart 1980.
8. Allen and Marquis 1965.
9. Schon 1967a.
10. See Schein 1990.
11. Writers have long debated the "deskilling" effect of new technology—i.e., the extent to which human skills were being embodied in technical systems, leaving only monitoring and mindless control functions as the province of the operator. Braverman (1974) documents the demise of machine tooling from craft to semiskilled labor upon the advent of numerically controlled machine tools. Sheridan (1980) names promotion to "button-pushing" as one of seven factors alienating people from computers. However, looking at aggregate data over time, Adler (1986) concludes that, on the whole, computer technology has upgraded people's skills. Studies have shown that the same technology can *both* devalue some skills and add the potential to apply other skills (see Buchanan and Boddy 1983).
12. Resistance to or acceptance of change depends on other factors as well, of course, including the way that the change is introduced and the person's general self-esteem. However, self-esteem may be based at least in part on signature skills, so the two are interdependent.
13. Van Maanen and Barley (1984) describe "occupational communities" of people whose

> identity is drawn from the work; who share with one another a set of values, norms and perspectives that apply to but extend beyond work related matters. [These occupational communities] create and sustain relatively unique work cultures consisting of, among other things, task rituals, standards for proper and improper behavior, work codes surrounding relatively routine practices and, for the membership at least, compelling accounts attesting to the logic and value of these rituals, standards and codes. (287)

14. 1990 (see 377–79).
15. Quoted in Cox and Roberts 1994, A-1.
16. Quoted in Cox and Roberts 1994, A-1.
17. See Schein 1987.
18. Leonard-Barton 1987a.
19. See Dougherty 1992 on the cross-disciplinary communication problems in new-product development stimulated by departmental "thought worlds."
20. Christensen and Leonard-Barton 1990, 4.
21. Kodama points to the transformation of Fanuc from a producer of mechanical machinery into the world leader in computerized numerical controllers for machine tools as an example of a company that successfully fused expertise in mechanics with electronics and materials development. Similarly,

Sharp has become a leader in liquid crystal displays by combining electronic, crystal, and optics technologies. "In each of these cases, the companies added one technology to another and came up with a solution greater than the sum of its parts—in technology fusion, one plus one equals three" (Kodama 1992, 71).

22. Coy et al. 1994.

23. Gross 1992. See also Bowonder and Miyake 1994.

24. Quoted in Hof 1993, 73.

25. Keirsey and Bates 1978, 17; italics in original.

26. Keirsey and Bates 1978, 18–19.

27. Writing about the inventive process, Weber and Perkins (1992) note:

    The tension between the needs for search expansion and search compression makes effective invention something of a balancing act. Lean too far toward expansion and you have an unmanageable option set. Lean too far towards compression and chances are you have squeezed out the powerful solutions that lead on to other things. Walking the tightrope requires immense commitment and mental agility. . . . (327)

28. Interview, February 28, 1994.

29. Interview, 16 November 1994.

30. Hampden-Turner 1981. Note however that descriptions of left and right brain activity are more metaphorical than physiologically precise.

31. Leonard-Barton 1985.

32. Granstrand et al. (1992) found in a study of three product lines (cellular phones, optical fiber systems, and refrigerators) that the number of subtechnologies in the technology base underlying all three increased between consecutive product generations. The increase was due to technological transitions from analogue to digital in all three, developments in man-made materials in all three, and the combination of electronics and physics (optronics) in optical fiber systems. For example, the first generation of cellular phone (early 1980s) required only electrical engineering; the third (mid-1990s) called on the disciplines of physics as well as electrical, mechanical, and computer engineering.

33. Iansiti 1993, 139.

34. One fairly long-standing exception is the systems engineering function. In his 1971 description of Bell Labs, Morton described such engineers as

    usually former specialists of considerable experience and judgment who have broadened their motivations and knowledge to include new disciplines, such as economics, sociology, and even psychology. In short, they are the interdisciplinary generalists of Bell Labs. . . . Because they are an integral part of Bell Labs, they are in constant touch with the R&D people who know the limitations and potential of science and technology. Together, systems engineers and R&D people work out measures of relevance and effectiveness for different areas of science and technology. By relating such science and technology to known or anticipated needs or opportunities, systems engineers develop proposals and plans for new systems developments. (57, 58)

35. As Allen (1977) notes:

    There is a great deal of overlap among the coding schemes of different organizations operating within the same culture. On the other hand, the nonoverlapping areas, however small, can potentially operate to produce semantic noise, and they can be even more troublesome because it can go undetected. Anyone who does not speak French knows his deficiency, but very often we think we know what someone from another organization is saying when in fact our understanding is very different from his. (139–40)

36. Based on tests of many different populations, Myers with Myers (1980) conclude that people preferring sensing "are drawn to occupations that let them deal with a constant stream of facts, whereas intuitives like situations in which they look at the possibilities" (158).

37. Interview, 10 December 1993.

38. Interview, 6 September 1994.

39. 1989.

40. For a discussion of this point, see Leonard-Barton 1991b and Schrage 1993.

41. Star and Griesemer 1989, 393.

42. Wheelwright and Clark 1992, 149.

43. Schrage 1993, 57; italics in original.

44. Clark and Fujimoto 1990, 109.

45. For a more extended discussion of the role of product concepts, see Leonard-Barton, Braithwaite, Bowen, Hanson, Titelbaum, and Preuss 1994.

46. White and Suris 1993, 1.

47. Clark and Fujimoto 1990, 113.

48. Bowen, Clark, Holloway, Leonard-Barton, and Wheelwright 1994.

49. Leonard-Barton, Braithwaite, Bowen, Hanson, Titelbaum, and Preuss 1994.

Chapter Four: Implementing and Integrating New Technical Processes and Tools

1. Clark, "Overhead Costs in Modern Industry," *Journal of Political Economics* (1927), quoted in Bohle 1967.

2. 1993.

3. The process of mutual adaptation was first noted in a ten-project study by Leonard-Barton (1988).

4. See Coch and French 1948 and, more recently, Locke and Schweiger 1979.

5. See von Hippel's 1994 discussion of the problems caused by this separation of knowledge and the "stickiness" of information.

6. For example, one experiment resulted in the finding that an "alternative" approach to software system design that explicitly draws upon the users' managerial "mental schemas" as well as on the software designers' schemas

produced a much richer and more inclusive design (Boland 1978). Other researchers report finding no evidence of improved output from a participative process (Ives and Olson 1984) or even negative relationships (Edstrom 1977). Ives and Olson point out that, at least for software, the hypothesis that a "system may be implemented successfully without user involvement" has been largely ignored in the information systems literature (1984, 600) and conclude that most research on the topic has been so flawed that "the benefits of user involvement have not been convincingly demonstrated" (586).

7. This case involves one of the two firms whose implementation of software was examined in the Alpha and Beta corporations study; see the box in Chapter 5 on page 128.

8. Doll and Torkzadeh 1989.

9. For a discussion of user involvement, see Leonard-Barton and Sinha 1993.

10. Von Hippel (1994) describes task partitioning in the creation of ASIC (semicustomized chips). The manufacturer encoded production information in a user-friendly CAD package that customers could use to customize chip specifications to their own needs, working within the constraints of the chip foundry equipment. The situation described here sounds somewhat similar, but there are two critical differences: in the apprenticeship mode, the users design *and produce* the product; moreover, the users *learn* the developers' knowledge base.

11. On the unfreezing of organizational routines, see Lewin and Grabbe 1962.

12. Keil 1992, 20.

13. Clark 1985. See also the discussion of design hierarchy in Chapter 7.

14. Tyre and Orlikowski 1994.

15. Employee "burnout" is hypothesized to be comprised of three components: (1) emotional exhaustion (a lack of energy and a sense that one's emotional resources are depleted); (2) a diminished sense of personal accomplishment (a tendency to evaluate oneself negatively); and (3) depersonalization (a tendency to treat others as objects rather than people). The first two of these are likely to be associated with the stress of fast-paced learning. See Cordes and Dougherty 1993 for a review of the literature on job-related burnout.

16. Goldstein and Klein 1988.

Chapter Five: Experimenting and Prototyping

1. Quoted in Levine 1989, 128.

2. Quoted in Cleese 1988, 128; Goldwyn Pictures was incorporated into Metro-Goldwyn-Mayer (MGM) in 1924.

3. Boeker (1989) points out that strategic change originates not only from the pressures of new technology or environmental changes but also as a "consequence of the interests of intraorganizational constituencies" (510).

4. This chapter covers technological experimentation. For a discussion of experimenting in the marketplace, see Chapter 7.
5. See Hayes 1985; Hamel and Prahalad 1989; and Mintzberg 1990.
6. This situation is analogous to traditional practices in creating large software programs. The developers used to spend the first two to three years of a project interviewing prospective users, constructing very elaborate descriptions of current operations, and writing up detailed specifications for the software program to automate those operations. Then they went into "production" mode, implementing their detailed plans. However, by the time they returned the software program to users, ready to run, the operations had often changed significantly. The target had moved, and their creation no longer fit the users' needs. In recent years, software developers have increasingly turned to the rapid creation of prototypes, which they employ to elicit user needs and to launch the actual coding of the software. This practice has enabled them to be much more responsive to changing user environments—and to deliver software faster.
7. See Kanter 1988; March 1978; Levitt and March 1988; Sitkin 1992; and Levinthal and March 1981. The need for variety seems embedded in the very nature of life itself. Researchers in biology have found tremendous redundancy and variety in nature that allows flexible responses to new circumstances.

   [O]rganisms contain much genetic information not committed to some particular function and therefore available for potential use in other circumstances. If every gene were absolutely specialized and committed to one particular function, the organism would work very well, but it would never survive very long. It would have no flexibility for change. . . . Creativity . . . is not predictable progress. It requires a measure of sloppiness, redundancy and potential for inherently unpredictable change. Its best metaphor, taking a clue from human invention, is not linear progress but rejuvenation. (Gould 1991, 18, 25)

8. Hamel and Prahalad 1989. Except that the examples cited are usually quite short and pithy, a strategic intent seems no different from a strategic vision as espoused by other academics. For instance, Hax and Majluf (1984) define a vision as "a rather permanent statement to communicate the nature of the existence of the organization in terms of corporate purposes, business scope and competitive leadership; to provide the framework that regulates the relationships among the firm and its primary stakeholders; and to state the broad objectives of the firm's performance" (294).
9. Quoted in Leonard-Barton and Pisano 1990, 1.
10. Koenig 1990, 1.
11. Even when the FDA gave approval for BST to be freely administered in the United States, the dairy industry continued to fight. See McFarling 1994.
12. Murray and Leonard-Barton 1994.

13. See Mahon 1982 and 1983.

14. See Badaracco 1979.

15. Strategic improvisation is akin to an "autonomous" strategic process (Burgelman 1991). A number of scholars have proposed similar categories for strategies. Mintzberg and Waters (1985) offer a spectrum anchored at one extreme by "deliberate" strategies (precise, common to all actors, realized as intended) and at the other by "emergent" strategies (order-consistent in action over time but with no intention about them). They identify a number of strategies that fall somewhere between the two poles, including "umbrella," which seems to correspond most closely with strategic intent, in that there is a "certain vision emanating from the central leadership" that "puts limits on the actions of others and ideally provides a sense of direction as well" (263). Their closest parallel to strategic improvisation would seem to be "unconnected," which describes action taken at the discretion of an organizational subunit. Initially perhaps clandestine, this strategy is watched by leaders and eventually "accepted and broadened" if it looks promising (266). See also Day 1994 for a discussion of top-down versus bottom-up champions of ventures.

16. The more high-cost, high-risk the venture undertaken, the more likely that it will require championing by someone in the top-management ranks (Tushman and Romanelli 1985).

17. Kanter 1988.

18. See Burgelman 1983 and 1994.

19. This is not to say that HP leaders always recognized opportunities. Pinchot (1985) recounts the harrowing experiences of Charles House, an intrapreneur who championed the electronic lens at HP. After a review of projects under way in the laboratory, David Packard declared, "When I come back next year, I don't want to see that project in the lab!" (27). The next year, it wasn't—only because the team had gotten it into the market. However, Packard forgave the team's defiantly literal interpretation of his order.

20. Hewlett-Packard company documents.

21. Vogel 1992.

22. Vogel 1992.

23. Andy Grove, quoted in Burgelman 1994, 38.

24. One of the best known is Kanter 1983.

25. Burns and Stalker 1961.

26. Van de Ven and Polley 1992.

27. Sitkin 1992; Levinthal and March 1993.

28. Cleese 1988, 126.

29. Sitkin (1992) suggests five characteristics of intelligent failures: "(1) they result from thoughtfully planned actions that (2) have uncertain outcomes and (3) are of modest scale, (4) are executed and responded to with alacrity,

and (5) take place in domains that are familiar enough to permit effective learning" (243).

30. Schon (1967a) distinguished between risk and uncertainty:

> Risk has its place in a calculus of probabilities. It lends itself to quantitative expression—as when we say that the chances of finding a defective part in a batch are two out of 1000. In the framework of benefit-cost analysis, the risk of an innovation is how much we stand to lose if we fail, multiplied by the probability of the failure.
>
> Uncertainty is quite another matter. . . . For example, a gambler takes a risk in an honest game of blackjack when, knowing the odds, he calls for another card. But the same gambler, unsure of the odds, or unsure of the honesty of the game, is in a situation of uncertainty. . . . A corporation cannot operate in uncertainty, but it is beautifully equipped to handle risk. (12)

Schon's MIT colleague Jay Forrester, inventor of the core memory for early computers, has a slightly different perspective, emphasizing the importance of the individual undertaking a risky endeavor:

> [Y]ou get in a situation where you have a person who undertakes something that others feel [is] tremendously unlikely and risky. . . . [T]his goes to the heart of this evaluation of risk that we teach in many of our courses. Risk is not something to be dealt with by statistics. A particular undertaking may be impossibly risky for Mr. A and essentially a sure thing for B because he already sees his way through as to how, one way at least, . . . he can succeed. And he finds better ways as he goes along. (Forrester 1982)

31. Quoted in Leonard-Barton 1992b, 32.
32. An exception may be the American tolerance for personal and business bankruptcy.
33. Macfarlane 1984.
34. Chase 1993.
35. Stalk 1988.
36. Maidique and Zirger 1985, 299.
37. Maidique and Zirger 1985, 306.
38. Experimentation provides a greater variety in potential organizational responses. As Levinthal and March (1993) note, success decreases search, and failure increases it.
39. Personal communication with the author, November 9, 1994.
40. Dumaine 1993, 104.
41. Schon and Wiggins 1992, 68.
42. Schrage 1993, 63.
43. Leonard-Barton 1987a.
44. Recounted to Dorothy Leonard-Barton's Management of Technology class, Massachusetts Institute of Technology, September 1982. Revised by Forrester, November 1994.

45. Chew, Leonard-Barton, and Bohn 1991.
46. Leonard-Barton 1990.
47. Hogarth and Makridakis 1981, 120.
48. Einhorn 1980.
49. See Wheelwright and Clark 1992.
50. Descriptions of this project are drawn from Leonard-Barton, Wilson, and Doyle 1994.
51. In the early 1970s, the University of Sussex conducted a study to determine the factors leading to the marketplace success of new products. Project SAPPHO identified twenty-nine product pairs in the first phase of the study, forty-three in a second phase; each pair consisted of one product that succeeded in the marketplace and one that did not. The other four factors distinguishing successful from unsuccessful projects were the extent to which the innovators (1) paid attention to marketing and publicity, (2) performed their development work more efficiently (but not necessarily faster), (3) used outside technology and scientific advice in the specific area targeted, and (4) had senior project leaders. SAPPHO researchers found that the probability of these distinctions' occurring by chance was less than one-tenth of 1 percent. See Rothwell et al. 1974.
52. Information was gathered through a combination of interviews and questionnaires directed toward engineers; middle-level managers; managers from the functions of R&D, marketing, and manufacturing; and the division's general manager. Three major questions were asked: (1) What steps were taken to develop the product definition? (2) In hindsight, what went right and what wrong in the development and use of the product definition? (3) How was the product definition used during the development phase? The study originally identified ten factors that distinguished successful projects from unsuccessful ones.
53. Translating user needs into product is the major subject covered in Chapter 7.
54. A follow-up study funded by the Sloan Foundation extended the audit to five other companies—IBM, GE, GM-Delco, Motorola, and Xerox. See Bacon et al. 1994.

Chapter Six: Importing and Absorbing Technological Knowledge from outside the Firm

1. Quoted in Weber 1989, 132.
2. Mathis 1992, 35.
3. Cohen and Levinthal 1990, 128.
4. Cohen and Levinthal (1990) originated the term *absorptive capacity*, which implies a much broader concept than they were able to operationalize in their empirical studies. They used R&D investment as a proxy for absorptive capacity.

5. Clark 1994.
6. Gomes-Casseres 1993.
7. An example of knowledge spillover in supply alliances is that product developers not only acquire expertise embodied in the parts they purchase but learn something about the underlying science as they integrate those components into the product design. In positioning alliances, sales and service personnel may learn considerable technical detail about the partner's products.
8. Pryzbylowicz and Faulkner 1993, 32.
9. McCullough 1987, 58.
10. Leonard-Barton 1987b.
11. See the distinction made between these two types of capability in Chapter 1.
12. Pryzbylowicz and Faulkner 1993.
13. Kearns and Nadler 1992.
14. For example, when GE acquired RCA, GE donated the Sarnoff Laboratory to a nonprofit research concern, SRI International. Bernstein and Nadiri (1988) estimate that companies have experienced private rates of return on R&D investment only half to one-tenth those of returns *to society.*
15. A survey of 140 firms affiliated with the Industrial Research Institute found that its members observed, during the 1980s, a definite shift away from centralized R&D toward more divisional R&D; they also observed strong drives to make the central laboratories more responsive to the business units and more involved in applications development research for *existing* markets as opposed to new markets (Bean 1989).
16. In the period 1980–1991, federal support for research and development dropped from an annual growth rate of 8.1 percent (1980–1985) to − 1.7 percent (1986–1991), and industry's went from almost 7.3 percent growth to 1.3 percent. Therefore, during this period, U.S. R&D expenditures have lagged those of foreign competitors (National Academy of Sciences, National Research Council 1992).
17. However, it did not top the list for spending per employee or as a percentage of sales. Biotechnology firms retained those honors, with Immunex spending 340 percent of sales and Genetics Institute almost 100 percent (Coy et al. 1994).
18. For example, Nicolaas Bloembergen's pioneering work at Harvard in nonlinear optics was financed as part of the Department of Defense's Joint Services Electronics Program. Karl Jansky discovered radio emissions from space in the course of applied research on improving radio telecommunications technology.
19. Armstrong 1994, 10, 11.
20. The real danger to this trend is not so much the requirement of relevance in research as the assumption that researchers should be developing *products.*

That assumption leads to unrealistic schedules for invention, the diversion of scientific talent to tasks for which the individuals may be ill suited, and the possibility that no resources may be allocated to creating the technological *capabilities* that will spawn tomorrow's products.

21. The literature on technological innovation is enormous and cannot be reviewed here. This discussion draws particularly upon the following sources: Tushman and Anderson 1986 (about competence enhancement or destruction); and Foster 1982 and 1986 (about S-shaped curves).

22. Henderson 1995.

23. Christensen 1992a, 346.

24. Christensen 1992a.

25. Leonard-Barton and Sviokla 1988; Kaewert and Frost 1990.

26. For further discussion of this kind of technology, see Pisano and Mang 1993.

27. Harrigan 1988. See also Kogut's (1988) study of 148 U.S. joint ventures, which found that most terminations occurred in the fifth or sixth year of the agreement, and a Coopers and Lybrand and McKinsey study that found as much as a 70 percent divorce rate for joint ventures (cited in Gomes-Casseres 1987).

28. Kogut (1988) describes a five-year relationship between Honeywell and L. M. Ericsson as successful despite its dissolution, and Gomes-Casseres (1987) points out that dissolution of a partnership may evidence flexibility in the face of changing environmental conditions.

29. In 1993, universities and colleges accounted for just over half the basic research conducted in the United States, and another 11 percent was done at the national research centers in universities. Industry represented only 18 percent. Investment in basic research at universities as a percentage of total research carried on at universities dropped from 77 percent in 1970 to 66 percent in 1993, but the proportion of research allocated to basic research at national research centers more than made up for that drop by increasing over the same time period from 36.5 percent to 53.8 percent. Industry's allocation to basic research of total research expenditures has held relatively steady—3.3 percent in 1970 and 4.2 percent in 1993 (National Science Board, National Science Foundation 1993, 333–34). Patents issued to U.S. universities grew from 434 in 1981 to 1,306 in 1991 (Buderi 1993, 78).

30. Personal communication, Alex Laats, Technology Licensing Officer, Massachusetts Institute of Technology, 2 August 1994. According to Parker (1993), only 25 percent of the licenses in California and Massachusetts universities reportedly return money to the universities.

31. Personal communication, Alex Laats 1994.

32. Wyatt 1992.

33. Gibson and Rogers 1994.

34. Coy et al. 1994.

35. Link and Bauer 1989.
36. Pope 1994, B4.
37. Granstrand et al. (1992) make a related point when they argue that general contracts, which rest on trust, imply greater integration than arm's-length transactions such as contract R&D (114–15).
38. See Hamilton 1985.
39. Harrigan 1985.
40. MacAvoy 1989.
41. Rosenbloom 1988.
42. Quoted in "Technology Transfer's Master" 1977, 120.
43. Granstrand et al. 1992.
44. Barker 1985, 23.
45. Gibbons 1992.
46. Allen 1977.
47. An interesting, potentially critical, and unexplored issue is the effect of such automated, targeted searches on the creativity of gatekeepers—and consequently, on the innovativeness of the entire organization. Historically, such individuals were among the most productive and innovative technical performers. They scanned materials to increase diversity of stimuli and thereby enhance their own creativity. Their service to the organization in disseminating information was a by-product of their own exploration routines. Will automated searches preclude the element of serendipity that is such an important ingredient in innovation? That is, if gatekeepers no longer "browse" personally, will they fail to see the apparently unrelated material that will stimulate creativity in their activity and that of others with whom they communicate? Information specialists relying on "keywords" that others provide them cannot be expected to see connections among apparently unrelated materials that experts might. Yet, as Chapter 3 suggests, creativity springs from juxtaposing hitherto unconnected planes of thought, and as Chapter 7 will argue, people with deep technical knowledge have an advantage in foreseeing its application in unexpected ways. Managers in the future will need to grapple with the issue of whether the capacity of the human mind to range widely over options and scan rapidly through large quantities of material in search of diffuse information can be mimicked by information technology.
48. Doz 1988; Kanter 1983; Niederkofler 1991.
49. Doz 1988.
50. Pisano and Mang 1993, 125.
51. For a discussion of tacit knowledge, see Polanyi 1967; for its specific role in an instance of technology transfer, see Gibson and Rogers 1994.
52. Niederkofler 1991, 245.
53. Gibson and Rogers 1994, 548.
54. Niederkofler 1991.

55. Harrigan 1985, 347.
56. Clark and Fujimoto 1991.
57. Ellison, Clark, and Fujimoto 1994, cited in Fujimoto 1994a (19).
58. The design of Chrysler's very popular minivan, which led the company out of bankruptcy, also owed much to the transfer of knowledge from the acquired Jeep company.
59. Fujimoto 1994b.
60. Fujimoto 1994a.
61. Technical accomplishments from this project, many of which were harbingers of recent innovations in computing, included the following: visual displays incorporating cathode-ray tubes on which an operator could "write" with a light pen; new switches, such as a crystal matrix switch, a magnetic matrix switch, and the cryotron; new vacuum-tube fabrication techniques and quality standards eliminating trace contaminants; techniques for sending digital data over telephone lines; simulation techniques by which hypothetical aircraft flights could be programmed into the computer; self-checking procedures to identify defective components and alert the operator; and the successful application of "synchronous parallel logic" design. See Redmond and Smith 1977.
62. Redmond and Smith 1977.
63. Forrester 1982.
64. Redmond and Smith 1977, 53.
65. Quoted in Redmond and Smith 1977, 59.
66. Forrester 1982.
67. Gibson and Rogers 1994. For a detailed look at the difficulties in getting the packaging/interconnect technologies out the door, see Preuss et al. 1991.
68. Gibson and Rogers 1994, 542.
69. See Argyris 1993 for examples of espoused versus enacted values.
70. Harrigan 1985, 341.
71. Cohen and Levinthal 1990, 128.
72. See also Niederkofler 1991, 244.
73. Gibson and Rogers (1994) note that a credible vision may be inspired by "first-level" influencers but that "[c]apable second-level influencers are required to enact such visions at the operational level" (543), and Harrigan (1985) finds that "[e]xperienced managers put scientists, engineers and plant managers on their negotiating teams, as well as their operating teams" (347).
74. Hof 1991, 86.
75. Harrigan 1985.
76. Harrigan 1985, 342.
77. Lyles 1988.
78. Niederkofler 1991, 252. See also Doz 1988; and Radtke, Fast, and Paap 1987.

79. Lyles 1988.

Chapter Seven: Learning from the Market

1. Landler 1991, 73.
2. Plato 1892.
3. Cooper 1986, 16.
4. Booz-Allen and Hamilton 1982.
5. Cooper 1986, 17.
6. Cooper and Kleinschmidt 1986.
7. See, for example, Hopkins and Bailey 1971; Cooper 1986; Canlantone and Cooper 1979; Souder 1987; and Gupta and Wilemon 1990.
8. For a discussion of dominant designs and excellent illustrations of how they emerge, see Utterback 1994.
9. Clark 1985, 243.
10. See Suris 1994; and Woodruff, Armstrong, and Carey 1994.
11. Consider that even to produce a next-generation car, the Saturn, General Motors managers separated the operation organizationally and geographically from Detroit and set up very different development routines.
12. Christensen 1992b, 114–15; italics in original.
13. Christensen 1992b, 150.
14. Itami with Roehl 1987.
15. Many of the Hewlett-Packard examples in this chaper are taken from Leonard-Barton, Wilson, and Doyle 1994.
16. Leonard-Barton, Wilson, and Doyle 1994.
17. Quotes from an interview with Dr. James Serum, group R&D manager, Analytic Group, Hewlett-Packard, October 23, 1992.
18. Interview with Dr. Joel Birnbaum, vice president and director, HP Laboratories, November 2, 1992.
19. Interview with Dr. Joel Birnbaum, vice president and director, HP Laboratories, November 2, 1992.
20. The word *serendipity* was coined and defined on 28 January 1754 by Horace Walpole, who wrote to Horace Mann (one of his eighteen hundred letters to Mann) about an accidental discovery

    which I call "serendipity," a very expresssive word, which . . . I shall endeavour to explain to you: you will understand it better by the derivation than by the definition. I once read a silly fairy tale, called The Three Princes of Serendip: as their Highnesses travelled, they were always making discoveries, by accidents & sagacity, of things which they were not in quest of: for instance, one of them discovered that a mule blind of the right eye had travelled the same road lately, because the grass was eaten only on the left side, where it was worse than on the right—now do you understand serendipity? One of the most remarkable instances of this accidental sagacity (for you must observe that no discovery of a thing you are looking for, comes under this description). . . .

This letter was reproduced in a book by Theodore G. Remer (1965), cited in Van Andel 1992. Van Andel cites seventeen "patterns of serendipity" and has catalogued a thousand! He discriminates three different forms of serendipity: (1) positive—a surprising discovery correctly understood; (2) negative—a surprising discovery not capitalized upon by the discoverer; (3) pseudoserendipity—finding what you were looking for, but in a surprising way (28). The serendipity referred to in new-product development is mostly the first type.

21. Arnst with Cortese 1994.
22. Landler 1991.
23. Quoted in "Infiniti Betting Smell Sells" 1992, G11.
24. Serafin 1993; Hauser, Urban, and Weinberg 1993.
25. For a discussion of the relationship between the level of respondents' knowledge about a product and their ability to evaluate a concept, see Reidenback and Grimes 1984.
26. Von Hippel 1988, 107; italics in original.
27. Leonard-Barton 1981.
28. Shiba et al. 1991.
29. Such techniques are often used as the "front end" for quality function deployment processes that translate user requirements into engineering specifications. See Hauser and Clausing 1988.
30. Zaltman and Higie 1993, 1; see also Coulter and Zaltman 1994.
31. The term originates from Leonard-Barton 1991b; see also Leonard-Barton, Wilson, and Doyle 1994. Empathic design differs from contextual inquiry precisely because it does not rely on inquiry; in the situations in which empathic design is most useful, inquiry is useless or ineffective.
32. A technique that informs such intuition is "value analysis," an economic assessment of the proposed product conducted by engineers or technical staff on behalf of potential customers, to determine the innovation's likely value. See Eliashberg, Lilien, and Rao 1994.
33. There are also situations in which a user product concept does not require high technology, of course. Robert Palmer, a retired Northwest Airlines pilot, invented the now-ubiquitous "Travelpro Rollaboard" suitcase, which has a retractable handle, is narrow enough (because it rolls on its end) to pass down airplane aisles, and is small enough to fit in an overhead compartment. Mr. Palmer built the first one for himself and had one hundred manufactured in the Far East after fellow pilots and flight attendants said they would buy one. It is worth noting that he has degrees in both engineering and marketing (O'Brian 1993).
34. Von Hippel 1988.
35. The $395 calculator performed trigonometric, logarithmic, and exponential

functions. It could handle larger and more complex problems with less memory than other models because of its powerful logic method called reverse Polish notation.

36. Of course, this close affinity to the market also misled both companies as to the importance of market research when the customer base changed and the developers were no longer representative of the people using their products.

37. Quoted in Wallace and Erickson 1992, 135.

38. Interview with Dr. James Serum, Hewlett-Packard, October 23, 1992, quoted in Leonard-Barton, Wilson, and Doyle 1994, 14.

39. This possible danger is exacerbated if high-level senior officials try to micromanage technical project details. In one company studied, project teams frequently complained that senior management "swooped down" midway through projects to "tinker" with technical details that they were no longer in a position to judge. Senior managers can also remain personally invested in an obsolete technology if it involves a signature skill base.

40. See Chapter 6 for an account of the company's acquisition history, including the all-important purchase of the high-tech Radiation, Inc., firm in 1967.

41. Flaherty 1980, 46.

42. Reported in Gold 1987.

43. Dumaine 1993.

44. Brown and Newman 1985.

45. This trend has been verified by surveys; in 1994, one of every ten meals purchased in a restaurant was likely to be consumed in a car, according to NPD Group, a Chicago company that tracks people's eating habits. That's about 25 percent higher than in 1985. Cited in Deveny 1994.

46. Kirkpatrick 1994, 78.

47. Miles 1989.

48. See, for example, Schwartz 1991.

49. Schwartz 1991.

50. Moore (1982) contrasts monadic with competitive testing of products, hypothesizing that monadic is preferable when it is difficult to identify direct competitors or when customers conduct little search prior to purchase.

51. Power 1992.

52. Robert Schmitz, director of market research for Lever USA, quoted in Power 1992, 46.

53. Quoted in "First Newton" 1993.

54. Slater and Gwennap 1992, 12–13.

55. R. Martin of The Chicago Corporation predicted in a 1993 America Online company report that the market for PDAs and other "handhelds" would grow from nothing in 1991 to an installed base of about 6.5 million in 1996 (Gomes-Casseres and Leonard-Barton 1994), and Gartner Group expected (.7 probability) that by 1997, 72 percent of all new portable

shipments (i.e., 23 million notebooks and handhelds) will incorporate PCMCIA slots, to enable data interchange between handheld PDAs and notebook computers. See Gartner Group 1993, 10.

56. Gomes-Casseres and Leonard-Barton 1994.

57. Itami with Roehl (1987) champion another kind of market experimentation—using a technology in high-volume consumer products so as to make advances in performance that can then be exploited in higher-priced products. He cites Sanyo's use of solar-cell technology as an example of this "premature" or "excessive" experimentation. The competitive edge in the market for amorphous solar cells comes from heat-exchange efficiency. Sanyo chose to commercialize its design in applications such as watches and calculators, which required only 3 percent efficiency, so as to speed development instead of waiting until efficiency reached 5 percent.

58. "What Makes Yoshio Invent" 1991.

59. Personal interview, 7 September 1994.

60. See Gomes-Casseres and Leonard-Barton 1994.

61. Stefflre 1965, 12.

62. See Freeze and Leonard-Barton 1992.

Chapter Eight: Transferring Product Development Capabilities into Developing Nations

1. Peterson 1990.

2. Quoted in Engardio 1993, 58.

3. Gomory 1983, 579.

4. Quoted in Hayes 1994, 4.

5. Quoted in Hayes 1994, 2.

6. In this chapter, quotations not otherwise referenced are from interviews I conducted in four Japanese subsidiaries of large U.S. electronics companies in 1988 or from interviews I conducted with joint venture partners of twelve U.S., Hong Kong, European, or Japanese firms in China during January and June of 1994.

7. Simon 1991, 9.

8. Reich and Mankin 1986, 80, 84, and 85, respectively.

9. Hayami and Ruttan (1971) write about three phases of transfer: the sale of new products or materials with no adaptation, the transfer of manufacturing capability, and the transfer of R&D capability. Baranson and Roark (1985) distinguish among technology-transfer situations according to whether they provide operational, duplicative, or innovative capabilities.

10. Austin 1990, 237, drawing upon Dahlman and Cortes 1984.

11. The astute reader will also remark some similarity between the four categories used in this chapter and the four types of interaction between product

developers and users during internal technology transfer as described in Chapter 4—delivery, consultancy, codevelopment, and apprenticeship.

12. In fact, of course, the recipient turned source now transfers its technological capabilities to multiple recipient points. Over the past twenty-five years, the "little tigers" in Asia—Hong Kong, Singapore, Taiwan, and Korea—have become prolific sources of technology for the world.

13. As noted in Chapter 4, implementation of new equipment in any situation usually requires adaptation of both the equipment and the operating system into which it is introduced. See Leonard-Barton 1988.

14. This is not an unusual occurrence; a study in Kenya found that a major reason why more sophisticated equipment was not being used was that it would have necessitated greater maintenance and operational knowledge than workers possessed (Gershenberg 1983, cited in Austin 1990).

15. Quoted in Hayes 1994, 4.

16. "Plugged In," 1993, 5.

17. Austin 1990, 249.

18. Quoted in Thill and Leonard-Barton 1993, case A, 4.

19. Bruijn and Jia 1993, 344.

20. Bruijn and Jia 1993, 344.

21. Nisbet 1986.

22. ISO9000 is a set of manufacturing standards developed by the International Organization for Standardization, based in Geneva, Switzerland. By documenting their processes and passing an on-site inspection, companies can receive certification that their production processes meet the strict requirements set up by this organization. ISO9000 certification is regarded as an indication of quality performance.

23. See Leonard-Barton 1990.

24. Quoted in "Sino-U.S. Joint Venture Develops New Product" 1993.

25. Quoted in Engardio 1993, 58.

26. Quoted in Thill and Leonard-Barton 1993, case A, 4.

27. The following descriptions of Fuji Xerox are drawn from McQuade and Gomes-Casseres 1991.

28. Quoted in McQuade and Gomes-Casseres 1991, 7.

29. Quoted in McQuade and Gomes-Casseres 1991, 14.

30. Interview with Fujisawa Manager Masayuki Narukawa, 31 August 1988.

31. Quoted in Bartmess and Cerny 1993, 89.

32. Bartmess and Cerny 1993, 90; italics added.

33. Bartlett and Ghoshal 1989, 125.

34. Engardio 1993.

35. Shaw and Meier 1993, 3.

36. Quoted in Gerace and Leonard-Barton 1994, 6.

37. The notion of "technocentrism," or the belief that a specific physical system

must and can be employed in the same way anywhere in the world, is set out in Maruyama 1989.

38. One of the preeminent scholars of diffusion noted over a decade ago that innovations are frequently reinvented by users. Rogers 1983, 174 ff.
39. Interview with Douglas Presley, Manager, IBM Japan, 2 September 1988.
40. See the discussion of organizational prototyping in Chapter 5.
41. Hofstede 1980.
42. For a discussion of traditional Chinese interaction and its implications for business, see Kao 1993.
43. Kanter and Corn 1994.
44. Knight 1992.
45. See Gerace and Leonard-Barton 1994, 9.
46. Quoted in Thill and Leonard-Barton 1993, case A, 4.
47. Langowitz and Wheelwright 1986.
48. Smith and Reinertsen 1991, 85–86.

Chapter Nine: Continuous Wellsprings

1. 1987, 45.
2. Schumpeter 1942.
3. Virany, Tushman, and Romanelli 1992; Tushman and Anderson 1986.
4. Benoit B. Mandelbrot of IBM's Thomas J. Watson Research Center coined the term *fractal* in 1975, deriving the word from the Latin *fractus,* meaning "to break." In 1983, his book *The Fractal Geometry of Nature* set off a flurry of interest in recreating, through the use of computers, the patterns found in nature that had not been recognized before as having an underlying mathematical regularity. Interest in his work parallels an evolution in chaos theory, which finds that many phenomena follow deterministic rules but are, in principle, unpredictable.
5. Jurgens, Peitgen, and Saupe 1990, 60.
6. McGuire 1991, 92; italics added. In the foreword to McGuire's book, the "father" of fractal mathematics, Benoit Mandelbrot, notes that his work on fractals falls "right between the two traditional beliefs, that 'simple rules can only generate simple effects' and that 'in order to generate complexity, one needs complicated rules' " (foreword).
7. Levinthal and March 1993, 101.
8. A variety of researchers and scholars have noted this search for higher learning as a key ingredient in personal and organizational renewal. Argryis's "double-loop" learning requires that a manager examine the most basic assumptions leading to action. See Argryis 1982. Fiol and Lyles (1985) note the differences between lower and higher learning.
9. Virany, Tushman, and Romanelli 1992.
10. Quoted in Burgelman 1994, 43.

11. Quoted in Burgelman 1994, 41. Departing so radically from the past was difficult, and some perceived Intel's exit as an admission of failure since the company was unable to compete in the market. As Burgelman's analysis shows, that causality is reversed. Decisions made by middle managers constrained Intel's performance in the DRAM business long before top management realized the need to shift concentration solely to logic chips.

R E F E R E N C E S

Abetti, Pier A., and R. W. Stuart. 1988. "Evaluating New Product Risk." *Research Technology Management* 31 (May–June): 40–43.

Adamson, R. E. 1952. "Functional Fixedness as Related to Problem-Solving: A Repetition of Three Experiments." *Journal of Experimental Psychology* 44:288–91.

Adler, Paul. 1986. "New Technologies, New Skills." *California Management Review* 29 (spring): 9–28.

Aguilar, Frank, and Arvind Bhambri. 1983. "Johnson & Johnson (A)." Case 384-053, Harvard Business School, Boston.

Allen, Thomas. 1977. *Managing the Flow of Technology: Technology Transfer and the Dissemination of Technological Information within the R&D Organization.* Cambridge, Mass.: MIT Press.

Allen, Thomas, and Donald Marquis. 1965. "Positive and Negative Biasing Sets: The Effects of Prior Experience on Research Performance." *IEEE Transactions on Engineering Management* EM-11 (4): 158–61.

Anderson, William, with Charles Truax. 1991. *Corporate Crisis: NCR and the Computer Revolution.* Dayton, Ohio: Landfall Press.

Argyris, Chris. 1982. "The Executive Mind and Double-Loop Learning." *Organizational Dynamics* 11 (autumn): 5–22.

———. 1990. *Overcoming Organizational Defenses.* Boston: Allyn & Bacon.

———. 1991. "Teaching Smart People How to Learn." *Harvard Business Review,* May–June, 99–109.

———. 1993. *Knowledge for Action: A Guide to Overcoming Barriers to Organizational Change.* San Francisco: Jossey-Bass.

Argyris, Chris, and Donald Schon. 1978. *Organizational Learning.* Reading, Mass.: Addison-Wesley.

Armstrong, John A. 1994. "Is Basic Research a Luxury Our Society Can No Longer Afford?" *The Bridge* (summer): 9–16. Cambridge: Massachusetts Institute of Technology.

Arnst, Catherine, with Amy Cortese. 1994. "PDA Premature Death Announcement." *Business Week,* 12 September, 88–89.

Arrow, Kenneth J. 1962. "Economic Welfare and the Allocation of Resources for Invention." In *The Rate and Direction of Inventive Activity,* edited by Richard Nelson, 609–26. Princeton, N.J.: Princeton University Press.

Ashley, Steven. 1992. "Engineous Explores the Design Space." *Mechanical Engineering* (February): 49–52.

Austin, James E. 1990. *Managing in Developing Nations: Strategic Analysis and Operating Techniques.* New York: Free Press.

Bacon, Glenn, Sara Beckman, David Mowery, and Edith Wilson. 1994. "Managing Product Definition in High Technology Industries: A Pilot Study." *California Management Review* 36 (3): 32–56.

Badaracco, Joseph L. 1979. "Allied Chemical Corporation (A)." Case 379-137, Harvard Business School, Boston.

Baranson, J., and R. Roark. 1985. "Trends in North-South Transfer of High Technology." In *International Technology Transfer: Concepts, Measures and Comparisons,* edited by Nathan Rosenberg and C. Frichtak, 24–42. New York: Praeger.

Barker, Robert. 1985. "Bringing Science into Industry from Universities." *Research Management* 28 (November–December): 22–24.

Barker, Virginia, and Dennis O'Connor. 1989. "Expert Systems for Configuration at Digital: XCON and Beyond." *Communications of the ACM* 32 (March): 298–318.

Barney, Jay B. 1986. "Organizational Culture: Can It Be a Source of Sustained Competitive Advantage?" *Academy of Management Review* 11 (3): 656–65.

Barrett, Randy. 1993. "A Day at Sandia Puts Technology Transfer in Far Sharper Focus." *Technology Transfer Business* (spring): 12–18.

Bartlett, Christopher, and Sumantra Ghoshal. 1989. *Managing across Borders.* Boston: Harvard Business School Press.

Bartmess, Andrew, and Keith Cerny. 1993. "Building Competitive Advantage through a Global Network of Capabilities." *California Management Review* 35 (2): 2–27.

Basadur, Min. 1992. "Managing Creativity: A Japanese Model." *Executive* 6 (2): 29–42.

Bean, Alden S. 1989. "Competitive Pressures and the Structure of the R&D Portfolio in the 1980s." Bethlehem, Pa.: Center for Innovation Management Studies, Lehigh University.

Benioff, Sarah C., and Richard Rosenbloom. 1990. "Du Pont Research and Innovation: 1945–1972." Case 391-009, Harvard Business School, Boston.

Berg, Sanford V., and Philip Friedman. 1981. "Impacts of Domestic Joint Ventures on Industrial Rates of Return: A Pooled Cross-Section Analysis, 1964–1975." *Review of Economics and Statistics* 63 (2): 293–98.

Bernstein, Jeffrey I., and M. Ishaq Nadiri. 1988. "Interindustry R&D Spillovers, Rates of Return and Production in High-Tech Industries." *American Economics Review* 78 (May): 429–34. (*Papers and Proceedings* 1987.)

"Big Expansion at VW's Shanghai Plant." 1992. *Motor Report International,* 3 February, 3.

Birch, Herbert G., and Herbert S. Rabinowitz. 1951. "The Negative Effect of Previous Experience on Productive Thinking." *Journal of Experimental Psychology* 41:121–26.

Blakeslee, Sandra. 1990. "Lost on Earth: Wealth of Data Found in Space." *New York Times,* 20 March, Sec. C:1.

Boeker, Warren. 1989. "Strategic Change: The Effects of Founding and History." *Academy of Management Journal* 32 (3): 489–515.

Bohle, Bruce. 1967. *The Home Book of American Quotations.* New York: Dodd, Mead.

Bohn, Roger. 1988. "Learning by Experimentation in Manufacturing." Working paper 188-001, Harvard Business School, Boston.

Bohn, Roger E. 1994. "Measuring and Managing Technological Knowledge." *Sloan Management Review* 36 (1): 61–73.

Boland, Richard J. 1978. "The Process and Product of System Design." *Management Science* 24 (9): 887–98.

Booz-Allen and Hamilton. 1982. *New Product Management for the 1980's.* New York: Booz-Allen and Hamilton.

Bowen, H. Kent, Kim B. Clark, Charles A. Holloway, Dorothy Leonard-Barton, and Steven C. Wheelwright. 1994. "Regaining the Lead in Manufacturing" ("Development Projects: The Engine of Renewal," "How to Integrate Work *and* Deepen Expertise," "Make Projects the School for Leaders"). *Harvard Business Review,* September–October, 108–43.

Bowen, H. Kent, Kim B. Clark, Charles A. Holloway, and Steven C. Wheelwright, eds. 1994. *The Perpetual Enterprise Machine.* New York: Oxford University Press.

Bower, Joseph, and Thomas M. Hout. 1988. "Fast-Cycle Capability for Competitive Power." *Harvard Business Review,* November–December, 110–18.

Bowonder, B., and T. Miyake. 1994. "Globalization, Alliances, Diversification and Innovation: A Case Study from Hitachi Ltd." *Creativity and Innovation Management* 3 (1): 11–28.

Braverman, H. 1974. *Labor and Monopoly Capital.* New York: Monthly Review Press.

Bresnahan, Timothy. 1985. "Post-entry Competition in the Plain Paper Copier Market." *American Economic Review* 75 (May): 15–19.

Brockhoff, Klaus. 1991. "R&D Cooperation between Firms: A Classification by Structural Variables." *International Journal of Technology Management* 6 (3, 4): 361–73.

Brown, John Seely, and Susan E. Newman. 1985. "Issues in Cognitive and Social Ergonomics: From Our House to Bauhaus." *Human-Computer Interaction* 1:359–91.

Brown, Kathi Ann. 1992. *Critical Connection: The MSS Story.* Rolling Meadows, Ill.: Motorola University Press.

Browning, Robert. "Andrea del Sarto" (called "The Faultless Painter").

Bruijn, Erik J. de, and Xianfeng Jia. 1993. "Managing Sino-Western Joint Ventures: Product Selection Strategy." *Management International Review* 33 (4): 335–60.

Buchanan, D. A., and D. Boddy. 1983. "Advanced Technology and the Quality of Working Life: The Effects of Computerized Controls on Biscuit-Making Operators." *Journal of Occupational Psychology* 56 (June): 109–19.

Buderi, Robert. 1993. "American Inventors Are Reinventing Themselves." *Business Week,* 18 January, industrial/technology edition, 78–82.

Buell, Barbara, Robert D. Hof, and Gary McWilliams. 1991. "Hewlett-Packard Rethinks Itself." *Business Week,* 1 April, 76–79.

Burgelman, Robert A. 1983. "A Process Model of Internal Corporate Venturing in the Diversified Major Firms." *Administrative Science Quarterly* 28: 223–44.

———. 1991. "Intraorganizational Ecology of Strategy Making and Organizational Adaptation: Theory and Field Research." *Organization Science* 2(3): 239–62.

———. 1994. "Fading Memories: A Process Theory of Strategic Business Exit in Dynamic Environments." *Administrative Science Quarterly* 39:24–56.

Burns, Tom, and George M. Stalker. 1961. *The Management of Innovation.* London: Tavistock Publications.

Cafasso, Rosemary. 1994. "Gerstner to Staff: Don't Relax." *Computerworld,* 15 August, 8.

Canlantone, R., and Robert G. Cooper. 1979. "A Discriminant Model for Identifying Scenarios of Industrial New Product Failure." *Journal of the Academy of Marketing Science* 7:163–83.

Carstairs, Robert T., and L. S. Welch. 1982. "Licensing and the Internationalization of Smaller Companies: Some Australian Evidence." *Management International Review* 22 (3): 33–44.

Caves, Richard E., and Sanjeev K. Mehra. 1986. "Entry of Foreign Multinationals into U.S. Manufacturing Industries." In *Competition in Global Industries,* edited by Michael Porter, 449–81. Boston: Harvard Business School Press.

Chase, Marilyn. 1993. "Demand for MS Drug May Help Chiron Corp. Emerge from the Pack." *Wall Street Journal,* 1 September, 1.

Chew, Bruce W., Dorothy Leonard-Barton, and Roger E. Bohn. 1991. "Beating Murphy's Law." *Sloan Management Review* 32 (3): 5–16.

"Chinese, U.S. Managers Sell Xerox Products in Shanghai." 1990. *Xinhua General Overseas News Service,* 23 November.

Christensen, Clayton M. 1990. "Continuous Casting Investments at USX Corporation." Case 391-121, Harvard Business School, Boston.

———. 1992a. "Exploring the Limits of the Technology S-Curve: Part I: Component Technologies." *Production and Operations Management* 1 (fall): 334–57.

———. 1992b. "The Innovator's Challenge: Understanding the Influence of Market Environment on Processes of Technology Development in the Rigid Disk Drive Industry." Ph.D. dissertation, Harvard Business School.

Christensen, Clayton and Dorothy Leonard-Barton. "Ceramics Process Systems Corporation." 1990. Case 9-691-028, Harvard Business School, Boston.

Clark, Kim B. 1985. "The Interaction of Design Hierarchies and Market Concepts in Technological Evolution." *Research Policy* 14:235–51.

Clark, Kim B., and Takahiro Fujimoto. 1990. "The Power of Product Integrity." *Harvard Business Review,* November–December, 107–18.

———. 1991. *Product Development Performance: Strategy, Organization, and Management in the World Auto Industry.* Boston: Harvard Business School Press.

———. 1994. "The Product Development Imperative: Competing in the New Industrial Marathon." In *The Relevance of a Decade: Essays to Mark the First Ten Years of the HBS Press,* edited by Paula Barker Duffy, 287–322. Boston: Harvard Business School Press.

Clark, Lindley H. 1994. "Intel to Sell Stake in VLSI, Partner in Chips." *Wall Street Journal,* 5 August, B3.

Cleese, John M. 1988. "No More Mistakes and You're Through!" *Forbes,* 16 May, 126 ff.

Coch, Lester, and John R. P. French Jr. 1948. "Overcoming Resistance to Change." *Human Relations* 1:512–32.

Cohen, Wesley, and Daniel Levinthal. 1990. "Absorptive Capacity: A New Perspective on Learning and Innovation." *Administrative Science Quarterly* 35:128–52.

Contractor, F. J., and P. Lorange, eds. 1988. *Cooperative Strategies in International Business.* Lexington, Mass.: Lexington Books.

Cooper, Robert G. 1975. "Why Industrial New Products Fail." *Industrial Marketing Management* 4:315–26.

———. 1983. "The Impact of New Product Strategies." *Industrial Marketing Management* 12:243–56.

———. 1986. *Winning at New Products.* Reading, Mass.: Addison-Wesley.

Cooper, Robert G., and Elko J. Kleinschmidt. 1986. "An Investigation into the

New Product Process: Steps, Deficiencies and Impact." *Journal of Product Innovation Management* 3:71–85.

———. 1990. "New Product Success Factors: A Comparison of 'Kills' versus Successes and Failures." *R&D Management* 20 (1): 47–63.

Cordes, Cynthia L., and Thomas W. Dougherty. 1993. "A Review and an Integration of Research on Job Burnout." *Academy of Management Review* 18 (October): 621–56.

Coulter, Robin Higie, and Gerald Zaltman. 1994. "Using the Zaltman Metaphor Elicitation Technique to Understand Brand Images." *Advances in Consumer Research* 21:501–7.

Cox, Meg, and Johnnie L. Roberts. 1994. "How the Despotic Boss of Simon & Schuster Found Himself Jobless." *Wall Street Journal,* 6 July, A-1, A-8.

Coy, Peter, Neil Gross, Silvia Sansoni, and Kevin Kelly. 1994. "What's the Word in the Lab? Collaborate." *BusinessWeek,* 27 June, 78–80.

Crawford, C. Merle. 1979. "New Product Failure Rates: Facts and Fallacies." *Research Management* 22 (5): 9–13.

———. 1990. *New Products Management.* 3d ed. Homewood, Ill.: Irwin.

Cyert, Richard M. 1985. "Establishing University-Industry Joint Ventures." *Research Management* 28 (January–February): 27–29.

Cyert, Richard M., and James G. March. 1963. *A Behavioral Theory of the Firm.* Englewood Cliffs, N.J.: Prentice-Hall.

Dahlman, Carl S., and Muriluz Cortes. 1984. "Mexico." *World Development* 12 (5–6): 601–24.

Davenport, Thomas H., Michael Hammer, and Tauno J. Metsisto. 1989. "How Executives Can Shape Their Company's Information Systems." *Harvard Business Review,* March–April, 130–34.

Day, Diana. 1994. "Raising Radicals: Different Processes for Championing Innovative Corporate Ventures." *Organization Science* 5 (2): 148–72.

Day, Diana L. Forthcoming. "The Curse of Incumbency: Cannibalism, Organizational Locations, and Innovativeness in Internal Corporate Venturing." *Organization Science.*

DeLacey, Brian, and Dorothy Leonard-Barton. 1986. "Solagen: Process Improvement in the Manufacture of Gelatin." Case 687-020, Harvard Business School, Boston.

Deutschman, Alan. 1994. "How H-P Continues to Grow and Grow." *Fortune,* 2 May, 90–92.

Deveny, Kathleen. 1994. "Movable Feasts: More People Dine and Drive." *Wall Street Journal,* 4 January, B1.

Dhebar, Anirudh. 1994. "'New-and-Improved' Products: Producer Speed and Consumer Recalcitrance." Unpublished paper, Harvard Business School.

DiMaggio, Paul J., and Walter W. Powell. 1983. "The Iron Cage Revisited: Institutional Isomorphism and Collective Rationality in Organizational Fields." *American Sociological Review* 48 (April): 147–60.

Doll, William J., and Gholamreza Torkzadeh. 1989. "A Discrepancy Model of End-User Computing Involvement." *Management Science* 35 (10): 1151–71.

"Don't Get Off Yer Bike." 1988. *The Economist,* 16 April, 81–82.

Dougherty, Deborah. 1992. "Interpretive Barriers to New Product Development in Large Firms." *Organization Science* 3 (2): 179–202.

Dougherty, Deborah, and Trudy Heller. 1994. "The Illegitimacy of Successful Product Innovation in Established Firms." *Organization Science* 5 (2): 200–18.

Doyle, John. 1985. "Commentary: Managing New Product Development: How Japanese Companies Learn and Unlearn." In *The Uneasy Alliance: Managing the Product-Technology Dilemma,* edited by Kim Clark, Robert Hayes, and Christopher Lorenz, 377–81. Boston: Harvard Business School Press.

Doz, Yves L. 1988. "Technology Partnerships between Larger and Smaller Firms: Some Critical Issues." In *Cooperative Strategies in International Business,* edited by Farok Contractor and Peter Lorange, 317–38. Lexington, Mass.: Lexington Books.

Dumaine, Brian. 1989. "How Managers Can Succeed through Speed." *Fortune,* 13 February, 54–74.

———. 1992. "Chaparral Steel: Unleash Workers and Cut Costs." *Fortune,* 18 May, 88.

———. 1993. "Payoff from the New Management." *Fortune,* 13 December, 103–4.

Duncan, Jerome L. 1982. "Impacts of New Entry and Horizontal Joint Venture on Industrial Rates of Return." *Review of Economics and Statistics* 64 (2): 339–42.

Duncan, Robert, and Andrew Weiss. 1979. "Organizational Learning: Implications for Organizational Design." *Research in Organizational Behavior* 1:75–123.

Duncker, K. 1945. "On Problem Solving." Translated by L. S. Lees. *Psychology Monographs* 58 (270): 1–112.

Edstrom, A. 1977. "User Influence and the Success of MIS Projects." *Human Relations* 30:589–606.

Edstrom, Anders, Bengt Hogberg, and Lars Erik Norback. 1984. "Alternative Explanations of Interorganizational Cooperation: The Case of Joint Programmes and Joint Ventures in Sweden." *Organizational Studies* 5 (2): 147–68.

Ehretsmann, J., A. Hinkly, A. Minty, and A. W. Pearson. 1989. "The Commercialization of Stagnant Technologies." *R&D Management* 19 (3): 231–42.

Einhorn, H. J. 1980. "Learning from Experience and Suboptimal Rules in Decision Making." In *Cognitive Processes in Choice and Decision Behavior,* edited by T. Wallsten, 1–20. Hillsdale, N.J.: Erlbaum.

Eliashberg, Jehoshua, Gary L. Lilien, and Vithala R. Rao. 1994. "Minimizing Technological Oversights: A Marketing Research Perspective." Paper presented at the Technological Oversights and Foresights Conference, 11–12 March, at Leonard N. Stern School of Business, New York University.

Ellison, David J., Kim B. Clark, Takahiro Fujimoto, and Young-suk Hyun. 1995. "Product Development Performance in the Auto Industry: 1990s Update." Working Paper 95-066. Boston: Harvard Business School.

Engardio, Peter. 1993. "Motorola in China: A Great Leap Forward." *Business Week,* 17 May, 58–59.

"Expert System Picks Key Workers' Brains." 1989. *Los Angeles Times,* 7 November, business, part D: 8.

Fiol, Marlene, and Marjorie A. Lyles. 1985. "Organizational Learning." *Academy of Management Review* 10 (4): 803–13.

"First Newton—The Message Pad—Hits the Market." 1993. *Business Wire,* 30 July.

Flaherty, Robert J. 1980. "Harris Corp.'s Remarkable Metamorphosis." *Forbes,* 26 May, 45–48.

Flam, Faye. 1992. "Japan Bids for US Basic Research." *Science* 258 (27 November): 1428–30.

Ford, David. 1985. "The Management and Marketing of Technology." In *Advances in Strategic Management,* edited by Robert Lamb and Paul Shrivastava, 104–34. Vol. 3. Greenwich, Conn.: JAI Press.

Fornell, Claes, Peter Lorange, and Johan Roos. 1990. "The Cooperative Venture Formation Process: A Latent Variable Structural Modeling Approach." *Management Science* 36 (10): 1246–55.

Forrester, Jay. 1982. Tape-recorded talk in Dorothy Leonard-Barton's Management of Technology class, Massachusetts Institute of Technology.

Foster, Richard. 1982. "A Call for Vision in Managing Technology." *Business Week,* 24 May, 24–33.

Foster, Richard N. 1986. *Innovation: The Attacker's Advantage.* London: Macmillan.

Freeze, Karen, and Dorothy Leonard-Barton. 1991. "GE Plastics: Selecting a Partner." Case study, Design Management Institute, Boston.

————. 1992. "Polymer Solutions: Tempest about a Teapot." Case study, Design Management Institute, Boston.

Fujimoto, Takahiro. 1994a. "The Dynamic Aspect of Product Development Capabilities: An International Comparison in the Automobile Industry." Working paper 94-F-29, Faculty of Economics, Tokyo University (August).

————. 1994b. "Reinterpreting the Resource-Capability View of the Firm: A Case of the Development-Production Systems of the Japanese Auto Makers." Working paper 94-F-20, Faculty of Economics, Tokyo University (May).

Gartner Group. 1993. "Mobile Hardware." Conference Presentation Report.

Gerace, Thomas, and Dorothy Leonard-Barton. 1994. "Emerson Electric in China." Case 694-064, Harvard Business School, Boston.

Geringer, J. Michael. 1991. "Strategic Determinants of Partner Selection Criteria in International Joint Ventures (IJV)." *Journal of International Business Studies* 22 (first quarter): 41–62.

Geringer, J. Michael, and Colette A. Frayne. 1990. "Human Resource Management and International Joint Venture Control: A Parent Company Perspective." *Management International Review (MIR)* 30 (special issue): 103–20.

Gershenberg, Irving. 1983. "Multinational Enterprises, Transfer of Managerial Know-How, Technology Choice and Employment Effects: A Case Study of Kenya." Working paper 28, International Labour Office, Geneva.

Gibbons, Ann. 1992. "In Biotechnology, Japanese Yen for American Expertise." *Science* 258 (27 November): 1431–33.

Gibson, David V., and Everett M. Rogers. 1994. *R&D Collaboration on Trial.* Boston: Harvard Business School Press.

Gold, Bela. 1982. "Managerial Considerations in Evaluating the Role of Licensing in Technology Development." *Managerial and Decision Economics* 3 (4): 213–17.

———. 1987. "Approaches to Accelerating Product and Process Development." *Journal of Product Innovation Management* 4 (2): 81–88.

Goldstein, Sabra B., and Janice Klein. 1988. "Owens-Illinois: Streator 10 Quad," "Owens-Illinois: Atlanta 10 Quad," and "Owens-Illinois: 10 Quad." Cases 688-110, 688-109, and 688-108, Harvard Business School, Boston.

Gomes-Casseres, Benjamin. 1987. "Joint Venture Instability: Is It a Problem?" *Columbia Journal of World Business* 22 (summer): 97–102.

———. 1993. "Computers: Alliances and Industry Evolution." In *Beyond Free Trade,* edited by David B. Yoffie, 79–128. Boston: Harvard Business School Press.

Gomes-Casseres, Benjamin, and Dorothy Leonard-Barton. 1994. "Alliance Clusters in Multimedia: Safety Net or Entanglement?" Paper presented at The Colliding Worlds Colloquium, 6–7 October, at Harvard Business School, Boston.

Gomory, Ralph E. 1983. "Technology Development." *Science* 220: 576–80.

Gould, Stephen Jay. 1991. "Creativity in Evolution and Human Innovation." In *Creativity & Culture: The Inaugural Mansfield American-Pacific Lectures, 1989–1990,* 11–25. Helena, Mont.: Falcon Press.

Grady, Barbara. 1992. "AT&T Says Acquisition of NCR Smooth One Year Later." *Reuter Business Report,* 15 September: 2–3.

Graham, Margaret B. W. 1986. "Corporate Research and Development: The Latest Transformation." In *Technology in the Modern Corporation,* edited by Mel Horwitch, 86–102. New York: Pergamon Press.

———. 1993. "Notes on Organizational Memory: Practice and Theory." Talk given at Xerox Palo Alto Research Center.

Granstrand, Ove, Erik Bohlin, Christer Oskarsson, and Niklas Sjoberg. 1992. "External Technology Acquistion in Large Multi-Technology Companies." *R&D Management* 22 (2): 111–33.

Gross, Neil. 1992. "Inside Hitachi." *Business Week,* 28 September, 92–100 passim.

Gupta, Ashok, and David Wilemon. 1990. "Accelerating the Development of Technology-Based New Products." *California Management Review* 32 (winter): 24–44.

Hakansson, Hakan, and J. Laage-Hellman. 1984. "Developing a Network R&D Strategy." *Journal of Product Innovation Management* 4:224–37.

Hall, Bronwyn H. 1993. "The Stock Market Valuation of R&D Investment during the 1980s." *American Economic Review* 83 (May): 259–64.

Hamel, Gary, Yves L. Doz, and C. K. Prahalad. 1989. "Collaborate with Your Competitors—and Win." *Harvard Business Review,* January–February, 133–39.

Hamel, Gary, and C. K. Prahalad. 1989. "Strategic Intent." *Harvard Business Review,* May–June, 63–76.

Hamilton, David. 1993. "AT&T Steps Up Effort in Asia to Bolster Presence in Telecommunications Market." *Asian Wall Street Journal,* 28 June, 3.

Hamilton, William. 1985. "Corporate Strategies for Managing Emerging Technologies." *Technology in Society* 7:197–212.

Hampden-Turner, Charles. 1981. *Maps of the Mind.* New York: Macmillan.

Hannan, Michael T., and John Freeman. 1977. "The Population Ecology of Organizations." *American Journal of Sociology* 83:929–84.

———. 1984. "Structural Inertia and Organizational Change." *American Sociological Review* 49 (April): 149–64.

Harrigan, Kathryn Rudie. 1985. *Strategies for Joint Ventures.* Lexington, Mass.: Lexington Books.

———. 1988. "Strategic Alliances and Partner Asymmetries." *Management International Review (MIR)* (special issue): 53–72.

Hauser, John R., and Don Clausing. 1988. "The House of Quality." *Harvard Business Review,* May–June, 63–73.

Hauser, John R., Glen L. Urban, and Bruce D. Weinberg. 1993. "How Consumers Allocate Their Time When Searching for Information." *Journal of Marketing Research* 30 (November): 452–66.

Hax, Arnoldo C., and Nicholas S. Majluf. 1984. *Strategic Management: An Integrative Perspective.* New York: Prentice-Hall.

Hayami, Y., and V. Ruttan. 1971. *Agricultural Development: An International Perspective.* Baltimore: Johns Hopkins University Press.

Hayes, Robert. 1985. "Strategic Planning—Forward in Reverse?" *Harvard Business Review,* November–December, 111–19.

———. 1994. "Sino-American Shanghai Squibb Pharmaceuticals Ltd." Case 694-105, Harvard Business School, Boston.

Hayes, Robert H., Steven C. Wheelwright, and Kim B. Clark. 1988. *Dynamic Manufacturing: Creating the Learning Organization.* New York: Free Press.

Hays, Laurie. 1994. "Gerstner Is Struggling as He Tries to Change Ingrained IBM Culture." *Wall Street Journal,* 13 May, A1, 8.

Hedberg, Bo. 1981. "How Organizations Learn and Unlearn." In *Handbook of*

Organizational Design, edited by Paul Nystrom and William Starbuck, 3–27. Vol. 1. New York: Oxford University Press.

Henderson, Rebecca. 1995. "Of Life Cycles Real and Imaginary: The Unexpected Long Old Age of Optical Lithography." *Research Policy,* November (Forthcoming).

Henderson, Rebecca, and Kim B. Clark. 1990. "Architectural Innovation: The Reconfiguration of Existing Product Technologies and the Failure of Established Firms." *Administrative Science Quarterly* 35:9–30.

Hitt, Michael, and R. Duane Ireland. 1985. "Corporate Distinctive Competence, Strategy, Industry and Performance." *Strategic Management Journal* 6:273–93.

Hof, Robert D. 1991. "Quantum Has One Tough Hurdle to Leap." *Business Week,* 8 July, 84, 86.

———. 1993. "Hewlett-Packard Digs Deep for a Digital Future." *Business Week,* 18 October, 72–75 passim.

Hofer, Charles W., and Dan Schendel. 1978. *Strategy Formulation: Analytical Concepts.* St. Paul: West Publishing.

Hofstede, Geert. 1980. *Culture's Consequences: International Differences in Work-Related Values.* Beverly Hills, Calif.: Sage.

Hogarth, Robin M., and Spyros Makridakis. 1981. "Forecasting and Planning: An Evaluation." *Management Science* 27 (2): 115–33.

Holusha, John. 1994. "New Kodak Strategy: Just Pictures." *New York Times,* 4 May, D1.

Hopkins, D. S., and E. L. Bailey. 1971. "New Product Pressures." *Conference Board Record* 8:6–24.

Hopper, Max D. 1990. "Rattling SABRE—New Ways to Compete on Information." *Harvard Business Review,* May–June, 118–25.

Hornstein, Harvey. 1986. *Managerial Courage.* New York: Wiley.

Horwitch, Mel, ed. 1986. *Technology in the Modern Corporation.* New York: Pergamon Press.

Hout, Thomas, Michael E. Porter, and Eileen Rudden. 1982. "How Global Companies Win Out." *Harvard Business Review,* September–October, 98–108.

Howard, R. W. 1987. *Concepts and Schemata: An Introduction.* London: Cassell Educational.

Howard, Robert. 1992. "The CEO as Organizational Architect: An Interview with Xerox's Paul Allaire." *Harvard Business Review,* September–October, 106–19.

Huber, George. 1991. "Organizational Learning: The Contributing Processes and the Literatures." *Organization Science* 2 (1): 88–115.

Hurstak, Johanna M., and Oscar Hauptman. 1990. "E-L Products (A)," "E-L Products (B)," and "E-L Products (C)." Cases 691-013, 691-014, and 691-015, Harvard Business School, Boston.

Hutchins, Edwin. 1991. "Organizing Work by Adaptation." *Organization Science* 2 (1): 14–39.

Hyatt, Josh. 1992. "Digital, Chairman Find a Rocky Road." *Boston Globe,* 27 April, 1, 6.

Iansiti, Marco. 1993. "Real-World R&D: Jumping the Product Generation Gap." *Harvard Business Review,* May–June, 138–47.

"Infiniti Betting Smell Sells." 1992. *Toronto Star,* 8 February, G11.

Ingelbrecht, Nick. 1993. "Busy Signals All over Asia." *Asian Business* 29 (September): 57–59.

Itami, Hiroyuki, with Thomas W. Roehl. 1987. *Mobilizing Invisible Assets.* Cambridge, Mass.: Harvard University Press.

Ives, Blake, and Margrethe H. Olson. 1984. "User Involvement and MIS Success: A Review of Research." *Management Science* 30 (May): 586–603.

Jelinek, Mariann. 1980. "Toward Systematic Management: Alexander Hamilton Church, Business History Review." *Business History Review* 54 (spring): 63–79.

Jelinek, Mariann, and Claudia Bird Schoonhoven. 1990. *The Innovation Marathon: Lessons from High Technology Firms.* Cambridge, Mass.: Basil Blackwell.

Jurgens, Hartmut, Heinz-Otto Peitgen, and Dietmar Saupe. 1990. "The Language of Fractals." *Scientific American* 263 (2): 60–67.

Kaewert, Julie W., and John M. Frost. 1990. *Developing Expert Systems for Manufacturing: A Case Study Approach.* New York: McGraw-Hill.

Kanter, Rosabeth. 1983. *Change Masters: Innovation & Entrepreneurship in the American Corporation.* New York: Simon & Schuster.

Kanter, Rosabeth Moss. 1988. "When a Thousand Flowers Bloom: Structural, Collective, and Social Conditions for Innovation in Organizations." In *Research in Organizational Behavior,* edited by Barry M. Staw and L. L. Cummings, 169–211. Vol. 10. Greenwich, Conn.: JAI Press.

Kanter, Rosabeth Moss, and Richard Ian Corn. 1994. "Do Cultural Differences Make a Business Difference: Contextual Factors Affecting Cross-Cultural Relationship Success." *Journal of Management Development* 13 (2): 5–23.

Kantrow, Alan. 1986. "Wide-Open Management at Chaparral Steel: An Interview with Gordon E. Forward." *Harvard Business Review,* May–June, 96–102.

Kao, John. 1993. "The Worldwide Web of Chinese Business." *Harvard Business Review,* March–April, 24–36.

Katz, Michael, and Janusz Ordover. 1990. "R&D Cooperation and Competition." *Brookings Paper: Microeconomics 1990:* 137–203.

Kearns, David T., and David A. Nadler. 1992. *Prophets in the Dark: How Xerox Reinvented Itself and Beat Back the Japanese.* New York: Harper Business.

Kehoe, Louise. 1992. "Digital to Cut Costs by $1 Billion a Year." *Financial Times,* 2 October, 30.

Keil, Mark. 1992. "Escalating Commitment: A Theoretical Basis for Explaining an IS Failure Phenomenon." Working paper CIS-92-03, College of Business Administration, Georgia State University, Atlanta.

Keirsey, David, and Marilyn Bates. 1978. *Please Understand Me: Character & Temperament Types*. Del Mar, Calif.: Prometheus Nemesis Book Company.

Kerr, Steven. 1975. "On the Folly of Rewarding A, While Hoping for B." *Academy of Management Journal* 18 (December): 769–83.

Killing, Peter J. 1978. "Diversification through Licensing." *R&D Management* 3:159–63.

Kimberly, J. R. 1987. "The Study of Organization: Toward a Biographical Perspective." In *Handbook of Organizational Behavior*, edited by J. W. Lorsch, 223–37. Englewood Cliffs, N.J.: Prentice-Hall.

Kirkpatrick, David. 1994. "A Look inside Allen's Think Tank: This Way to the I-Way." *Fortune*, 11 July, 78–80.

Kline, Stephen J., and Nathan Rosenberg. 1986. "An Overview of Innovation." In *The Positive Sum Strategy: Harnessing Technology for Economic Growth*, edited by Ralph Landau and Nathan Rosenberg, 275–302. Washington, D.C.: National Academy Press.

Knight, Charles F. 1992. "Emerson Electric: Consistent Profits, Consistently." *Harvard Business Review*, January–February, 57–70.

Kodama, Fumio. 1992. "Technology Fusion and the New R&D." *Harvard Business Review*, July–August, 70–78.

Koenig, Richard. 1990. "Tricky Roll-Out: Rich in New Products, Monsanto Must Only Get Them on Market." *Wall Street Journal*, 18 May, 1, A1.

Koestler, Arthur. 1964. *The Act of Creation*. New York: Dell.

Kogut, Bruce. 1988. "Joint Ventures: Theoretical and Empirical Perspectives." *Strategic Management Journal* 9:319–32.

Landler, Mark. 1991. "The 'Bloodbath' in Market Research." *Business Week*, 11 February, 73–74.

Langer, Ellen. 1989. *Mindfulness*. Reading, Mass.: Addison-Wesley.

Langowitz, Nan S., and Steven C. Wheelwright. 1986. "Plus Development Corporation (A)" and "Plus Development Corporation (B)." Cases 687-001 and 689-073, Harvard Business School, Boston. Joint copyright with Stanford University.

Lavin, Douglas. 1993. "Straight Shooter: Robert Eaton Thinks 'Vision' Is Over-rated and He's Not Alone." *Wall Street Journal*, 4 October, 1.

Leonard-Barton, Dorothy. 1981. "The Diffusion of Residential Solar Equipment in California." In *Marketing of Solar Energy Innovations*, edited by Avraham Shama, 145–83. New York: Praeger Press.

———. 1985. "Experts as Negative Opinion Leaders in the Diffusion of a Technical Innovation." *Journal of Consumer Research* 11 (4): 914–26.

———. 1987a. "The Case for Integrative Innovation: An Expert System at Digital." *Sloan Management Review* 29 (1): 7–19.

———. 1987b. "A New CAE System for Shield Electronics Engineers." Case 687-081, Harvard Business School, Boston.

————. 1987c. "New Technology at World Aluminum Corporation: The Jumping Ring Circulator." Case 687-050, Harvard Business School, Boston.

————. 1988. "Implementation as Mutual Adaptation of Technology and Organization." *Research Policy* 17:251–67.

————. 1990. "Implementing New Production Technologies: Exercises in Corporate Learning." In *Managing Complexity in High Technology Organizations,* edited by Mary Ann Von Glinow and Susan A. Mohrman, 160–87. New York: Oxford University Press.

————. 1991a. "Chaparral Steel: Rapid Product and Process Development." Case 692-018, Harvard Business School, Boston.

————. 1991b. "Inanimate Integrators: A Block of Wood Speaks." *Design Management Journal* 2 (3): 61–67. Reprint 9123LEO61.

————. 1992a. "Core Capabilities and Core Rigidities: A Paradox in Managing New Product Development." *Strategic Management Journal* 13:111–25.

————. 1992b."The Factory as a Learning Laboratory." *Sloan Management Review* 34 (1): 23–38.

————. 1992c. "Management of Technology and Moose on Tables." *Organization Science* 3 (4): 556–58.

Leonard-Barton, Dorothy, H. Kent Bowen, Kim B. Clark, Charles A. Holloway, and Steven C. Wheelwright. 1994. "How to Integrate Work *and* Deepen Expertise." *Harvard Business Review,* September–October, 121–30.

Leonard-Barton, Dorothy, Douglas Braithwaite, H. Kent Bowen, William Hanson, Michael Titelbaum, and Gil Preuss. 1994. "Guiding Visions." In *The Perpetual Enterprise Machine,* edited by H. Kent Bowen, Kim Clark, Charles A. Holloway, and Steven C. Wheelwright. New York: Oxford University Press.

Leonard-Barton, Dorothy, and Brian DeLacey. 1987. "Skunkworks at Digital Equipment Corporation: The Tale of XCON." Case 687-051, Harvard Business School, Boston.

Leonard-Barton, Dorothy, and William A. Kraus. 1985. "Implementing New Technology." *Harvard Business Review,* November–December, 102–10.

Leonard-Barton, Dorothy, and Gary Pisano. 1990. "Monsanto's March into Biotechnology (A)." Case 690-009, Harvard Business School, Boston.

Leonard-Barton, Dorothy, and Everett M. Rogers. 1981. "Horizontal Diffusion of Innovations: An Alternative Paradigm to the Classical Diffusion Model." Working paper 1214-81, Sloan School of Management, Massachusetts Institute of Technology, Cambridge.

Leonard-Barton, Dorothy, and Deepak Sinha. 1990. "Dependency, Involvement and User Satisfaction: The Case of Internal Software Development." Working paper 91-008, Harvard Business School, Boston.

————. 1993. "Developer-User Interaction and User Satisfaction in Internal Technology Transfer." *Academy of Management Journal* 36 (5): 1125–39.

Leonard-Barton, Dorothy, and John Sviokla. 1988. "Putting Expert Systems to Work." *Harvard Business Review,* March–April, 91–98.

Leonard-Barton, Dorothy, Edith Wilson, and John Doyle. 1994. "Commercializing Technology: Imaginative Understanding of User Needs." Technical note 694-102, Harvard Business School, Boston.

Levine, Jonathan B. 1989. "Keeping New Ideas Kicking Around: HP's Free-Thinking Scientists Help Hone Its Market Edge." *Business Week,* special issue, 128–34.

Levine, Jonathan B., and Leslie Helm. 1989. "HP: Now No. 1 in Workstations." *Business Week,* 24 April, 30.

Levinson, Marc, with Nancy Hass. 1994. "Bound to the Printed Word." *Newsweek,* 20 June, 52–53.

Levinthal, Daniel, and James G. March. 1981. "A Model of Adaptive Organizational Search." *Journal of Economic Behavior and Organization* 2:307–33.

———. 1993. "The Myopia of Learning." *Strategic Management Journal* 14: 95–112.

Levitt, Barbara, and James March. 1988. "Organizational Learning." *Annual Review of Sociology* 14:319–40.

Lewin, Kurt, and P. Grabbe. 1961. "Principles of Re-education." In *The Planning of Change: Readings in the Applied Behavioral Sciences,* edited by Warren G. Bennis, Kenneth D. Benne, and Richard Chin, 503–509. New York: Holt, Rinehart and Winston.

Lewis, Jordan D. 1990. *Partnerships for Profit: Structuring and Managing Strategic Alliances.* New York: Free Press.

Lieberman, Marvin B. 1989. "The Learning Curve, Technology Barriers to Entry, and Competitive Survival in the Chemical Processing Industries." *Strategic Management Journal* 10 (September–October): 431–47.

Link, A., G. Tassey, and Robert W. Zmud. 1983. "The Induce versus Purchase Decision: An Empirical Analysis of Industrial R&D." *Decision Science* 14:46–61.

Link, Albert N., and Laura L. Bauer. 1989. *Cooperative Research in US Manufacturing: Assessing Policy Initiatives and Corporate Strategies.* Lexington, Mass.: Lexington Books.

Litterer, Joseph A. 1963. "Systematic Management: Design for Organizational Recouping in American Manufacturing Firms." *Business History Review* 37 (winter): 369–91.

Locke, E. A., and D. M. Schweiger. 1979. "Participation in Decision-Making: One More Look." In *Research in Organizational Behavior,* edited by Barry Staw, 265–339. Vol. 1. Greenwich, Conn.: JAI Press.

Lohr, Steve. 1994. "On the Road with Chairman Lou." *New York Times,* 26 June, section 3, 1.

Loomis, Carol J. 1993. "Dinosaurs?" *Fortune,* 3 May, 36–42.

Lowe, Julian F., and Nicholas K. Crawford. 1983. "New Product Development and Technology Licensing for the Small Firm." *Industrial Management and Data Systems* (September–October): 26–29.

Lyles, Marjorie A. 1988. "Learning among Joint Venture Sophisticated Firms." *Management International Review (MIR)* (special issue): 85–98.

MacAvoy, Thomas C. 1989. "Technology Strategy for a Diversified Corporation Note" and "Technology Strategy." Unpublished Papers, UVA-OM-0659 and UVA-OM-0656, Darden Graduate School of Business, University of Virginia, Charlottesville.

Macfarlane, Gwyn. 1984. *Alexander Fleming: The Man and the Myth.* Cambridge, Mass.: Harvard University Press.

Machalaba, Daniel. 1993. "Burlington Northern Shows Risks of Hiring an Outsider as CEO." *Wall Street Journal,* 6 April, 1.

MacMillan, Ian, Mary Lynn McCaffery, and Gilles Van Wijk. 1986. "Competitors' Responses to Easily Imitated New Products—Exploring Commercial Banking Product Introductions." *Strategic Management Journal* 6:75–86.

Madeuf, B. 1984. "International Technology Transfers and International Technology Payments: Definitions, Measurement and Firms' Behavior." *Research Policy* 13 (3):124–40.

Mahon, John F. 1982. "A Note on the Chemical Industry, Changing Public Perceptions, and Governmental Regulations." Case BU 741-101, Harvard Business School, Boston.

———. 1983. "Superfund (A)—The Early Maneuvering." Case BU 741-102, Harvard Business School, Boston.

Maidique, Modesto A., and Billie Jo Zirger. 1985. "The New Product Learning Cycle." *Research Policy* 16 (December): 299–313.

Mansfield, Edwin. 1975. "International Technology Transfer: Forms, Resource Requirements and Policies." *American Economic Review* 65 (May): 372–76.

March, James. 1978. "Bounded Rationality, Ambiguity and the Engineering of Choice." *Bell Journal of Economics* 9:587–608.

Martin, Linda Grant. 1975. "What Happened at NCR after the Boss Declared Martial Law." *Fortune,* September, 100–4, 178–81.

Maruyama, Magoroh. 1989. "Cultural Models of International Borrowing." *Human Systems Management* 8:213–16.

Mathis, James F. 1992. "Turning R&D Managers into Technology Managers." *Research-Technology Management* 35 (January–February): 35–38.

McAllister, Robert. 1992. "Avia Aims to Be on the Cutting Edge." *Footwear News* 48 (47): 19.

McClelland, Kevin, Betsy Joseph, and Rick Bolander. 1993. "NCR's CEO Talks Shop." *Harbus* 57 (4 October): 1, 8.

McCullough, Tim. 1987. "Six Steps to Selling A.I." *A.I. Expert* 2 (December): 55–60.

McDonnell, John F. 1994. Speech to CEO Conference, 26 April, Amsterdam. Quoted in *Executive Speaker* 15 (July): 9.

McFarling, Ursha Lee. 1994. "Hormones for Cows Create a Row." *Boston Globe,* 3 February, 21, 25.

McGuire, Michael. 1991. *An Eye for Fractals.* Redwood City, Calif.: Addison-Wesley.

McQuade, Krista, and Benjamin Gomes-Casseres. 1991. "Xerox and Fuji Xerox." Case 391-156, Harvard Business School, Boston.

McWilliams, Gary. 1993. "A Radical Shift in Focus for Polaroid." *Business Week,* 26 July, 66–67.

Meyer, Michael. 1994. "Ripe for a Change." *Newsweek,* 29 August, 40.

Miles, Gregory L. 1989. "Specialty Metals That Are Special Indeed." *Business Week,* special issue, 129.

Miller, Danny. 1990. *The Icarus Paradox.* New York: Harper Business.

Mintzberg, Henry. 1990. "Strategy Formation: Schools of Thought." In *Perspectives on Strategic Management,* edited by J. W. Fredrickson, 105–235. New York: Harper & Row.

Mintzberg, Henry, and James A. Waters. 1985. "Of Strategies, Deliberate and Emergent." *Strategic Management Journal* 6:257–72.

Mirvis, Philip H., and Mitchell Lee Marks. 1992. "The Human Side of Merger Planning: Assessing and Analyzing 'Fit.' " *Human Resource Planning* 15 (3): 69–92.

Mitchell, G. R., and W. F. Hamilton. 1988. "Managing R&D as a Strategic Option." *Research Technology Management* 31 (May–June): 15–22.

Moore, William L. 1982. "Concept Testing." *Journal of Business Research* 10:279–94.

Morehead, John W. 1984. "Advantages of New Product Search." *Les Nouvelles* 19 (June): 100–2.

Morgan, Gareth, and Rafael Ramirez. 1983. "Action Learning: A Holographic Metaphor for Guiding Social Change." *Human Relations* 37 (1): 1–28.

Morison, Elting E. 1966. *Men, Machines and Modern Times.* Cambridge, Mass.: MIT Press.

Morone, Joseph G. 1993. *Winning in High-Tech Markets: The Role of General Management.* Boston: Harvard Business School Press.

Morton, J. A. 1971. *Organizing for Innovation: A Systems Approach to Technical Management.* New York: McGraw-Hill.

Mowery, David C., and Nathan Rosenberg. 1991. *Technology and the Pursuit of Economic Growth.* Cambridge, England: Cambridge University Press.

Murray, Kenneth L., and Dorothy Leonard-Barton. 1994. "Monsanto's March into Biotechnology (C)." Case 694-061, Harvard Business School, Boston.

Myers, David G. 1987. *Social Psychology.* New York: McGraw-Hill.

Myers, Isabel Briggs, with Peter B. Myers. 1980. *Gifts Differing.* Palo Alto, Calif.: Consulting Psychologists Press.

National Academy of Sciences, National Research Council. 1992. Academy

Industry Program, "Corporate Restructuring and Industrial Research and Development." Washington, D.C.: National Science Board Committee on Industrial Support for R&D, the Competitive Strength of U.S. Industrial Science and Technology: Strategic Issues (August).

National Science Board, National Science Foundation. 1993. "Science and Engineering Indicators." Washington, D.C.: U.S. Government Printing Office.

Nelson, Kelly. 1992. "A High Tech Success." *China Business Review* 19 (January–February): 36–38.

Nelson, Richard, and Sidney Winter. 1982. *An Evolutionary Theory of Economic Change.* Cambridge, Mass.: Harvard University Press.

Nelson, Richard R. 1982. "The Role of Knowledge in R&D Efficiency." *Quarterly Journal of Economics* 97 (August): 453–70.

"Networking: Sourcing Goods and Parts." 1993. *Business China* 19 (5 April): 3–4.

Niederkofler, Martin. 1991. "The Evolution of Strategic Alliances: Opportunities for Managerial Influence." *Journal of Business Venturing* 6:237–57.

Nisbet, Stephen. 1986. "Quality First—What's That? Ask Chinese." *Reuters North European Service,* 21 June.

Nonaka, Ikujiro. 1992. "Managing Innovation as an Organizational Knowledge Creation Process." Paper presented at Technology Strategies in the Nineties conference, 21 May, Rome.

O'Brian, Bridget. 1993. "Hot Suitcase Brings Success—and Stress." *Wall Street Journal,* 27 September, B1.

Ohmae, Kenichi. 1989. "Companyism and Do More Better." *Harvard Business Review,* January–February, 125–32.

Olleros, Francisco-Javier. 1986. "Emerging Industries and the Burn-out of Pioneers." *Journal of Product Innovation Management* 3 (March): 5–18.

Parker, Douglas D. 1993. "University Technology Transfers: Impacts on Local and US Economies." *Contemporary Policy Issues* 11 (April): 87–99.

Pavitt, Keith. 1991. "Key Characteristics of the Large Innovating Firm." *British Journal of Management* 2:41–50.

Peters, Tom. 1992. "Rethinking Scale." *California Management Review* 35 (1): 7–29.

Peterson, Donald K. 1990. Remarks to the New England–Canada Business Council, reported in *Executive Speeches* 8 (22 February): 56.

Pettigrew, Andrew. 1979. "On Studying Organizational Cultures." *Administrative Science Quarterly* 24:570–81.

Pfeffer, Jeffery. 1981. "Management as Symbolic Action: The Creation and Maintenance of Organizational Paradigms." *Research in Organizational Behavior* 3:1–52.

Pinchot, Gifford, III. 1985. *Intrapreneuring.* New York: Harper & Row.

Pisano, Gary P., and Paul Y. Mang. 1993. "Collaborative Product Development and the Market for Know-How: Strategies and Structures in the Biotechnology Industry." In *Research on Technological Innovation, Management and Policy*, edited by Robert A. Burgelman and Richard S. Rosenbloom, 109–36. Greenwich, Conn.: JAI Press.

Pitta, Julie. 1993. "It Had to Be Done and We Did It." *Forbes*, 26 April, 148–52.

Plato. 1892. *The Dialogues of Plato*. Translated by B. Jowett. New York: Macmillan Company. Copyright renewed by Oxford University Press, 1920.

"Plugged In." 1993. *Business China*, 31 May, 5–6.

Polanyi, Michael. 1967. *The Tacit Dimension*. New York: Doubleday.

Pope, Kyle. 1994. "Staid EDS Cuts Loose with Interactive Multimedia Push." *Wall Street Journal*, 25 March, B4.

Power, Christopher. 1992. "Will It Sell in Podunk? Hard to Say." *Business Week*, 10 August, 46–47.

Prahalad, C. K., and Gary Hamel. 1990. "The Core Competence of the Corporation." *Harvard Business Review*, May–June, 79–91.

Preuss, Gil, Dorothy Leonard-Barton, Marco Iansiti, and David Gibson. 1991. "MCC: The Packaging and Interconnect Program." Case 692-020, Harvard Business School, Boston.

Pryzbylowicz, Edward P., and Terrence W. Faulkner. 1993. "Kodak Applies Strategic Intent to the Management of Technology." *Research-Technology Management* 36 (January–February): 31–38.

Quinn, Brian. 1980. *Strategies for Change: Logical Incrementalism*. Homewood, Ill.: Irwin.

Radtke, M., N. D. Fast, and J. Paap. 1987. *Corporate Partnering in the 1980s. Venture Intelligence Focus Report*. Wellesley Hills, Mass.: Venture Economics.

Redmond, Kent C., and Thomas M. Smith. 1977. "Lessons from 'Project Whirlwind.'" *IEEE Spectrum* 14 (October): 50–59.

Reich, Robert B., and Eric D. Mankin. 1986. "Joint Ventures with Japan Give Away Our Future." *Harvard Business Review*, March–April, 78–86.

Reidenbach, Eric R., and Sharon Grimes. 1984. "How Concept Knowledge Affects Concept Evaluation." *Journal of Product Innovation Management* 4:255–66.

Remer, Theodore G., ed. 1965. *Serendipity and the Three Princes. From Peregrinaggio of 1557*. Norman: University of Oklahoma Press.

Replogle, Douglas. 1988. "Guidelines for a Product Technology Strategy." *Planning Review* 16 (November–December): 12–18.

Roberts, Edward B. 1980. "New Ventures for Corporate Growth." *Harvard Business Review*, July–August, 134–42.

Roberts, Edward B., and R. Mizouchi. 1989. "Inter-firm Collaboration: The Case of Japanese Biotechnology." *International Journal of Technology Management* 4 (1): 43–61.

Rock, Stuart. 1990. "VolksChairman." *Director* (October): 69–72.

Rogers, Everett M. 1983. *Diffusion of Innovations.* New York: Free Press.

Rogers, Everett M., and Judith K. Larsen. 1984. *Silicon Valley Fever.* New York: Basic Books.

Rosenbloom, Richard S. 1988. "From Gears to Chips." Presentation to the Business History Seminar: Technology, the Workplace, and Competition, 1880–1988; 15 February, at Harvard Business School, Boston.

Rothwell, Roy, Christopher Freeman, A. Horsley, V. T. P. Jervis, A. B. Robertson, and J. Townsend. 1974. "SAPPHO Updated—Project SAPPHO Phase II." *Research Policy* 3:258–91.

Rumelhart, D. E. 1980. "Schemata: The Building Blocks of Cognition." In *Theoretical Issues in Reading Comprehension,* edited by R. J. Spiro, B. C. Bruce, and W. F. Brewer, 33–58. Hillsdale, N.J.: Erlbaum.

Rumelt, Richard. 1974. *Strategy, Structure, and Economic Performance.* Boston: Harvard Business School Press. Reprint edition, Harvard Business School Classics, Boston: Harvard Business School Press, 1986.

Sagawa, Paul, and Dorothy Leonard-Barton. 1990. "The Carnegie Group." Case 690-033, Harvard Business School, Boston.

Schein, Edgar. 1984. "Coming to a New Awareness of Organizational Culture." *Sloan Management Review* 25 (winter): 3–16.

———. 1987. "Career Anchors: Discovering Your Real Values." Available from University Associates, Inc., 8517 Production Avenue, San Diego, Calif. 92121.

———. 1990. *Organizational Culture and Leadership.* San Francisco: Jossey-Bass.

Schon, Donald A. 1967a. "The Fear of Innovation." In *Uncertainty in Research, Management and New Product Development,* edited by Raymond M. Hainer, Sherman Kingsbury, and David B. Gleicher, 11–25. New York: Reinhold Publishing Corp.

———. 1967b. *Technology and Change: The New Heraclitus.* New York: Delacorte Press.

Schon, Donald A., and Glenn Wiggins. 1992. "Kinds of Seeing in Designing." *Creativity and Innovation Management* 1 (2): 68–74.

Schrage, Michael. 1993. "The Culture(s) of Prototyping." *Design Management Journal* 4 (1): 55–65.

Schumpeter, Joseph A. 1942. *Capitalism, Socialism, and Democracy.* New York: Harper. Reprint edition, London: Unwin Paperbacks, 1987.

Schwartz, Peter. 1991. *The Art of the Long View: Planning for the Future in an Uncertain World.* New York: Doubleday Currency.

Sen, Falguni, and Albert Rubenstein. 1989. "External Technology and In-House R&D Facilitative Role." *Journal of Product Innovation Management* 6 (2): 123–38.

Senge, Peter. 1990. "The Leader's New Work: Building Learning Organizations." *Sloan Management Review* 32 (1): 7–23.

Serafin, Raymond. 1993. "The Information Accelerator and Me." *Advertising Age,* 22 March, 47.

Shahrokhi, Manuchehr. 1987. *Reverse Licensing: International Transfer of Technology to the United States.* New York: Praeger.

Shapiro, James, Jack Behrmann, William Fischer, and Simon Powell. 1991. *Direct Investment and Joint Ventures in China.* New York: Quorum Books.

Shaw, Stephen M., and Johannes Meier. 1993. " 'Second Generation' MNCs in China." *McKinsey Quarterly* 4:3–16.

Sheridan, Thomas B. 1980. "Computer Control and Human Alienation." *Technology Review* (October): 61–73.

Sherrid, Pamela. 1983. "Breaking away from the Bunch." *Forbes,* 5 December, 45.

Shiba, Shoji, Richard Lynch, Ira Moskowitz, and John Sheridan. 1991. *Step by Step KJ Method.* CQM document no. 2. Wilmington, Mass.: Center for Quality Management, Analog Devices.

Simon, Denis Fred. 1991. "China's Acquisition and Assimilation of Foreign Technology: Beijing's Search for Excellence." Testimony to Joint Economic Committee, U.S. Congress, January 1.

Simon, Herbert A. 1969. *The Sciences of the Artificial.* Cambridge, Mass.: MIT Press.

"Sino-U.S. Joint Venture Develops New Product." 1993. *Xinhua General Overseas News Service,* 23 November.

Sitkin, Sim B. 1992. "Learning through Failure: The Strategy of Small Losses." In *Research in Organizational Behavior,* edited by B. M. Staw and L. L. Cummings, 231–66. Vol. 14. Greenwich, Conn.: JAI Press.

Slater, Michael, and Linley Gwennap. 1992. "EO Announces First Personal Communicator." *Microprocessor Report* 12:12–16.

Slutsker, Gary. 1989. "To Catch a Particle." *Forbes,* 23 January, 88–89.

Smith, Preston G., and Donald G. Reinertsen. 1991. *Developing Products in Half the Time.* New York: Van Nostrand Reinhold.

Snow, Charles C., and Lawrence G. Hrebiniak. 1980. "Strategy, Distinctive Competence, and Organizational Performance." *Administrative Science Quarterly* 25:317–35.

Souder, William. 1987. *Managing New Product Innovations.* Lexington, Mass.: Lexington Books.

Springer, Sally P., and Georg Deutsch. 1981. *Left Brain, Right Brain.* San Francisco: Freeman.

Stalk, George, Philip Evans, and Lawrence E. Shulman. 1992. "Competing on Capabilities: The New Rules of Corporate Strategy." *Harvard Business Review,* March–April, 57–69.

Stalk, George, Jr. 1988. "Time—The Next Source of Competitive Advantage." *Harvard Business Review,* July–August, 41–51.

Star, Susan Leigh, and James R. Griesemer. 1989. "Institutional Ecology, 'Translations' and Boundary Objects: Amateurs and Professionals in Berkeley's Museum of Vertebrate Zoology, 1907–39." *Social Studies of Science* 19:387–420.

Starbuck, William H. 1983. "Organizations as Action Generators." *American Sociological Review* 48:91–102.

Stefflre, Volney. 1965. "Simulation of People's Behavior toward New Objects and Events." *American Behavioral Scientist* 8:12–16.

Stonham, Paul. 1993. "The Future of Strategy: An Interview with Gary Hamel." *European Management Journal* 11 (June): 150–57.

Sun, Lin. 1990. "China Follows the Long Road to Telecom Growth." *Telephony,* 28 May: 22–30.

Suris, Oscar. 1994. "Californians Collide with Folks in Detroit over the Electric Car." *Wall Street Journal,* 24 January, A1.

Sviokla, John. 1990. "An Examination of the Impacts of an Expert System on the Firm: The Case of XCON." *Management Information Systems Quarterly* 14 (June): 127–40.

Sykes, Hollister B. 1986. "The Anatomy of a Corporate Venturing Program: Factors Influencing Success." *Journal of Business Venturing* 1 (3): 275–93.

"Technology Transfer's Master." 1977. *Business Week,* 10 October, 120–24.

Teece, David J. 1977. "Technology Transfer by Multinational Firms: The Resource Cost of Transferring Technological Know-How." *The Economic Journal* 87:242–61.

———. 1988. "Capturing Value from Technological Innovation: Integration, Strategic Partnering and Licensing Decisions." *Interfaces* 18 (May–June): 46–61.

———. 1989. "Inter-organizational Requirements of the Innovation Process." *Managerial and Decision Economics* 1–2:35–42.

Teece, David J., Gary Pisano, and Amy Shuen. 1990. "Dynamic Capabilities and Strategic Management." Working paper 90-8, Consortium on Competitiveness and Cooperation, Center for Research in Management, University of California at Berkeley.

Thiessen, Arthur E. 1965. *A History of the General Radio Company.* West Concord, Mass.: General Radio Company.

Thill, George, and Dorothy Leonard-Barton. 1993. "Hewlett-Packard: Singapore (A)," "Hewlett-Packard: Singapore (B)," and "Hewlett-Packard: Singapore (C)." Cases 694-035, 694-036, and 694-037, Harvard Business School, Boston.

Thunman, Carl G. 1988. *Technology Licensing to Distant Markets: Interaction between Swedish and Indian Firms.* Stockholm: Amnqvist & Wiksell International.

Tichy, Noel, and Ram Charan. 1989. "Speed, Simplicity, Self-Confidence: An Interview with Jack Welch." *Harvard Business Review* 67 (September–October): 112–20.

Tushman, Michael, and Philip Anderson. 1986. "Technological Discontinuities and Organizational Environments." *Administrative Science Quarterly* 31:439–65.

Tushman, Michael, and Elaine Romanelli. 1985. "Organizational Evolution: A Metamorphosis Model of Convergence and Reorientation." In *Research in Organizational Behavior,* edited by Barry Staw and Larry L. Cummings, 171–222. Vol. 7. Greenwich, Conn.: JAI Press.

Tyre, Marcie J., and Wanda J. Orlikowski. 1994. "Windows of Opportunity: Temporal Patterns of Technological Adaptation in Organizations." *Organization Science* 5 (1): 98–118.

Urrows, Elizabeth, and Henry Urrows. 1986. "Campbell Soup Company." *PC Week* 3:57.

Utterback, James. 1994. *Mastering the Dynamics of Innovation.* Boston: Harvard Business School Press.

Van Andel, Pek. 1992. "Serendipity: 'Expect also the Unexpected.'" *Creativity and Innovation Management* 1 (March): 20–32.

Van de Ven, Andrew, and Douglas Polley. 1992. "Learning while Innovating." *Organization Science* 3 (February): 92–116.

Van Maanen, John, and Stephen R. Barley. 1984. "Occupational Communities: Culture and Control in Organizations." *Research in Organizational Behavior,* edited by Barry Staw and Larry L. Cummings, 287–365. Vol. 6. Greenwich, Conn.: JAI Press.

Virany, Beverly, Michael L. Tushman, and Elaine Romanelli. 1992. "Executive Succession and Organization Outcomes in Turbulent Environments: An Organization Learning Approach." *Organization Science* 3 (1): 72–91.

Vogel, Carl. 1992. "30 Products That Changed Our Lives." *R&D* 34 (11): 42.

Von Braun, Christoph-Friedrich. 1990. "The Acceleration Trap." *Sloan Management Review* 32 (1): 49–58.

Von Glinow, Mary Ann. 1985. "Reward Strategies for Attracting, Evaluating and Retaining Professionals." *Human Resource Management* 24 (2): 191–206.

Von Hippel, Eric. 1986. "Lead Users: A Source of Novel Product Concepts." *Management Science* 32 (July): 791–805.

———. 1987. "Cooperation between Rivals: Informal Know-How Trading." *Research Policy* 16:291–302.

———. 1988. *The Sources of Innovation.* New York: Oxford University Press.

———. 1994. "'Sticky Information' and the Locus of Problem Solving: Implications for Innovation." *Management Science* 40 (4): 429–39.

Wallace, James, and Jim Erickson. 1992. *Hard Drive.* New York: Wiley.

Weber, Joseph. 1989. "Going over the Lab Wall in Search of New Ideas." *Business Week,* special issue, 132.

Weber, Robert J., and David N. Perkins. 1992. *Inventive Minds: Creativity in Technology.* New York: Oxford University Press.

Weitzman, Martin L., and Douglas L. Kruse. 1990. "Profit Sharing and Productivity." In *Paying for Productivity,* edited by Alan S. Blinder, 139. Washington, D.C.: The Brookings Institution.

Welch, Lawrence S. 1985. "The International Marketing of Technology: An Interaction Perspective." *International Marketing Review* 2 (spring): 41–53.

Wender, Paul H. 1968. "Vicious and Virtuous Circles: The Role of Deviation Amplifying Feedback in the Origin and Perpetuation of Behavior." *Psychiatry* 31:309–24.

"What Makes Yoshio Invent." 1991. *The Economist,* 12 January, 61.

Wheelwright, Steven, and Kim Clark. 1992. "Creating Project Plans to Focus Product Development." *Harvard Business Review,* March–April, 70–82.

Wheelwright, Steven C., and Kim B. Clark. 1992. *Revolutionizing Product Development: Quantum Leaps in Speed, Efficiency, and Quality.* New York: Free Press.

White, Joseph B., and Oscar Suris. 1993. "New Pony: How a 'Skunk Works' Kept Mustang Alive—On a Tight Budget." *Wall Street Journal,* 21 September, 1, 12.

Wiegner, Kathleen K. 1990. "Good-bye to the HP Way?" *Forbes,* 26 November, 36–37.

Wilke, John R. 1991. "Digital Equipment Inching Forward in Uneasy Search for Olsen's Successor." *Wall Street Journal,* 4 November, 1, B4.

———. 1992. "Digital's Offer to Employees Proves Popular." *Wall Street Journal,* 1 June, B6.

Wind, Yoram, and Vijay Mahajan. 1988. "New Product Development: A Perspective for Re-examination." *Journal of Production Innovation Management* 5 (4): 304–10.

Woodruff, David, with Larry Armstrong and John Carey. 1994. "Electric Cars: Will They Work? And Who Will Buy Them?" *Business Week,* 30 May, 104–14.

Wrubel, Robert. 1992. "The Ghost of Andy Carnegie?" *Financial World,* 1 September, 50.

Wyatt, Edward A. 1992. "Another Breathtaking Breakthrough: U.S. Alcohol Stirs the Speculative Juices." *Barron's* 72 (10 February): 27–28, 37–38.

Yates, JoAnne. 1989. *Control through Communication: The Rise of System in American Management.* Baltimore: Johns Hopkins University Press.

———. 1990. "For the Record: The Embodiment of Organizational Memory, 1850–1920." In *Business and Economic History,* edited by William J. Hausman, 172–82. Vol. 19. Williamsburg, Va.: Business History Conference, College of William and Mary.

Zachary, G. Pascal. 1993. "Climbing the Peak: Agony and Ecstasy of 200 Code Writers Beget Windows NT." *Asian Wall Street Journal,* 27 May, 1, 24.

Zahra, Shaker A., and Diane Ellor. 1993. "Accelerating New Product Development and Successful Market Introduction." *SAM Advanced Management Journal* 58 (January): 9–15.

Zaltman, Gerald, and Robin A. Higie. 1993. "Seeing the Voice of the Customer: The Zaltman Metaphor Elicitation Technique." Report 93-114. Cambridge, Mass.: Marketing Science Institute.

Zhao, Liming, and Arnold Reisman. 1992. "Toward Meta Research on Technology Transfer." *IEEE Transactions on Engineering Management* 39 (1): 13–21.

INDEX

ABOUT THE AUTHOR

Dorothy Leonard is the William J. Abernathy Professor of Business Administration at the Harvard Business School, where she teaches classes on new product and process development, manufacturing, technology strategy, and technology implementation. She is also a faculty member of Harvard Programs on Enhancing Corporate Creativity and Managing International Collaboration. She has been at Harvard for twelve years; previously she taught at the Sloan School of Management at MIT. At Harvard, MIT, Digital, AT&T, Johnson&Johnson, and other corporations, she has conducted executive courses on a wide range of technology-related topics, such as cross-functional interfaces and technology transfer during new product and process development.

Professor Leonard's major research interests and consulting expertise are in technology development and commercialization. She is currently undertaking an international study of these topics in the multimedia industry, with special emphasis on managing geographically dispersed new product development teams. As a consultant, she has worked with governments such as Sweden, Jamaica, and the United States and major corporations such as Kodak, Monsanto, and Silicon Graphics on technology management. Professor Leonard has written more than twenty-five articles for books and journals and dozens of field-based studies.